DATE DUE

DE 8'00			
AP 1 6'07			
MY 1 0 07			
AG 7 08			

DEMCO 38-296

Prime-Time Feminism

University of Pennsylvania Press
Feminist Cultural Studies, the Media, and Political Culture

Mary Ellen Brown and Andrea Press, Editors

A complete list of books in the series is available from the publisher.

Prime-Time Feminism

Television, Media Culture, and the
Women's Movement Since 1970

Bonnie J. Dow

PENN

University of Pennsylvania Press

Philadelphia

Library of Congress Cataloging-in-Publication Data

Dow, Bonnie J.
    Prime-time feminism : television, media culture, and the women's
movement since 1970 / Bonnie J. Dow
        p.   cm.—(Feminist cultural studies, the media and
political culture)
    Includes bibliographical references and index.
    ISBN 0-8122-3315-8 (hardcover : alk. paper).—ISBN 0-8122-1554-0
(pbk. : alk. paper)
    1. Women in television—United States.   2. Women and television—
United States.   3. Feminism—United States.   I. Title.
II. Series.
PN1992.8.W65D69   1996
305.4'0973—dc20   96-5604
                                                                CIP

For
John and Lisa,
my favorite back porch scholars

Contents

Acknowledgments

This book has been in process for a number of years. Portions of it began as a dissertation at the University of Minnesota. I would like to thank Karlyn Kohrs Campbell for her incisive direction of that project, for educating me as a critic, and for her continuing encouragment, support, and friendship.

As this book has moved from a proposal to a reality, a number of people have influenced its shape. Celeste Condit's comments on the original proposal influenced my thinking more than she probably thought they would. Patricia Smith, the Women's Studies acquisitions editor at the University of Pennsylvania Press, has my gratitude for reacting so enthusiastically to the proposal, for pursuing the project, and for being consistently helpful at every stage in its completion. During the review process, the comments of Mimi White and Nina Leibman were generous, insightful, and tremendously valuable in guiding this book to what I hoped it would become.

Time and again the research necessary for this book overreached the resources of the NDSU library. Time and again, the Interlibrary Loan staff managed to get me what I needed, quickly and efficiently, never complaining about my endless requests and my absentmindedness about due dates. They have my deepest appreciation, as does Laurie Baker, my graduate student, who did some last minute research and fact checking for me that greatly helped in the final stages of preparing the manuscript.

I would like to acknowledge the assistance of the Speech Communication Association, which granted permission to reprint portions of Chapter 1 that first appeared in "Hegemony, Feminist Criticism, and *The Mary Tyler Moore Show,*" *Critical Studies in Mass Communication,* 7 (Fall 1990): 261–274, and portions of Chapter 3 that first appeared in "Performance of Feminine Discourse in *Designing Women,*" *Text and Performance Quarterly,* 12 (1992): 125–145. In addition, portions of Chapter 4 first appeared in "Femininity and Feminism in *Murphy Brown,*"

Southern Communication Journal, 57 (Winter 1992): 143–155. They are reprinted here with permission of the Southern Speech Communication Association.

For authors, time is a valuable commodity. Two successive department chairs at North Dakota State University, Robert Littlefield and Tim Sellnow, supported this book by providing me with release time from teaching. My spouse, John Murphy, created a home environment that allowed me to use that time to the fullest. In addition to providing peace and quiet and taking on almost all of the household responsibilities, he never complained about endless viewing of *The Mary Tyler Moore Show* or *Dr. Quinn, Medicine Woman,* and he never refused to read and comment on yet another draft of a chapter. He is, in short, my most valuable colleague and a pretty good wife.

My most profound thanks go to Lisa Hogeland, who was my Women's Studies colleague at the University of Cincinnati for two years and has become my most valuable resource for understanding contemporary feminism. She championed this project from the beginning, read (and patiently discussed) every chapter, and saved me from many mistakes in the process. Her willingness to share her knowledge of feminist history, theory, and politics has enriched every part of this book, and her intellectual and emotional companionship has enriched every part of my life.

Finally, I wish to acknowledge the less direct but crucial contributions made by those who have comprised my overlapping personal, feminist, and scholarly collectives, now scattered across the country, for the past decade or so: Mari Tonn, Kristin Vonnegut, Tom Burkholder, Debra Petersen, Steve Depoe, Susan Huxman, and Debbie Chasteen. Their friendship has enhanced the quality of my thinking and of my life.

Preface

This book is about television entertainment, feminism, and their intersections, a focus that arises from my interests in these two areas—interests both scholarly and personal. I am a passionate television watcher,
critic, and aficionado, and I have been so from a young age. As a child,
I was allowed to watch all of the television that I wanted. Much of my
knowledge about programs that were on prime-time when I was not yet
born or was too young to understand them comes as much from my extensive viewing of television reruns on countless afternoons throughout
my childhood as it does from the reading of television programming history. My parents' indifference to the volume of my viewing was linked, I
think, to the fact that they saw no ill effects from it. I was a fine student,
a voracious reader, and a fairly well-adjusted child (at least, I think so). I
hasten to point that out whenever I can, especially to academic colleagues convinced that television is at the root of the decline of our students (and of human civilization as they know it).

Television entertainment programming is problematic in many ways,
but so is much of popular culture, from Barbie dolls to professional football to some computer games. Yet, it has become peculiarly fashionable,
particularly for those on the Right (although Democrats increasingly are
jumping on the bandwagon as well), to attack television as a primary
cause of America's moral decline. I am troubled by an unrelenting focus
on television as a social problem because such an attitude inevitably
blinds us to the complexity of television programming as, simultaneously, a commodity, an art form, and an important ideological forum for
public discourse about social issues and social change. As a television fan,
I appreciate television's capacity to amuse, to entertain, and to give pleasure. As a television critic, I recognize the problems of those pleasures
while often admiring, at the same time, the skill and artistry that goes
into producing them. As a feminist, I believe that patriarchy is alive and
well, that women's attempts at self-definition and self-determination continue to be marginalized, silenced, and stymied in myriad ways (despite

descriptions of contemporary times as "postfeminist"), and that popular culture and television play key roles in that process. The confluence and contradictions of these three subjectivities—fan, critic, and feminist—motivate and inform this book.

To love television as I do and to be a committed feminist, as I believe myself to be, will seem oxymoronic to many. When I first began to study feminism and popular culture, I found that a large part of my motivation was to understand my own experience and the contradictions that emerged from it. I have, at one time or another, been an avid consumer of the various forms of popular culture specifically targeted at white, middle-class women. When I travel by plane, which I dislike, I often survey airport newsstands and choose two or three women's magazines to see me through the journey. I could justify this behavior as necessary for my work, as I often integrate material or insights gained from such reading into my scholarship. However, I also know that I get pleasure from it and find it soothing. Even so, as a critic and a feminist, I found much of Naomi Wolf's *The Beauty Myth* (1992) tremendously persuasive.

As a teenager, I devoured cheap romance novels, to my mother's disapproval. I defended my addiction by telling her that because the novels were often set in exotic locales, I learned a great deal about other cultures from them. That claim was absolutely true, but I also knew, even then, that what satisfied me was the repetitive form of the books. I became adept, when browsing used bookstores, at reading the back covers and choosing the stories most likely to meet my expectations. When I encountered Janice Radway's *Reading the Romance* (1984) years later, I found that her arguments for the appeal of romance storylines had great explanatory power for me.

To this day, despite my own arguments about its rather timid feminist vision, I find *The Mary Tyler Moore Show* (hereafter abbreviated *Mary Tyler Moore*) one of the most pleasurable sitcoms to watch. In fact, I originally decided to write about *Mary Tyler Moore* in 1988, when I was in graduate school, because of my attachment to the show. When I moved to Minneapolis to attend the University of Minnesota in 1987, I was lonely and scared, a bit overwhelmed by a large and unfamiliar city. When I discovered that a local independent station showed reruns of *Mary Tyler Moore* every evening, I used daily viewing of this familiar sitcom as a reassuring anchor in a strange place. It was a show that had been a family favorite when I was growing up, and viewing it comforted me in an inexplicable way.

I can honestly say that I have never written about any kind of television programming that I did not enjoy watching. Thus, part of what I do in my work is attempt to dissect my own pleasures and interests. This, it seems to me, is the preferred way to do one's work, whether the object of study is literature, politics, or history. The myth of the critic as a disinterested and wholly detached reporter has long since been deconstructed, and, in my mind, critics of popular culture should favor a swing in the opposite direction. We should look askance at anyone who purports to understand and to evaluate a text that s/he claims not to appreciate on its own terms.

Television has become the popular art form easiest to vilify. This vilification, particularly in forums such as Congressional hearings and newspaper editorial pages, is often accomplished by those least qualified to do it because, as they openly admit, they do not watch such trash. Academic television critics sometimes exhibit their own version of this attitude, what I term the "It's a dirty job but someone's gotta do it" approach. Such critics offer their conclusions about television's ideological function with little indication that they, or anyone else with any taste or intellect, get any pleasure from the medium. Some of this attitude can be traced to the norms of scholarly writing, which discourage personal expression. However, some of it also is about academic critics' internalization of disdain for television's aesthetic dimensions. We expect literary critics to find beauty and pleasure in literature, but a similar reaction toward television programming from media critics is somehow improper. It is as if television critics find it necessary always to maintain the distinction between their own superior insight and the false consciousness of the hapless masses who consume popular culture.

I believe in critics' ability, by virtue of training and expertise, to analyze and explain the strategies and implications of television that are often invisible to the ordinary viewer, but I also believe it is a mistake to act as though we are immune to television's influences ourselves. I study television because I think it is important, because I think it could be better, and because I want people to take it seriously. I also study it because I like it.

Another aspect of some current television criticism is to use various television texts to illustrate some larger theoretical or conceptual argument. This is a trend connected as much to the race for theory in the humanities academy at large as to the disdain for television as a worthy object of study in its own right. However, what often happens in this kind of writing is that the television programming becomes decontextualized as it is abstracted from its historical, cultural, and televisual milieux— the very elements, in my mind, that create its meaning for audiences. As the writing in this book will demonstrate, I am not opposed to theory; rather, I am opposed to a kind of theorizing about television that does not account for the role of television programming as public discourse that carries important meanings for its viewers, meanings that cannot be separated from their links to the larger context in which television is created and received. As Lynn Spigel and Denise Mann have put it:

> Such theoretical generalizations have done little to explain television's specific discursive functions as they are played out in different cultural and social contexts. By attending to television's textual systems and to the specific historical frameworks in which television is received, we might better understand how mass media help to produce, transmit, and at times transform the logic of cultural fantasies and practices. (1992, p. xiii)

My particular concern is with how television programming has contributed to the cultural conversation about feminism in this country at different historical moments over the past twenty-five years. Theory, particularly feminist theory and genre theory, is vital to explaining the rhetoric of this programming. However, equally important is the historicization of the programming: its placement within a cultural and intertextual milieu that influences how audiences "make sense" of the visions of feminism it offers.

Much of my perspective on television can be traced to the fact that I was trained not in media studies but in rhetorical studies. My graduate education was in departments of speech communication, and my emphasis, until well into my doctoral program, was on American public address: the speeches and public writings of various political and social leaders and their function in persuading publics to accept philosophies and policies for social change. In fact, I became interested in the study of feminism through the study of speeches from the nineteenth-century woman's rights movement. Much of my work over the past decade has analyzed the rhetoric of women like Frances Willard, Elizabeth Cady Stanton, and Abby Kelley—nineteenth-century advocates for temperance, woman suffrage, and abolition, respectively. In that work, I attempted to explicate the strategies used by these rhetors to communicate feminist ideology in ways that would attract women to their efforts and would persuade the larger public of the legitimacy of their claims.

When I began to study television, and eventually focused my doctoral dissertation, the genesis of this book, on television programming, I brought the biases of a rhetorical perspective with me. Key among them was a belief in the importance of context. For example, to understand the discourse of nineteenth-century female reformers, it is necessary to understand the daunting situational obstacles they faced, including the cultural myths about "true womanhood" and the proper "sphere" of women. They tailored their rhetoric in specific ways to confront these myths or, in the case of reformers like Frances Willard, to work with them rather than against them. Aristotle's definition of rhetoric, "the faculty of observing . . . the available means of persuasion" (p. 24) and, more recently, Donald Bryant's, "adjusting ideas to people and people to ideas" (1953, p. 413), are useful for understanding not only the rhetoric of social reformers but also the attempts of television producers to respond to a changing social climate.

My interest in studying the treatment of feminism as a theme in entertainment television programming was the fruit of the intersection of my background in public address studies and my lifelong fascination with television. I am most interested, as a result, in television that works rhetorically to negotiate social issues: to define them, to represent them, and, ultimately, to offer visions of their meanings and implications. I am convinced that entertainment television does some of the cultural work that formerly was done through public speeches. In the nineteenth and early twentieth centuries, public speeches by important reformers and politicians were a popular form of entertainment. They drew huge crowds and were discussed and debated by the public. Cultural occasions like the Fourth of July were celebrated with long, patriotic speeches in which rhetors defined what it meant to be an American.

In very different times, and in different ways, I see television entertainment as serving a similar function of interpreting social change and managing cultural beliefs. In this study, I offer a series of case studies of television entertainment that have been important in defining what it means to be a "liberated woman." I discuss five popular television series since 1970—*The Mary Tyler Moore Show, One Day at a Time, Designing Women, Murphy Brown,* and *Dr. Quinn, Medicine Woman*—which have done important cultural work in representing feminism for the American public. My view of this process is influenced by the notion of television as a cultural forum, which holds that

contemporary cultures examine themselves through their arts, much as traditional societies do via the experience of ritual. Rituals and the arts offer a metalanguage, a way of understanding who and what we are, how values and attitudes are adjusted, how meaning shifts. . . . In its role as central cultural medium, [television] presents a multiplicity of meanings rather than a monolithic dominant point of view. It often focuses on our most prevalent concerns, our deepest dilemmas. . . . The emphasis is on process rather than product, on discussion rather than indoctrination, on contradiction and confusion rather than coherence. (Newcomb and Hirsch, 1987, pp. 458–459)

Although, as Newcomb and Hirsch assert, television is rarely final in its definitions of issues, I do not believe that it features debate without direction. That is, television's treatment of ongoing cultural concerns is conditioned and constrained by its aesthetic conventions, by its social context, and by its intersection with other forms of cultural discourse. My claims about the construction of feminism in each of the series examined in this book is based on analysis of the intersections of their textual strategies—genre, plot, character development, narrative structure—with the confluence of discourses, produced by and about feminism, in the time period during which they were produced and originally received.

This emphasis on the intersections of textual strategies and cultural contexts was possible for me to imagine because of the steady growth in recent years of feminist scholarship about the mass media, particularly television, and because of the appearance of several fine historical treatments of the contemporary women's movement.[1] I attempt to integrate insights gained from both of these areas in this book because my purposes are both historical and critical. The "history" I offer, however, is not so much a record of events in contemporary feminism as it is an attempt to understand how feminist rhetoric and events were absorbed, structured, and represented in media discourse for public consumption. My primary focus is on popular television entertainment, but my analysis of that medium is contextualized by representations of feminism produced by other media as well—newspapers, magazines, television news, bestselling books, and feature films—all of which make up a "media culture" that has had a great deal to say about contemporary feminism and its impact on American life. In short, what this book adds to more traditional histories of feminism is a shift in focus from movement events and the rhetoric and actions of individual feminists and feminist groups to the ways in which those events, discourses, and actions are *interpreted* by various media, but particularly by popular television series. It is, of course, vital to know "what really happened," but it is also illuminating to know what popular media told us was happening; that is, how the "meaning" of feminism was (and still is) translated into public discourses that are consumed by millions of Americans.

I date the beginning of this process to 1970, a watershed year in American second-wave[2] feminism and in American prime-time television programming. Change and difference, of course, are always recognized through comparison. It is not the case, in either television or American society, that the years between World War II and 1970 were a time of total and untroubled acceptance of traditional gender roles. I maintain, however, that the debut of *Mary Tyler Moore* and a wave of media attention to women's liberation in 1970 marked a qualitative shift in public consciousness of the presence of an organized feminist movement. Prior to that time, entertainment television's preferred mode of representing women in series television was as contented housewives in popular shows such as

The Adventures of Ozzie and Harriet (1952–66), *Father Knows Best* (1954–63), *Leave It to Beaver* (1957–63), *The Donna Reed Show* (1958–66), and *The Dick Van Dyke Show* (1961–66).

Scholars such as Nina Leibman (1995) and Suzanna Danuta Walters (1992) have argued that these shows are more complicated than they appear and that their narratives actually had to work quite hard at masking the contradictions lurking beneath their seemingly placid surfaces. Likewise, other critics have commented on the resistance to traditional domesticity enacted by such rebellious housewives as Lucy Ricardo of *I Love Lucy* (1951–61) (Mellencamp, 1986), Alice Kramden of *The Honeymooners* (1955–56), or Samantha Stevens of *Bewitched* (1964–72) (see Douglas, 1994). Certainly, the post–World War II containment of women's aspirations and abilities was not instant or easy, particularly given the expansion of their roles that women had experienced (and enjoyed) during the war (Douglas, 1994; Meyerowitz, 1994). However, the pockets of rebellion that feminist critics find in popular culture of this period occurred in a social context that lacked public awareness of feminism or of the existence of any organized political resistance to women's oppression.

Nuclear family hegemony was not total on television; although they were few and far between, single woman-centered shows appeared on prime-time before 1970. Early shows of this variety, such as *Our Miss Brooks* (1952–56), *Private Secretary* (1953–57), and *How to Marry a Millionaire* (1957–59), although not necessarily discounting their female characters' competence as working women, tended to highlight their obsessive husband-hunting. In the late 1960s, shows such as *Julia* (1968–71), about a widowed nurse with a small child, and *That Girl* (1966–71), about a young actress trying to make it in New York City, introduced slightly more progressive potential. However, because the lead character in *Julia* was black, attention to the sitcom's treatment of race overshadowed the possibilities of its portrayal of an intelligent, highly competent working woman (Bodroghkozy, 1992). *That Girl*'s rather ditzy heroine also lived on her own, but her pursuit of an acting career turned out to be little more than a premarital fling closely monitored by her father and her boyfriend. By series end, she was headed for the altar. Marlo Thomas, the star of *That Girl*, became a visible feminist in the 1970s (Cohen, 1988), adding some feminist resonance to the show after it had left prime-time. However, *Mary Tyler Moore*'s greater longevity (in prime-time and syndication), the greater maturity and autonomy of its lead character, and its timing in relation to the women's liberation movement made it, then and now, television's breakthrough feminist representation.

All of the programs I have mentioned in this brief review are situation comedies. Since the beginning of television, woman-centered dramas have been few and far between. In the 1950s and 1960s, the most popular dramatic series were law and order shows (focusing on cops, private detectives, or lawyers) and westerns. These shows did have female characters, a few of whom, like Miss Kitty of *Gunsmoke* (1955–75), Della Street of *Perry Mason* (1957–74), and Victoria Barkley of *The Big Valley* (1965–69), were regulars. Yet, as Diana Meehan (1983) has noted, the most likely functions of female characters in such dramas were to support male heroes, to serve as victims to be rescued or as temptations to be vanquished. Conventional wisdom in the television industry held that a woman could not carry a drama. To a considerable extent, this belief still seems to hold sway. Today, women are visible in popular ensemble dramas such as *E.R.* (1994–present), *Chicago Hope* (1994–present), and *NYPD Blue* (1993–present), but they are still outnumbered and upstaged by male characters (Douglas, 1995a). As of this writing, there are two dramas on prime-time television centered on female leads: *Murder, She Wrote* (1984–present) and *Dr. Quinn, Medicine Woman* (1993–present).[3] In this book, I devote a chapter to *Dr. Quinn*, but for reasons I have given here, and others that I discuss in Chapter 1, I am concerned primarily with situation comedy. This is the type of programming in which women are most often and most centrally represented and from which television's most resonant feminist representations have emerged.

However, I wish to be clear that I consider the programs discussed in this book to be interesting and important *in themselves*, as well as for the generalizations they reveal about the construction of feminism for audiences. This is a key aspect of my rationale for organizing the book as a series of case studies rather than as thematic chapters. Each program, as I argue in individual chapters, is noteworthy for its place within the trajectories of television history, feminist history, and the evolution of televisual representations of feminism. Each is also important to analyze for its own unique appeal and its distinctive rhetorical strategies. This is why, for example, I have chosen programming of demonstrated popularity and influence among critics and general audiences. Indeed, I believe that each of the series analyzed is an example of quality television that deserves sustained discussion.

Fans of these programs may not always agree with the arguments I make about the programs they enjoy, but I am hopeful that they will agree that I took them seriously and attempted informed judgment. I would like for this book to be useful both to readers interested in conclusions about the treatment of feminism in popular culture and to those who are interested in reading about specific programs. I see work such as this as contributing to what David Bianculli calls "teleliteracy," an "acknowledgment and understanding of the elements of TV's past and future that are likely to survive well into the future" (1992, p. 5). In short, I write this book because I believe television's contribution to our common culture is important and meaningful (and not just as a social problem). To attempt to understand past and present reactions to feminist movements without attending to television's frequent attempts to offer visions of the "new women" produced by women's liberation is to overlook the medium's considerable power in making sense of social change. Moreover, it is also to dismiss the pleasure that those representations have brought to many viewers, particularly those who, like me, searched for progressive portrayals of women among prime-time schedules filled with passive housewives, sultry sex objects, and helpless female victims.

The type of contextualized analysis of television that I advocate has become more common among feminist media scholars in recent years. Several critics have published analyses of television that, to greater and lesser degrees, stress the interrelationships among industry and commercial imperatives, textual strategies, political and social climates in the United States, and television audiences. For example, Lynn Spigel's (1992) analysis of the introduction of television into post–World War II American homes, and the gendered politics of that process, is a fine example of the intersections of criticism and social history. The same can be said for Ella Taylor's (1989) study of the family motif in prime-time television, for Elayne Rapping's (1992) work on made-for-television movies, for Susan Douglas's (1994) analysis of post–World War II popular culture directed at women, and for Julie D'Acci's thorough treatment of the fascinating history of *Cagney and Lacey* (1994). Insights from all of these works inform my perspective in this book; like these authors, I emphasize television's role in mediating social change, in reproducing assumptions about women's "appropriate" roles, and in appealing to and constructing a subjectivity for women as a television audience.

Moreover, I also share with these critics an awareness of television's economic stake in representing women. To this point, I have been discussing my perspective on television's ideological work as public discourse. However, television programming's ideological role is not incidental to its status as a commodity but, rather, is thoroughly implicated in it. The television industry, including the networks and the producers who create shows for them, creates prime-time programming that is designed to appeal to a particular "market" or target group of viewers. When a television program is successful, it can attract more advertisers and collect additional revenue. The overall purpose of television as a commercial system is to deliver an audience for the messages of advertisers. Advertisers, in turn, have two goals: "to reach the largest possible audience, and to reach the ideal (target) audience for their products" (Jamieson and Campbell, 1988, p. 123). Thus, the ratings for television programs demonstrate how many persons are watching that show, and the demographic research conducted by the networks indicates what social subgroups are watching that program (Gitlin, 1983, pp. 58–60). Both of these factors are crucial in selling the program to advertisers. As Eileen Meehan notes: "Television is always and simultaneously an artifact and a commodity that is both created and manufactured; television always and simultaneously presents a vision for interpretation and an ideology for consumption to a viewership that is always and simultaneously a public celebrating meaning and an audience produced for sale in the market place" (1986, p. 449).

The emphasis on commercial viability in television has special implications for women. Women between the ages of eighteen and forty-nine are the prime consumer group that advertisers wish to target because this group makes the majority of consumption decisions (Jamieson and Campbell, 1988). In other words, television executives and producers strive to create programming that is attractive to women. However, advertisers also require that the programming directed at this audience should provide a suitable forum for their messages, limiting the creative choices. In essence, this means that television producers and advertisers are not as interested in finding out what appeals to women as in constructing (or reinforcing) an identity for women that is favorable to what advertisers hope to sell (Nightingale, 1990). For example, Mary Beth Haralovich (1992) has argued that the suburban sitcoms of the late 1950s and early 1960s can be studied for their role in encouraging the growth of middle-class suburbs and the emergent and complementary consumerist role of middle-class housewives.

E. Ann Kaplan notes that "television's reliance on constructing numbers of viewers as commodities involves reproducing female images that accommodate prevailing (and dominant) conceptions of 'woman,' particularly as these satisfy certain economic needs" (1987, p. 223). Thus, advertisers resist characterizations that would inhibit women's incentive to purchase certain products. This means, for example, that women on television tend to dress expensively, to wear makeup, and generally to project the message that attractiveness, particularly to the opposite sex, is important. Advertisers reason that ads for cosmetics, toiletries, and clothing are less effective without such a backdrop.[4] Similarly, family values are reinforced on television because a great deal of consumption is done on the basis of family needs. To undermine the dominance of heterosexuality, for instance, is seen as subverting such interests.[5] Finally, middle- and upper-class characters are featured more prominently and positively on television because these are the classes to which most viewers are believed to aspire. Not only do those segments of the population consume more, reinforcing advertisers' messages, but aspiration to middle-class and upper middle-class status can be enacted through consumption of advertised goods and services.

Maintaining traditional notions of women's roles, duties, and responsibilities is an important part of constructing women's identities as consumers. As times have changed, advertisers have acknowledged that women's physical location is no longer restricted to the home (a perception that applied only to certain, limited segments of the female population anyway, although those segments were particularly attractive to advertisers). However, the qualities, responsibilities, and/or characteristics associated with "woman's place" in the private sphere are still expected from women, both inside and outside television discourse. Such qualities include specific caretaking behaviors ranging from cooking, cleaning, and child-rearing to more general qualities of nurturance and emotional support. Advertisers (and, consequently, television executives) assume that "women are implicated in their own exploitation through love, through the desire to first please their husbands, fathers, and children" (Nightingale, 1990, p. 29).

However, the sexism (and heterosexism) visible in television programming is not solely due to economic motives, and a purely economic analysis distorts a thoroughly overdetermined phenomenon. Americans generally are ambivalent about feminism because it represents significant changes in traditional ways of thinking and acting. Television producers understand this point; they are unlikely to create programming that wholeheartedly endorses ideas that make many people in their audience uncomfortable. If the show makes you uncomfortable, you might turn it off, and then you would not see the commercials. Moreover, television producers work within a medium with established aesthetic conventions, narrative patterns, and expectations. Those constraints are important factors affecting the messages television sends about women and feminism.

For example, as I discuss further in Chapter 1, television programming generally embraces individualism, depicting issues at the level of specific characters and their experiences. Particularly in formats like situation comedy, problems that are social in origin, like sexism, are packaged by television entertainment as solely personal difficulties to be solved by the characters in a half-hour episode. Television implicitly supports a view of the world that discounts the ways in which cultural norms and values affect people's lives. The medium's individualistic view of the world implies that most problems can be solved by hard work, good will, and a supportive family. Television programming does not deal well with complex social issues; it prefers the trials and tribulations of the individual. This logic works well with advertising, which operates on the presumption that an individual's purchasing decision can make an enormous change in his or her life. For example, rather than critiquing unrealistic cultural standards for female appearance, television advertising works on the logic that such standards are unquestionable; what is questionable is which diet aid you should buy in order to meet those standards. The personal buying decision—the individual action—is the way to solve a problem.

Although the bulk of television advertising still relies on appeals to women's senses of their traditional roles within the family or a general framework of heterosexual relationship expectations, advertisers have also incorporated feminist rhetoric into advertising strategies that clearly attempt to appeal to, or to construct, a new feminist consumer. As I discuss in later chapters, television producers also have seen incorporation of feminist discourse as a way to appeal to newly perceived consumer categories, such as working women. Thus, "in the culture industry, feminism and femininity have come to represent a range of strategies for capturing market share," and advertisers, like television producers, have developed a repertoire of signifying practices "which connote independence, participation in the work force, individual freedom, and self-control" (Goldman, Heath, and Smith, 1991, pp. 333, 337).

Indeed, from *Mary Tyler Moore* to *Dr. Quinn, Medicine Woman,* television representations of feminism have always been driven as much by economic goals as by cultural awareness or sensitivity. As I discuss in Chapter 1, *Mary Tyler Moore* was part of CBS's shift to "relevant," socially sensitive programming in the early 1970s, a shift motivated by the network's desire to attract young, urban viewers with disposable income. *Dr. Quinn,* in contrast, has been a gold mine for CBS in the 1990s because it does something that few network drama series have been able to accomplish in recent years: it attracts a family audience on Saturday nights. However, commercial television's relentless profit motive is one of the elements that makes it such a useful cultural barometer. In its attempt to capture the zeitgeist and to attract a large audience, it "feeds off itself and other media, and in this way its images both echo and participate in the shaping of cultural trends" (Taylor, 1989, p. 4).

Thus, a study of television's treatment of feminism is, to some degree, a study of mass-mediated cultural attitudes toward feminism. Analysis of some of television's most powerful and popular visions of liberated women is a journey through phases of popular consciousness over the past quarter century. Television entertainment, as much as a sociological study, can tell us what we like about feminism, what we fear about feminism, and, perhaps most interesting, what aspects of feminism we simply refuse to represent in popular narrative.

I attempt as much as possible to discuss these (tele)visions of feminism on their own terms, rather than evaluating them through some ideal template in order to test their correspondence (or lack thereof) to "true" versions of feminist ideology existing outside of the television text. However, because I also attempt to place these texts within a cultural context, I highlight the ways they pick and choose among available discourses about feminism that are circulating in the times in which the texts are produced. I am concerned, then, with how these texts limit, even omit, some aspects of feminist ideology while emphasizing others. To that extent, I treat feminism as a set of political ideas and practices— developed through feminist movements, dedicated to the progress of women and the transformation of patriarchy[6]—that resides inside and outside of television discourse.

As is true of mass media at large, television's representations of feminism are almost exclusively filtered through white, middle-class, heterosexual, female characters. This focus on the experiences of white, middle-class, heterosexual women has dominated contemporary feminism, although not without contestation (see hooks, 1989), and is, importantly, congruent with the demographics of television's target audience. Television programming, therefore, both draws from and contributes to the consolidation of a racially, sexually, and economically privileged *version* of feminism that, for the American public, has come to represent feminism *in toto*. Because this kind of feminism has the most presence on television, it has the most presence in this book; however, in later chapters I discuss the implications of the absence, in prime-time, of attention to the differences in women's experiences of feminism that are linked to race, class, and sexual identity.

It also should be clear by now that I make a distinction in this project between television's representation of *feminism* and its representations of *women*. Feminist critics have rightly argued that television representations of women always have implications for feminism, and valuable critical work has emerged from that perspective. However, my own purposes are more specific in that I have chosen to focus on popular, long-running programs that were produced during or after the second wave of American feminism (1966–82),[7] that feature unmarried women as lead characters, that contain explicit themes made visible by second-wave feminism (e.g., women in the workplace, sexual freedom, single motherhood, women in male-dominated professions, the conflicts of motherhood and career, social construction of gender roles), and that are described in the discourse that surrounds them (reviews, star interviews, popular press coverage) as offering progressive portrayals of women.

These parameters include a number of programs, such as *Cagney and Lacey* and *Kate and Allie*, that I do not closely analyze. Other programs, such as *Maude* and *Roseanne*, while they do not closely fit the parameters above, clearly have feminist implications. In later chapters, I discuss these programs and many others in terms of their role in forming a context for the case studies. To some extent, any choices that I might make in a book that includes only five case studies could seem arbitrary. My choices were influenced by chronology, by access, by my own familiarity with certain shows, and by my desire to choose case studies that would allow for important comparisons as well as for telling contrasts. I have tried to be thorough and responsible in my claims, but this book is not exhaustive.

Although all of the series I examine contain common threads that I argue are important hallmarks of feminist television, all also highlight different implications of American feminism and use different rhetorical strategies to do so. Moreover, I have chosen programs that I believe represent different *phases* in reactions to feminism because of their positions in different time periods; thus, I analyze two programs from the 1970s (*Mary Tyler Moore* and *One Day at a Time*), a peak time for radical feminist activity and visibility; two that began in the mid- to late 1980s (*Murphy Brown* and *Designing Women*), a time characterized by antifeminist backlash and the construction of "postfeminism"; and one that I argue reflects the late 1980s/early 1990s influence of maternalist feminism particularly well (*Dr. Quinn, Medicine Woman*).

These choices also reflect a desire to study differing *premises* for feminist programming. *Mary Tyler Moore*, for example, is the paradigmatic "working-woman sitcom" that influenced (indirectly and directly through spin-offs) a number of sitcoms developed in the 1970s. *One Day at a Time* (hereafter abbreviated *One Day*) was the first successful sitcom with a divorced, single mother as the lead character and was also a Norman Lear production, tying it to the school of socially conscious sitcoms that included programs such as *All in the Family*. *Murphy Brown* has, since its debut in 1988, become the icon of feminist programming for its time—a position, I argue, solidified by the program's similarities to and differences from *Mary Tyler Moore*. *Designing Women*, an ensemble comedy almost exclusively populated by women, is an interesting shift from the tradition of feminist programming that focuses on a single female lead character. *Designing Women* is also interesting because of its frequent incorporation of specific feminist issues, such as sexual harassment, pornography, and spouse abuse, in its storylines. In contrast to the other sitcoms, *Designing Women* has a less explicitly feminist premise but much more explicitly feminist rhetoric.

This lineup is heavily skewed toward sitcoms, for reasons I explain in Chapter 1 that have to do with sitcom's historical role in introducing controversial issues to American television and with my own desire to counterweight the emphasis in feminist television criticism on dramatic programming, particularly daytime soap opera and prime-time serials such as *Dallas* and *Dynasty*. My inclusion of a case study of *Dr. Quinn, Medicine Woman* is motivated by factors both textual and extratextual. When *Dr. Quinn* made its debut in January of 1993, it was a surprising success, and this success was consistently attributed to its ability to draw a family audience that embraced the strong female role model offered by its lead character, a female doctor on the post–Civil War Colorado frontier. In my own anecdotal experience, the attraction of *Dr. Quinn* for an adolescent female audience is remarkably strong. Textually, *Dr. Quinn* also is interesting, because of its combination of nostalgia appeals (a trend generally in cultural products since the late 1980s revival of the western) and because of its reframing of contemporary issues in a historical context.

Following this Preface, and preceding Chapter 1, is an Introduction that addresses some current theoretical debates in academic television criticism. This Introduction is important in explaining my assumptions to other academic critics and to outlining my general perspective on the rhetorical power of television. Readers who are not interested in these issues should feel free to go directly to Chapter 1, where this book's narrative about prime-time feminism begins. I am hopeful that what follows will be a contribution to the conversation, both inside and outside of the academy, about the necessity of feminism, the importance of criticism, and the possibilities of television.

Notes

1. See, for example, Davis, 1991; Echols, 1989; Kaminer, 1990.
2. "Second wave" is a term used to distinguish the contemporary feminist movement, beginning in 1966, from the "first wave" of feminism represented by the woman's rights movement of the nineteenth and early twentieth centuries. The first wave culminated in the 1920 passage of the Nineteenth Amendment, which granted women the right to vote.
3. The inclusion of *Sisters* (1991-present), an ensemble drama focusing on the lives of four sisters, would bring this count to three.
4. Gloria Steinem has insightfully explained this kind of logic and its implicit disrespect for women in "Sex, Lies, and Advertising," her analysis of the relationship between advertisers and women's magazines (see Steinem, 1990).
5. There has been some slippage in this generalization in recent years, although it still largely applies to prime-time network television. Targeted cable networks have more freedom to resist the compulsion to attract the largest number of people and offend the smallest number of people, leading to noteworthy events such as HBO's 1993 production of an original movie based on Randy Shilts's book, *And the Band Played On* (1988), about the spread of AIDS and its effect on the gay community. Even the minor storylines about gays or lesbians included in prime-time continuing series such as *thirtysomething*, *L.A. Law*, and *Roseanne* on the "big three" networks have created controversy and network dis-

comfort. A 1994 episode of *Roseanne*, in which Roseanne kissed a lesbian in a gay bar, was preceded by a "viewer discretion" warning from ABC (Roush, 1994).

6. What "counts" as progress and what *kind* of transformation patriarchy needs do, of course, differ according to what kind of feminist thought one is dealing with. At various points in the chapters to follow, I deal with different varieties of second wave political feminism (liberal, radical, cultural) and their varying visibility in television and in American cultural discourse.

7. I believe that the feminist movement is, in many ways and on many levels, ongoing. However, I make distinctions, in later chapters, between different phases of feminist activity. I date the beginning of organized second-wave feminism around 1966–68 because of the founding of the National Organization for Women in 1966, the formation of women's liberation groups in the fall of 1967, and the highly visible protest against the Miss America protest staged by radical feminists in Atlantic City in 1968 (Echols, 1989). However, I argue in Chapter 1 that second-wave feminism did not develop significant visibility for the general public until 1970, when it became the focus of extensive media coverage. In Chapter 3 I use 1982, the year in which the Equal Rights Amendment was defeated, to indicate a shift, at least in the eyes of the mass media and the general public, to what came to be labeled the "postfeminist" era.

Introduction: The Rhetoric of Television, Criticism, and Theory

Academic television criticism has come a long way in the past two decades if you date its birth, as I do, with the publication of Horace Newcomb's *TV: The Most Popular Art* in 1974. Its increasing theoretical sophistication is evident, and is made most clear, perhaps, by the meta-criticism that has developed to interrogate the assumptions of critical practice. Television criticism has become an increasingly self-conscious and self-reflexive activity that requires definitions, explanations of perspective, and defense of positions before a critic can even begin to engage with a text (a term that also cannot be taken at face value).

This chapter is my attempt to situate this project within the myriad perspectives that constitute television study. In that process, I engage with debates that I will not resolve: my primary concern here is to explain why I approach the texts that I analyze in the way that I do, as well as to explain what I see as the merits of that approach. I organize this discussion around a series of key terms—*criticism, text, audience* and *theory*—that I will use repeatedly in this book and which I view as central to the practice of television criticism at this point in time. I begin with an explanation of my view of what criticism, both broadly and with regard to television, is about; specifically, I offer my perspective on its social, theoretical, and political functions. In the following sections on text, audience, and theory, I discuss some current debates over these concepts as I sketch my own position relative to those issues. Related to my discussion in the Preface, what emerges from this discussion is my view of television as a rhetorical medium and my belief that television criticism is a rhetorical activity.

Television and Criticism

Criticism is a social activity because it is written for an audience. As Said writes, "there is always an Other; and this other willy nilly turns interpretation into a social activity, albeit with unforeseen consequences, audiences, constituencies and so on" (1983, p. 137). For example, I view myself as addressing several audiences simultaneously in this book: television critics, feminist critics, fans of the programming I study, students. Each of these communities will no doubt have different uses for and reactions to various parts of this book. I expect and welcome that. One can never, as Said indicates, be cognizant of all of the ways one's work might be received.

Even so, this discussion of my views of criticism is designed to sketch some parameters for how I would prefer my criticism to be understood. It is, in a sense, my contract with imagined and potential readers, intended to tell them what to expect from me and my work. The expectations that readers have of the criticism they read is a central, but rarely articulated, concern to television critics. For example, at one level, the debates within television studies over the relative values of studying texts (or content) versus studying audiences (or reception) and the validity of the conclusions derived from studying either often seem to me to be linked to the issue of expectations.

The growth of attention to reception in studying television has given television scholars new questions to consider as they study television's role in making meaning for audiences. Although I do not do reception study myself, I find it interesting and useful, particularly because it has expanded the possibilities for television study and because it produces a *different* kind of knowledge from that produced by textual analysis of television. However, to say that reception study is valuable because it produces a different kind of knowledge is not the same as saying that it produces better or more valid knowledge, an unfortunate conclusion that can be inferred from reading some of the work on reception theory. Textual analysis, it is sometimes implied, cannot tell us what we *really* need to know: what actually goes on in the minds of viewers (as opposed to what the textual critic *speculates* goes on in their minds). As Charlotte Brunsdon puts it, "the pursuit of the audience" can be characterized "as a search for authenticity, for an anchoring moment in a sea of signification" (1990, p. 68).

The most powerful claim of audience studies has been that "real" viewers often resist the dominant messages of television and interpret programming in ways that suit their own interests, a claim that has cast suspicion on the claims that textual critics make for the oppressive or hegemonic function of texts (or for any predictable function of texts). Intentional or not, such judgments cast the differences between approaches within the framework of a zero-sum game in which only one party can be right, making the other automatically wrong.[1]

What troubles me most about this kind of thinking is that it assumes that it is proper to expect television study to reveal the "truth" of how texts work to produce various effects upon their receivers. Disagreements over how "open" texts are, how "active" audiences are, and how possible it is for viewers to "resist" the hegemonic message of a text are issues we must settle on our way to discovering how to access that truth. There are problems with this assumption at various levels, many of which I discuss later in this chapter. What I question at this point, however, is why critics feel the need to ground the value of criticism on "truth" in the first place.

Linked to my background in rhetorical studies, I view criticism as a species of *argument* rather than as a quest for truth, and I view skeptically any assurance of greater truth value derived from method. Moreover, linked to my awareness of feminist critiques of science and knowledge production, I view criticism as a kind of argument that, whatever its value to the reader, articulates the interests of the arguer first. This does not mean that all criticism is ultimately solipsistic or self-centered; however, it does mean that it is always the product of socially situated persons who make arguments that are enabled but also limited by their experiences and perspectives.

However, there is no such thing as the totally isolated, individualistic, idiosyncratic reading of a text. Because all critics are socially situated members of communities, their interpretations of texts are the product of social life. Membership in a community is always partially linguistic (anyone who tries to read works on postmodernism without first learning the jargon has lived this realization) and to the extent that you speak or write so that others can understand you, you are acting socially. Criticism is a particular kind of writing, one that I view as fundamentally rhetorical. By rhetorical, I mean that it assumes an audience, that it attempts to persuade, and that its "truths" are social, reflecting what we agree to believe, based on the evidence and our interpretation of it, at a particular point in time. Because of the wealth of things that a critic might write about and the wealth of things that might be said about them, any access to knowledge provided by the critical act is necessarily partial and contingent.

Moreover, because the critic must make choices, his or her work is rhetorical. Criticism "takes up a text and re-circulates it, that is, 'says' or "does" that text differently, and asks the listener or reader to re-understand and re-evaluate the text, to see and judge it in new ways suggested by the critic" (Nothstine, Blair, and Copeland, 1994, p. 3). Given this perspective, criticism is not about discovering or reporting the meaning in texts. Rather, it becomes a performative activity that is, in some sense, dedicated to creating meaning. This distinction is particularly important for feminist criticism, given that

> a fully politicized feminist criticism has seldom been content to ascertain old meanings and . . . take the measure of already constituted subjectivities; it has aimed, rather, at bringing into being *new* meanings and *new* subjectivities. . . . In this respect it may be said to have a performative dimension—i.e., to be *doing* something beyond restating already existent ideas and views, wherever these might happen to reside. (Modleski, 1991, p. 49)

This perspective assumes that texts are *polysemous*—that is, they can mean in different ways at different times. However, my use of polysemy here differs from its current meaning in cultural studies, in which it is used to refer to the possibility that audiences can decode texts in varying ways (Fiske, 1986). Rather, I use the term as it applies to critical activity as opposed to audience activity. In his *Anatomy of Criticism* (1957), literary critic Northrop Frye explained the necessity for critics to accept that there are manifold critical approaches to a text by arguing that the alternative was to choose a school of critical thought "and then try to prove that all the others are less legitimate. The former is the way of scholarship and leads to the advancement of learning; the latter is the way of pedantry" (1957, p. 72).

Certainly, undiscriminating pluralism has its limits, and not all criticism is equally valuable. A work of criticism can be poorly supported, poorly argued, or simply unconvincing. However, the motive for diversity in critical approaches should not be a search for the holy grail of truth but an exploration, with unavoidable twists and turns, toward the many, sometimes contradictory, possibilities of understanding. This perspective does not see criticism as an attempt to provide the most accurate retelling of how a text is received or as an attempt to account for the widest variety of interpretations; rather, it views criticism as an argumentative activity in which the goal is to persuade the audience that their knowledge of a text will be enriched if they choose to see a text as the critic does, while never assuming that that particular "way of seeing" is the only or the best way to see that text (or that all audiences do, in fact, see it that way). Thus, even when a critic writes as though s/he is "discovering" or "revealing" a meaning in a text (and I often find myself using such language), what s/he has "discovered" is the *possibility* of meaning rather than its certainty. This perspective is not a maneuver to avoid standing behind the arguments we make as critics or a descent into endless relativism; instead, it is a responsible position that acknowledges the contingency of the claims that we as humans make about any human activity.

As a critic, then, I argue for the possibility and the usefulness of understanding a text in a particular fashion. The power of the arguments I make depends upon how well they interpret the text, the strength of their evidence and theoretical underpinnings (which I address more specifically later), and, ultimately, their heuristic value. The heuristic value of criticism, in my view, is both theoretical and political. In theoretical terms, it means that the argument should, in addition to revealing something interesting and useful about the text itself, reveal something interesting and useful about the *kind* of symbolic activity that the text represents, whether it is music, literature, or television programming. That is, given the recombinance of symbolic activity (which is especially true for television), arguments that help to explain *Mary Tyler Moore* might also help to explain rhetorical processes in other sitcoms, or in other programming that deals with feminism. I view the kind of grounded theory that arises from and can be used for the study of concrete texts as the most useful kind.

Politically, the heuristic value of criticism, specifically the feminist criticism that I practice, is its capacity to engage our thinking about the political implications of discursive practice. To the extent that criticism teaches us something about television and how it works, it tells us something about the world and how it works. The poststructuralist insight that everything is discourse, and that we therefore cannot separate discursive practice from "real life," is quite useful here. Whether or not television "reflects" reality outside the tube is beside the point: we watch television and it is therefore part of life. Rather than existing in some autonomous realm outside of political life, media is part of it. What criticism can do is to accentuate the importance of that realization and offer specific arguments for its meaning.

In this book, for example, I argue that one of the ways that programs such as *Mary Tyler Moore* and *Murphy Brown* function politically is that they offer visions of what feminism "means." They are fictional, to be sure, and to some extent we are aware of their artificiality. However, to deny that they influence our thinking about women, women's roles, and the impact of social change is, it seems to me, to be dangerously naive. It is possible for television to be acknowledged as fiction and yet be experienced as realistic in its characterization or treatment of issues (Deming, 1990, p. 41). As I discuss in Chapter 5, the controversy engendered by then-Vice-President Dan Quayle's attack on Murphy Brown's decision to have a baby out of wedlock is a vivid illustration of the symbolic possibilities that can reside in a fictional character. As a feminist critic, the political task that I see for my work is to give presence to such possibilities, to articulate them in a way that can provide some insight into the world in which we all live and which shapes us in myriad ways. Feminist literary critic Annette Kolodny calls this the "altered reading attentiveness" (1985, p. 158) that a feminist critic can bring to a text:

> All the feminist is asserting, then, is her own equivalent right to liberate new (and perhaps different) significance from these same texts: and, at the same time, her right to choose which features of a text she takes as relevant because she is, after all, asking new and different questions of it. In the process she claims neither definitiveness nor structural completeness for her different readings and reading systems, but only their . . . applicability in conscientiously decoding woman as sign. (1985, p. 160)

Finally, at the most basic level, this work is intended to continue the conversation about feminism—what it has meant and can mean—because the more talk there is about it, the more likely it is to live on as a viable, dynamic, and fertile set of ideas and practices. As Modleski writes, "It remains importantly the case that feminist critical writing is committed writing, a writing committed to the future of women" (1991, p. 47).

Television as Rhetorical Text

At this point, if not earlier, the term *text*, as I use it, deserves some attention. Already, I have used "text" in the broad sense that many critics use it—to refer to the artifact, or the "thing" to be analyzed. However, because television programming, unlike a poem or a speech (at least as we traditionally understand them), is capable of being divided or "textualized" in so many ways, it makes sense to be specific. All of the television series that I analyze in this book—*The Mary Tyler Moore Show, One Day at a Time, Murphy Brown, Designing Women*, and *Dr. Quinn, Medicine Woman*—constitute what I consider my primary texts.

I make arguments that explain what I see as patterns occurring within each series and which give each series a distinctive rhetorical function in defining feminism. Generally, then, I define "text" at the level of the series, rather than the episode. Because it is my contention, which I treat in more detail in Chapter 1, that texts are interpreted in relation to other texts, my analysis also treats as "texts" a variety of other kinds of discourse. For example, I use what John Fiske (1987a, p. 85) has called "secondary texts"—journalistic criticism, reviews, advertisements, promos, interviews with stars and producers—to argue for the way that treatment of programming in mass media can both enable and constrain interpretation (see also Allen, 1992, p. 132). On a broader level, I will also discuss the interaction of these television texts with other culturally produced "texts" about feminism found in press coverage of the movement and its effects.

In short, my approach to the specific television texts I analyze is to place them within a context that I believe sheds light on how they might be understood. Given my contention that television draws from and contributes to the larger cultural conversation about feminism, a major part of my approach to these texts is based on contextual concerns. Much as rhetorical critics view speeches as responses to specific situations and as affected by audience expectations regarding genre and occasion, I view television discourse about feminism as situated and constrained by its relationship to other forms of cultural discourse about feminism, to previous televisual representations, to secondary texts, to industry practice and commercial demands, and to the expectations attached to established televisual genres. I view all of these factors as constraints that work to channel the messages that television presents (and that viewers receive) about feminism in particular directions.[2]

I believe that it is a mistake to treat texts as ahistorical entities that can be abstracted out of their historical/cultural milieux and given timeless meanings. It is particularly a mistake for my purposes in this book. Because my purpose is to discuss the interaction of television and feminism at different points in time since 1970, I treat these texts as products of their time, directed at audiences in their time and contributing to the cultural conversation about feminism in their time. Although I certainly cannot avoid bringing my historical hindsight, as a critic writing in 1995, to a text like *Mary Tyler Moore*, which went off prime-time in 1977, my case study of the program attempts, as much as possible, to create an understanding of its feminist discourse as a product of the 1970s. As Celeste Condit has argued, such an approach leads away from simplistic praise or blame of programming and toward

a calibrated understanding of the particular role [programming] played in introducing certain limited pieces of information to different ranges of audiences at different times. Critical analysis should therefore, at least at times, be rhetorical; it should be tied to the particularity of occasion; specific audiences, with specific codes or knowledges, addressed by specific programs or episodes. (1989, p. 115)

Underlying Condit's perspective, and my own, is a conception of television texts as rhetorical entities that can be interpreted as performing particular functions at particular times. These are *persuasive* functions that work to make some ideas, positions, and alternatives more attractive, accessible, and powerful to audiences than others. Particularly when television programming is studied with an eye toward its role in social change, it is useful to view it as rhetorical discourse that works to accomplish some end(s).

Kenneth Burke (1973, p. 1) notes that we can think of "any work of critical or imaginative cast as the adopting of various strategies for the encompassing of situations." Thus, all artistic work can be approached as "the *functioning* of a structure" that is designed to accomplish something (Burke, 1973, p. 74). If we assume that a work is designed to "do something" for its audience, then "we can make the most relevant observations about its design by considering the poem [or creative work] as the embodiment of this act" (Burke, 1973, p. 89). Within such a rhetorical perspective, works of art are "strategies for selecting enemies and allies, for socializing losses, for warding off evil eye [sic], for purification, propitiation, and desanctification, consolation and vengeance, admonition and exhortation, implicit commands or instructions of one sort or another" (Burke, 1973, p. 304).

A rhetorical perspective, then, assumes that symbolic acts function to accomplish an end, and that they do so through the employment of strategies that influence audiences. However, this is not a one-way process in which texts impose meaning upon audiences. As Burke indicates, rhetorical discourse is strategic because of its ability to interact with, draw from, and respond to the context in which it occurs and in which its audiences are situated (1973, pp. 1–3).

Within this general perspective, there are still a variety of ways to analyze or interrogate a text. The angle that I take on the texts I examine in this study is directed at their role in negotiating the meaning of social change wrought by feminism. The meanings offered by television are rarely direct, often contradictory, and never final. Certainly, it is the central dynamic of series television to rework the same problematic over and over. Thus, the persuasive function of television is not so much to provide solutions to cultural conflicts but, rather, to negotiate the parameters for the debate. This is why, for example, one of the central concerns of this project is not so much an evaluation of the success or the failure of television's feminist visions but, rather, an understanding of how entertainment programming has functioned to influence cultural perceptions of feminism.

My view is consonant with that of critics who claim that those who produce television programming function as "cultural interpreters" (Newcomb and Hirsch, 1987, p. 458), and that television acts to "*articulate* the main lines of the cultural consensus about the nature of reality" (Fiske and Hartley, 1987, p. 602). The interpretation and articulation that occur in television entertainment involve choices at many levels. Thus, the rhetorical critic of television is interested in such questions as

why an artist chose to deal with certain topics (and not others); why the artistic elements chosen were structured as they were (and not some other way); why certain characteristics of the medium . . . are emphasized (and others are not emphasized); what purpose, among all those possible, seems to be governing these choices; and to what audience the work addresses itself with what potential effect. (Medhurst and Benson, 1984, p. x)

Such questions do not require a determination of intent. Any work can have effects beyond those for which it was designed. A rhetorical critic is concerned with the purpose, strategies, and functions that can be discerned from an understanding of the television text and its potential interaction with audiences.

Television and Audiences

Although, as I said above, I do not wish to engage in a contest over the truth-seeking potential of criticism, there are several good reasons to revisit the issues involved in debates over audience activity and textual power. The most important reason is that such debates force critics to consider, to articulate, and, ultimately, to make more precise our always present but often implicit arguments about how texts and audiences interact. Indeed, it is my contention that the best way to deal with this issue is to treat it as a collection of *arguments* that use different types (and strengths) of evidence and reasoning to support different positions. And, because arguments are always susceptible to fallacies, my organization of this section is based on a discussion of the various manifestations of what I see as a recurring fallacy in this species of argument: the false choice.

To provide a quick overview, here are some of the troublesome dichotomies that I see at work in what, for lack of a better term, I call the powerful text/active audience debates: hegemony versus polysemy (of the text), passive versus active viewing (by audiences), critics versus audiences (as the makers of meanings), and dominant culture versus subculture (as the major determinant of social subjectivity).[3] I also discuss another dichotomy that I believe should be strengthened rather than dissolved: that between culture and politics.

To begin at the top, the concept of hegemony, based on the writings of Italian Marxist Antonio Gramsci, refers to "the myriad ways in which the institutions of civil society operate to shape, directly or indirectly, the cognitive and affective structures through which men [and women] perceive and evaluate problematic social reality" (Femia, 1981, p. 24). The ideological function of this process is made clearer by Becker, who describes it as "the cultural, intellectual, and moral direction exercised by the dominant classes over other classes. In part, hegemony is the imposition of one or more classes' ideology on other classes" (1984, p. 69). Media's role in the maintenance and reproduction of hegemony has been the topic of much cultural studies research, including that produced by British scholars such as Stuart Hall (1982) and other members of the Birmingham group, as well as that produced in the United States by scholars such as Todd Gitlin (1980, 1982). For example, Gitlin has argued that, in television entertainment,

major social conflicts are transported *into* the cultural system, where the hegemonic system frames them, form and content both, into compatibility with dominant systems of meaning. Alternative material is routinely *incorporated*: brought into the body of cultural production. Occasionally oppositional material may succeed in being indigestible; that material is excluded from the media discourse and returned to the cultural margins from which it came; while *elements* of it are incorporated into the dominant forms. (1982, p. 527)

Scholars critical of this perspective argue that it presents texts as closed, as offering only the possibility of absorption of the ideology offered, and thus positioning the audience as passive receivers. In contrast, it is the textual critic who actively makes meaning from the text by articulating its structures of domination (and assuming these strategies are usually invisible to the audience). Given this framework, the dominant ideology as disseminated through media, education, religion, and so on (what Althusser [1971] would call the "ideological state apparatuses"), has an enormous amount of power to mold the subjectivity of audiences so that they are persuaded to think and behave in ways that are not necessarily in their interests as defined by their social experience (or, as it is often expressed, as defined by their subcultural identities as, for example, workers, women, members of oppressed racial or ethnic groups, gays, or lesbians, to name a few hardly distinct categories).

As John Fiske has put it, such an account makes hegemony appear "almost irresistible" (1987a, p. 40). Or, as another writer recently explained her decision to disregard Marxist-influenced analyses of popular culture: "To embrace the Frankfurt school position on the hegemony of state capitalism, for instance, is necessarily to see the television viewer as a figure essentially passive, held captive by the communications apparatus of the capitalist interests, at best a prisoner of false consciousness" (Tichi, 1991, p. 9).

On the other side of this series of dichotomies are those who argue for the polysemy of the text—that is, its capacity to invite different meanings from different viewers. From this perspective, viewers are actively making meanings as they watch television, and these meanings do not necessarily reflect those "preferred" by the text. Audiences, rather than critics, are thus makers of meaning. Finally, the subjectivities of active audiences (that is, the way they see themselves and the relations through which they operate in the world) are much more determined by their specific (again, often termed "subcultural") social experience than by the ideological operations of the dominant culture. The implication of this perspective, again in the words of John Fiske, is that

textual studies of television now have to stop treating it as a closed text, that is, as one where the dominant ideology exerts considerable, if not total, influence over its ideological structure and therefore over its reader. Analysis has to pay less attention to the textual strategies of preference or closure and more to the gaps and spaces that open television up to meanings not preferred by the textual structure but that result from the social experience of the reader. (1987a, p. 64)

This quotation, in fact, efficiently expresses the distance that at least some see between the dichotomies I have suggested.

Having established, albeit briefly, the substance of these positions, I would like to mediate between them, blurring their boundaries while carving out my own position on the relationship between texts and audiences. Although I explore a variety of issues, it is for the purpose of coming back to where I began, with a rationale for an essentially *rhetorical* approach to television study. Generally, my position throughout this discussion is that critics' understanding and employment of the concepts of hegemony and polysemy (and the terms and concepts that radiate from these central ideas) would benefit from more nuanced explanation of our motives and reasoning for employing them in particular situations at particular times for particular purposes.

For example, those critics who work with the concept of hegemony are accused of adhering to the position that television viewers are passive cultural dupes who are caught up in the static, totalistic, and inescapable web of ideology emanating from commercial television. Tichi's illustrative comment is that "the resistant figure . . . has no legitimate place in [the] Frankfurt school [of] thought" (1991, p. 9). If we look past Tichi's unfortunate tendency to lump all Marxist cultural analysis under the aegis of the Frankfurt school, the most crucial oversight in this view is that it discounts the fact that hegemony theory *assumes* oppositional thinking; that is why the hegemonic process must be dynamic, flexible, and "leaky" (Gitlin, 1982, p. 526). As Gitlin rather emphatically points out in what has become a central work on hegemony and television: "One point should be clear: the hegemonic system is not cut-and-dried, not definitive. It has continually to be reproduced, continually superimposed, continually to be negotiated and managed, in order to override the alternative, and, occasionally, the oppositional forms" (1982, p. 527). Moreover, even the Frankfurt school perhaps has been judged more harshly than necessary, as Thomas Streeter argues: "Horkheimer and Adorno did not arrive at their pessimistic views because they failed to take into account social difference, plurality, and resistance. Their despair should not be taken for an orthodox, mechanistic understanding of social domination. On the contrary, their fear was that plurality and difference has [sic] been thoroughly accommodated to the modern order" (1989, p. 16, quoted in Rapping, 1992, p. xxx).

The question becomes, then, not whether or not resistance or oppositional thinking exists—hegemony theorists have always assumed that—but how powerful or effective they are relative to the hegemonic process and, moreover, what role the media play in facilitating them. This question goes to the heart of arguments about the polysemy of texts. While some researchers have claimed that the television text is an " 'empty vessel' that can be all things to all people" (Barkin and Gurevitch, 1987, p. 18), the position advanced by John Fiske is more representative of claims for the "open" text. Fiske describes the television text "as a structured polysemy, as a potential of unequal meanings, some of which are preferred over, or proffered more strongly than, others, and which can only be activated by socially situated viewers in a process of negotiation between the text and their social situation" (1987a, p. 65).

Although Fiske admits that the "dominant" ideology at work in a television text can usually be discerned (1987a, pp. 51–52), there is no guarantee that audiences will receive the text in the intended fashion; instead, "the dominant ideology . . . can be resisted, evaded, or negotiated with, in varying degrees by differently socially situated readers" (1987a, p. 41). Generally, it is impossible to disagree with this position. The fact that feminist critics can and do perform feminist readings of patriarchal texts means that there is no reasonable way to claim that a text is closed. However, the power of the dominant ideology, or preferred meaning, of the text is visible in Fiske's formulation, given that every possibility he offers is a *reaction to the preferred meaning*. In short, resistance or opposition assumes that the viewer "gets" the preferred meaning of the text (to the extent that there is ever only one preferred meaning) prior to resisting it (Evans, 1990, p. 150).

For example, when I watch a program, such as the NBC drama *Law and Order*, that is often deeply at odds with my politics (although I consider the program superbly done and eminently watchable), I often find myself verbally resisting (I talk back to the set and deconstruct certain characterizations). I think of myself, at these times, not as making a different meaning from that intended by the program, but, rather, of evaluating the preferred meaning negatively. What I experience, in short, is more akin to what Celeste Condit has called *polyvalence*—the process through which audiences *receive* essentially similar meanings from television texts but may *evaluate* those meanings differently depending upon their value systems. She notes that "different respondents may similarly understand the messages that a text seeks to convey. They may, however, see the text as rhetorical—as urging positions upon them—and make their own selections among and evaluations of those persuasive messages" (Condit, 1989, pp. 107–108).

Condit's analysis of the limits of polysemy is instructive in a number of ways. She urges critics to consider the possibilities of polysemy and resistance in a social context, stressing the differential resources and efforts necessary to construct truly oppositional or resistant meanings. Part of the power of the ideology offered by television is that "it *relays* and *reproduces*, and *processes* and *packages*, and *focuses* ideology" that is at work elsewhere in society as well (Gitlin, 1982, p. 510). A "preferred" reading does not happen in isolation and does not rely solely on the power of the text; it partakes of the competencies and discursive codes that are reinforced throughout the different areas of social life (not to mention those, like genre, narrative pattern, and intertextuality, that are learned from television itself). In short, even if we agree that viewers negotiate the meanings of television, "their definitions do not match the discursive power of a centralized storytelling institution" (Carragee, 1990, p. 88).

Condit points out that "oppositional and negotiated readings require more work of viewers than do dominant readings" (1989, p. 109), and, moreover, that the possibility of these nonpreferred decodings is dependent upon the codes available to the viewer. So, for example, while television viewers (assuming they are moderate consumers of media) can easily acquire the codes necessary for preferred readings, the acquisition of codes for negotiated or oppositional readings is more difficult and less common (Budd, Entman, and Steinman, 1990, p. 177). The likelihood of counterreadings may have been exaggerated, Condit argues, because audience researchers have tended to study groups that have access to oppositional codes (1989, pp. 110–112).[4] In the end, "it is not the case that all human beings are equally skilled in responding to persuasive messages with countermessages. The masses may not be cultural dupes, but they are not necessarily skilled rhetors" (1989, p. 111).[5]

Of course, audience researchers have claimed that oftentimes it is the social experience of viewers, as members of subcultures or interpretive communities, that provides them with the resources to resist television's hegemonic messages. For example, as Fiske explains this position, "the actual television viewer is a primarily social subject. This social subjectivity is more influential in the construction of meanings than the textually produced subjectivity which exists only at the moment of reading" (1987a, p. 62). Two assumptions in this position trouble me. First, it posits the social subjectivity of the viewer (linked to membership in a subculture or interpretive community) as autonomous from, rather than overlapping with, and substantially affected by, media subjectivity (see

Budd, Entman, and Steinman, 1990, p. 174). Second, it overlooks the strong possibility that television texts, because of their repetitive nature and their participation in a wide-ranging system of cultural hegemony, produce a subjectivity that is hardly momentary and isolated from other sources of reinforcement.

Membership in a subculture may indeed provide a strong sense of subjectivity that can be used to combat the insinuations of the dominant culture. However, it seems a mistake to assume that all viewers are members of coherent subcultures or, for that matter, that all subcultures are critical. As Budd, Entman, and Steinman note, "Subcultures can be reactionary or accept most elements of the status quo" (1990, p. 175). Let us say, however, that we decide to grant that subcultures do routinely provide viewers with the resources to interpret television against the grain. Then, staying with the theme of placing claims for audience resistance within a wider social context, the next question that seems natural to ask is, to what end does this interpretation occur? What does it mean, if anything?

If we celebrate the active audience to prove that viewers are not dominated by cultural hegemony, then what have we proven when their resistance does not go beyond negotiating with the messages of television? Or, as Elayne Rapping puts it, while we seem to have established that people can watch television in different ways, "we have not been asking how they watch it in similar ways, or, more to the point, how they receive and use it in ways similar enough to lead to potential changes in power relations" (1992, p. xxvi). This is a serious gap if we are to take audience research as having political implications (which is clearly the hope of scholars like John Fiske [see 1986, p. 394], for instance). Budd, Entman, and Steinman succinctly summarize this problem: "Researchers have yet to demonstrate that the active thinking and resistance to hegemonic principles that may accompany the viewing of TV entertainment spills over into direct thinking about and behavior in politics" (1990, p. 178). In the end, there is still a power structure that benefits a few people; the people who make television programming continue to get richer; and, of particular concern to me, women continue to live in patriarchy.

A summary of the arguments articulated thus far is useful at this point. First, hegemony, rather than assuming an all powerful, closed text, presumes the possibility of resistance and opposition. Moreover, this position is not inconsistent with Fiske's claim that

the hegemony of the text is never total. . . . The meanings within the text are structured by the differential distribution of textual power in the same way that social groups are related according to the differential distribution of social power. All meanings are not equal, nor equally easily activated, but all exist in relations of subordination or opposition to the dominant meanings proposed by the text. (1987a, p. 93; see also Fiske, 1992, pp. 291–292)

However, as I have argued, it is possible that what critics have called polysemy is, in many cases, polyvalence—that is, the possibility of viewers creating different *evaluations* of a text, rather than different meanings.

Another argument I have offered here is that it is a misnomer to call viewers passive if we believe they accept the ideology of a text and active if we believe they resist it. Decoding is always work and always requires competence from audiences, denying the label of "dupes." Our concern should, rather, be with the resources available for decoding and with the *kind* of decoding we wish to analyze (Evans, 1990, p. 150). This position also carries caution about our assumptions regarding the distance between what textual critics do and what audience researchers do. In the end, we are all making arguments based on the evidence we choose to examine.

For critics stressing hegemony, that evidence consists of the text and the codes of the dominant culture. For audience researchers, that evidence is the behavior and discourse of audiences, to which we give meaning based, oftentimes, on subcultural codes or the competencies of interpretive communities. This realization, I suggest, dissolves the dichotomy between critics and audiences as meaning makers in different types of studies. In both textual studies and audience studies, the act of interpretation and argument by the researcher (whether ethnographer or critic) is paramount.

Finally, given the evidence of the world around us, we should be careful about the extent to which we claim that the influence of subcultural codes necessarily overrides dominant cultural codes or is critical of or resistant to them. Also imbricated in this issue is the need to recognize that television has codes of its own, that, as George Gerbner has said, "People are now born into the symbolic environment of television and live with its repetitive lessons throughout life. . . . Living with television means growing up in a symbolic environment" (quoted in Tichi, 1991, p. 3). This environment is not separate from the social experience of a subculture or a dominant culture but interacts with, affects, and is affected by, both.

Ultimately, what I have suggested is that positions that have at times been taken to be dichotomous can, rather, be characterized as sharing some of the same strengths and weaknesses. As I said earlier, I am troubled by the drawing of differences between textual criticism and audience research, or between the hegemony or polysemy of the text, that cast the two activities or perspectives as opposing players in a zero-sum game: that is, if one kind of activity is "right," the other must be "wrong." This kind of thinking is implicit, for example, in a quotation from John Fiske I used above, in which he asserts that "textual studies of television now *have to* stop treating it as a closed text. . . . Analysis *has to* pay less attention to the textual strategies of preference or closure and more to the gaps and spaces that open television up" (1987a, p. 64; my emphasis). Obviously, Fiske is not suggesting that critics have to become audience researchers, although he uses the conclusions of audience research to support his claims about the polysemy of the text. However, he is suggesting that there is no question that analyzing the polysemic potential or the "gaps and spaces" in a text is more valuable, more useful, and, I suspect, more "accurate" in terms of how texts are used than is analysis of the hegemonic functions of texts.

At this point, it seems to me, we verge into a dangerous area that is hardly supportive of critical pluralism. At the point that we assert that one kind of work is more worthy than another, we must ask on what basis that evaluation is made. As the arguments reviewed above indicate, the basis for claiming greater access to truth through interpretive audience research is rather shaky. Those arguments also suggest that texts have both hegemonic and polysemic dimensions and that the articulation of either is largely a function of the choices and the emphasis of the researcher.

This state of affairs should not leave us at a relativistic impasse, however. Instead, I suggest that it underscores the importance of examining and articulating the motives, purposes, and possible consequences of whatever kind of television analysis we attempt to do. That is, we should choose our approach to the objects we study because of what we want to find out, because of the problem(s) that we want to solve, rather than because we are convinced that one approach leads to truth and the other to conjecture. At the same time, we must always realize that we cannot solve *all* of the problems or explore *all* of the possibilities that the text (whether it is a television program or audience discourse *about* a television program) presents.

Television and Theory

The division of topic implied by a new heading is rather artificial at this point, particularly because "theory" has been an implicit or explicit presence in everything I have discussed thus far. However, I wish to make some broad statements about the uses of theory as well as to continue explicating my approach to the texts in this study. Because, as a rhetorical critic, my aim is always to make an argument about how a text can be understood, I value theory most for its explanatory potential and for the vocabulary or set of assumptions it provides to make sense of symbolic processes, to solve the "problem" that a text, or group of texts, presents. Critics always situate their arguments within implicit or explicit theoretical constructs, although to differing degrees. The more foregrounded the theory, the more likely it is that the artifact illustrates the theory. Conversely, the more foregrounded the artifact, the more likely it is that the theory helps understand the artifact. Recognizing that a bit of both of these scenarios is true in every piece of good criticism, I tend toward the latter.

However, it is also clear by this point that I am working with some broad assumptions about how television texts function as part of cultural discourse. I find it necessary, then, to articulate my theoretical assumptions at two levels. First, I reiterate my broad assumptions about how television texts function as a part of cultural hegemonic processes, explaining my motives, as a critic and a feminist, for choosing this framework. Second, I explain my essentially inductive approach to the individual texts I analyze in the case studies to follow. This move is not as contradictory as it seems. Although I am working with hegemony theory as a broad rubric, I suggest that each of these texts illustrates unique rhetorical strategies and deserves considered critical attention on its own terms. Each series reproduces hegemonic assumptions about women and feminism, yet each does so in different ways and to different degrees.

Television and Cultural Hegemony

As is no doubt evident by this point, I tend to favor a view of the text as powerful in its potential to persuade viewers to perform preferred readings. I believe in hegemony because the evidence for its power is, in my experience, quite good. The problems that I am trying to solve in my study of these texts is a product, then, of my social experience as a feminist and a teacher and of my purposes as a critic. As a bridge to further explication of my motives, it is useful to review Todd Gitlin's explanation of why Antonio Gramsci was led to develop hegemony theory. According to Gitlin, Gramsci was stimulated by the desire to understand why the working class in Italy, given its social experience, was not revolutionary and, instead, yielded to fascism (1982, pp. 507–508). Hegemony, the "bourgeois domination of the thought, the common sense, the life-ways and everyday assumptions of the working class," provided an explanation for Gramsci of the failure of the working-class movement (Gitlin, 1982, p. 508).

At a general level, hegemony makes sense to me, as a feminist, in a similar fashion. For example, it allows me to understand and to analyze why women themselves have historically been the most powerful enemies of feminism. From the anti-suffrage organizations of the late nineteenth and early twentieth centuries to the contemporary STOP ERA movement, the historical record provides a number of examples. Closer to home is my continuing bewilderment at the attitudes of college-age women in my classes who see feminism as irrelevant to their lives and goals. The young women who claim, during a discussion of the rhetorical/ideological function of women's magazines, that the glamorous images are unrealistic and do not affect them, are the same young women who, from their appearance in my classroom, spend hours in tanning booths (in North Dakota, tans in the winter and early spring are, by necessity, artificial), at cosmetic counters, in department stores, in hair salons, and in front of mirrors. These kinds of contradictions interest and concern me, and I think hegemony helps explain them.

I do not assume, however, that my female students are cultural dupes, incapable of resistance toward the dominant culture. They often, as I mention above, are astute about media attempts to manipulate them (although we must remember that they are critical when I *ask* them to be). Rather, I question the quality or power of that resistance in the face of the repetitive and consistently reinforced hegemonic media messages that they consume. In fact, to consider my students cultural dupes would be to place myself, to some extent, in that category as well. As I discussed in the Preface, an additional part of my motivation in this project is to understand the contradictions in my own responses to cultural products. For feminist critics, awareness of such contradictions provides a useful sense of our commonality with the viewers we write about. As Modleski suggests, our motivation to insist that audiences can glean emancipatory meanings from commercial popular culture "often seems to be based on an unspoken syllogism that goes something like this: 'I like *Dallas*; I am a feminist; *Dallas* must have progressive potential' " (1991, p. 45). However, in our rush to confirm that hegemony can be resisted "we are in danger of forgetting the crucial fact that like the rest of the world even the cultural analyst may sometimes be a 'cultural dupe'—which is, after all, only an ugly way of saying that we exist inside ideology, that we are all victims, down to the very depths of our psyches, of political and cultural domination (even though we are never *only* victims)" (Modleski, 1991, p. 45).

Although some have implied that the danger of believing too strongly in the power of hegemony is a kind of cynicism about the possibilities of social change, the opposite, a romantic faith in the power of individuals to resist ideology, has its dangers as well. By celebrating people's abilities to make the best of a bad situation, we may lose sight of the need to address the situation itself. As Gitlin argues: "Culture, of course, is streaked with politics. So, indeed, is pleasure. But it is pure sloppiness to conclude that culture or pleasure *is* politics. Culture is mistaken for politics only by default—only in a society stripped of opportunities for serious politics. . . . Scholastic radicalism, in other words, serves the theorist as a shield against practical resignation" (1990, p. 192). Elayne Rapping has a similar concern about romanticizing individual resistance to the extent that we end up "redefining the word *political* to fit these inherently noninstrumental views of cultural use" (1992, p. xxiv). This does not mean that audience research that stresses resistance by viewers is not meaningful and useful; it simply means that we should be judicious about our claims for its implications. The same, of course, is true for our claims about the power of the text. As an academic feminist critic, my belief that culture is political is an underlying premise of my work. Yet, as a woman who lives in "white supremacist capitalist patriarchy" (hooks, 1994), I also believe that collapsing culture and politics is short-sighted and naive.

I do not rely on hegemony theory in this project because I believe that viewers are victims of an inescapable ideology to which I am immune and therefore capable of explicating. Instead, my motivation is rhetorical and pragmatic: I believe that the concept of hegemony is useful in interpreting the specific phenomenon that I wish to examine: the construction of feminism, as a set of beliefs, practices, and effects, in selected U.S. popular prime-time television programs since 1970. I am interested in elucidating a set of dominant discourse practices that I argue were shared by prime-time television and other forms of cultural discourse. I will be relying on the premise that viewers are likely to interpret television according to the dominant codes available to them as members of American society and as consumers of American media. This perspective assumes that viewers outside the white, middle-class, heterosexual "mainstream" to whom television always presumes it is speaking still understand the "rules" for preferred readings, even as they might work to deconstruct them.

Thus, I focus my analysis of the potential function of these texts on what is shared by viewers rather than what is not. This is consistent with my rhetorical perspective; rhetorical critics traditionally are concerned with how people are persuaded to adhere to positions as members of a public with common beliefs, attitudes, and values. This perspective is useful for understanding television because

television's political functions are not confined to its address to the pleasures of individuals. In addition, television "makes present" particular codings in the public space. Once such codings gain legitimacy they can be employed in forming public law, policy, and behavior. Even if they are not universally accepted, their presence gives them presumption (the right to participate in formulations, and even the need for others to take account of them in their policy formulations). . . . Hence, television, or any mass medium, can do oppressive work solely by addressing the dominant audience that also constitutes the public. (Condit, 1989, p. 112; see also Rapping, 1992, p. xxxi)

This perspective does not mean that television discourse is always and only reflective of dominant interests. The gaps, spaces, and contradictions that interest resistance theorists are also present, and their presence is always a qualification of claims for the hegemonic functions of a text. As John Fiske (1986) has rightly argued, such polysemic potential is what makes television watchable by so many people and what allows its popularity. However, what I am maintaining here is that it is as legitimate and useful to emphasize the function of television as dominant, public discourse as it is to study the gaps and spaces it contains that may facilitate differential private decodings.

The very premise of this project belies a vision of hegemony as totalistic and static. To claim, as I do, that feminist ideology has been manifested in television entertainment in a variety of ways over the past twenty-five years is to presume the flexibility and adaptability of hegemonic practice and to acknowledge its inability to contain completely the possibilities of social change. If nothing else, the (tele)visions of feminism that I analyze here demonstrate the television industry's willingness to engage with (some of) the questions that feminism has raised in American society. It is not my intent, either, to discuss television's treatment of feminism only to argue for the many ways in which feminist ideology as been coopted and depoliticized to serve dominant interests. I address these processes at length, but I also address the ways in which, despite efforts to contain it, feminism has established a presence on American television that has not just changed but often progressed over time.

Because I view the (tele)visions of feminism that I analyze as contributions to the evolution of cultural debate about feminism, I am interested in, to use Fredric Jameson's terms, both the "ideological" and the "utopian" dimensions of their role in the "transformational work" of mass culture (1979, pp. 144, 141). Jameson posits that mass culture texts possess intersecting ideological and utopian (or transcendent) dimensions; the ideological dimension encompasses the ways in which a text facilitates "legitimation of the existing order" (1979, p. 144) and functions hegemonically. Jameson also maintains, however, that texts have a simultaneous utopian dimension that "remains implicitly, and no matter how faintly, negative or critical of the social order from which, as a product and a commodity, it springs" (1979, p. 144). For Jameson, then, "social and political anxieties or fantasies" must "have some effective presence in the mass cultural text in order subsequently to be 'managed' or repressed" (1979, p. 141). Once that "presence" is established, it cannot be totally erased; it has become part of cultural discourse.

Ultimately, one of the biggest challenges to commercial television entertainment, which I will return to throughout this book, is the need to respond to social change and the desire of audiences for representations of "the new woman" (as she is defined at different moments in time) while working within perceived economic and institutional constraints. The situation I described in the Preface regarding the place of women within television's economic context obviously invites analysis that emphasizes the hegemonic processes of television; that is, that focuses on the set of practices in which oppositional or alternative ideology is packaged or framed to limit, undermine, or contradict its power. However, given the contradictions that exist both within and across television discourse, through both programming and advertising, its hegemonic function can never be complete.

The Rhetorical Uniqueness of the Television Text

Up to this point, I have been detailing the broad assumptions under which I am working because of my overall purpose in this book. Beyond those assumptions and the general worldview developed through my training as a rhetorical critic, I do not consider myself to be working at all times within a given theoretical tradition, such as psychoanalytic criticism or even cultural studies (which represent quite a large umbrella in the first place).

Thus, although I bring with me some broad assumptions about how television does its cultural work, I also assume that the strategies through which that work is accomplished *differ* across programming. That is, I can assume that television operates hegemonically at a broad level and yet still assume that different examples of television discourse will manifest hegemonic functions in distinct ways. This is particularly true for this project because I argue that television representations of feminism change over time, just as the conversation about feminism in other areas of cultural life changes over time.

At the level of analyzing individual texts, then, my approach is inductive rather than deductive. I begin with the programming that I wish to understand and to explain, and I gain a thorough familiarity with it. For example, I have been a long-time viewer of all the programming discussed in this book. In the case of programs such as *The Mary Tyler Moore Show, Murphy Brown, Designing Women,* and *One Day at a Time,* not only was I a faithful viewer during their lives on prime-time, but I have had continued exposure during their "afterlives" in syndication. Indeed, the popularity of all of these sitcoms in syndication is one of the factors that attracted me to them as potential case studies. In the case of more recent and short-lived programming, such as *Dr. Quinn, Medicine Woman,* I have followed the series since its debut.

My experience with the text itself governs the approach I will take to it, reflecting the belief that "working out from the particular (rather than applying ready-formed analytical systems) gets critics closer to the subject *before* deciding which analytical systems are appropriate and with what limitations" (Deming, 1990, p. 48). Thus, while I have an overarching purpose in this book to explore the ways in which programming constructs feminism over time, the critical tools that enable my discussion of each unique text differ because each text functions differently. This is why, for example, my analysis of *Designing Women* relies heavily on theories of women's use of language and conversation, while my analysis of *Murphy Brown* pays a great deal of attention to intertextuality.

This inductive approach leads to the case study organization of this book in which I perform close analysis of relatively few examples of programming. I prefer to study television at the level of the series. When a series becomes an artifact for a critic, it becomes possible to do the kind of close reading that reveals patterns of plot and character, recurring rhetorical strategies, and, ultimately, repetitive rhetorical function, that I find interesting and useful. This focus on what Caren Deming calls "concrete particularity" means "resisting, or at least suspending, the manly inclination to argue deductively from principles assumed to apply to all television equally" (1990, p. 59).

Generally, my concern is with understanding the functions of this programming as part of cultural debates about feminism, rather than with using these texts to promote a new way of understanding television. Following Kenneth Burke's (1973) admonition to "use all there is to use," I attempt to integrate the insights offered by theorists and critics that will help me to make the arguments that I wish to make about the programming that I discuss. To the extent that the case studies reveal continuity between strategies of representation of feminism over time (as I believe they do), I am hopeful that this book produces a kind of grounded, historically situated theory that can be helpful to scholars studying the uses of feminism in popular culture.

Notes

1. For example, some of the fine work done by the Birmingham group, which joins textual analysis and ethnographic approaches, is highly sophisticated and extremely useful (see, e.g., McRobbie, 1991) and does not attempt to value one approach at the expense of the other. A recent example of this kind of research that specifically treats women and U.S. prime-time television is Andrea Press's

Women Watching Television (1991), an elegant melding of textual and audience approaches that is extremely responsible in pointing out the limitations and possibilities of each.

2. Todd Gitlin offers an interesting variation on this perspective with regard to the television production process. In *Inside Prime-Time* Gitlin discusses the reliance of television producers on mass media to discover ideas for programming, with the result that

> the ideas about public opinion circulating through these channels are the ideas that find their way into network offices. By keeping up to the minute, executives try to stay flexible, but their flexibility is bounded by the conventional wisdom that circulates through their favored media. Their periodicals put issues in their mental agendas. They also certify vague ideas, or fragments of personal experience, or potentially marketable ideas worth taking seriously. Ideas form about the ebb and flow of popular feelings, and the genres that might or might not correspond to them. (1985, pp. 204–205)

3. At times in this discussion, I will appear to be collapsing the distinction between the activities of textually based critics who argue for the polysemy of the text (i.e., its potential for different meanings) and researchers who study the activity of audiences as they make different meanings. Obviously, these are not the same kind of activity. However, they are intertwined in important ways because both assume that the power of audience subjectivity is equal to or greater than that of the subjectivity offered by the text. Moreover, textual critics who argue for polysemy often rely on the conclusions of audience studies to support their arguments (see, e.g., Fiske, 1987a, chapters 5 and 6).

4. There is also a tendency to take viewer responses to *some* television as representative of their response to *all* television. Audiences researchers have not attempted to verify if all types or genres of programming are likely to provoke the negotiated or oppositional readings that they have argued occur in relation to a limited sample of programming. As Carragee notes, much of this research ignores "the likelihood that actions in particular environments will vary depending on the characteristics of particular texts or genres" (1990, p. 89).

5. Another difficulty with taking resistant audience claims at face value is the fact that the presence of a researcher necessarily affects the responses to television offered by the audiences being studied. As Modleski writes in reference to David Morley's study of the audience for *Nationwide*: "To what extent is the respondents' critical attitude merely a function of the fact that the ethnographer places them in a situation where they are *required* to be critical? When people are watching television in ordinary situations, as one of Morley's respondents observes, the critical attitude is relaxed. The media's messages might easily slip past the vigilant censor into the viewer's unconscious" (1991, p. 38). Similarly, Evans notes that "interpretivists' findings indicate an assumed parity between reported behavior (including meaning-making) and that which actually transpired" (1990, p. 153). Obviously, this is a problem with all interpretive social science and is certainly not specific to audience studies.

Chapter 1
1970s Lifestyle Feminism, the Single Woman, and *The Mary Tyler Moore Show*

If television scholars had established a canon of "great works" akin to that which exists (although not without challenge) in literature, *The Mary Tyler Moore Show* surely would be included in it. A sitcom focusing on the life of thirtyish, unmarried, working woman Mary Richards and her network of friends and co-workers at WJM-TV in Minneapolis, *Mary Tyler Moore* was described by reviewers and critics as an example of original programming both during and after its seven seasons on CBS (1970–77). The claim to originality was based, among other things, on production factors, such as its status as the first of a series of highly successful programs that would be created by its parent company, MTM Enterprises (Feuer, Kerr, and Vahimagi, 1984; Gitlin, 1983), on its contribution to the situation comedy format as an exemplar of the move from domestic or home-based situations to situations based in the workplace (Gitlin, 1983; Newcomb, 1974), and on its social sensitivity and timeliness as a program focused on the life of a career-oriented, single woman (Feuer et al., 1984; Gitlin, 1983; Marc, 1984).

Mary Tyler Moore is generally acknowledged as the first popular and long-running television series clearly to feature the influence of feminism. Although the show's creators consistently claimed that *Mary Tyler Moore* was about character, not politics (an implied contrast to *All in the Family*), writer-producer James Brooks observed that "we sought to show someone from Mary Richards' background being in a world where women's rights were being talked about and it was having an impact" (quoted in Bathrick, 1984, pp. 103–104). *Mary Tyler Moore* was not the first working-woman sitcom. Yet it is generally acknowledged as the first to assert that work was not just a prelude to marriage, or a substitute for it, but could form the center of a satisfying life for a woman in the way that it presumably did for men. This was, perhaps, the most consistent and explicit profeminist statement made by the sitcom. As one of *Mary Tyler Moore*'s writers asserts, "To me, Mary [Richards] represented a new attitude, that you could be single and still be a whole person, that you didn't need to be married to have a complete life" (quoted in Alley and Brown, 1989, p. 50).

Other "single woman on her own" programs that followed *Mary Tyler Moore* would take this basic theme in different, more progressive directions, but the shadow of *Mary Tyler Moore* hangs over them. It was the first sitcom "to draw upon feminist consciousness raising as a contextual frame," and it worked to establish the working-woman sitcom as the "preferred fictional site for a 'feminist' subject position" (Rabinovitz, 1989, p. 3). *Mary Tyler Moore* was not just innovative, it was also tremendously successful. It launched three spin-offs[1] and is still popular in syndication almost twenty years after it left prime-time.[2] That television producers recognized the power of its formula is evident in the numerous attempts to duplicate its premise throughout the 1970s and 1980s (attempts that I discuss in Chapter 2), and in the fact that *Mary Tyler Moore* still serves as a standard, or starting point, against which progressive televisual representations of women are judged, at least in popular media.[3]

However, at the same time that they note the popularity and importance of *Mary Tyler Moore* as the generator of "a new representational space for female audiences" (Deming, 1988, p. 208), television critics and historians take care to note the ways in which *Mary Tyler Moore* offered a very qualified feminist vision that blended discourses of the "new woman"—working and living on her own outside of the confines of past domestic sitcoms—with traditional messages about the need for women to continue fulfilling traditional female roles as caretakers and nurturers in the cobbled together "family" of the workplace (Dow, 1990; Gitlin, 1983, pp. 214–217).[4] Ella Taylor is perhaps most explicit about this judgment in *Prime-Time Families* (1989, p. 124) when she argues that "the combination in Mary [Richards] of girl-next-door sweetness and 'old-fashioned' attachment to honesty and integrity, on the one hand, and spunky New Woman, on the other, allows *The Mary Tyler Moore Show* to ride the currents of social change, endorsing modernity at the same time as it hallows tradition." Through her functions as mother, daughter, and sister within her work-family, Mary "becomes the 'career True Woman' as a television producer who nonetheless retains the equable charm and mediating skills of the well-brought-up girl." As Taylor concludes, the appeal of such a character might lie in the fact that "this is a difficult reconciliation to pull off in life, and therefore it is very satisfying—for men as well as women—to see on the small screen" (p. 125).

Andrea Press's work on middle-class women's responses to television indicates that this appeal was quite strong for some women in *Mary Tyler Moore*'s demographic target group (1991, pp. 77–79). From her interviews with middle-class women, some of whom identify themselves as feminists, Press describes the viewers' "specific identification" with Mary Richards, and their interpretation of *Mary Tyler Moore* as a realistic and positive representation of female independence which demonstrated that a woman could be "popular" and attractive as well as autonomous and successful (p. 79).[5] As I argue in this chapter, this kind of reaction indicates how well-calibrated *Mary Tyler Moore*'s feminism was: It embraced social change in a noticeable fashion, becoming a forerunner in the 1970s "turn toward 'relevance' " cemented by the January 1971 debut of *All in the Family* and the 1973 debut of *M*A*S*H*, also on CBS (Gitlin, 1983), while simultaneously quieting the fears (of men *and* women) raised by the increasing visibility of feminist activism in the early 1970s.

For various reasons that I have mentioned to this point, and unlike other programming I discuss in this book, *Mary Tyler Moore* has received substantial attention from television scholars. What I attempt in this chapter is to broaden and deepen previous conclusions about *Mary Tyler Moore* (including my own, in Dow, 1990) by situating them within the context of a variety of discourses that I argue can be viewed as framing and guiding interpretations of the sitcom. These discourses include popular understandings of second-wave feminism encouraged by media coverage of feminist activity, the generic parameters and functions of situation comedy, and the history of televisual representations of women. This chapter introduces and exemplifies the kind of analysis I perform in each of the case studies to follow. *Mary Tyler Moore* is a fitting "baseline" example because of its popularity, longevity, and resonance in American cultural memory. *Mary Tyler Moore* created important parameters for future television discourse representing feminism, parameters that include a focus on working women (and a concomitant avoidance of a critique of the traditional patriarchal family), the depiction of women's lives without male romantic partners, the enactment of a "feminist lifestyle" by young, attractive, white, heterosexual, female characters, and a reliance on the tenets of second-wave liberal or equity feminism.

Mary Tyler Moore and Second-Wave Feminism

Mary Tyler Moore made its debut in September of 1970, on the heels of a rash of publicity generated by feminist activity related to the enormous (and surprising, even to feminists) success of the August 26, 1970, "Women Strike for Equality" demonstration. Women all over the country, but most visibly on Fifth Avenue in New York City, marched as part of what outgoing National Organization for Women President Betty Friedan called "a twenty-four hour general strike . . . of all women in America against the concrete conditions of their oppression" (quoted in Davis, 1991, p. 115). Held on the fiftieth anniversary of the date on which the Nineteenth Amendment granting women the right to vote was ratified in 1920, the demonstration prompted extensive coverage by national media, including stories in *Newsweek* and *Time* (with a cover featuring *Sexual Politics* author Kate Millett), a lengthy story in *Life*, and front page coverage by the *New York Times*.

Second-wave feminism's resurgence can be dated, variously, from the publication of Betty Friedan's *The Feminine Mystique* in 1963, from the 1966 founding of the National Organization for Women, from the formation of women's liberation groups in 1967 (Echols, 1989), or from the Miss America pageant protest in 1968 (at which, cultural legend erroneously has it, feminists "burned their bras").[6] Although press coverage of second-wave feminist ideas and activities appeared in the late 1960s,[7] 1970 saw the first sustained attempts by the national media to treat the themes and interpret the implications of the women's liberation movement (Davis, 1991, chapter 6; Freeman, 1975, pp. 84–85). In February of 1970, for example, women's liberation was the subject of a cover story in *Saturday Review* (Komisar, 1970), entire issues of *Atlantic Monthly* and *Mademoiselle*, followed in March by a "Special Report" story in *Newsweek* (Dudar, 1970) and a lengthy article in the *New York Times Magazine* by feminist Susan Brownmiller, headlined as "A Member of the Women's Liberation Movement Explains What It's All About" (Brownmiller, 1970a). Several weeks before the August demonstration, *Ladies Home Journal* included an eight-page insert on "The New Feminism" (written by feminists themselves) in its August issue, an action prompted by the famous "sit-in" held by a coalition of New York feminists at editor John Mack Carter's office on March 18, 1970 (Davis, 1991, pp. 111–114). Also in 1970, NBC and CBS each broadcast a series of stories on the women's movement in addition to their regular coverage of events such as the Strike for Equality.[8]

Because many of the articles in the wave of press attention in 1970 were written by movement supporters or members of feminist groups (e.g., Brownmiller, 1970a, 1970b; Janeway, 1970; Komisar, 1970; Rossi, 1970) or because the experience of reporting on the movement resulted in the conversion to feminism of a heretofore "objective" writer (e.g., Dudar, 1970; Gross, 1970), the print coverage was often sympathetic and fairly accurate in terms of representation of ideology and issues. For example, press accounts make clear that second-wave feminism was not monolithic, although they tended to group it into "reformist" and "radical" wings, often eliding the differences among radical groups. Mainstream writing on the movement also tended to focus on what the writers would term "leaders," even though radical feminism was resolutely anti-hierarchical.[9] Radical feminist philosophy that called for cultural transformation of patriarchy and, in cases, elimination of marriage and the traditional family received a great deal of attention in 1970 and 1971 because of its sensationalism and because of the publication of books like Kate Millett's *Sexual Politics* (1970), Shulamith Firestone's *The Dialectic of Sex* (1970), *Sisterhood Is Powerful* (an anthology of feminist writings edited by Robin Morgan, 1970), and Germaine Greer's *The Female Eunuch* (1971). Ultimately, the effect of this media convergence was that information on the goals and ideology of the movement reached women and men all over the country.

Press accounts of feminist ideology and goals tended to focus the myriad issues involved into two broad areas: discrimination in the public sphere (primarily in employment and education) and the broad critique of sex-role conditioning (related to media images of women as sex objects and traditional roles within the patriarchal family).[10] The former theme was most often associated with reformist feminist groups such as NOW and leaders such as Betty Friedan, and the latter with radical feminist groups such as the New York Feminists or Redstockings and ideologues such as Ti-Grace Atkinson or Kate Millett. Obviously there is crossover between these areas: Friedan, for example, relied on analysis of sex-role conditioning to make her case for the need for women to work outside the home in *The Feminine Mystique*, and radical feminists who called for elimination of marriage often did so on the grounds that it exploited women's unpaid labor, stunting their desires and opportunities for success in the public sphere.[11]

Susan Douglas argues that media coverage ultimately functioned to divide the women's movement into "legitimate feminism and illegitimate feminism" that, generally, followed the divide between liberal, reformist feminism and radical feminism calling for cultural transformation (1994, p. 186). The arguments purporting to demonstrate the existence of public discrimination against women received, by and large, more sympathetic treatment in the press. Wage disparity, discriminatory laws, and the low percentage of women in certain professions were easily documented with statistics, were understandable in terms of basic American values like equal opportunity, and were located in the public sphere, which reporters saw as the realm where legitimate news resided. The critique of sex roles, the patriarchal family, and the false consciousness created by the mythology of romance and heterosexuality were treated with much more skepticism and, often, outright ridicule (pp. 186–189). These issues were associated with the "angry" and "militant" radical feminists who were depicted as "ugly, humorless, disorderly man-haters desperately in need of some Nair" (p. 189).

Radical feminist activity was difficult for journalists to cover in comparison to the activities of groups like NOW or the equally reformist National Women's Political Caucus (formed in 1971). For one thing, radical feminists feared the misinterpretations they suffered at the hands of the mainstream press and often refused interviews and access to their meetings (Davis, 1991, pp. 108–109; North, 1970). Also, the core of radical feminist activity was the small, leaderless group for which the purpose was often personal transformation of members achieved through consciousness-raising. The public orientation of NOW, and the visible public events it created, were easier to report. Finally, many of the radical feminist groups disbanded by the mid-seventies for a variety of reasons, including internal dissension (Echols, 1989, p. 284) and the fact that they had "served their purpose" by radicalizing their members (Davis, 1991, p. 142). As a result, "almost by default, liberal feminism became the mainstream of the second wave" (Davis, 1991, p. 136) making NOW "a major beneficiary of radical feminism's disintegration" (Echols, 1989, p. 294).

The ascendance of liberal feminism, both in terms of actual membership and in terms of media presence, was fairly obvious, in retrospect, by 1972. Liberal feminism's most visible symbol by this time was the attractive, thoroughly heterosexual, thirtyish, never married Gloria Steinem. Steinem's popularity with powerful men and her glamorous single woman lifestyle were the subject of a number of profiles (e.g., Boeth, 1971; Levitt, 1971; "Woman of the Year," 1972). On *Newsweek*'s cover, Steinem was labeled "The New Woman" and the magazine's story on Steinem was headlined "A Liberated Woman Despite Beauty, Chic, and Success" (Boeth, 1971, p. 51). An *Esquire* writer called her "the intellectual's pin-up," and "the one the ad men meant when they wrote 'You've Come a Long Way, Baby,' " (Levitt, 1971, p. 88).

Steinem was obviously attractive to the media, which was largely responsible for turning her into the feminist heroine of the 1970s. In contrast to antimarriage and antisex radical feminists such as Ti-Grace Atkinson or controversial bisexuals such as Kate Millett,[12] Steinem was a movement spokesperson who was also a glamorous celebrity who could attract both women and men. She was a package that combined the single-woman adventurism preached by Helen Gurley Brown in *Sex and the Single Girl* (1962) and in the pages of *Cosmopolitan*[13] with the increasingly reformist, lifestyle-oriented liberal feminism that would dominate the pages of *Ms.* magazine (Hogeland, 1994b). *McCall's* magazine chose Steinem as its 1972 "Woman of the Year" because of her ability "to bridge the gap between the early militants, whose vehemence frightened away the people they wanted most to reach, and the thoughtful, dedicated women who understand that woman's status *must* change. She is, in short, a transitional figure, proof that change is not so frightening after all" ("Woman of the Year" 1972, p. 67). Steinem was "the exemplar of the new, liberated young woman; she was the compromise the news media had been looking for, a feminist who looked like a fashion model" (Douglas, 1994, p. 230).

With Steinem as editor-in-chief, *Ms.* magazine put out its first issue in July of 1972, further cementing Steinem's status as the model moderate feminist and media spokesperson.[14] By March of 1973, Betty Friedan, writing in the *New York Times Magazine* on the tenth anniversary of the publication of *The Feminine Mystique*, was predicting that the mainstream, represented by NOW and the ERA supporters, would triumph over "the man-hating fringe" represented by lesbian feminists and radicals such as Ti-Grace Atkinson (1973, p. 37). The campaign for the ERA, which became a unifying focus for feminist groups between 1972 and 1982 and the most visible feminist issue for the public at large (particularly after the abortion victory in *Roe v. Wade* in 1973), further brought liberal feminism, and its emphasis on equal opportunity in the public sphere, to the forefront of popular consciousness (Davis, 1991, chapter 18).[15]

Mary Richards and Careerist Feminism

Read against this background, the premise of *Mary Tyler Moore* has a number of features easily decoded as representative of liberated womanhood. In the first episode of the series, "Love Is All Around,"[16] Mary Richards leaves her hometown and family to make it on her own in Minneapolis. Mary's journey is depicted in the opening montage of leave-taking and traveling scenes that flashes behind the credits and is accompanied by the show's theme song, which begins, "How will you make it on your own? This world is awfully big, and girl, this time you're all alone." At thirty, however, Mary is not a "girl" biding her time until marriage (as was *That Girl*'s Ann Marie [1966–71]), but a woman who has chosen to pursue a career instead of a man. Indeed, at the end of the first episode, given a chance to reconcile with her boyfriend (whom she left because he reneged on a promise to marry her when he finished medical school), she refuses. Her rejection of the possibility of marriage (to a doctor, yet!) in favor of an independent working life is a key moment in setting the "situation" for this comedy.

Also in the first episode, Mary lands a job in the all-male enclave of the WJM-TV newsroom, a job that her boss, Lou Grant, tells her he presumed would be filled by a man. Mary's discomfort and mild indignation when Lou asks her personal questions about religion and marital status in the interview ("You've been asking a lot of questions that have nothing to do with my qualifications for this job") bring echoes of equal-opportunity rhetoric into the narrative. These echoes are strengthened when Lou reveals that the associate producer's job he offers her pays less than the secretary's job she was originally seeking. As Darrell Hamamoto notes, "The unspoken implication was that the ten dollar differential between the window dressing secretarial job and the position of substance as associate producer represented the price of 'making it' in a male-dominated profession" (1989, p. 115). Indeed, when Mary wonders why she was hired, her new colleague, newswriter Murray Slaughter, tells her explicitly that she will be their "token woman." From the beginning, then, Mary's work role is laden with implications of second-wave feminist discourse. Viewers rightly suspect that Mary gives up money for a meaningless title (Lou tells her that if she will take even less money he will make her a producer), a choice she would not have to make if she were male (indeed, a later episode reveals that Mary's salary is considerably less than that paid to her male predecessor). As the "token woman" hired for her sex rather than her qualifications, Mary does not begin her job with the presumption of equality; rather, she will have to earn it.

That Mary and others recognize that her gender does make a difference is meaningful; however, that Mary accepts this situation with good humor, and is grateful for the job, is equally meaningful. This kind of situation will become one of Mary's trademarks: she is a woman sophisticated enough to recognize sexism when she sees it, but she is not necessarily assertive enough to do anything about it.

While feminist-inspired equal-opportunity discourse dominates the premise of *Mary Tyler Moore*, the debut episode also includes some allusions to the radical feminist critique of sex roles. For example, when Phyllis, Mary's old friend and apartment manager, informs Mary that her boyfriend will be visiting, she urges Mary to reconsider marrying him. She tells Mary that marriage can be "beautiful," if you "face the fact that it means a certain amount of sacrificing, unselfishness, denying your own ego, sublimating, accommodating, surrendering. . . ." Phyllis grows steadily more agitated as she delivers this line, tightening her grip on Mary's hand. This is a clearly comic, but still potentially meaningful recognition of the suffocation second-wave feminists attributed to traditional marriage. Phyllis, at this point the only regular female character who is married (and whose husband is *never* seen), is hardly an argument for marital bliss, and acts as reinforcement for Mary's choice to say a permanent goodbye to her boyfriend.

Before her boyfriend arrives, however, Mary receives a surprise visit from her new boss. Lou, obviously drunk, announces that his wife is out of town. Mary replies, "*Now* I know why you're here," inferring that she was hired by Lou for her "great caboose." Lou does not, in fact, come on to her, but Mary's manifest indignation at the possibility of sexual harassment, and at her potential status as a sex object for Lou, has made its point, bringing with it additional elements of feminist awareness.

This brief survey of *Mary Tyler Moore*'s debut episode suggests that the sitcom appropriated and adapted a variety of feminist themes circulating in popular media of the time, simultaneously developing a prototype of television's own "new woman"—the young, single, white, attractive, middle-class working female—who possessed a number of the same qualities that made Gloria Steinem so popular as a movement symbol. *McCall's* magazine called Steinem "the women's movement's most persuasive evangelist," supporting this claim with an article praising Steinem's warmth, friendliness, style, and modesty (Mercer, 1972, p. 68). Indeed, to the extent that Steinem functioned as a "transitional figure" that made change seem less frightening ("Woman of the Year," 1970, p. 67), so did Mary Richards. What Mary Richards and Gloria Steinem had in common was the potential to make liberation marketable. To claim, as its producers and various critics have, that *Mary Tyler Moore* was about *lifestyle*, whereas *All in the Family* was about *politics*, does not necessarily detract from the sitcom's feminist resonance for viewers. At least in media interpretations, feminism increasingly was equated with lifestyle, especially the kind of lifestyle exemplified by media star Gloria Steinem.

Mary Richards and TV Womanhood

Part of CBS's rationale for developing programming such as *Mary Tyler Moore* was to appeal to a youthful audience, including the single-woman market, and to replace its lineup of shows like *Petticoat Junction* (1963–70), *Mayberry RFD* (1968–71), and *Green Acres* (1965–71), which appealed to an older, rural, viewer (Feuer et al., 1984, pp. 3–5; Gitlin, 1983, pp. 205–220). The network's new demographic strategy of seeking a "quality" audience (younger, urban, and with greater disposable income) included a number of programs, such as *M*A*S*H* (1972–83) and *All in the Family* (1971–83), that drew themes from 1960s radicalism, which, by the early 1970s, was distant enough to be made comic.[17] At the same time that CBS sought to develop new markets, however, it did not discard conventional wisdom about audiences. When developing the concept for *Mary Tyler Moore*, for example, Mary Tyler Moore envisioned Mary Richards as a divorcée, an idea that network executives quashed because of their belief that viewers were not ready for a divorced woman (Feuer et al., 1984, p. 6), and because of the identification of Mary Tyler Moore with the role of "perfect wife" Laura Petrie on *The Dick Van Dyke Show*.[18]

The compromise made on Mary Richards's marital status because of Mary Tyler Moore's relation to a previous highly popular television character illustrates the key role of intertextuality in potential interpretations of *Mary Tyler Moore*. Although *Mary Tyler Moore* clearly drew much of its power as a representation of the "new woman" from its temporal relationship to women's liberation discourse, it also drew meaning from its relationship to previous television representations of women, particularly single women. Robert Deming suggests that viewers' " 'television archives,' " consisting of "our memories of past programs and surrounding discourses," predispose us "to assume various positions of identification and to accept a range of ideas, actions and behaviors" that frame our interpretation of programming (1992, p. 207). Although Deming is stressing the possibility for viewers to interpret programming in relation to their experiences with other *similar* programs, it is equally possible that this kind of intertextual reading enables recognition of *difference* as well.

An early review of *Mary Tyler Moore* illustrates this kind of comparative reading as a way to make sense of the "difference" the sitcom presented. John Leonard, writing in *Life* magazine in an article entitled "The Subversive Mary Tyler Moore" (1970) begins with a critique of the banality of female characters on contemporaneous domestic sitcoms, specifically *The Brady Bunch* (1969–74) and *Nanny and the Professor* (1970–71). Leonard allows that his dissatisfaction is the outcome of his consciousness raising on the "Woman Question," which also leads him to criticize television's attempts to depict women who are, in some way, professional, single, or powerful:

If women have a profession, it's usually nursing, where they minister to men. If they are superior to men, it's because they have magical powers. If they are over 30 years old, they've got to be widows, almost always with children, so that they can't run around enjoying themselves like real people. And they're guaranteed to be helpless once every fifteen minutes." (p. 8)

In this paragraph, Leonard alludes to a number of programs, including *Julia* (1968–71) (focusing on a widowed nurse), *Bewitched* (1964–72), *I Dream of Jeannie* (1965–70), and *The Flying Nun* (1967–70) (sitcoms about women with supernatural powers), and, possibly, *The Partridge Family* (1970–74), *The Doris Day Show* (1968–73),[19] *Here's Lucy* (1968–74), and *The Ghost and Mrs. Muir* (1968–70) (all sitcoms about widowed mothers). In contrast, Leonard praises *Mary Tyler Moore* as "subversive" because the main character is "over thirty without being either a widow or a nurse" and can take care of herself. He concludes that "if *The Mary Tyler Moore Show* ever goes into weekday reruns, vampirized homemakers may get their consciousness raised to the point where they will refuse to leave their brains in the sugar canister any longer" (1970, p. 8).

Leaving aside Leonard's unkind characterization of some female viewers, his review exemplifies the tendency to recognize innovation in *Mary Tyler Moore* through explicit comparison to previous sitcoms. Other secondary texts from the early years of the show also "read" the sitcom in this way. In a *TV Guide* article on "TV and the Single Girl," Diane Rosen gives qualified praise to *Mary Tyler Moore* by comparing it to *That Girl* (1966–71), a sitcom focusing on a would-be actress in New York City, living alone but well-protected by her father and boyfriend. Noting that both Mary Richards and Rhoda Morgenstern are "surviving without the comfort of a brood of children or a steady boyfriend," Rosen also points out that, unlike *That Girl*'s main character, Mary Richards's charm is not based on incompetence (1971, p. 14).[20]

Thus, *Mary Tyler Moore* can be viewed as disrupting hegemonic practices of female representation on television in at least two ways. First, and most obviously, it was a departure from the "goodwife" character type (Meehan, 1983) which dominated popular domestic sitcoms from the beginning of television, including *Mama* (1949–56), *The Adventures of Ozzie and Harriet* (1952–66), *Father Knows Best* (1954–63), *Leave It to Beaver* (1957–63), and *The Dick Van Dyke Show* (1961–66). As Mary Beth Haralovich has argued, such sitcoms worked to "naturalize woman's place in the home" (1992, p. 112), and, as the Leonard review quoted above indicated, at the time of *Mary Tyler Moore*'s debut, sitcoms depicting women within familial settings were still a dominant form. The significance of the shift from this premise was underscored by the career trajectory of Mary Tyler Moore herself, who moved from playing an exemplary goodwife in *The Dick Van Dyke Show* for most of the 1960s to the consummate career woman of the 1970s, a fact noted in press coverage of *Mary Tyler Moore* (e.g., Whitney, 1970).[21]

Second, as Leonard pointed out in his review of the show, *Mary Tyler Moore* expanded the limited parameters of the single adult woman comedy, which, although existent since the beginning of television, was hardly a dominant form in the way that domestic sitcom was. At the very least, *Mary Tyler Moore* liberated single-woman sitcoms from narratives dominated by husband hunting (e.g., *Our Miss Brooks* [1952–56], *Private Secretary* [1953–57], *The Lucy Show* [1962–68]), charming incompetence and/or troublemaking (e.g., *That Girl* and *I Dream of Jeannie*), or widowed motherhood.

Mary Richards signaled a major difference from previous representations because she was single by choice, had no explicit familial protection, and saw her job as a career rather than as a stopgap on the journey toward marriage. Moreover, as an associate producer, Mary was in a job traditionally assigned to a man, ending the string of single-woman teachers and secretaries in past sitcoms. As I discuss later in this chapter, these innovative elements were contradicted, domesticated, and negotiated in various ways during the life of the series (for example, although Mary's title is associate producer, the work she is actually seen doing *looks* secretarial a great deal of the time).

However, given its cultural context, the innovative aspects of *Mary Tyler Moore* should not be dismissed. Resistance by some audiences to the sitcom's original premise can be inferred by the fact that *Mary Tyler Moore* was not an unqualified ratings success until its second season (when it followed the popular and controversial *All in the Family*),[22] and by the fact that a preview audience for the first episode in 1970 tagged the Mary Richards character as a "loser," Rhoda Morgenstern as "too abrasive," and Phyllis Lindstrom as "not believable" (Feuer et al., 1984, pp. 6–7).[23]

Mary Tyler Moore and Situation Comedy

That *Mary Tyler Moore* achieved solid popularity through its pairing with the most explicitly "relevant" sitcom of the 1970s, *All in the Family*, underscores the extent to which "relevance" became associated, both then and now, with situation comedy. CBS's new demographic strategy for the 1970s produced relevant dramas as well (e.g., *Headmaster* [1970–71], *The Interns* [1970–71], and *Storefront Lawyers* [1970–71]), but they were short-lived, leaving *M*A*S*H*, *All in the Family*, and *Mary Tyler Moore* as the most memorable manifestations of entertainment television's attention to social change (Marc, 1989, chapter 5; Taylor, 1989, pp. 44–49). That these three shows were all sitcoms provides part of the explanation for their success at negotiating the shoals of topicality and provides an additional part of the interpretive context for *Mary Tyler Moore*.

In this chapter, I have been using the terms "sitcom" or "situation comedy" in a taken-for-granted fashion, assuming that readers (and viewers) understand the generic typing that dominates television. Television is an intensely generic medium; we understand what "happens" on the screen in terms of its adherence to the conventions that define a type of programming, such as the police show, the news magazine, or the soap opera (Attallah, 1984, p. 227). Genres are made up of bundles of expectations that viewers come to know and receive pleasure from repeating in various guises, a process that is a "historical internalization of the institution by the audience" (Attallah, 1984, p. 234; see also Schatz, 1981). Though generic understanding may be commonsensical, it is not neutral. In literature, we surely understand that the same story told as an epic poem will be written and understood differently from the way it is told in a novel; likewise, content will be handled differently, and received differently when "told" as a sitcom versus a melodrama. The fact that the popular critics I cited above compare *Mary Tyler Moore* to other sitcoms, rather than to prime-time dramas or to soap operas, indicates the power of generic conventions in thinking about television.

The power of genre is its ability to channel meaning, or to "control the audience's reaction by providing an interpretive context" (Feuer, 1992, p. 144). The power of generic direction comes not only from television but also from its presence in our experience of any kind of discourse. Kenneth Burke writes that "repetitive form, the restatement of a theme by new details, is basic to any work of art, or to any other kind of orientation, for that matter. It is our only method of 'talking on the subject' " (1968, p. 125). Burke argues that all understanding relies on some form of comparison, a creation of links between discrete experiences: "The formal aspects of art . . . enable the mind to follow processes amenable to it. . . . They can be said to have a prior existence in the mind of the person hearing or reading the work of art" (pp. 142–143). Prior experience with similar forms guides interpretation of the forms one encounters; "the new is made familiar through the recognition of relevant similarities" (Miller, 1984, p. 157). In short, form tells us how to interpret content: "form shapes the response of the reader or listener to substance by providing instruction, so to speak, about how to perceive and interpret; this guidance disposes the audience to anticipate, to be gratified, to respond in a particular way" (p. 159).

Television situation comedy has its own structural characteristics, adapted from radio comedies and developed since the early days of television, and I will turn to these in a moment. However, working from Fredric Jameson's (1981, p. 41) claim that "genre is essentially a sociosymbolic message . . . immanently and intrinsically an ideology in its own right," we can link sitcom's general ideological potential to the social commentary that has been a part of comedy from its classical beginnings.

Hugh Duncan notes that comedy has always been used for the negotiation of social change because "under the guise of play, our most sacred values are opened to reason" (1962, p. 398). Comedy in general, and situation comedy in particular, are oriented toward resolution of conflict. Comic characters do not become alienated or die, as they do in tragedy; rather, they learn from their mistakes and are reintegrated into the group: "We submit to the discipline of comedy because we believe it is necessary to social solidarity and group survival. Communication is kept open and free through laughter because laughter *clarifies* where tragedy *mystifies*" (p. 388). Efforts at rhetoric and social change are tied to a comic perspective, making situation comedy a likely rhetorical form: "Rhetoric usually is comic because, given its commitment to the efficacy of deliberation and social action, it must opt to emphasize rationality, the community, cyclical survival, and progress" (Campbell, 1980,

p. 308). Comedy thus becomes a vehicle for social discussion. The portrayal of social conflicts and their resolution through comedy can lend guidance to a culture that faces adjustment to social change.[24] As Taylor notes in reference to situation comedy, "Comedy is a more flexible form than drama because it can create multiple, conflicting and oppositional realities within the safe confines of the joke" (1989, p. 27).

The "all's well that ends well" motif of classical comedy and situation comedy is visible in Horace Newcomb's (1974) brief description of the structure of sitcom: a problem arises that threatens the situation, the group, or a character within it, the characters attempt to deal with it, and the problem is resolved by the end of the episode, returning the situation to "normalcy" (pp. 40–41). This structure influences other characteristics of the form. For example, for audiences to be invested in the continuing integrity of a group of characters, those characters must have stable and familiar relationships. Situation comedy almost invariably operates within an actual or metaphorical family relationship, which leads to reiteration of stock character types, such as the patriarchal father figure, the nurturing mother figure, or the sibling rivals (Mintz, 1985; Taylor, 1989). Another result of sitcom's repetitive nature is the extent to which the form makes use of stock storylines. In workplace sitcoms, for example, episodes centering on a character's dilemma about whether to take another job (therefore sundering the work "family") are common.[25]

The ideological effect of these parameters is fairly obvious. When sitcom brings social issues into the family, it personalizes them, making them the problems of individual characters rather than tying them to structural and political circumstances. Classically, comedy stresses the triumph of the individual and the possibilities of social integration. Situation comedy is much the same in its emphasis on individualism in the context of family support. Herman Gray has commented on this tendency in the television representation of blacks:

> The primacy of individual efforts over collective possibilities, the centrality of individual values, morality, and initiative, and a benign (if not invisible) social structure are the key social terms that define television discourse about black success and failure. . . . Viewers question individual coping mechanisms rather than the structural and political circumstances that create and sustain racial equality. (1994, pp. 179, 183)

Gray's conclusions can be equally applied to situation comedy's treatment of women in feminist-inspired programming like *Mary Tyler Moore*, creating what he calls "the hegemony of the personal and personable" (1994, pp. 184, 185).[26] This individualistic philosophy is manifested in television's fondness for representations stressing liberal, or equal opportunity, feminism in which female characters are placed in roles, situations, and/or jobs formerly reserved for men. The implication of such representations is that *access* is the major problem for women; that is, given the same opportunities as a man, a woman's success or failure from that point on is solely a matter of individual choice and/or ability. This stance severely restricts the depth and breadth of the feminist critique offered by television programming because it accepts as desirable the cultural standards established through male hegemony and it focuses almost exclusively on women's equality in public life.

Not only is this the version of feminism preferred and publicized by mainstream media, it is also the easiest for television programming to incorporate because it "perpetuates the values of the status quo and limits the possibility of challenges to those values" (Jaggar, 1983, p. 197). Of course, what liberal feminism does not account for is that, even when a woman fills a "man's" job, she does not cease to be a woman, and the gender role expectations that are a part of every woman's life, to varying degrees, do not disappear. As Josephine Donovan notes, liberal feminism does not seriously consider "that the division of the world into public and private and the assumption that women uphold the domestic world—including the duty of child-rearing—might interfere with women's ability to enjoy equal rights and opportunities, even if they were granted" (1993, p. 27).

Indeed, the working-woman sitcom, and *Mary Tyler Moore* in particular, is a good example of the perseverance, in the public sphere, of gender-role expectations developed in the private sphere. The reliance on a family model means that workplace sitcoms never really escape family/ gender politics as much as they superficially seem to do. Intertextually, Mary Richards's liberation from domesticity is one of the key elements defining her character as a feminist representation. In that sense, the workplace sitcom focused on a woman contains at least an implied awareness of the problems of the nuclear family for women.[27] However, workplace sitcom's tendency to structure characters and relationships within a nuclear family metaphor often replicates rather than questions family politics. The " 'mirror' " family of the workplace can be seen as a "utopian" vision of the family, one that shows "love and work merged in an essentially harmonious universe that represented a throwback to a less corporate age—a residual ideology" (Feuer, 1986, p. 108; see also Taylor, 1989, p. 50).

Problems are solved, whether through individual initiative or with group support, in a way that preserves the integrity of the "family"; one of the recurring themes of workplace sitcoms is that the unity and stability of the family represent a paramount value and a "higher goal than personal ambition" (Feuer, 1986, p. 108). Individualism is thus limited by the need to retain the integrity of the group. In the end, the premise of traditional domestic sitcoms and workplace comedies is often the same: "Family" is still the source of love, fulfillment, and support within which the "problem" presented by that week's episode is solved. Indeed, given the dominance of domestic situation comedy since television's beginnings, the viewing audience for the new workplace sitcoms of the 1970s was thoroughly "trained" to interpret the workplace sitcom's group dynamics within a familial framework. The foundation of a belief in the power of genre as an interpretive frame is that it relies on "the consistent maintaining of a principle under new guises. . . . By varying a number of details, the reader is led to feel more or less consciously the principle underlying them" (Burke, 1953, p. 125).

Family is a wide-ranging term, and it is important to remember that second-wave feminist critiques of "the family" presumed the traditional, idealized, patriarchal, nuclear family and its attendant gender-role stereotypes that are a product of an ongoing dichotomy (real and socially constructed) between the public and private spheres (Eisenstein, 1983). In the most neutral sense, "family" can refer to the notion that all of the group members care about one another, are committed to their relationships with one another, and compose a unit of sorts. While this definition applies to most situation comedy, it does not necessarily include the problematical male/female stereotypes that arise in sitcoms which adhere to a traditional family structure that is inherently patriarchal, in which female characters enact particular roles, characteristics, and functions that position them as naturally nurturing, affective, intuitive, and submissive to the needs of others.

The term "patriarchal" is, at base, a descriptor of gender hierarchy and power relations that, while they may be modeled on the family, are replicated throughout society on a number of levels. As Adrienne Rich defines it, patriarchy refers to "any kind of group organization in which males hold dominant power and determine what part females shall and shall not play, and in which capabilities assigned to women are relegated generally to the mystical and aesthetic and excluded from the practical and political realms" (1979, p. 78). One of the ways in which the coercion that feminists identify in patriarchy is masked is through arguments that claim women choose and/or embrace their roles as defined within patriarchy or that, in fact, they do not choose them because they simply "come naturally" to women. This kind of refutation of the radical feminist analysis of patriarchy was common in media coverage of second-wave feminism. Reporters seeking to balance their news stories on women's liberation, or women's magazines seeking to protect a gendered constituency, routinely featured such arguments as articulated by women themselves. For example, the *New York Times* coverage of the 1970 Strike for Equality was "balanced" by an article entitled "For Most Women, 'Strike Day' Was Just a Topic of Conversation" (Lichtenstein, 1970; see also Bernays, 1970; Fosburgh, 1970).

The Domestication of Mary Richards

Given this lengthy review of the historical context that framed *Mary Tyler Moore*, the sitcom is most usefully viewed, I think, as featuring and adapting a confluence of discourses drawn from feminist rhetoric, single-woman lifestyle imagery, television history, and generic conventions. Each of these discourses is featured to varying degrees at different points in the history of the series. The premiere episode, as I have discussed, features a moderate dose of equal opportunity rhetoric as well as a subtle but clearly present valorization of single womanhood as a positive alternative to traditional marriage. Because of the absence of such themes from prior sitcoms, *Mary Tyler Moore* draws a large portion of its meaning from intertextual difference.

Generally, the ongoing source of *Mary Tyler Moore*'s feminist resonance is that embedded in the show's premise—the independent woman trying to "make it on her own." Over seven seasons, various episodes treat issues that can be explicitly linked to women's liberation. Some examples include plots in which Mary asks for a raise ("The Good-Time News"), hires a female sportscaster ("What's Wrong with Swimming?"), encourages her friend Georgette to stand up to Ted Baxter's mistreatment ("The Georgette Story"), and goes after—and gets—a promotion to producer ("Mary Richards: Producer"). While these episodes and others depend upon the context provided by the women's movement, they are a small number of the 168 episodes that comprise the series. Far more consistent and repetitive is the emphasis on the construction and protection of the *Mary Tyler Moore* "family" and Mary Richards's key position within it. Within her family of co-workers, Mary functions in the recognizable roles of idealized mother, wife, and daughter—roles familiar from decades of reinforcement in popular culture generally and sitcom specifically. Mary alternately nurtures, mediates, facilitates and submits, bringing the accessible, other-centered, emotionally skilled "True Woman" to the workplace (Bathrick, 1984). In *Mary Tyler Moore*, "woman's place" is transformed from a matter of location to one of function.

The patterns of interaction of characters on the show indicate that Mary Richards plays two major roles: that of daughter and wife to Lou Grant, and that of mother to Lou and other characters on *Mary Tyler Moore*. As many episodes illustrate, these roles are not always distinct;

Mary can be submissive and nurturing in the same episode. However, her interaction with other characters (usually male, but sometimes female as well) consistently depicts her fulfilling one of these gendered familial roles. The exception to this pattern is Mary's relationship with her home-based friends, Rhoda and Phyllis, which has a different dynamic.

The paternal role that Lou Grant plays in relation to Mary Richards and her submission to his authority on both personal and private matters demonstrate the perseverance of patriarchal relationship patterns in *Mary Tyler Moore.* Mary consistently seeks Lou's approval and goes to him for advice on personal and professional matters while Lou, in turn, guides and protects her. In "Sue Ann Falls in Love," an example of conflict resolution illustrates this relationship. Before an awards dinner, Sue Ann Nivens's boyfriend makes a pass at Mary. Mary becomes upset and takes her problem to Lou, who offers to "kill him." Mary refuses this offer but later takes Lou's advice that she should tell Sue Ann. When Mary explains what happened to Sue Ann, Sue Ann cries and Mary comforts her. By the end of the episode, Sue Ann's confidence is restored when she wins an award.

The handling of the problem in this show reinforces the patriarchal politics of Lou and Mary's relationship. In the beginning, it underscores Lou's protective feeling toward Mary, and by the end, it completes the pattern of the classic father and child problem-solving plot familiar from *Father Knows Best* or *Leave It to Beaver.* The child has a problem and goes to the father, who tells the child to do "the right thing," which the child intuitively knows she should do anyway. With the advice and pressure of the parent, the child overcomes her reluctance, does what is required, and the situation is resolved happily, reaffirming the wisdom of the father.

"Look at Us, We're Walking," an episode in which Mary and Lou ask for a raise, further illustrates the parent/child nature of Mary and Lou's relationship. When Mary wants a raise, Lou tells her that they must confront the station manager as a package, arguing that the station could afford to lose one, but not both, of them. When they are refused, they threaten to quit, and the station manager does not object. Mary is thoroughly demoralized by unemployment, but Lou is confident that the station manager will eventually give in. At the end of the episode, she and Lou go back to see the station manager, who offers them a large raise, double what Mary first expected, to split between them. Once again, despite Mary's reluctance, the course of action Lou recommended proves to be the successful one.

The significance of these examples, which demonstrate Lou's patriarchal superiority, is underscored by the negative consequences that result in episodes in which Mary refuses to follow Lou's advice. In "What's

Wrong with Swimming?" Mary meets a female swimmer who she is convinced would make a good sportscaster. Lou ridicules the idea, and Mary accuses him of sexism. However, Lou tells Mary that, as the producer of the news, she has the authority to hire anyone she likes, and Mary hires the woman. In her first broadcast, the new sportscaster reports nothing but swimming, ignoring baseball and football. The woman later reveals to Mary that she does not believe in contact sports and will not report them. Mary is forced to fire her. At the conclusion, Mary tells Lou that she was wrong about the sportscaster, bemoaning her failure to strike a blow for women. Lou assures her that she has indeed proven something, "that a woman has the chance to be just as lousy in a job as a man."

The implicit lesson from the episode is that Mary should have listened to Lou in the first place. Like a good parent, he allowed her to make her own mistakes, which taught her a lesson. This episode is troublesome because it implies that Mary needs Lou's paternal guidance in order to make correct decisions even when the nature of her job as producer should allow her to make them independently.[28] On another level, this plot's resolution is also interesting because of its illustration of the limits of equal-opportunity feminism. B.J., the female sportscaster, is fired because she refuses to play by the rules of male-defined sportscasting, in which exclusively male professional sports are most important. Her ostensibly feminist value of eschewing violence is considered inappropriate by everyone, including Mary (and the episode's laugh track encourages the audience to conclude similarly). B.J.'s experience is a microcosm of the general dynamic within which Mary operates: They are both allowed access to "man's world" but are not allowed to question its rules for appropriate behavior.

At different points in the series, Lou explicitly acknowledges that he views Mary as a daughter (in "Mary Gets a Lawyer," he even gives her hand in marriage to a friend of his), and the father-daughter dynamic between the two is the most clear-cut example of a traditional relational pattern. However, in less explicit ways, Mary also functions as a nurturing wife/mother to Lou and other characters. It is her responsibility to maintain the interpersonal relations within the members of the group, and she does this through personal advice, support, and mediation of conflict.[29]

Mary is constantly accessible; her friends, who drop by at any time of the day or night, are received warmly. In "Ted and the Kid," Ted Baxter, the station's anchorman, cannot father a child. He comes to Mary, who reconciles him to the idea of adoption. In "Not with My Wife, I Don't," Ted has sexual problems, and his wife, Georgette, comes to Mary for advice. When Sue Ann feels threatened by her sister's success in Minneapolis in "Sue Ann's Sister," she seeks comfort from Mary. Later in this same episode, Sue Ann becomes so demoralized that she takes to her bed, convinced that she is no longer wanted or needed. Although Sue Ann has consistently treated Mary unkindly, Mary feels responsible for cheering her up. In "The Square-Shaped Room," Lou decides to redecorate the living room as a surprise for his wife. He seeks Mary's advice, who enlists Rhoda, her neighbor, for the job. Moreover, it is Mary who sees Lou through his painful divorce and his wife's remarriage. During this crisis, he frequently turns up at Mary's apartment for dinner, seeking the wifely/motherly functions that he misses. Whenever a "woman's touch" is needed, Mary is there.

Mary is the ideal wife/mother surrogate in these situations. Like other typical sitcom mothers such as Harriet Nelson or June Cleaver, she is other-directed, sublimating her own feelings or needs to those of her "family." That this "comes naturally" to Mary is made clear in an episode, "My Son, the Genius" in which Murray chides Mary for being too giving, and recommends that she read *The Importance of Being Selfish*, a book that he says will change her life. After embracing the philosophy of the book, she refuses Murray's request for a favor, trying her best to be selfish. She clearly wants to help him, however, and is relieved when he convinces her that she can disregard the book in this instance.

Those moments in *Mary Tyler Moore* when Mary is forced, by conscience, prodding, or circumstance, to be less than "nice," are milked for the comedy of her extreme discomfort. Moreover, it is not uncommon for Mary to suffer for those occasions when she does manage to assert herself. For example, in "Feeb," after Mary complains about an incompetent waitress, the woman is fired. Mary's guilt leads her to get the woman a job at WJM, with disastrous consequences. In "Mary and the Sexagenarian," when she briefly dates Murray's father, a much older man, Mary feels the disapproval of others. At a party, she delivers an impassioned speech in which she defends their relationship and accuses the others of being small-minded. Moments later, she discovers that Murray's father has dumped her for an older woman.

Of course, it is most difficult for Mary to be assertive in her own "family." The importance of Mary's "womanly" functions to the group is reinforced in the rare instances in which she flatly refuses to perform them. Even when she attempts to assert herself, she returns to her accommodating patterns by the end of the episode. For example, in "Hail the Conquering Gordy," a former WJM staff member returns for a visit, and Lou decides a party at Mary's home would be appropriate (most social interaction outside the office takes place in Mary's apartment). Mary refuses to go along with this imposition, suggesting that Lou have the party at his house. She arrives at his home early that night to assist him in last-minute preparations, only to find that the entire place is a mess, and Lou is making no effort to get ready for his guests. He clearly assumes that Mary will take over and clean up for him, but she recognizes this manipulation and refuses to help. However, when Lou suggests that the guests will assume that she helped him anyway, and that she will be blamed for the mess, she frantically begins to clean.

Two aspects of this situation are significant. The first is that Mary is obviously concerned about others' assessments of her traditional "womanly" qualities and does not want to be viewed as messy or unprepared. Second, this episode emphasizes Mary's role as social facilitator for the group. His confidence that Mary would take over the preparations demonstrates Lou's realization of her role, and Mary's acceptance of it is clear when she gives in and begins to clean. Even though Mary refused to fulfill a traditional role in her own home at the beginning of the episode, she ends up assuming it at Lou's house. The nurturing aspect of Mary's character is not just an extension of her status as a "nice" person. Certainly Murray Slaughter, her friend and the newswriter at WJM, would be described as a nice person; however, he does not nurture and facilitate interpersonal relationships as Mary does. Indeed, the importance of Mary's interpersonal skills is briefly forecast in her job interview in *Mary Tyler Moore*'s first episode, in which Lou Grant tells her, "If I don't like you, I'll fire you. If you don't like me, I'll fire you." Here is the first clue that Lou's standards for Mary are based on personal factors rather than professional ones, indicating that Mary's success in the newsroom will be dependent upon her likability rather than her professional merit.

Mary's sensitivity, relationship skills, and willingness to spend her time and energy on the problems of others are symptomatic of her status as mother to the group. Like the traditional mothers of domestic sitcoms, her value as a person comes from what she can do for others. The new lyrics to the *Mary Tyler Moore* theme song that appear in the show's third season echo this idea: "Who can turn the world on with her smile?/ Who can take a nothing day and suddenly make it all seem worthwhile?" In *Mary Tyler Moore* Mary is a woman in a man's world, and her primary function is to enhance the lives of others in ways a male supposedly cannot. As Adrienne Rich has claimed, "The patriarchy looks to women to embody and impersonate the qualities lacking in its institutions . . . such qualities as intuition, sympathy, and access to feeling" (1979, p. 80).

Although *Mary Tyler Moore* took the sitcom from the home to the workplace, it did not alter significantly the traditional male/female roles of the genre. The sitcom's reliance on a family paradigm with Mary Richards as its center is a comforting vision of *adjustment* without *change*. That is, the genre adjusted to a new location (the workplace) and a new kind of character (the careerist woman) and then proceeded to slot these new elements into familiar structures (the family) and role expectations (the accessible, nurturing, submissive woman). In this process, the feminist challenge posed by Mary Richards is contained and made less threatening to audiences who have palpable fears about what women's liberation might mean. The repeated characterization of radical feminists as angry, militant, and aggressive in media coverage of the second wave indicates the key attributes of unwomanliness, attributes that are conspicuously absent (or, when present, very short-lived) in Mary Richards (just as profiles of Gloria Steinem in the early 1970s also made a point to stress how polite, soft-spoken, and empathic she was).[30]

Although Mary's niceness and docility within her "family" temper the feminist implications of the sitcom, those implications are still available for viewers who want to see them. Moreover, as I discuss in the conclusion, *Mary Tyler Moore*'s lasting contribution to feminism on television is its inauguration of a tradition of feminist representation built around the single woman with something to prove. The individualist philosophy and equal-opportunity feminism that *Mary Tyler Moore* emphasized would become a major theme in popular culture representations of feminism across media and genres.

The Female Community in *Mary Tyler Moore*

Another theme present in *Mary Tyler Moore* during its first four seasons is also key in 1970s representations of feminism—friendship between women. Serafina Bathrick (1984), in particular, has argued that the interaction among Mary, Rhoda, and Phyllis contributes some of the most progressive discourse to emerge from *Mary Tyler Moore*. For example, Bathrick links the daily conversations among these women in Mary's apartment to the heightened awareness of the importance of women's talk created by the spread of consciousness-raising among women during the early 1970s (1984, p. 118). Alexander Doty takes this facet of *Mary Tyler Moore* even further, suggesting that the sitcom can be read as lesbian, because of its "crucial investment in constructing narratives that connect an audience's pleasure to the activities and relationships of women" (1993, p. 41). To a large extent, I agree with these arguments; the female solidarity and pleasure in female companionship represented by Mary and Rhoda's relationship in particular is an antidote to television's frequent isolation of women within the suburban family or its caricature of female friendship as largely competitive. However, it is no accident, I think, that this solidarity is relegated to the private sphere of Mary's home life and is absent from the workplace, where it would be much more threatening. At work, Mary is still an isolated woman, a token.

An example of *Mary Tyler Moore*'s use of female support and cooperation as a theme is found in "Rhoda the Beautiful," an episode focusing
on Rhoda's loss of twenty pounds in a weight watching group.[31] The
change in her appearance leads to an invitation to participate in a beauty
contest at Hempel's Department Store where she is a window-dresser. A
repetitive issue in this episode is Rhoda's refusal to acknowledge her attractiveness and the frustration this causes for Mary, who showers Rhoda
with praise and encouragement. Ultimately Rhoda wins the contest and
is finally able to take some pleasure in her new appearance.

This episode has a number of interesting facets to it. First of course, is
the fact that Mary is completely supportive of Rhoda, wanting her friend
to succeed and feel good about herself. Moreover, Rhoda wins the contest and experiences a clear surge in self-confidence as a result. These
are certainly positive elements to the storyline. At the same time, resting
so much self-esteem on physical appearance (and a beauty contest is
surely the apotheosis of this kind of obsession) is not exactly a progressive feminist message.

Indeed, as is so often the case in *Mary Tyler Moore*, the gender politics
are acknowledged but not necessarily confronted. Rhoda notes in a conversation with Murray and Mary that the women at the department store
voiced some objections to the idea of a beauty contest, based on "the
whole thing that it's the wrong way to think about a woman and all," a
reference easily traced to the much publicized protest by feminists at the
Miss American Pageant in 1968 (Davis, 1991, p. 107). The store's response, Rhoda continues, was that "if they call it '*Ms.* Hempel,' it evens
things out." Actually, this statement could serve as a metaphor for the
episode's treatment of the issue, a mixture of parody of the absurdity of
such pageants with a clear investment in the emotional payoff for Mary,
Rhoda, and, presumably, the viewing audience, when Rhoda wins the
contest.

As Rhoda is dressing for the pageant, she and Mary stage a parody of
typical contestants' answers to questions such as "What are your hobbies?" or "What is your goal in life?" Rhoda's answers to the questions
are, respectively, "My favorite hobbies are cheerleading, liking people,
and living in America," and "I would like to become a brain surgeon—
or a model." This is the kind of satire that could come only from Rhoda's
mouth; it simply would not seem that absurd coming from Mary, who
probably *was* a cheerleader in high school.

Indeed, much of Rhoda's positive function in *Mary Tyler Moore* arises
from her ability to make the wry comment about a woman's position that
is seconded by Mary but would not originate with her. As press accounts
and even the show's creators point out (see Alley and Brown, 1989),
Rhoda is the "brassy" contrast that serves as a foil to Mary's perky perfec-

tion (an issue to which I return in a moment). As two single women who share their lives and problems, they often offer a powerful statement about the alternative to the nuclear family (Bathrick, 1984). Unfortunately, this dynamic ends in 1974 when Rhoda leaves *Mary Tyler Moore* to become the leading character in her own sitcom (Phyllis departs for the same reason one season later). After this point, Mary's life becomes almost entirely defined by her relations with co-workers and the facilitative functions she performs for the "work family" composed almost entirely of men. Indeed, Doty notes that these changes "signaled the program's switch from lesbian narratives to more heterosexual(ized) ones" (1993, p. 49).

Sue Ann Nivens enters *Mary Tyler Moore* in 1973 as the host of the "Happy Homemaker" show at WJM. Although she is seen in the newsroom, she does not work there, and she does not provide Mary with an opportunity for female bonding. Sue Ann's job and her interests reflect traditionally female concerns. She is man-hungry and constantly in pursuit of Lou, which makes her relationship with Mary competitive rather than cooperative. After the departures of Rhoda in 1974 and Phyllis in 1975, the role of Georgette Franklin Baxter, Ted's girlfriend and later his wife, is expanded, providing the only opportunity for Mary to interact with a woman on a genuinely friendly basis. However, Georgette, like the men, uses Mary as a problem-solver and confidante; she treats Mary more like a mother-figure than a peer.

Particularly after the fifth season (but, in some ways, since the beginning of the series), Mary is portrayed as the token successful female within her environment. Certainly, Mary is specified as the target for identification in the title for the sitcom, a device that would become common in single-woman sitcoms. To a large extent, other female characters function as foils for Mary, for they invariably embody some *lack* in comparison to her. Mary is constructed as a thoroughly positive, sympathetic character. She is bright, attractive, and well-liked, has a good job, and is generally happy. In contrast, the other female characters on *Mary Tyler Moore* do not fare well. Sue Ann is constantly seeking fulfillment through men; Georgette is an addle-brained blonde who is devoted to the egocentric and insensitive Ted Baxter; Rhoda has a less than satisfying job, little confidence in her attractiveness, and is unsuccessful in romantic relationships; and Phyllis is an eccentric, narcissistic wife and mother who often is frustrated by her circumscribed role. Moreover, Rhoda and Phyllis cannot get along with each other despite their common friendship with Mary, again reinforcing the idea that only Mary can be successful in all contexts. Mary's superiority is attested to by the various episodes in which all of these women—even Sue Ann—turn to Mary for advice and help.

Mary's isolation as the sole female in the newsroom and her portrayal as the only completely successful and fulfilled female in *Mary Tyler Moore* are evidence of her tokenism. Her success in the public realm can be linked to her willingness to fulfill traditional female roles within the work-family. Mary is successful, likable, and admirable in the eyes of the other women and men on *Mary Tyler Moore* because she has successfully adapted herself to the male culture. In comparison to Mary, the other women fall short in some way. Rhoda is too abrasive, Phyllis too self-centered, Sue Ann too predatory, and Georgette too naive.

Moreover, Mary's isolation as the only thoroughly positive female character in the private realm promotes perception of her as an ideal woman who is different from most.[32] The token woman is "separate[d] from the wider female condition; and she is perceived by 'ordinary' women as separate also, perhaps even stronger than themselves" (Rich, 1986, p. 6). In the context of Mary's relationship to other female characters on *Mary Tyler Moore*, this is certainly true. As the sole well-adjusted female character, Mary is figuratively isolated from and literally outnumbered by the unfulfilled female characters of Rhoda, Phyllis, and Sue Ann, re-inforcing basic liberal ideology that stresses women's success as "isolated individuals rather than as members of a collective group" (Press, 1991, pp. 37–38).

In the end, Mary is no one's equal. She is inferior to other, specifically male, characters in the public realm, where her success is more dependent on interpersonal qualities than professional skill, and she is superior to other female characters in the private realm, where her success and general happiness are a marked contrast to the other women. In their own ways, Rhoda, Phyllis, and Sue Ann are depicted as incapable of meeting the demands of patriarchy. Mary has adapted well, however, and she is rewarded for her efforts. Mary's tokenism fits well with the individualistic philosophy of sitcom: The fault is not in the expectations but in the failure of women to meet them. The episodes featuring Rhoda's pursuit of romance or Phyllis's self-improvement schemes (for herself, her child, and her marriage) make it clear that the pursuit of the kind of perfection that Mary embodies is expected and natural, if often humorous and usually unsuccessful.

The dynamics of the *Mary Tyler Moore* "family" are consistent, repetitive, and present through the last episode of the series. In "The Last Show," as the WJM "family" prepares to split up after the station has been sold, Lou, in his paternal role, arranges to bring Rhoda and Phyllis back to console Mary. Even on this occasion, Phyllis and Rhoda bicker over Mary's attention, reinforcing Mary's superiority and bringing her mediating skills to the fore. Significantly, in her speech at the end of the show, Mary acknowledges the relationships she has formed, saying, "Thank you for being my family."

Mary Tyler Moore, Television, and Feminism

One of the contentions underlying this book is that television programs like *Mary Tyler Moore* provide opportunities for viewers to "make sense" of feminism. In my view, this means that television discourse both produces and is produced by feminist discourse. *Mary Tyler Moore* draws on the presence of second-wave feminism as a way of giving "relevance" to its rhetoric; at the same time, it produces a vision of feminism that is a selection, deflection, and reflection of various available discourses (Burke, 1968). The codes and logics of television as a medium are key elements in this process.

Mary Tyler Moore is a sitcom. The logic of situation comedy operates through the disturbance of stability (the source of the "comedy") followed by the restoration of stability (a return to the "situation"). A dominant tradition in sitcom is that the disturbance represents some kind of threat to the family that characters represent, a threat that must be resolved so that the family can remain intact. This formula does not mean that characters cannot change and grow in some ways, but it usually means that the important dynamics of the group are protected over time. As the seasons wear on, Mary can grow more confident and assertive on the job; for example, her use of pointed sarcasm and ridicule in dealing with Ted and Sue Ann increases over time. However, she can never go so far as to relinquish her deference toward Lou (symbolized by her inability to call him anything but "Mr. Grant"), for such a move would destroy the basic father-daughter dynamic between them and eliminate the basis for countless plots.

Sitcom is basically repetitive; it uses stock characters and recycles variations on the same plot over and over. The appeal of the form does not come from suspense or the pleasure of decipherment; rather, the nature of the resolution to come is known and expected. What gives pleasure is the comedy and humor experienced along the way. The role of key characters in the creation of disturbance and the attainment of resolution are important indicators of the politics of sitcom, a claim well illustrated by Patricia Mellencamp's argument that *I Love Lucy* offered a repetitive dynamic of rebellion followed by containment. Lucy Ricardo was "constantly trying to escape domesticity," and her attempts were always thwarted in the end (1986, p. 87). Because the audience knows that Lucy will ultimately fail and will be restored to her place in the domestic sphere, the thoroughly *active* nature of her character is amusing rather than threatening (although, as Mellencamp discusses, some women may have found her antics briefly liberating).

Mary Richards, in contrast, is essentially a reactive character, what Ella Taylor calls, in a narrower sense, the "ethical straight woman" (1989, p. 123). Mary does not create problems; rather, they are thrust upon her or she is drawn into them because of her nurturing, empathic instincts. Mary is much more likely to seek to restore equilibrium than she is to provoke its disturbance. For the most part, Mary is the classic "goodwife" in a new location; she solves the problems of her "family" through her superior insight and interpersonal skills. On those rare occasions when Mary is the source of the problem, she, like Lucy, must give in and regret her rebellion or suffer some embarrassing consequence.

The construction of Mary Richards as an essentially passive character is just another of the strategies that were part of *Mary Tyler Moore*'s finely tuned negotiation of tradition and change. Because Mary was not contained by location, she was contained by character definition. In the public sphere of the workplace, she functioned, in many ways, in the familiar relational patterns of female domestic characters on past sitcoms situated within patriarchal families. Those patterns, and the discourse they derived from, were familiar to many viewers in a way that the emerging women's liberation movement was not. Women's lib gave *Mary Tyler Moore* relevance and no doubt attracted female viewers sympathetic to feminism, but it did not require the alteration of traditional ideology about how "good" women operate (through intuition, empathy, and submission to the needs of others) and what their job in the world really is (facilitating and mediating relationships between loved ones). The big difference was that these traditional activities were given a new location.

Does the argument that Mary Richards, the key figure for identification in *Mary Tyler Moore*, functioned as an office wife/mother/daughter negate the feminist potential of the sitcom? Not necessarily. Although I do not subscribe to the belief that all discourses are equal, I also do not believe that to argue that one wins (i.e., that it exerts more influence over an interpretation) is necessarily to argue that the influence of the others is eliminated. Based on the power of repetition and familiarity, I believe that the lion's share of the rhetorical appeal of *Mary Tyler Moore* derives from its reiteration of a conventional female character, enmeshed in a familiar complex of relationships and problems. These familiar elements are made interesting and "new" because they reside in a new location and because the members of the family are diverse and well-rounded characters, providing the possibility for a new range of "problems."

Certainly, hegemony is at work in *Mary Tyler Moore*. Mary's independence is consistently compromised by her submission to others' needs, and the sitcom's naturalizing of her "true woman" qualities (particularly in comparison to other female characters) reflect little awareness of the radical feminist critique of gender roles. A potentially threatening idea (a woman on her own) is made less threatening when she is slotted into familiar roles and relationships that assure the audience that little has really changed. As Ella Taylor has succinctly put it, "*The Mary Tyler Moore Show* is almost as likely to appeal to antifeminists as it is to feminists" (1989, p. 123).

To admit that *Mary Tyler Moore* offers a compromised and contradictory feminism is not to say that those critics and viewers who have viewed it as the first effort at feminist television are victims of false consciousness. Rather, it is to view the sitcom as a historically situated collection of rhetorical choices that attempted to combine the marketability of single womanhood with the timeliness of feminism. At the same time, it attempted to avoid the most controversial aspects of feminist rhetoric, that is, those requiring the most fundamental change in norms of thought and action.

Locating Mary Richards outside of the traditional patriarchal family and placing her in a man's job in an all-male office are key markers of *Mary Tyler Moore*'s liberal feminist lifestyle politics. The young, unmarried woman living outside of the nuclear family, pursuing a career in an urban setting (and the rejection of domesticity and patriarchal authority that these characteristics implied) was becoming the representative carrier of feminist resonance during the years in which *Mary Tyler Moore* enjoyed its greatest popularity. One of the ways that mass media in general packaged feminism was to depict it as the concern of a certain kind of woman who had chosen (or hoped to choose) a specific lifestyle, one which emphasized access to and opportunities in the public sphere (Faludi, 1991, p. 76).

The Virginia Slims cigarette ads that appeared in the early seventies are a prime example. Picturing a young attractive, fashionable, smoking woman, the tag line for these ads was "You've Come a Long Way, Baby." The slogan referred to the historical "flashback" included in each ad that pictured some earlier time in history in which women were punished for smoking. Smoking in public, as a lifestyle marker, was represented as a benefit of liberation. The Virginia Slims slogan, and its feminist overtones, became a favorite in pop culture addressing feminism. The title of *Time*'s August 1970 article on women's liberation was "Who's Come a Long Way, Baby?" and the *TV Guide* article on the premiere of *Mary Tyler Moore* was entitled "You've Come a Long Way, Baby" (Whitney, 1970, p. 34). The transformation of women's liberation into a lifestyle or set of attitudes was aided by the growth of the single-woman market and by the appearance of pop culture heroines who could symbolize the meaning of liberation. Mary Richards was just such a heroine, and she had her real-life counterpart in Gloria Steinem.

The popularization of liberal feminism and its emphasis on woman's success in man's world occurred in tandem with feminists' focus on the ERA. By the time that *Mary Tyler Moore* ended its prime-time run in 1977, the Equal Rights Amendment, passed by the Senate in 1972, was the dominant issue for mainstream feminists and the mass media (Davis, 1991; Ryan, 1992). As most radical feminist groups disbanded and their leaders slipped out of the headlines, liberal feminism ascended, as did its emphasis on women's equality in public life, symbolized by the ERA. The rhetorical power of equal-opportunity feminism is that its emphasis on public life leaves intact the distinction between the public and the private sphere. It elides the possibility that gender roles developed in the private sphere carry over to the public sphere or that women, because of biology or traditional responsibilities in the private sphere, are ill-equipped to compete in the public sphere (Hartmann, 1979; Kanter, 1977). A focus on the unmarried career woman as the primary audience for and beneficiary of women's liberation enables avoidance of such issues altogether. The message was that "feminism . . . should only redraw the workplace, and this only slightly. Other regions of society, like a man's home, his marriage, his family, should be cordoned off from feminist surveyors" (Douglas, 1994, p. 187).

Mary Tyler Moore relies on such an implicit distinction between the public and private spheres. The single women work in the public sphere (Mary, Rhoda, Sue Ann), and the married women work in the home (Lou's wife Edie,[33] Murray's wife Marie, Ted's wife Georgette). This means that although *Mary Tyler Moore* offers an alternative to traditional womanhood (at least in terms of location), it does so without an explicit critique of the problems of traditional womanhood. Feminism becomes a matter of lifestyle choice, not systemic oppression or social transformation. Even Mary's rejection of the possibility of marriage at the end of the first episode is a rejection of a *particular man* who has been inconsiderate and unreliable. Her decision is *individual* rather than political, in keeping with sitcom's general individualistic philosophy.

The "commodification" of feminism implicit in viewing it as a lifestyle rather than an ideology carries obvious class implications. Mary's ability to choose the life she does is a function of her status as an educated, middle-class, white woman. Historically, of course, it is the middle class that has created an ideology of womanhood that sees wage-earning and domesticity as incompatible, a separation that women of lower classes have rarely been able to afford (Epstein, 1981). That *Mary Tyler Moore* preserves such an implicit ideology reveals its classist assumptions. Mary Richards is precisely the type of woman most well-equipped to benefit from emerging feminist ideology without creating uncomfortable disso-nance. She is not married or a mother (and thus does not have to bal-ance work and the domestic sphere), she is educated (and thus can pursue a career rather than simply have a job), she is definitively hetero-sexual, attractive, and socially active (and thus not a "man-hater"), and she is white (and thus does not face racial politics).

This stereotype of the feminist heroine worked well for pop culture and its almost always assumed middle-class audience, but not so well for feminist politics. Not only did it make identification difficult for women not privileged by class or race, but it was easily used to create a devil-figure for many white, middle-class homemakers and mothers. Phyllis Schlafly's successful STOP ERA campaign, begun in 1972, exploited the dark side of the stereotype by arguing that ERA would benefit only lim-ited numbers of childless, man-hating, careerist women while negatively affecting the millions of white, middle-class women invested in home and family.

Schlafly's claim that ERA had the power to transform private relations between men and women by, for example, forcing women to contribute to the economic support of families, or making divorce easier for men, were powerful and created substantial opposition to the ERA among white, middle-class women (Davis, 1991, chapter 18; Mansbridge, 1986, chapter 9). The claims were not true, but they made sense through a kind of syllogistic reasoning. That is, feminists supported ERA, and much feminist rhetoric had attacked the traditional family; thus, the ERA must be an attack on the traditional family. What had begun as a measure that seemed only to extend previously denied public protec-tions and benefits to women, a move consonant with American traditions of individualism and equal opportunity, became a battle over sacred territory, the family. Most important, the battle pitted women against women, a tactic with historical precedent in the anti-woman suffrage campaign of the late nineteenth and early twentieth centuries (Kraditor, 1981). Schlafly managed to convince her audience that the ERA would make feminist lifestyle options a mandate rather than a choice. From unisex toilets to homosexual marriage, the power of her arguments about the effects of the ERA was derived from perceived intrusion into the private sphere.

Although viewers may have attached such meanings to *Mary Tyler Moore*, the text does not encourage them. *Mary Tyler Moore*'s (tele)vision of feminism as an individualistic lifestyle choice offers a parallel, but not competing, world to domesticity. In this sense it was a product of its times; while *Mary Tyler Moore* was a limited vision of what feminism could mean for women, it was also a hopeful and innocent one. Women such as Mary Richards could achieve fulfillment without serious challenge to dearly held beliefs about man's world and woman's place in it. Mary's life was an alternative to domesticity but not a reprisal of it, especially given her performance of womanly functions in the workplace. The issues that came to plague feminism's public image in later years—the "man short-age," woman's biological clock, conflicts between responsibilities at home and in the workplace, the New Right's profamily line, and battles over reproductive freedom—were not yet in the forefront of public con-sciousness. The first clear indications of a what would become a sus-tained anti-feminist backlash emerged at the International Women's Year Conference in Houston held in 1977, the year *Mary Tyler Moore* left prime-time (Ryan, 1992, p. 75).

In the meantime, however, other feminist-inspired—and *Mary Tyler Moore*-inspired—sitcoms had hit the airwaves. *Rhoda* (1974–78) and *Phyllis* (1975–77) were direct offshoots, but they were joined by other shows that breached the timid limits *Mary Tyler Moore* had set. *Maude* (1972–78), for instance, introduced a married, loudmouthed, suburban feminist. The short-lived *Fay* (1975–76) and the long-running *One Day at a Time* (1975–84) each offered a divorced woman as a lead character, a move too controversial five years earlier. Between roughly 1975 and 1980, television screens were populated with a succession of single women intent on finding themselves and exploring liberation. These shows, discussed in the next chapter, were the legacy of *Mary Tyler Moore.*

Notes

1. After a slow start, the show was consistently among the top twenty rated pro-grams for six of the seven years it was broadcast (Brooks and Marsh, 1985). Spin-offs from *Mary Tyler Moore* included *Rhoda* (1974–78), *Phyllis* (1975–77), and *Lou Grant* (1977–82). The last of these is noteworthy because of a shift in genres that was highly unusual for spin-offs. *Lou Grant* was an hour-long dramatic series that gained its premise from the life of a character originally developed in a sitcom.

2. As I write this, *Mary Tyler Moore* is shown daily on *Nick at Nite,* a national cable channel that bills itself as offering "classic TV."

3. For examples of journalistic evaluations of female representation that rely on *Mary Tyler Moore* as a standard by which to measure progress on television, see Theroux, 1987, Rebeck, 1989, and Waters and Huck, 1989. *Mary Tyler Moore* also is prominent in journalistic reviews of television history. The special issue of *People* magazine celebrating television's fiftieth anniversary named Mary Tyler Moore as one of television's top twenty-five stars, noting that *Mary Tyler Moore* "changed TV's portrayal of women" ("Mary Tyler Moore," 1989, p. 35). In 1993, in *TV Guide's* fortieth anniversary issue focusing on the "all-time best TV," Mary Tyler Moore is named as one of the "best comic actresses" and is called "the role model for a generation of working women" ("The Best Comic Actresses," 1993, p. 22). In Chapter 4, I specifically discuss the ways in which journalists frequently used comparisons with *Mary Tyler Moore* in their discussions of the "progress" represented by *Murphy Brown.*

4. For examples of this type of evaluation, see Bathrick, 1984; Deming, 1992, p. 208; Hamamoto, 1989, pp. 114–115; Jones, 1992, pp. 194–202; Marc, 1989.

5. This appeal, at least among Andrea Press's respondents, was limited by class. Working-class women replied that they did not enjoy *Mary Tyler Moore* and several indicated that they "actively disliked" the character of Mary Richards. Press does not explore the reasons for this rejection beyond noting that working-class women would find it harder to identify with a lead character in a program with a decidedly middle-class look and orientation (1991, pp. 79–81). One of the most interesting aspects of Press's work is that it does not support the notion that these working-class women find a way to decode *Mary Tyler Moore* so that it speaks to their differing social experience, as the work of some polysemy advocates and audience researchers suggests they would be likely to do. Rather, the working-class women perceive that the message of *Mary Tyler Moore* does not fit their lives, and they reject it. On the other hand, at least on the basis of Press's sample, *Mary Tyler Moore*'s mixed messages about feminism are quite rhetorically effective with the middle-class female audience its advertisers most want to reach. This realization brings to mind Celeste Condit's claim that television, or any mass medium, can do oppressive work solely by addressing the dominant audience that also constitutes the public. It is her contention that because television "makes present in public" a vocabulary that prefers the dominant audience's interests, the dominant audience gets the most pleasure from television and television actively promotes its interests (1989, p. 112).

6. As historians of feminism have been noting for years, although protestors tossed various symbols of women's oppression as sex objects, including bras and high-heeled shoes, into a trash can, the can was not set on fire (Davis, 1991, p. 107; Freeman, 1975, p. 112).

7. Examples of early coverage, which vary in the degree of sympathy for the movement's ideas, include Martha Weinman Lear, "The Second Feminist Wave," *New York Times Magazine,* March 10, 1968; Peter Babcox, "Meet the Women of the Revolution, 1969," *New York Times Magazine,* February 9, 1969; Gloria Steinem, "After Black Power, Women's Liberation," *New York,* April 7, 1969; and Sara Davidson, "An 'Oppressed Majority' Demands Its Rights," *Life,* December 12, 1969.

8. In her book, *Where the Girls Are: Growing Up Female with the Mass Media* (1994), Susan J. Douglas provides an insightful analysis of media treatment of the movement in the late 1960s and early 1970s. Her discussion of television coverage in chapter 8 is particularly useful.

9. In late 1970, largely because of the publication of her book *Sexual Politics,* Kate Millett was often represented as a leader in news stories (see, e.g., "Who's Come a Long Way, Baby?" 1970; Prial, 1970). The attempts of journalists to create leaders in order to facilitate their stories, and the problems this caused among radical feminists, are discussed in Echols, 1989, chapter 5.

10. For a sampling of this press coverage, which includes articles written by feminists as well as writers uninvolved in the movement, see Klemesrud, 1970a; "The New Feminism," 1970; Wilkes, 1970; "Who's Come a Long Way, Baby?" 1970; Woman's Place," 1970.

11. Although the Strike for Equality involved a broad coalition of feminist groups, the event was Friedan's idea, and the explanation of the goals for the strike featured in news stories reflected the ideology of Friedan and of NOW. The feminist demands cited most often in press accounts of the August 1970 Strike for Equality were equality of opportunity in education and employment, free access to abortion on request, and twenty-four-hour child care for working mothers,

all issues tied to the goal of women's greater participation in the public sphere (see, e.g., Charlton, 1970; Klemesrud, 1970a; "Who's Come a Long Way, Baby?" 1970).

12. Although *The New York Times*, for instance, dubbed her "a high priestess of the current feminist wave" in its coverage of the Strike for Equality (Prial, 1970, p. 30), Millett's star fell quickly after she revealed that she was bisexual at a public meeting in November of 1970. As a result, in a December issue, *Time* magazine ran a vicious column that claimed she had discredited herself and the movement and quoted a number of critics who excoriated *Sexual Politics*, which the same magazine had called "remarkable" in its August cover story on Millett. The incident accelerated tensions over the lesbian/heterosexual divide in the women's movement itself, as well as demonstrated the power of lesbianism as a negative for the movement in the eyes of the media and the public (Davis, 1991, pp. 267–268; Klemesrud, 1970b, p. 47; "Women's Lib: A Second Look," 1970, p. 50).

13. Barbara Ehrenreich and Deirdre English provide a useful description of the single-girl culture of the 1970s and its attractiveness to advertisers in *For Her Own Good: 150 Years of the Experts' Advice to Women* (1978; rpt. 1989, pp. 285–297). Also see McCracken (1993, pp. 158–162) for an analysis of the sexually liberated, single-woman philosophy of *Cosmopolitan*.

14. Steinem became involved in the movement through her work as a journalist writing about women's liberation (see Steinem, 1969, 1970). She was not a member of a women's liberation group and has never been considered an ideologue. She emerged as a potential leader in the eyes of the media at the August 1970 Strike for Equality, one of the first feminist events in which she participated.

15. As Ellen Willis argues in "Radical Feminism and Feminist Radicalism," the liberal feminism that became visible in the mid-1970s was not so much a distinct alternative to radical feminism as a cooptation and deradicalization of radical feminist issues: "*Ms.* and the new liberals embraced [radical feminist] issues but basically ignored the existence of power relations. Though they supported feminist reforms, their main strategy for improving women's lives was individual and collective self-improvement" rather than structural transformation (1984, p. 108).

16. The episode titles that I use in this analysis are taken from Alley and Brown, 1989, which includes a complete listing of all of the episodes in *Mary Tyler Moore*.

17. Feuer et al., argue that the placement of *Mary Tyler Moore* in a Saturday night lineup with *M*A*S*H* and *All in the Family* was a major factor in its success, both because *Mary Tyler Moore*'s "relevant" aspects seemed tame in comparison to the much more overtly political *All in the Family*, and because the lineup as a whole (which also included *The Bob Newhart Show* by 1973) came to be considered "the most impressive evening of comedy ever to appear on any American television network" (1984, p. 7).

18. In *Inside Prime-Time*, Todd Gitlin quotes a CBS vice-president who supposedly said to *Mary Tyler Moore* creators Allan Burns and James Brooks, "Fellas, they're going to think she's divorced Dick Van Dyke. We can't have that" (1983, p. 214).

19. Interestingly, although *The Doris Day Show* began as a sitcom about a widowed mother, in the 1971 season it was transformed into a show about a single working woman, as the children and other members of the supporting cast disappeared, bringing the show into the "urban career girl format popularized by *The Mary Tyler Moore Show*" (Brooks and Marsh, 1985, p. 233).

20. Another useful contrast between *That Girl* and *Mary Tyler Moore* involves the sexual practices of their lead characters. In *That Girl*, Ann Marie's relationship with her boyfriend, later fiancé, was chaste; there was no hint that they ever spent the night together. In *Mary Tyler Moore*, there were subtle, recurring indications that Mary Richards was sexually active (including one rather famous veiled reference to the fact that she was on the pill). In an interesting intertextual move, Ted Bessell, the actor who played Ann Marie's fiancé, showed up in late seasons of *Mary Tyler Moore* as a steady boyfriend of Mary's, with whom she clearly had a sexual relationship.

21. Another facet of press coverage of *Mary Tyler Moore* and its star, however, is the emphasis on Mary Tyler Moore's happy home life, with her then-husband, MTM executive Grant Tinker, to whom Moore attributed much of her success (see, e.g., Whitney, 1970; "Rhoda and Mary—Love and Laughs," 1974). Thus, the star discourse around Moore testified to the benefits of traditional domesticity at the same time that *Mary Tyler Moore* presented an alternative to it (Bathrick, 1984, pp. 101–102).

22. At the beginning of the 1971 season, *Mary Tyler Moore* was in a Saturday night lineup in which it followed *All in the Family*, *Funny Face* (a short-lived sitcom about a college girl/actress played by Sandy Duncan), and *The New Dick Van Dyke Show* and preceded *Mission: Impossible*. In contrast, in the 1970 season, *Mary Tyler Moore* was preceded by *Mission: Impossible*, *My Three Sons*, and *Arnie* (a sitcom about the adjustments faced by a dock foreman after he was promoted to an executive position), and followed by *Mannix*. By 1973, CBS had perfected its Saturday night comedy lineup in which four sitcoms (which varied from year to year, although they always included *Mary Tyler Moore* and *Bob Newhart*) were followed by *The Carol Burnett Show*.

23. Having read this anecdote about the preview audience's perception in more than one account of the production of *Mary Tyler Moore*, I am always struck by the fact that all of the perceived negatives in the program were attached to the female characters.

24. However, this process involves a balance that is not always achieved. Comedy can also encourage resistance to social change "by making ridiculous, absurd, or laughable whatever threatens social order," an issue to which I give more attention in Chapter 4 (Duncan, 1962, p. 376).

25. *Mary Tyler Moore* has at least three such episodes that explicitly deal with this problem: one centering on Murray ("One Producer Too Many"), one on Ted Baxter ("Ted's Moment of Glory"), and one on Mary herself ("Party Is Such Sweet Sorrow"). The value placed on family unity in such narratives, sometimes in defiance of common sense, is perhaps best exemplified by the fact that the employees of WJM are actually concerned about the loss of Ted Baxter when he threatens to take another job, even though he is consistently acknowledged as a thoroughly incompetent news anchor and, in many ways, an unattractive personality.

26. This tendency operates across television, to differing degrees, although it carries more ideological power in some genres than in others. Elayne Rapping, for example, offers a fine analysis of the personalization and familialization of social issues in the genre of television movies in *The Movie of the Week* (1992).

27. Of course, another way to read this is that the workplace sitcom allowed producers who wished to capitalize on feminism to *avoid* the critique of the family in any explicit sense by constructing feminism as the preserve of single, working women. I discuss this issue in the conclusion.

28. Interestingly, the proscription against incest that would exist in a true father-daughter relationship is implicitly revealed in "Lou Dates Mary," an episode late in the series in which Mary asks Lou for a date. Lou comes over to Mary's house for dinner, and both are extremely nervous and uncomfortable. They decide to end the suspense and they kiss, during which both begin to giggle. Agreeing that a dating relationship will never work, they settle down to talk about the office. Clearly, the patterns created in their father-daughter relationship prohibit romance.

29. Mary's implicit role as a fantasy mother/wife figure was acknowledged in a 1977 episode, "My Three Husbands," in which Murray, Lou, and Ted each fantasize about Mary as their wife.

30. Susan Douglas makes the interesting point that Mary's compliance, rather than simply symbolizing submission, might have struck a realistic chord with female viewers: "Through Mary, women's desires for independence, autonomy, and respect were expressed and validated, yet also choked off, swallowed, muted. We identified powerfully with this pas de deux, for few real life dramas for women in the 1970s were more difficult than that tension between speaking the truth and hedging it, or even, in the end, keeping quiet" (1994, p. 207).

31. From the beginning of the show, despite producers' initial attempts to disguise it, Rhoda is a thoroughly attractive woman; she just is not model thin and glamorous in the same Midwestern Protestant sense that Mary is. The emphasis on Rhoda's lack of attractiveness in comparison to Mary is one of the ways in which Rhoda acts as a foil to emphasize Mary's superiority, an issue I discuss later in this chapter.

32. Of course, some episodes of *Mary Tyler Moore* acknowledge Mary's perfection by building humor around her temporary inability to live up to it. One of the most vivid of these episodes is "Put On a Happy Face," in which Mary must attend an awards ceremony even though she is sick and feels and looks miserable. She wins an award and must accept it looking absolutely terrible.

33. The requirement that a wife be restricted to the private sphere is a theme in a 1971 episode ("The Boss Isn't Coming to Dinner") in which Lou's wife, Edie, goes back to school, prompting a serious conflict in the marriage. Lou is the one who gives in, and peace is ostensibly restored. However, this episode is a precursor to Lou and Edie's divorce in the sitcom's fourth season ("The Lou and Edie Story"). Although the handling of the divorce is fairly progressive (the divorce is Edie's idea; she wishes to be more independent, to make a life for herself alone, to work), it reinforces the dichotomy between the public and private spheres for women. That is, Edie cannot achieve independence and satisfying work and remain a wife. Her departure allows Lou to become even more dependent on Mary's wifely/motherly functions.

Chapter 2
Prime-Time Divorce: The "Emerging Woman" of *One Day at a Time*

The success of *The Mary Tyler Moore Show* spawned numerous attempts to cash in on the "single woman on her own" theme, providing a perfect example of what Todd Gitlin calls the "recombinant culture" of television (1983, p. 63). The women that began populating the airwaves in increasing numbers in 1970s sitcoms shared a number of key characteristics with Mary Richards: they were white, heterosexual, unmarried, middle-class (at least in origin) and usually were faced with the task of exploring their independence after a life change, ranging from a divorce (*Diana* [1973–74], *Fay* [1975–76], *One Day at a Time* [1975–84]), to the death of a spouse (*Phyllis* [1975–77], *Alice* [1976–85]), to moving to a new city or a new job (*Funny Face* [1971], *The Sandy Duncan Show* [1972]).[1]

Rhoda (1974–78), the most popular and long-lived of the *Mary Tyler Moore* spin-offs, incorporated a number of these elements in its four-year run. Rhoda Morgenstern moved back to New York from Minneapolis in the fall of 1974. Originally living with her parents, she moved out to live with her sister, who was also single (making it clear that a "woman alone" premise does not mean literally alone, but simply "without a man"). During this time she fell in love, and within a couple of months she was married and a housewife, realizing the goal that had animated her character on *Mary Tyler Moore*. Bored with being at home, she started her own business. By the 1976 season of *Rhoda*, she was separated, again a "single woman on her own." In the fall of 1977, Rhoda, now divorced, began an entirely new job with a new cast of co-workers.

The producers of *Rhoda* defended the many changes in the show by arguing that wedded bliss was simply boring for a character who had always been interesting for her "underdog" status as a single woman (Davidson, 1976, pp. 25–26). The implication that female television characters derive their appeal from exploration of their vulnerability is somewhat disturbing. However, that Rhoda's separation and divorce was a ploy to *improve* ratings in 1976 shows how far television had come in six years. Indeed, although a divorced woman as a lead character was taboo when *Mary Tyler Moore* was being planned in 1970, the lives of women after divorce became a popular premise for sitcoms in the mid- to late 1970s. One could speculate that the success of *Mary Tyler Moore* (which did, after all, have a brief storyline about divorce among supporting characters) made producers less wary of the controversy. Moreover, making a female lead a divorcée was a way to add a new twist to the single-woman formula.

One Day at a Time and Prime-Time Politics

One Day at a Time is generally credited as the first sitcom to feature a divorced woman as a lead character; more accurately, it was the first *successful* sitcom with such a premise. *Diana*, a sitcom about an English divorcée who moves to New York to start anew had a brief life from September of 1973 to January of 1974,[2] and *Fay*, focusing on a middle-aged woman who has divorced her unfaithful husband and is exploring sexual freedom, premiered a few months before *One Day* in the fall of 1975 but did not last a full year. *One Day*, in contrast, continued for nine seasons and regularly ranked in the twenty top-rated programs (Brooks and Marsh, 1992). *Fay* was, in truth, a bit more adventuresome than *One Day*. Unlike Ann Romano of *One Day*, Fay Stewart did not have children at home to curtail her independence and her new swinging single lifestyle. Fay was a mature (fortyish), attractive, sexually interested woman with no one to "control" her—a fairly scary premise. She certainly lacked the docility and "good girl" persona of Mary Richards.

In the character of divorced mother Ann Romano, *One Day* picked a path between Mary Richards and Fay Stewart. Like Mary Richards, Ann Romano is a young woman (thirty-four) who recently moved to the city (Indianapolis) from the suburbs, and is independent for the first time in her life (she married at seventeen). Unlike Mary, she is divorced and the mother of two teenagers. Parenthood gives her authority and responsibility of a type that Mary did not have. Indeed, the recurring dynamic of *One Day* in its early seasons is Ann's negotiation of her own growth process while directing that of her daughters. Like Fay, Ann Romano is more self-consciously liberated than Mary Richards; she has taken back her maiden name and prefers to be addressed as *Ms.* Romano.

Several critics, popular and academic, have commented on the feminist leanings of *One Day*. Rick Mitz calls Ann Romano "TV's first feminist" (1980, p. 365), and Ella Taylor identifies a "populist feminism" in the sitcom, arguing that "Ann discovers the energies of the women's movement organically, through the experience of standing alone in a man's world" (1989, p. 89). Suzanna Danuta Walters (1992, p. 133) acknowledges that there is a feminist *ethos* to *One Day*, but compares the show unfavorably to the more radical *Maude* (1972–78). Although I disagree with Walter's conclusion that *One Day* is "generally an uninspired show" (p. 132), a comparison of *One Day* and *Maude* is useful for what it reveals about the diversity of prime-time feminism in the 1970s.

Maude, of course, has little in common with *One Day* in terms of premise; in fact, *Maude* is somewhat of an anomaly in the single-woman tradition of prime-time feminism that I focus on in this book. Maude Findlay was an upper-middle-class suburbanite in her late forties, married to her fourth husband, and sharing her home with her divorced daughter and her daughter's young son. Maude's was not a "lifestyle" feminism (she did not work outside the home and, in fact, always had a live-in housekeeper); rather, it was feminism represented by large doses of explicit feminist rhetoric emanating from both Maude and her daughter, Carol. *Maude* built episodes around explicit explorations of feminist issues, many of which were television taboos, including abortion, menopause, and sexual harassment.

In many ways, Maude was the flip side of Mary Richards; if Mary was the fantasy figure of feminism, Maude was its nightmare. She was large, loud, deep-voiced, disrespectful of almost everyone (including her husband), and, as Ella Taylor puts it, she was "generally angry on principle" (1989, p. 86). Maude first emerged as a character on *All in the Family*, from which *Maude* was a spin-off. As Edith Bunker's outspoken, politically liberal cousin, she was a sparring partner for the equally outspoken, stubborn, but politically conservative Archie. Maude was not an evolving feminist, feeling her way in a man's world; rather, she appeared on the television screen as a fully formed, self-confident ideologue.

Importantly, Maude also represented a privileged and protected feminism. Supported by her husband's business, her controversial views could not lead her to lose her job. Given her domestic servants, she was hardly an oppressed household drudge. Older, married to a man who apparently loved her for what she was, she had no fear of being perceived as a man-hater or a woman whose politics would impede her love life. Maude could announce her views daily without real fear of repercussions (Douglas, 1994, p. 203). Her most famous decision—to have an abortion—was controversial, and Maude did some soul-searching before making up her mind (Beale, 1992). However, because of her economic status, that process was untouched by such issues as accessibility or affordability, primary concerns for many women. Maude is perhaps the perfect example of Gloria Steinem's adage that women become more radical as they age; however, part of the explanation for that phenomenon could be that they can do so because they have less to lose.[3] Women have told me that they found Maude's feminist diatribes liberating, and I suspect that much of Maude's appeal for many viewers came from the sheer *spectacle* of her unrepentant feminism, a "thrilling catharsis" as Douglas calls it (1994, p. 203), facilitated by its distance from the material realities most of us experience.

One Day offers an entirely different appeal, although it was, like *Maude*, created by Norman Lear, the acknowledged king of topical television by the mid-1970s (Arlen, 1975; "King Lear," 1976). Given that *One Day* emerged from the same mind that created *All in the Family, Sanford and Son,* and *Good Times*, critics probably expected more explicit social consciousness from the sitcom than it actually delivered, particularly in comparison with *Maude*. *One Day* was more in the tradition of *Mary Tyler Moore*, with its emphasis on a formerly sheltered woman exploring her independence and trying to make it on her own without a man. Ann Romano was another example of the transitional woman—what Lear himself called the "emerging woman" (Levine, 1975, p. 21)—designed to tap into the social consciousness about women's roles produced by the women's liberation movement. As an "emerging" woman, rather than a mature and self-confident one such as Maude, Ann Romano's appeal was the possibility of identification by all of those women in the television audience with growing pains of their own. Although popular critics clearly identified *One Day*'s place within the genre of "independent woman" sitcoms (e.g., O'Connor, 1975, p. 79), they did not view it as controversial in the same vein as *All in the Family* or *Maude*. A review in *TV Guide* introduced *One Day* with "Don't look now but there's another woman out there all alone in the great big cruel world," acknowledging the popularity of the premise but still praising the sitcom (Amory, 1976, p. 27). After the first three seasons of *One Day*, a writer for *Ms.* magazine claimed that the show came closer than any other sitcom "to portraying a feminist point of view" (Weller, 1978, p. 45). Interestingly, this *Ms.* article also noted that Bonnie Franklin, the actor who portrayed Ann Romano, was being pursued by ERA activists in California to act as a spokesperson for the Amendment.

As Ella Taylor has noted, *One Day*'s feminism was more organic than explicitly political (1989, p. 88). I view the sitcom's feminist rhetoric as more powerful than Taylor does, who has said that the show is as much guided by "a highly contemporary psychological sensibility" as by feminism (p. 89). I differ from Taylor in that this "psychological sensibility" which she identifies as *separate* from feminism I see as an *outgrowth* of feminism, specifically of consciousness-raising, as I discuss in this chapter. Certainly, *One Day*'s radicalism (in television terms) pales in comparison to *Maude*. Although *Maude*'s producers received a large volume of mail in response to the famous abortion episode (Beale, 1992), *One Day*'s most controversial moments occurred before the sitcom aired for the first time when it became embroiled in controversy engendered by television's "family hour."

As a Norman Lear production, *One Day*, in its planning stages, came under close scrutiny by CBS censors. Lear was, of course, known for his commitment to realistic television and for his taste for social controversy. In early 1975, acknowledging the rise of concern over sex and violence on television and hoping to forestall government-imposed regulation, network executives agreed upon a self-censoring tactic, labeled the "family hour," that would prohibit programming with content unsuitable for children to be broadcast between 8:00 PM and 9:00 PM ET, the first hour of prime-time (Taylor, 1989, pp. 53–54). Program pilots by independent producers like Lear consequently required approval by network censors before the network would agree to buy the program for placement in its schedule (Levine, 1975, p. 21).

CBS objected to a number of items in the pilot for *One Day*, including remarks indicating disrespect for religion, varied levels of sexual innuendo, and mild profanity ("damn" and "hell"). Lear, committed to offering a realistic portrayal of an adult woman and of the language and attitudes of teenage girls, saw the restrictions as "the beginning of a terrible repression. They're going to stop every piece of realistic human behavior on television in the name of something called the 'family hour,' which nobody has the courage to define" (quoted in Levine, 1975, p. 20). Beyond the language issues that primarily drove CBS's reaction to *One Day*, censors no doubt saw an obvious contradiction in airing a sitcom about divorce (which was written to present divorce as the right choice for its main character) during the family hour. As Richard Levine, the writer of a *New York Times Magazine* article about the *One Day*/family hour saga, put it, CBS "was not about to let a Norman Lear script about a divorced woman pass . . . with a wink and a nod" (1975, p. 92).

Originally planned for September of 1975, *One Day* did not air until December because of the various problems afflicting the pilot. In the end, CBS asked Lear to rush production of the show because the network desperately needed to fill a hole in its schedule occasioned by the disastrous ratings of a number of new fall programs. One consequence was that *One Day* received the very popular *M*A*S*H* as a lead-in show on Tuesday nights. However, this meant that *One Day* would be airing after the family hour (at 9:30 PM ET), making much of the previous controversy moot (Levine, 1975, p. 96).[4] Levine implies that the controversy and changes in *One Day* undermined some of the radical potential of the sitcom, resulting in a show focused more on "parent-child conflict" than on adult relationships. For example, the pilot was rewritten so that Ann Romano's divorce was already a year old rather than in the process of occurring, as was the case in the original pilot, prompting Levine to comment that the sitcom might simply become "an updated version of *Bachelor Father*" (p. 95).

Of course, Levine's prediction was based on the pilot episode alone. Moreover, his easy assumptions that parent-child conflict is not interesting and that single parenthood by an economically struggling, formerly sheltered, divorced woman is no different from single parenthood by a wealthy bachelor with domestic help (*Bachelor Father* actually focused on a man raising his orphaned niece) indicate a certain insensitivity to the innovative features of *One Day*. In my view, the pilot has some strong doses of feminist sensibility, and other episodes from the early seasons of *One Day* had even more.

Consciousness-Raising and the Legacy of Radical Feminism

In contrast to *Mary Tyler Moore*, which never really acknowledged the existence of radical feminist activity and preferred to emphasize the lifestyle implications of women's liberation, *One Day* premiered at a point when radical feminist groups and visibility had almost disappeared. Alice Echols (1989) dates her history of radical feminism in America from 1967 to 1975; Flora Davis notes that "by 1975, most of the early women's liberation groups had vanished" (1991, p. 138); and Barbara Ryan calls 1975 a "watershed year" for feminism because of fragmentation in the movement, the clear eclipse of radical feminism by liberal feminism, and the resultant power plays within NOW (1992, pp. 69–73). The year 1975 marked a new phase of feminist action, one in which liberal feminist concerns like the ERA would dominate the movement and the media. Indeed, a sitcom like *One Day*, which was much more straightforward than *Mary Tyler Moore* about feminist influence, may have been made possible by the decline of radical feminism (i.e., only when radical feminism was no longer a visible threat could some of its issues receive sustained treatment in prime-time). However, radical feminism made some lasting marks on public consciousness, and one of the most important of these was the heightening of women's self-awareness produced by consciousness-raising.

In 1973, American women involved in consciousness-raising groups numbered 100,000, "making it one of the largest ever educational and support movements of its kind for women in the history of this country" (Shreve, 1989, p. 6). In consciousness-raising groups, women gathered to share their personal experiences and feelings about being women in a male-defined and male-dominated culture. The maxim that governed this process—"the personal is political"—reflected the belief that "women would come to understand that what they had previously believed were personal problems were, in fact, 'social problems that must become social issues and fought together rather than with personal solutions'" (Echols, 1989, p. 83). To have one's consciousness raised was to begin to understand the *political* position of women as members of an oppressed group (see Eisenstein, 1983, chapter 4).

Not all women in such groups were committed feminists or would ever participate in feminist action beyond consciousness-raising. Moreover, feminists were and still are divided over the function of consciousness-raising. In the early 1970s, many radical feminists saw consciousness-raising as the foundation for feminist theory analyzing women's oppression. Others feared that the groups were substituting talk for action and that consciousness-raising functioned more as therapy and self-help than as the basis for social transformation (Echols, 1989, pp. 85–88). There is some truth in both positions. Certainly, consciousness-raising was used to produce radical feminist theory (Echols, 1989); however, it also had strong effects on the personal lives of the women who participated in it (Shreve, 1989).

Generally, disagreements over consciousness-raising reflected deep tensions in 1970s feminism over the relationships between individual and social change and between personal life and politics. These tensions also emerged in other forms, such as debates over the politics of *Ms.* magazine and over NOW's cooptation of some elements of radical feminism. *Ms.*, for example, was attacked by radical feminists for what Alice Echols calls its "'pull-yourself-up-by-your-bootstraps' brand of feminism" which stressed self-improvement rather than social transformation (1989, p. 199). Likewise, NOW's recasting of radical feminist techniques and ideas in liberal terms was also a sore spot for radical feminists. For example, around 1974, NOW created consciousness-raising groups, led by feminist therapists, in response to requests from members (Freeman, 1975, pp. 85–86). Of course therapy, even feminist therapy, is still about personal solutions. Moreover, the leaderless, nonhierarchical group, in which no woman had more power than another, was an important element in radical feminist consciousness-raising theory. NOW's institutionalization of consciousness-raising and its use of therapists as facilitators were violations of this principle.

Radical feminism's heyday, in terms of membership, visibility, and power, was short. However, it did not disappear; many of the issues originally raised by radical feminists (e.g., abortion) were simply redefined as liberal feminist issues by the mid-1970s. One of the most powerful instruments of radical feminism, consciousness-raising, was the most thoroughly coopted. Anita Shreve argues that consciousness-raising "not only . . . transform[ed] the lives of most of the women who participated, but it also did so for women who did not participate but who benefited from the phenomenon as feminist thinking began to pervade the culture" (1989, p. 15).[5]

As with other aspects of women's liberation, elements of consciousness-raising were incorporated into popular culture directed at white, middle-class women. The therapeutic and self-help dimensions of consciousness-raising translated easily into the self-improvement ideology of women's magazines,[6] for example, which were incorporating feminism in varied ways. In the early 1970s, Betty Friedan began writing a column, "Betty Friedan's Notebook," for *McCall's*, in which she would discuss her activities on behalf of feminism as well as comment on changes in the movement. During the same period, *McCall's* also published a regular feature, "The Working Woman," written by feminist Letty Cottin Pogrebin (a friend of Gloria Steinem and contributor to *Ms.*).

Pogrebin's writing, in particular, had a strong feminist tone, as she addressed issues such as sex discrimination at work, maternity rights, the sharing of housework by dual-career couples, and sexism in labor unions. While Pogrebin's solutions were oriented toward self-help, her primary purpose was education and self-awareness. She devoted a number of columns to disseminating a gentler version of radical feminist ideology. For example, in a May 1972 column, Pogrebin adds up the cost of all of the services a housewife performs and proceeds to analyze why the housewife's role gets so little respect. She notes that "no matter what her talent and temperament, every women is expected to fulfill the role of housewife at some point in her life. It is difficult to explode and examine such a pervasive myth—especially when men have a psychological and economic investment in maintaining the status quo" (Pogrebin, 1972, p. 32). Much of this column sounds like a gentler version of Pat Mainardi's "The Politics of Housework," originally published in *Notes from the Second Year* (Firestone and Koedt, 1970), a radical feminist journal. Indeed, at the end of her article, Pogrebin recommends that readers send for a copy of Mainardi's essay. Pogrebin also includes recommendations for how to go about establishing a consciousness-raising group for couples.

A modified form of consciousness-raising was often performed by articles, like Pogrebin's, that purported to challenge "myths" about womanhood.[7] A *Ladies Home Journal* article titled "Myths That Keep Women Down" from November of 1971 illustrates this type well. Caroline Bird takes on myths such as "women enjoy being women," " 'feminine' women have better sex lives," and "women should be fulltime mothers" and refutes them with statistics and testimony from experts

(1971, pp. 69–70). A *Mademoiselle* article on the National Women's Political Caucus contains such consciousness-raising statements as this, from
Betty Friedan: "It is a remnant of our own self-denigration, the put-down
we finally do to ourselves, to think that a woman is 'pushy' or 'unfemi-
nine' or 'elitist' or on an 'ego-trip' to want to run for political office. It is
to be hoped that there are thousands of us sufficiently liberated now to
take on the responsibility and demand the rewards of running for political office" (quoted in Comer, 1972, p. 188).

The adaptation of consciousness-raising processes and insights by
women's magazines took a variety of forms. Bird and Friedan offer fairly
straightforward deductive arguments designed to alter opinions about
women and their possibilities. While the form of their rhetoric does not
fit the consciousness-raising model (e.g., it is not necessarily based on
personal experience or presented inductively [Campbell, 1973]), their
common purpose of challenging myths about what it means to be a
woman is easily traceable to consciousness-raising's key goal of " 'awak-
en[ing] the latent consciousness that . . . all women have about our oppression' " (quoted in Echols, 1989, p. 83).

In contrast, a 1972 article in *Mademoiselle* took a more explicit approach by reporting on a consciousness-raising session created among
nine female *Mademoiselle* staffers.[8] In an article entitled "Are Women's
Minds or Lives Really Changing?" the magazine published the discussion
among the women, including their answers to such questions as "What
do you think of the Women's Liberation Movement?" and "How do the
men in your life . . . feel about Women's Liberation?" (1972, pp. 124–
125). In this same issue of *Mademoiselle*, a self-identified member of the
movement writes a frank, first-person narrative about the changes in her
identity since becoming an active feminist. Using her own personal experience and that of other women, she draws such conclusions as:
"Women's Liberation . . . invites women to leave the safety of their own
preconceived, socially certified image of themselves and to abandon the
game with all its prizes, security, marriage, even love. It has suggested,
for the first time, that the prizes aren't worth it if they are only to be had
at the expense of the self" (Durbin, 1972, p. 162).

That this rhetoric is targeted at women rather than men indicates that
one of the primary tasks of consciousness-raising was to disabuse women
themselves of naturalized notions of womanhood. Indeed, one of the
problems of the self-improvement ethos favored by women's magazines
is that they often posit a change in women's attitudes alone as the goal of
women's liberation. These essays often fail to acknowledge the existence
of patriarchal interests actively resisting women's progress. However, regardless of the radicalism (or lack thereof) of the analysis or of the solutions, the dissemination of a consciousness-raising mindset through

feminist activities, feminist writings,[9] and women's popular culture made awareness of the problems of cultural definitions of womanhood a major legacy of radical feminism.

One Day at a Time and Therapeutic Feminism

The influence of consciousness-raising is particularly visible in early episodes of *One Day*. One of the key differences between *Mary Tyler Moore* and *One Day* is the heroine's self-consciousness about her situation and her choices as a divorced single mother. Mary Richards, an old-fashioned woman in a new situation, adapted traditional ideals of womanhood to the workplace. Ann Romano, in contrast, is acutely aware that "all the rules by which she'd lived her life were no longer applicable" (Jones, 1992, p. 232). The theme song for *One Day* (as well as the title of the sitcom) is a reminder of this premise with such lines as "This is it! Straight ahead and rest assured you can't be sure at all. / So while you're here enjoy the view and keep on doin' what you do. / Hold on tight, we'll muddle through—one day at a time."

For the first couple of seasons of *One Day*, the theme song is the background for a series of traveling scenes. Ann Romano and her daughters are seen loading a station wagon in front of their middle-class suburban home, traveling the highway into the city, and pulling up in front of their new, very modest, apartment house. In the last of these scenes, they collapse, exhausted, onto the sofa in their new apartment filled with jumbled boxes and furniture. Eerily reminiscent of the opening for the early seasons of *Mary Tyler Moore*, these scenes clearly set the premise for the sitcom: A single mother and her children have moved to the city to forge a new life.[10]

As with all pilot episodes, the first episode of *One Day* serves to set the situation and introduce the main characters, who include Ann Romano, Julie and Barbara Cooper (Ann's daughters), Dwayne Schneider (the apartment building's superintendent), and David Kane (Ann's twenty-six-year-old divorce lawyer, persistent suitor, and neighbor in the building). The entire episode, as is the case with most episodes of *One Day*, takes place in Ann's apartment, placing *One Day* firmly within the family sitcom tradition. Although Ann's work life became more visible in later episodes, she did not land a steady job until the second season of *One Day*.

Reflecting Norman Lear's penchant for realism, the economic consequences of Ann's divorce are apparent from the outset, both in the drabness and limited size of the apartment and from references to money issues in several episodes. The living area of the apartment, where most scenes take place, is small enough to be seen almost entirely in one camera shot. The living room, eating area, and kitchen are all part of one room, with the kitchen somewhat separated by a counter. The doors to the bathroom and the two bedrooms are visible in a short hallway leading off the living room. The fact that there is little privacy in the apartment is often a contributor to comic moments.

Adding to the lack of privacy is the tendency of the building super, who is almost always referred to as "Schneider," to enter the apartment unannounced, using his passkey. In early episodes, Schneider is distinguished by his lasciviousness and constant sexual come-ons directed at Ann. For example, in the pilot, he offers her his sexual services, saying "Here you are, a woman of the divorced persuasion. Go ahead, use me." Later, he reminds her that "the ladies in this building don't call me 'super' for nothing." From the beginning, it is clear that Schneider is mostly bluster. His character is softened and made more likable over time as it is revealed that he has the proverbial heart of gold beneath his attempts at machismo. In fact, Schneider is the only male character to last the entire lifetime of the series, and he becomes a somewhat eccentric and often irritating member of the Romano/Cooper family.

Ella Taylor describes Schneider as one of "a long line of castrated males in television entertainment, men who make themselves absurd with tough macho talk, who are safe because they have been stripped of the sexual challenge that complicates relations between men and women, and who melt into vulnerability and loving support when the chips are down" (1989, p. 87).[11] On a descriptive level, Taylor is absolutely on target. However, there is also an interesting evaluative dimension to Schneider's character. That he is so clearly a caricature of a certain type of male braggadocio, and that he is so easily dismissed by Ann, adds to the feminist potential of *One Day*. Indeed, the only character truly annoyed by Schneider is David, who often competes with Schneider for Ann's attention and generally resents Schneider's interference in her life. The frequent sniping between the two men, in which Schneider questions David's masculinity and maturity (Schneider to Ann: "How could you marry a man who might pass away at any moment from massive diaper rash?"), and David taunts Schneider for his lack of education and lower class tastes ("Schneider, if you don't get out of here immediately, I'm going downstairs and scratch the custom mural on your camper"), generally positions Ann as more mature and sensible than both of the men.

Despite Lauren Rabinovitz's claim that featured male characters such as Schneider or David functioned as "symbolic patriarchs" in 1970s single-mother sitcoms (1989, p. 8), one of the recurring dynamics of *One Day* is that almost every male character that enters Ann Romano's life is eventually proven less wise than Ann herself. David, for example, is a central character in the first year of *One Day*, during which he serves as a confidant and sounding board for Ann's parenting crises and repeatedly asks her to marry him. However, Ann's most final rejection of this offer (which I discuss shortly) precipitates his departure from the sitcom.

The characters of Barbara and Julie, Ann's two daughters (approximately ages fifteen and seventeen, respectively), also reflect Lear's desire for realism. Julie, the eldest, is often truly obnoxious and troublesome. She is rebellious, self-centered, and loud, taunts her sister, and displays histrionics to try and get her way with her mother. Barbara is the quieter, prettier, and gentler of the two, but she, too, can be dramatic and is able to respond to her sister's taunts in kind. The two girls frequently call each other "jerks" and quite openly discuss boys, their bodies, and sex (displaying some of the realistic teen language and behavior that Lear fought for).

Julie is the trigger for the crisis Ann negotiates in the pilot episode. Ann refuses Julie's request to go on a co-ed camping trip, and the two have a discussion about Ann's discomfort with the sexual possibilities of the situation. Julie turns hysterical, threatening to leave and live with her father if she is not allowed to go on the camping trip. Ann, rather than back down on her decision, hands Julie the bus fare.

It is clear to the viewer that this confrontation is difficult for Ann. After Julie leaves, Barbara asks, "Mom, why did you let her go?" and Ann replies: "I had to make a decision. For the first seventeen years of my life my father made the decisions. And the next seventeen my husband made the decisions. The first time in my life I make a decision on my own and I blow it." This statement is the first clear indicator of Ann's self-awareness of how her life as a traditional woman has handicapped her, a theme that dominates the early seasons of *One Day*. Despite her insecurity, however, Ann refuses offers to help her with the decision. Earlier, when David offered to mediate between Ann and Julie, saying, "Look, Ann, I am a lawyer. I can stand back and be totally objective," Ann responded with "Then stand back and stay out of the way."

When Julie unexpectedly returns, having decided on her own not to return to her father, Ann thanks her, and asks the two girls to sit down for the following speech:

> When your father and I broke up, I was scared, plenty scared. But I didn't want you kids knowing it because you were pretty rocky yourselves. So I played it very big, took back my maiden name—Annie Romano, liberated woman, master of her fate. Well, the master had a disaster. But I have learned a lot today. From now on, we level with each other. I don't know everything, maybe I don't know anything. But I am trying. So stick with me, huh? We'll make it. I promise.

Ann goes on to tell Julie that while she still does not approve of the camping trip she will allow Julie to go, "because I'm just not sure." Moments later, Ann overhears Julie telling her friend on the phone that Ann has forbidden the trip. Ann smiles and the credits begin.

The resolution to this episode is, in several ways, ambiguous. Ann's retreat from a stance of unyielding parental wisdom, particularly when contrasted with the all-knowing TV patriarchs of years past, is grounds for arguing that *One Day* showcases feminine indecisiveness and insecurity, undermining the feminist premise of the sitcom. However, another interpretation is that Ann has consciously rejected a style of parenting that she is not comfortable with, and that the new style she is fashioning is a product of her personal process of consciousness-raising. From this viewpoint, Ann's remark that she "blew it" by taking a hard line with Julie reflects an awareness that she does not wish to replicate, with her own daughters, the same kind of unquestionable parental authority that she was subjected to for most of her life.

Instead, as her final speech illustrates, she desires a different model of parenting. In this model, responsibility for decisions and the reasoning behind them are shared between parent and child, so that her daughters will not experience the same kind of powerlessness and resentment that led to her divorce.[12] Ann's willingness to let Julie make her own decision about the camping trip is a product of this new awareness. Following this interpretation, Julie's ultimate decision not to go on the trip reflects the success of Ann's new approach. Once Julie is given a stake in the decision, her need to rebel is lessened and she respects her mother's reservations about the trip.

Based on other, similar episodes, this is the interpretation that I prefer and that I believe was likely for many viewers, particularly women, who watched the show for its new permutation on the family sitcom as well as its feminist sensibilities. Suzanna Danuta Walters, for example, although seeing a number of flaws in *One Day*, has offered this reaction to the sitcom:

As the daughter of a single parent with two teenage sisters of my own, I felt "One Day at a Time" legitimized and validated a family form that was consistently underrepresented in popular culture. . . . I too knew what it meant to learn how to be responsible to my siblings and to my mother in an entirely different way than before her divorce. I suspect many of my generation felt a similar resonance. It's heartening to be *represented*, even if that representation is lacking aesthetically and politically. (1992, p. 246 n.6)

Certainly, some of the parental decision-making in *One Day* can be explained as application of basic child psychology, but I also discern a feminist-inspired philosophy at work, one that is the product of Ann's voiced realizations about the negative effects of the traditional roles men and women play. In another episode centered on parental decision-making, Julie and Barbara wish to buy an old car, very cheaply, from a friend. Ann will not allow it, reasoning that any car that cheap cannot be reliable. In the midst of this dispute, the girls' father, Ed Cooper, visits, having just returned from a trip to Hawaii with his new wife.[13] Feeling guilty and out of touch with his daughters (e.g., "Ann, don't you think I should've been told that my daughter's a different dress size?"), he magnanimously offers to buy the girls a new car, undermining Ann's position that the proper solution is for the girls to save until they can buy a decent one themselves. After Julie and Barbara rush off to research new cars, Ed and Ann proceed to argue the issue. They begin by arguing about which of them, Ann or Ed, possesses ultimate parental authority. Ann resents Ed for undermining her decision in front of the girls, and Ed accuses Ann of resisting the car because of an "ego trip," saying that she will deprive Julie and Barbara of a new car simply to prove that she is "head honcho now." In the end, however, Ann convinces Ed that her resistance to the car is based on her desire for the girls to become more self-sufficient than she is:

> *Ann*: Ed, you're going to make them as dependent on you as I was.
> *Ed*: But you didn't complain. Now it's their time at bat.
> *Ann*: All those years of being pampered didn't do me any good. I'm often scared, I'm always insecure—do you want them to be the same way?

Ed agrees with Ann's reasoning and even offers to be the one to tell Julie and Barbara that they will not be getting a new car. Ann's victory is clear when Julie says, accusingly, "You dominated Dad!" and Ann replies, grinning, "I did?"

The character of Ed Cooper appears infrequently on *One Day*, but often enough for it to be clear that he is a likable, if old-fashioned and domineering, man. His daughters adore him and he and Ann get along fairly well. There is no basis to believe that Ann divorced Ed because he was unfaithful, abusive, or a poor father. In short, there is no easy explanation for the divorce (as there was in *Fay*, for instance, in which the ex-husband was a philanderer). Viewers are forced to accept the reasoning Ann offers: that she divorced Ed because he treated her like a child and would not allow her to have any independence, a pattern she does not wish repeated for her daughters.

In short, Ann rejected her marriage because of its politics, under which she had no power. This is one of the aspects of *One Day* that makes the sitcom more radical that it might have been; that is, unlike the widows of *Alice* or *Phyllis*, Ann *chose* her status explicitly for purposes of self-actualization. In an episode in which Julie and Barbara have mistakenly inferred that Ann and Ed are reconciling, Ann explains to Barbara why the divorce was necessary:

> *Barbara*: Why couldn't it be a happy ending?
> *Ann*: Oh, honey, it is a happy ending. . . . Your father tries to protect us from the world and nobody can do that. We all have to get out and make it on our own. Your Dad and I both want to protect you, but, oh, my darlings, I don't want you to grow up the way I did. . . . I want you to start growing up before you're thirty.
> *Barbara*: Why couldn't you tell Dad that and fix it up?
> *Ann*: I did, . . . the last four years of the marriage. What do you think all that yelling and crying was all about?

Self-actualization, and achieving independence and fulfillment, were the reigning feminist themes of *One Day* for its first four seasons. And, as came to be the case in other 1970s pop culture influenced by feminism, the presence of a male partner (even a positive, seemingly liberated one) was constructed as a threat to the heroine's self-actualization.[14] In *One Day*, for example, the departure of the character of David Kane at the beginning of the sitcom's second season was precipitated by Ann's realization, on the eve of her wedding to David, that to marry him would be a retreat from her hard-won independence. Over the course of *One Day*'s first season, Ann and David had become steadily more involved, emotionally and sexually, although Ann continued to put off his frequent marriage proposals.

However, when David receives a fabulous job offer in California, he convinces Ann to marry him and move there with him. Her initial reluctance to seriously consider remarriage is couched in the language of self-actualization: "I'm just beginning to discover myself as a human being, as an individual." David, in turn, assures her that he has no wish to dominate her, that this marriage will be different from her first one: "I don't want to jeopardize your independence. I promise. Look, anything that I might do that would diminish you as an individual would just be hurting me." This storyline is played out over two episodes. Although Ann still seems unsure at the end of the first episode, by the beginning of the second, the apartment is being packed for the move to California, and she is trying to decide what to wear for the wedding the following day. Ann is clearly nervous and edgy, and David's casual revelation that he assumes they will have additional children provokes the discussion in which Ann realizes why she cannot marry him.

Initially, they simply argue over Ann's refusal to have more children.

Her explanation of her feelings is, again, tinged with the desire for self-actualization: "I've had my kids. I've been all through that baby bit—the months of blimpdom, the waking up in the middle of the night, the four hour feedings. . . . I had Julie when I was eighteen years old. I've been raising children half of my life. Now I have a chance to begin raising myself." Ultimately, however, when it appears that David will give in on the issue of children, Ann finally realizes that children are not the real stumbling block: "It's not children, it's me. It's me. It's what I gotta do with my life. David, it's not going to work. . . . I can't share my life with you or with anyone until I find out what that life is."

The shift to Ann's self-examination is a key moment in the politics of this storyline. The often oppressive nature of child-rearing (which both Ann and David assume will be primarily Ann's responsibility) and its impact on women's lives are hinted at and then dropped.[15] At the point that Ann explicitly locates the problem between her and David in her own psyche, the deeply political issues raised in their conflict, including the unequal burden of parenting for men and women and the sense of patriarchal entitlement that leads David to try to convince Ann to have a child *for him* against her judgment, simply vanish. Calling herself "selfish," Ann confesses that "I've been using you, David. I've been using you as a sounding board, a lover, a friend, a surrogate father to the girls. . . . It's wrong, David. It's wrong for you and for me. I can't need that anymore."

One Day, although addressing the politics between men and women fairly frequently and self-consciously (much more so than *Mary Tyler Moore*, to be sure) ultimately recasts material issues of power between the genders into therapeutic obstacles to be conquered through self-transformation. Ann and David's breakup, then, is not about the ways in which David, despite his liberated stance, is revealed to desire the same prerogatives as Ann's first husband. Instead, the breakup is about Ann's recognition of her psychological need for dependence and her resolution to fight it. This interpretation is strengthened by the final moments of this episode. Ann, alone in the apartment after David departs, begins to sob, saying, "I'm scared, I'm scared," as she realizes that she is finally, truly, alone.

This therapeutic turn in *One Day*'s feminism is the sitcom's most consistent hegemonic strategy.[16] Ann's self-awareness demonstrates how thoroughly elements of feminist consciousness-raising had infiltrated popular consciousness. At the same time, however, the residue of consciousness-raising manifested in popular culture targeted at women was largely limited to self-help solutions. Even *Ms.* magazine, considered by many to be the most accessible and representative voice of feminism, "could only offer a vision of feminism as self-blame and self-transformation, as the same kind of women's 'self-help' the mainstream press found acceptable" (Hogeland, 1994b, p. 301). The implicit individualism and psychological emphasis of popularized consciousness-raising lacked key elements of the radical feminist theory of consciousness-raising. For radical feminists, consciousness-raising was opposed to individualism in that it located women's problems in the political structure of patriarchy rather than in women's psyches. Moreover, the insights gained from consciousness-raising were to lead to analysis of patriarchy, and its eventual transformation, not to self-help solutions for individual women (Echols, 1989).

Indeed, the fact that Ann Romano is a "woman alone," not just in the sense of being without a man but also in the sense of lacking regular adult female companionship, makes depiction of any kind of *sisterhood* virtually impossible in *One Day*. In an interesting fourth-season episode, the possibility of sisterhood, in feminist terms, is presented. Joyce and Fred, a married couple and friends of Ann's from her married days, come for a visit. Fred is a representation of a benign patriarch, who regrets Ann's divorce and views her in need of protection, illustrated by such comments as "Honestly, Annie, I think it would be better for you and the girls if there were a man around the house." Ann, to her credit, responds with a popular feminist saying: "Oh, Fred, haven't you heard? A woman without a man is like a fish without a bicycle."

Joyce is silent during this exchange and, after Fred leaves for a walk, reveals why. Inspired by her perceptions of Ann's glamorous single life, she has decided to leave Fred, believing that there must be more to life than being a housewife. In a hilarious speech, she describes her frustration: "Oh, Annie, I feel trapped, trapped, trapped. I mean, you know, I keep having this nightmare. I'm locked in a supermarket with a whole bunch of other housewives, and this giant roll of toilet paper keeps running after us trying to squeeze us." The implicit critique of the idiocy of consumer culture directed at women contained in Joyce's remarks is a nice touch (remember those "Please don't squeeze the Charmin" commercials?).

Joyce goes on to reveal that the contrast between her life and media representations of liberated women has contributed to her dissatisfaction: "Oh, Annie, all around me women like you are conquering new fields. I see what's going on. I look at the papers, I watch television, I read *Cosmopolitan*." From the ensuing conversation with a concerned Ann, it becomes apparent that Joyce is not truly unhappy. Rather, she is suffering the lack of self-esteem that comes from being left behind and perceiving that her work as a housewife is no longer valued. Using reverse psychology, Ann begins to agree with Joyce's low opinion of herself, taunting Joyce about the mundane tasks that fill her days. Predictably,

Joyce is roused to defend her life and, in the process, convinces herself that being a good wife and mother is indeed important.

The most interesting facet of this episode, to me, is its image of feminism as a contagious trend rather than a politics. Joyce wants to "keep up" with what's going on "out there"; her problem, as she tells it, is self-esteem, perhaps boredom, but not oppression. Joyce's consciousness has been raised to the degree that she can envision alternatives to her life; however, the source and the solution to her problem are internal rather than external. Ann's response to Joyce's admiration of Ann's liberated life is "You're not me," further underscoring the notion that feminism is about individual psychology, not structural and cultural constraints that afflict women as a group.

One of the elements that made the early *Mary Tyler Moore* so appealing (and to which Serafina Bathrick [1984] attributes feminist implications) was the interaction between Mary and Rhoda. Two women (three if you include Phyllis), similar enough to share experiences and to support each other's perspectives, present at least the possibility of group solidarity and sisterhood. In *One Day*, Ann Romano lacks such a community. Despite liberation, her most constant companions are her children or Schneider.

In *One Day*'s second season, the hole left by the departure of David Kane was filled, for one year, with a new female neighbor, Ginny Wrobliki. A savvy, working-class cocktail waitress with multiple divorces, Ginny was more similar in temperament and background to Schneider than she was to Ann. In her first appearance as Ann's new neighbor in the 1976 season, Ginny barges into Ann's dispute with a furniture upholsterer who has wildly exceeded his original estimate and is holding the furniture hostage until Ann pays up. Ginny, more experienced with this particular brand of con artist, recognizes the scam and rescues Ann. Although Ann initially is put off by Ginny's brassy demeanor, she recognizes a potential new friend.

Ginny's function in most episodes, however, is to provide the kind of comic relief that Schneider does—humor laden with sexual innuendo and working-class wisdom. Different in class, background, and experiences, Ginny and Ann only rarely share moments of insight about their shared position as women. However, one such moment occurs in a second-season episode that illustrates the recurring *One Day* pattern of raising an important feminist issue only to dissolve politics into psychology. In this episode, Ann and Schneider are surprised to learn that Ginny has a young daughter who has been living with her father. Although Frank, the father, intended to care for the child, Lori, only until Ginny could provide a stable home for her, he has recently decided to ask for permanent custody.

Schneider and Ann instantly surmise that Ginny will fight for custody herself, and vow to help her. However, when Ann and Ginny are alone, Ginny reveals that she believes Lori would be better off with her ex-husband ("I can't hack motherhood. Lori knows that"). Ann sympathizes, thinking that Ginny is nervous about the responsibility of raising a child. However, as the conversation continues, Ginny makes it clear that she is simply uninterested in motherhood ("I don't think like a mother. I don't feel like a mother") but, at the same time, feels enormously guilty about her lack of maternal instinct, leading to the following exchange:

Ginny: The problem is me. Every mother should want to be a mother. I'm not natural.
Ann: Not every woman is cut out to be a mother. . . . Ever since we were born we have had it drummed into our head that the ultimate proof of womanhood is to be a mother. If you're not a mother, you're nothing. You're not nothing, Ginny. You're a terrific woman.

Ann's speech is additional proof of her raised consciousness, her ability to question the taken-for-granted wisdom about womanhood. The joys of family life and the rewards of motherhood are seldom questioned in prime-time television, given the importance of these concepts in American culture generally and consumer culture specifically. There are, of course, "bad mothers" in television, but they are not generally positive characters, as Ginny is clearly meant to be.

Indeed, according to Bonnie Franklin's interview in *Ms.*, this episode's plotline was controversial on the set of *One Day.* Franklin revealed in the interview that in the original script, Ginny felt no guilt about giving up her child, but

the men on the show wouldn't buy that. They couldn't see how any quote-unquote *good* woman wouldn't want her children with her twenty-four hours a day, so they came up with this contrived plot that had her go through all kinds of emotional agony before reaching her decision. Every woman on the set protested that a woman *could* feel she was a better person by honestly admitting she wasn't a classically *good* mother. We finally won out. (Weller, 1978, p. 46)

Given the way this episode ends, however, it is difficult to see exactly what Franklin believed was won in the battle. Frank arrives to tell Ginny that he has had a change of heart and that he will not fight for custody. When Ginny tells him that she does not want custody of Lori, his immediate response is, "Oh, Ginny, don't you love her?" Ginny protests that she does love Lori, "but what kind of a mother would I make? I'm up all night, I go to bed at sunrise. The only person who wants a mother like that is Bela Lugosi." After Frank leaves, Ginny, with Ann's support, reassures herself that she "did the right thing."

From the beginning to the end of this episode, Ginny's guilt is a major theme; clearly the women of *One Day* did not win that particular battle, despite what Franklin implies. More disturbing, however, is the collapse of Ginny's *lack of interest* in motherhood with her *lack of ability* at motherhood. Both Franklin's discourse and *One Day*'s dialogue conflate these issues. In the original script, according to Franklin, the character "wasn't interested in the daily process of being a mother, and she didn't feel any guilt about it." By the end of her description of the episode, however, Franklin is defending a woman's right to admit that she isn't a "classically 'good' mother" (Weller, 1978, p. 46). The *One Day* episode follows a similar trajectory. In the beginning, Ginny simply is not interested in being a mother. By the end, her position is that she would not be a good one because of the kind of life she leads.

In each case, the distinction is lost between two very different issues. Assertion of a lack of interest in motherhood is far more radical than arguing that, given the circumstances, one would be a poor mother. The former is a challenge to cultural dictates and the prescribed feminine role; the latter is simply to acknowledge a lack of resources. Put another way, the former is self-centered and rooted in self-determination; the latter is other-centered and rooted in concerns about the well-being of the child. *One Day* elides the distinction, transforming an abstract recognition of the politics of femininity ("Not every woman is cut out to be a mother") into an individualized response to a particular situation ("What kind of mother would I make?").

One Day's recurring deradicalization of the feminist issues it raises is traceable both to television's general tendency to individualize social issues (Gray, 1994) and to the cultural transmutation of feminism in the mid- to late 1970s. *One Day*'s vision of self-help feminism fit easily into the cooptation of feminist thinking by mass culture. In the adaptation of marketable aspects of women's liberation, consciousness-raising became psychological self-awareness, and "the primacy of individual consciousness as the site of feminism" was the result (Hogeland, 1994b, p. 301). Feminism also became the province of the young, those women in the best position to practice a feminist "lifestyle," which generally meant to live without a man. The absence of men in television's representations of feminism—or the presence of only unsuitable men—underscored the emphasis on women as the site of feminist transformation. By and large, pop culture representations of feminism ignored both men's stake in perpetuating patriarchy *and* the possibility that men as well as women need to change for feminist goals to be realized.

In *One Day*, for example, Ed Cooper, Ann's ex-husband, is the most consistent carrier of patriarchal ideology. However, Ed is a rather benign patriarch; he is simply misguided, behind the times, and not very self-aware rather than actively oppressive. A fourth-season episode is illustrative. Claiming his business is failing and he is nearing bankruptcy, Ed tells Ann that he must cease child support payments. Knowing of Ed's lavish lifestyle with his second wife, Vickie, Ann has little sympathy and threatens to go to court: "We need that money and there are state agencies to help women collect."

Ann's militancy is tempered the following day, however, when Ed, having gotten so drunk the night before that he is forced to spend the night in Ann's apartment, reveals the true causes of his distress. He is afraid that Vickie will leave him if she discovers his financial failure. Apparently, his hope was that if he could cut corners elsewhere (e.g., by ending child support) Vickie would not have to give up her maid or her new house. Strangely enough, this bit of self-disclosure elicits sympathy from Ann and her daughters. They counsel Ed, convincing him that he must share his problems with his wife and that Vickie will surely stand by him. The issue of child support is glossed over with Ann's assurance to Ed that "we'll work it out."

In *One Day*, patriarchy, like feminism, is reducible to the individual psyche. Ann's first reaction is a political one: Ed is attempting to avoid his financial obligation to his children, a move that many men got away with in the 1970s (and still do), given judicial bias and lax enforcement of child support rulings (see Davis, 1991, pp. 289–298). The divorce rate increased 100 percent between 1963 and 1975 and brought with it an increase in the number of impoverished female-headed families, what Flora Davis calls the "nouveau poor" (1991, pp. 287, 286). The fact that men's standard of living usually rose after divorce, whereas that of their ex-wives and children usually dropped, is linked to women's disadvantage in the labor market and the courts' failure to order or enforce adequate child-support payments. That Ann recognizes this situation is clear when she says, "Look, Ed, you have a responsibility to these girls. Skipping child support may be the national pastime, but you're not gonna get away with it." Later, Ann admits to the girls that the court battle will not be easy, and that they will have to hope for a "fair, impartial *woman* judge."

Ann's consciousness of the unfairness of the system, and her anger at Ed's willingness to take advantage of and to benefit from that unfairness, evaporate when Ed adds an emotional dimension to his situation. Yet, regardless of Ed's emotional trauma, he is still a man who is willing to endanger the financial welfare of his children in order to preserve his own lifestyle. That truly disturbing fact is not erased by his eventual realization that he should have more faith in his wife.

One Day, Television, and Feminism

One Day's strategy of raising complex feminist issues only to dissolve them into the personal psychology of individual characters, thereby suppressing their larger political meaning, is not a strategy unique to this sitcom or, indeed, to television in general. As Fredric Jameson (1979) argues, all mass culture texts have such contradictory functions. However, *One Day*'s utopian dimension is really rather powerful, both historically and rhetorically. Viewing television pragmatically, as I do, means acknowledging at the outset that it will never offer uncontradicted oppositional ideology. To evaluate television on the basis of how faithfully it reflects radical feminist politics, for instance, is to embark on a project with a foregone conclusion. However, as Jameson indicates, in order to contain the disturbing aspects of feminism, television is forced at least to raise the topic. *One Day* "raises the topic" in a variety of ways, and on a variety of levels, that were highly unusual in television entertainment.

One Day acknowledged the presence and the impact of second-wave feminism (while, like most television, avoiding actual use of the "f-word") in the life of a quite ordinary woman. Sexual freedom, gender stereotypes, class issues, and the impact of divorce on children—these were issues that simply had not been explored on television in a recurring fashion, at least not from a female, protofeminist point of view. Although its premise was linked to pop culture notions of lifestyle feminism, *One Day* went beyond lifestyle issues in the problems it raised. To some extent, the show deserves notice simply for doing that, and for doing it in a somewhat responsible way. For example, one sign of *One Day*'s responsibility was that it treated its issues seriously. Characters such as Schneider, and the wisecracking of Julie and Barbara, provided comic relief necessary to preserve the tone of a sitcom while making it possible for the show to contain very dramatic scenes that explored the emotional reactions of characters in a fashion reminiscent of soap opera. *One Day* also regularly extended storylines over more than one episode, rebelling against the sitcom dictate that all problems are solvable in a half-hour.[17]

One Day's *rhetorical* difference from earlier representations also deserves notice. In contrast to Mary Richards, who might notice sexism but was too compliant or well-mannered to protest it seriously, and Maude Findlay, who had no problem protesting sexism but rarely seemed to suffer much from it, Ann Romano noticed sexism, talked about it, and lived a life very much affected by it.[18] Feminism is a powerful ideology because it is rooted in the experiences of women. *One Day* provided glimpses of the kinds of experiences that made feminism meaningful for many women. The vision of feminism offered in *One Day* was rooted in the possibility of identification by the women who watched it. The same women who might reject the "feminist" label because it conjured up visions of the deep-voiced, irreverent, obstreperous Maude might embrace the goals that seemingly drove Ann Romano's choices: a desire for independence and autonomy, economic opportunity, well-adjusted children, and a satisfying egalitarian relationship with a man.

Of course, the power of this vision was mitigated by the eventual relocation of Ann's problems to her own or others' psyches and by Ann's lack of a female community. These factors constitute, in Jameson's terms, the ideological dimension of *One Day*. *One Day*'s vision of an individualistic feminism rooted in self-help solutions is one of the easiest and least disruptive kinds of feminism for audiences to absorb because it plays into several assumptions that are crucial to the maintenance of patriarchy. For example: If television is willing to admit that women have a legitimate need to change their lives (and *One Day* does admit this), the subsequent adjustment will be so much simpler if:

1. by placing the source of the problem in individual situations (one woman's stifling marriage) or persons (one unenlightened, sexist man) rather than social/cultural structures (patriarchy), television assures us that only *selected* women need/desire such change; and
2. the site of change for those women who need/desire it is their individual consciousness rather than society as a whole (or the behavior/consciousness of others, e.g., men).

These moves, exemplified in *One Day*, use feminism as support for good old-fashioned individualism, and, at the same time, negate the need for and possibilities of sisterhood. Given that competition among women and their isolation from one another are key barriers to the kind of gender solidarity that would pose a profound threat to patriarchy, the triumph of individualist feminism is an important rhetorical/ideological strategy in *One Day*. If the solution to patriarchy is all in women's minds, then they can fix it without having to upset anyone else. Given the immense power of individualism in American culture, this is a comforting fiction for many men and women.

From its "emerging woman" themes in early years, the trajectory of *One Day*'s narrative gradually developed into a feminist Horatio Alger story. The most interesting and explicit treatments of feminist themes appear in the first four years of *One Day*, from which I take the episodes closely examined in this chapter. In later years, these themes are replaced by a stronger focus on the lives of Julie and Barbara as both marry and start homes of their own (although both daughters and their husbands live with Ann for brief periods).[19] Ann's professional life became more visible and important during these years. She succeeded at her job as an advertising account executive and left it in 1980 to do freelance advertising. She had two different partners in her freelance business. The first, Nick Handris, became her lover as well as her partner. His death after one year resulted in Ann's caring for his young son, Alex, for the next two years. Ann's next partner, Francine Webster, was a calculating and competitive character, a smart woman, but not one to be trusted. Her function was to provide a contrast to Ann, and their relationship reinforced stereotypes about competition between women rather than supplying Ann with sisterhood.

In short, the conflicts over the liberationist themes of self-actualization, independence, and the boundaries of womanhood that were frequent in the first half of *One Day*'s life on prime-time were replaced in later years with more standard sitcom fare derived from the domestic/relational crises of Julie and Barbara, the demands of Ann's professional life, and assorted family issues (e.g., Ann's developing relationship with Alex and her conflicts with her mother, who moved to Indianapolis in the 1980–81 season). In 1983, her self-actualization presumably complete after she has indeed "made it on her own," Ann marries again. The series closes when Ann and her new husband decide to move to London, where Ann has been offered a job.

Within the narrative of the series taken as a whole, Ann's feminist self-awareness in early seasons is a phase that she travels through on her individual journey toward self-actualization and economic success. Having helped Ann to overcome her *personal* barriers (e.g., her need for dependence), feminism has done its job. In some interesting and noteworthy ways, *One Day*'s evolution illustrates the evolution of radical feminism's critique of patriarchy into liberal feminism's focus on individualistic solutions into, finally, the postfeminist ethos of the 1980s (exemplified by the fact that Julie and Barbara seem to have few of the doubts about marriage and children that their mother voiced just five years earlier).

Popular culture's featuring of therapeutic feminism in the mid- to late 1970s was not a case of creating a new feminism out of whole cloth; rather it was a selection of a particular variation of feminism from the available options. *One Day* did not make feminism into something it wasn't; self-help feminism existed already in the pages of women's magazines, including *Ms. One Day* simply limited the discourses of feminism to those that would fit easily into its institutional and generic parameters. A key part of television's hegemonic function is limiting the menu of what we are encouraged to think about to those ideas that television can represent easily and well. As I discuss in a variety of ways in this book, this means that certain elements of feminism will get a great deal of attention and others will be virtually ignored (or ridiculed). The bottom line, however, is that entertainment television has been offering selected visions of feminism, in various genres,[20] since 1970. Moreover, those visions have changed and evolved as feminism, and cultural reaction to it, have changed and evolved. During radical feminism's peak, the most popular feminism-influenced programming was the rather timid *Mary Tyler Moore*. However, as radical feminism evolved (or devolved, some would say) into liberal feminism and it became clear that many feminist goals could be integrated with basic American ideals (individualism, equal opportunity), entertainment television became braver about explicitly representing feminist thinking.

By the early 1980s, *One Day* was the sole survivor of the wave of "single woman on her own" shows that had defined feminism for a decade of television. Of the new shows with clear feminist influence, *Kate and Allie* (1984–89) came closest to the single-woman tradition, but was also different in important ways, as I discuss in Chapter 3. The growth of a political climate hostile (or, perhaps, more *overtly* hostile) to feminism, and challenges from within feminism itself presented a new set of issues to be grappled with in the feminist representations of the mid- to late 1980s. The 1970s sitcoms, for all of their problems, eventually made it clear that women could "make it on their own." In the 1980s, the issue was no longer whether or not women could succeed but how they would handle the consequences of that success.

Notes

1. A 1975 article in *Ms.* magazine implicitly identified the feminist implications of the wave of single-woman sitcoms and praised both *Fay* and *Phyllis* as television attempts "to present what is actually happening out there [with widowed and divorced women] with some healthy accuracy and some even healthier laughter" (Berman, 1975, p. 62).

2. I give little attention to *Diana* in contrast to *Fay* in this chapter because the former received so little notice during its brief lifetime, whereas *Fay* was specifically singled out by *Ms.* as an example of television's new attention to women's lives.

3. For an excellent essay on the perceived costs of feminism for young women, an analysis that implicitly reveals how different the situation can be for older women, see Hogeland, 1994a.

4. Lear and other producers (including Allan Burns, one of the producers of *Mary Tyler Moore*) and members of the Writers' Guild would file suit against the Federal Communications Commission, the National Association of Broadcasters, and the networks, arguing that the family hour was an unwarranted restriction on free speech (Levine, 1975; Taylor, 1989, p. 53). They were successful, and in 1977 the networks were prohibited from officially continuing the family hour. However, as Taylor argues, despite the official demise of the family hour, "the networks had backed themselves into a corner; they could hardly retreat from a measure designed, as they had loudly proclaimed, to protect children" (1989,

p. 53). As a result, the chill on provocative programming during the early hour of prime-time continued unofficially and the later prime-time hours were used for exploitative programming such as *Charlie's Angels* and *Starsky and Hutch* (p. 54).

5. Consciousness-raising was, however, a largely white, middle-class activity. As Ellen Willis has said, "Another of the problems in interpreting data gleaned from consciousness-raising was, to what extent did it reveal patterns of male-female relations in general, and to what extent did it reflect the situation of women in particular social groups?" (1984, p. 95). To the detriment of the movement, many of the insights radical feminists gained from consciousness-raising were falsely universalized to all women, regardless of race, class, or sexual identity (see Echols, 1989, pp. 89–101).

6. Marjorie Ferguson has concluded that women's magazines "proclaim self-help as the doctrine of salvation for all areas of a woman's life from the most public to the most private" (1983, p. 185).

7. Karlyn Kohrs Campbell has argued that consciousness-raising is a rhetorical strategy that exists in public discourse as well as in small groups. As a rhetorical strategy, consciousness-raising works to "'violate the reality structure'"—that is, to question and/or attack accepted beliefs and norms that have "great mythic power" (Campbell, 1973, pp. 81–82).

8. In 1970, *Mademoiselle* had published "A Report on a Consciousness-raising Group," which recorded the discussion of a preexisting group. The introduction to the discussion described consciousness-raising as "a group of, say, six to ten women meeting regularly to talk to one another about being women" but did not mention any political function of the process ("A Report on a Consciousness-Raising Group," 1970, p. 80).

9. For example, in addition to explicitly political feminist publications such as *Ms.* or *Notes From the Second Year*, a number of feminist consciousness-raising novels were published in the late 1970s, including Alix Kates Shulman's *Burning Questions* (1978) and Marilyn French's *The Women's Room* (1977). Lisa Hogeland argues that "the novels and the women's liberation writings created an audience for each other, further fostered by extensive media coverage of feminism in the mainstream press and by the development of a specifically feminist press as well" (1995, p. 605).

10. In later seasons, while the theme song remains the same, the traveling scenes are eliminated. The opening visuals are simply brief scenes taken from earlier episodes and focusing on various characters.

11. In a similar vein, Lauren Rabinovitz includes Schneider in the tradition of the "featured male" often found in single-mom sitcoms. Such a character is "necessarily established as an unsuitable mate for the woman through his difference in age, class, political biases, or sexual preference" (1989, p. 8).

12. It is made generally clear in various references that the divorce was Ann's idea, brought on by her feeling of suffocation in her traditional marriage. In one episode in which she feels that David is threatening her independence, she tells him that "one of the biggest problems in my marriage was that I thought there had to be more to life than being supported by another person."

13. Ed's fairly lavish lifestyle with his new wife, especially in contrast to Ann's constant concerns about money, is a topic in a number of episodes over the life of the series. *One Day*'s frequent references, implicit and explicit, to the differing economic consequences of divorce for men and women is one of the most progressive and realistic aspects of the sitcom.

14. At differing levels (sometimes resulting in the dissolution of the relationship), this conflict between romance and independence is played out in films such as *Alice Doesn't Live Here Anymore* (1975), *An Unmarried Woman* (1978), and *My Brilliant Career* (1979) as well as in the best-selling feminist novel *The Women's Room* (1977).

15. For example, when David protests that he desperately wants a son to play Little League with, Ann retorts: "You want to have all the fun while I stay home and do all the work." Incredibly, David responds, "I want this experience and I think you're the one who's being damned selfish in not allowing me to have it."

16. "One day at a time" is, of course, a slogan attached to the twelve-step self-help program of Alcoholics Anonymous, adding an additional layer of potential meaning to the title of the sitcom, particularly in terms of its therapeutic dimensions.

17. In *One Day's* first season, for instance, a storyline in which Julie ran away with her boyfriend lasted four episodes.

18. *One Day* contains some interesting intertextual references to these other "feminist" sitcoms. The "niceness" of Mary Richards, for instance, is alluded to in an episode in which Barbara, vowing to be a better person, says, "I'm gonna make Mary Tyler Moore look like the bride of Frankenstein." In another episode, Ann counsels a friend of Barbara's who is suffering an identity crisis as he realizes that, against his father's wishes, he does not want to be a lawyer. When the boy's father arrives to confront Ann for interfering in his plans for his son, he says, "I pictured you more like that woman on television, that Maude." Through such allusions, *One Day* participates in the drawing of intertextual contrasts between its own representation of feminism and those that preceded it.

19. Extratextual factors occasioned some changes in the sitcom. For example, Julie and her husband moved out of town in the 1979–80 season because Mackenzie Phillips, who played Julie, was in drug rehabilitation (Westover, 1980). Julie returned to the sitcom in 1981, and produced a granddaughter for Ann, but deserted her family in the 1983 season (Phillips was written out of the show again because of physical problems). During this time, the increasing focus on the character of Barbara reflected not only Phillips's absences, but also the enormous growth in popularity of Valerie Bertinelli, the actress portraying Barbara (Davidson, 1981).

20. For an entertaining and thoughtful discussion of the incorporation of feminism into 1970s female-centered dramatic programming (e.g., *Police Woman, Charlie's Angels, The Bionic Woman, Wonder Woman*), see chapter 9 in Douglas, 1994.

Chapter 3
"After the Revolution": 1980s Television, Postfeminism, and *Designing Women*

In 1986, Peter Jennings hosted an ABC news special entitled "After the Revolution." The special was promoted in *Working Woman* magazine as addressing "how women's lives continue to be affected by the sexual revolution and the women's movement," even though the title of the program implied that the revolution and the movement were over (Bosworth, 1986, p. 110). The year 1986, as I discuss in this chapter, was a key moment in the "posting" of feminism, signaled by specials such as this, by the publication of books such as *A Lesser Life: The Myth of Women's Liberation in America* (Hewlett, 1986), by various "trend" stories in print media on the aftermath of feminism, as well as by shifts in television programming.

For many feminists, the 1980s as a whole represent a depressing time for feminism. This view has gained credence from the persuasive arguments in Susan Faludi's successful book *Backlash: The Undeclared War Against American Women* (1991). Faludi extends her arguments about the backlash against feminism to prime-time television, excoriating popular and critically acclaimed programming such as *thirtysomething* (1987–91) for its regressive politics (pp. 160–167). Faludi makes a powerful case for the decline of television's interest in and support for feminism, pointing out that in the 1980s, unlike the 1970s, shows built around single career women almost vanished entirely (a point that helps explain the intense reaction to the appearance of *Murphy Brown* in 1988), or, like *Cagney and Lacey*, faced constant pressure to mute their feminist implications (pp. 149–153; see also D'Acci, 1994).

Although the "backlash" has become a catch-phrase for many feminists as a result of Faludi's book, and has become a handy way of understanding the 1980s retreat from many feminist goals, it has also glossed over subtleties in 1980s responses to feminism. "Backlash" implies a wholesale rejection of feminist ideals, an attempt to demonize women's liberation and to return women to the subordinate roles of a bygone era. As Faludi describes it, "the last decade has seen a powerful counter-assault on women's rights, a backlash, an attempt to retract the handful of small and hard-won victories that the feminist movement did manage to win for women" (1991, p. xviii). However, some 1980s reactions to feminism do not reflect such a clear-cut attitude. As I discuss in this chapter, some discourse that has been labeled "backlash" is more fittingly labeled "postfeminist," a distinction recognizing that some discourse which questions certain feminist issues and/or goals assumes the validity of other feminist issues and/or goals.

Judith Stacey's definition of postfeminism as "the simultaneous incorporation, revision, and depoliticization of many of the central goals of second-wave feminism" is a useful indicator of this distinction (1987, p. 8). For example, the outcome of women's liberation that has been most thoroughly absorbed into popular consciousness is a woman's right to pursue employment and education. Statistics indicate that by the end of the 1980s, more women than men were high school graduates, and that women lagged only slightly behind men as college graduates (Cowan, 1989, p. 8Y). Moreover, whatever their attitudes toward feminism, most women would continue to work for wages even if they had no economic need to do so (Brenner, 1993, p. 110). Of the young women (under age twenty-five) polled in a 1982 survey, 98 percent expected to work for wages (Bolotin, 1982, p. 106–107).

One of the implications of postfeminism, signified by the prefix "post," is that feminism is over. Although, as Faludi documents, women are far from equal in terms of pay, opportunity, or representation in all sectors of the workforce, media accounts often assume that opportunity for women has exploded, thus confirming the belief that feminism has triumphed, at least in the public sphere (1991, pp. ix–xv).[1] Basic opportunity is taken for granted, and success beyond that is a result of individual initiative. For example, although 77 percent of women polled in 1989 believed that "the women's movement has made life better," only 33 percent would label themselves feminists, and 76 percent say they pay " 'not very much' or 'no' attention to the women's movement" (Wallis, 1989, p. 82). I have no doubt that a backlash exists—the New Right alone provides ample evidence for that claim (see Faludi, 1991, pp. 229–256)—but I am also convinced from my own experience of dealing with young women in the classroom since 1985 that shifting attitudes toward feminism do not always represent a *rejection* of women's liberation as much as an *adjustment* to it. As I discuss below, some of this adjustment is a product of cultural influence, including the backlash discussed by Faludi, and some of it is a reaction to women's material lives. What postfeminism represents, I think, is a hegemonic negotiation of second-wave ideals, in which the presumption of equality for women in the public sphere has been retained. This presumption, serving as the "essence" of feminism, requires the least ideological adjustment from men and from the culture at large (and, concomitantly, the most adjustment from women themselves). At the same time, the most radical aspects of feminism, those centered in sexual politics and a profound awareness of power differences between the sexes at all levels and in all arenas, have been discarded as irrelevant or threatening.

"Posting" Feminism in the 1980s

The contours of a postfeminist landscape in the United States began to surface in the early 1980s, but they did not emerge, as one might predict, from disgruntled patriarchs. The publication of Betty Friedan's *The Second Stage* in 1981, for example, is an important moment in the construction of postfeminism. Friedan's thesis in *The Second Stage*, that second-wave feminists ignored the needs of the family, the differences between men and women, and the power of women's traditional roles, was perhaps not the first, but the most visible, in a wave of "feminist recantation" (Faludi, 1991, p. 319). Sylvia Ann Hewlett, also a self-identified feminist, wrote a book with similar themes, *A Lesser Life: The Myth of Women's Liberation in America*, in 1986. What Friedan and Hewlett had in common, along with lesser luminaries and vehement anti-feminists (see Faludi, 1991, pp. 90–92; 289–312), was their rhetorical strategy of blaming women's current troubles with combining marriage, motherhood, and work or with finding suitable mates (two central post-feminist issues) on the misguided goals of second-wave feminists. The lack of social policies to support working mothers (e.g., federally sponsored day care, guaranteed maternity leave), economic discrimination against women, and the attitudes of men (whom Friedan depicts as liberated and ready to cooperate, an assumption contradicted by the research in Arlie Hochschild's *The Second Shift* [1989]) are somehow exempted from this analysis (or feminists are blamed for not working hard enough to change them). Importantly, patriarchy escapes responsibility in these descriptions of women's dire situation.

These arguments are crucial to the development of a postfeminist perspective which assumes that second-wave feminism ignored the family except to attack it. What they neglect is that second-wave feminists did not simply attack the family as an impediment to women's self-actualization (the premise that Friedan and Hewlett both work from) but they also attacked it as a source of material oppression manifested in a gendered division of labor, domestic violence, marital rape, and unequal divorce laws.[2] Moreover, as Barbara Ehrenreich argues so persuasively in *The Hearts of Men: American Dreams and the Flight from Commitment* (1983), men began to reject marriage long before feminism came along. Clearly, Friedan's and Hewlett's arguments had resonance for women, and many of their claims carry tremendous truth. Working mothers do not get enough support, from their families, their employers, or the government, for the many demands that they juggle. However, I find it interesting that Hewlett and Friedan found it necessary to lay these problems largely at feminism's door, as though, somehow, the reforms necessary to ameliorate these problems were on the way in the 1970s and women's liberation derailed them.

This strategy found its way into popular media treatments of postfeminism in the 1980s. A 1982 cover story in *The New York Times Magazine* (Bolotin, 1982), although written by a self-identified feminist dismayed with what she found, details the rejection of the feminist label by women in their twenties. A refrain in this article is young women's conviction that feminism is the province of angry, bitter women too dedicated to pointing out the problems of being female. Although these young women assume their right to equality of opportunity in the workplace—as well as their right to a fulfilling personal life—they are unwilling to admit that if barriers to those goals exist in 1982, they cannot be overcome through rugged individualism. One law student, for example, claims, "Sure, there's discrimination out there, but you can't just sit there feeling sorry for yourself. It's the individual woman's responsibility to prove her worth. Then she can demand equal pay" (1982, p. 31). As Bolotin puts it, "not one woman I spoke to believes that women receive equal pay for equal or comparable work, but it does not occur to most of them to use the power of the feminist movement to improve their position" (p. 103).[3]

In some sense, according to the women Bolotin interviewed, to admit the need for continued feminist activism is to admit a lack of self-sufficiency, a lack of control over one's life. As one of Bolotin's interviewees expressed, "My abandonment of feminism was a process of intellect. It was also a process of observation. Look around and you'll see some happy women, and then you'll see these bitter, bitter, women. The unhappy women are all feminists. You'll find very few happy, enthusiastic, relaxed people who are ardent supporters of feminism. Feminists are really tortured people" (1982, p. 31). Certainly, the realizations that come from a feminist consciousness can often be profoundly depressing, and young women's "fear of feminism" can be partially traced to their resistance of the anger, and sometimes hopelessness, that such realizations create (Hogeland, 1994a).

However, uniting the perspectives of Friedan, Hewlett, and the women Bolotin interviewed is the notion that feminism is (or was) about ideology that is not relevant to the conditions of women's lives. *Time* magazine, in a story on Hewlett's book, notes her argument that their reaction against the 1950s cult of motherhood "led many modern feminists in an ideological direction that culminates in a 'blind spot' toward the crucial issues of motherhood and family" (Leo, 1986, p. 63). In a similar move, the subtitle of a 1983 *Time* story on women authors, "Postfeminism: Playing for Keeps," approvingly notes that "from novels to humor, women are moving beyond doctrine" (Reed, 1983, p. 60).

The review that follows, of work by Toni Morrison, Alice Walker, Joyce Carol Oates, Joan Didion, and others, makes the somewhat incredible claim that women writers are maturing because they no longer write about—you guessed it—women: "While some, like Marilyn French (*The Women's Room*), continue to dissect the feminine psyche and situation, a growing cadre of women has enlarged and honored the literary mainstream" by writing books "characterized by less dogmatic treatments of both men and women, and with themes expanded to include family, children, and political events" (Reed, 1983, p. 60). In fact, Marilyn French's *The Women's Room* deals with family, children, and political events in some detail but is presumably too dogmatic to count as part of the literary mainstream.

The impression that feminist doctrine has little connection to "the mainstream of America life" is echoed by Sylvia Hewlett in a 1986 *People* magazine piece on *A Lesser Life*. Hewlett's claim that second-wave feminists ignored the fact that 90 percent of women would wish to work *and* become mothers is the crux of her attack on the movement (Powell, 1986, p. 101). Although it is difficult to tell if American women lay the blame for the difficulties of reconciling work and motherhood at feminism's door quite as squarely as Hewlett, a subsequent *Time* magazine poll indicated that women see "'helping women balance work and family'" as the "most important goal for the women's movement" (Wallis, 1989, p. 86).

Indeed, "family" issues seem to be at the center of much postfeminist angst, according to media representations and the polling data they offer. A 1986 *Newsweek* story on working mothers included poll results showing that only 50 percent of women believed that a woman could work fulltime and "adequately fulfill her responsibilities to her child" (Kantrowitz, 1986, p. 51). The story also emphasized the ways in which women were lowering their career expectations in order to spend more time with their children. A 1989 *New York Times* poll found that 48 percent of women felt that they "had had to sacrifice too much for their gains," and "respondents of both sexes cited children and family life as the primary casualties" (Cowan, 1989, p. 1). A December 1989 issue of

Time found that 42 percent of women believed that children suffered "when women try to have it all" (Wallis, 1989, p. 86).

This central postfeminist issue demonstrates the still powerful romanticization of heterosexuality, the nuclear family, and motherhood as well as the disappearance of "sexual politics," the term Judith Stacey uses to describe radical feminist efforts to "struggle against the systemic, structural subordination of women. Reflecting the ambiguous, double meaning of the word 'sexual,' feminist sexual politics has included efforts to transform both gender and sexuality . . . both in the public sphere and individually in the 'privacy' of our kitchens and bathrooms" (1983, p. 561).

The very fact that postfeminist polls enquire about how *women* are coping with dual-career families, or how *women* are coping with child-care encourages (or reinforces) a view of these issues as female responsibilities and overlooks the sexual politics that naturalize such a view. As Stacey argues, "For many, this politicization of intimate relationships, particularly male-female relations, was the most explosive and threatening aspect of feminist sexual politics,"[4] and the retreat from this analysis of power has become a key characteristic of postfeminism (1983, p. 561). Indeed, euphemistic postfeminist references to moving beyond "ideology," "doctrine," or "dogma" can easily be read as dismissal of sexual politics.

That feminist challenges to the politics of the private sphere were inherently controversial had already been demonstrated in the battle over the ERA. The success of the arguments of Phyllis Schlafly and the STOP ERA forces—that the ERA would deprive women of the joy and fulfillment of traditional roles—cemented the notion that feminism entailed an anti-family ideology (Mansbridge, 1986; see also Solomon, 1979). This strategy also dovetailed nicely with the rhetoric of the increasingly powerful New Right, which viewed the ERA, in the words of Jerry Falwell, as "a satanic attack on the home" (quoted in Faludi, 1991, p. 232).

For many, no doubt, the defeat of the ERA in 1982 "posted" feminism. Feminist organizations and agitation did not disappear but became even more professionalized and fragmented, a process that had been ongoing since the mid-1970s (Davis, 1991, pp. 152–153). Without a central, unifying goal such as the ERA, feminism, as a movement, lost grass-roots membership and dropped out of the media spotlight. Specific but varied feminist issues—for example, domestic violence, abortion, legal reform, and women's studies—were pursued by specific organizations that functioned more as interest groups than as activist collectives.[5] The "posting" of feminism intersected with and was enabled by broad changes in economic and political reality. Some of the values of postfeminism, such as celebration of the family and rugged individualism, were consonant with the rhetoric of the New Right and the Reagan/Bush administrations. Little government support for feminist ideas, combined with an increasingly troubled economic life for the middle and lower classes (including the feminization of poverty), provided motivation for the retreat from radical feminism, while "a return to traditional ethics, values, and lifestyles became the response to disruption and decay" (Ryan, 1992, pp. 100–102). Judith Stacey, drawing conclusions from her research into postfeminist attitudes in Silicon Valley families, argues that because of the economic consequences of postindustrialization,

> many women (and men) have been susceptible to the appeals of the antifeminist backlash, and especially to pro-family ideologies. Because of its powerful and highly visible critique of traditional domesticity, and because of the sensationalistic way the media disseminated this critique, feminism has taken most of the heat for family and social crises that have attended the transition from an industrial to a postindustrial order in the U.S. . . . Feminism serves as a symbolic lightning rod for the widespread nostalgia and longing for "lost" intimacy and security that presently pervades social and political culture in the United States. (1987, p. 11)

The result is that many women see feminism as irrelevant, or even threatening, to their personal lives. For older women, feminism might "intensify the pain and difficulty of the compromises most women must make in order to mediate the destructive effects of postindustrial society on family and interpersonal relationships" (Stacey, 1987, p. 23). For younger women, in contrast, "there is a high level of agreement with feminist goals in combination with a weakening perception that there is still a need for feminist activism" (Ryan, 1992, p. 110). To some extent, as Stacey comments, this perception seems linked to a refusal to acknowledge the continuing existence of sexism (1987, p. 22).

This discussion of broad themes in postfeminist attitudes indicates that postfeminists and backlashers, while sometimes conflated, operate from somewhat different premises. Postfeminism acknowledges, or even takes for granted, the positive gains of women's liberation in certain areas such as access to employment and education while denying the need for continued feminist action (Rosenfelt and Stacey, 1987, p. 358).[6] Friedan and Hewlett, for example, operate from the premise that feminism's primary legacy has been a cult of careerism for women, resulting in a feminist hegemony that assumes women want to "clone the male competitive model in the marketplace" (Hewlett, 1986, p. 186). Importantly, however, Friedan and Hewlett can be differentiated from backlashers in that neither advocates women's retreat from the labor market as a solution to the problems they face.

Moreover, postfeminists are likely to assume that with basic access assured by feminism, women's economic success is dependent on individual initiative and does not require collective action. As Rosenfelt and Stacey say of Hewlett's *A Lesser Life*, the postfeminist perspective "fails to analyze male power or to hold men accountable for sustaining the unjust economic and social conditions" that many postfeminist women experience (1987, p. 349). Indeed, this characteristic of postfeminist thought is closely linked to the general rejection of sexual politics, including the critique of the nuclear family. The problems of the nuclear family (e.g., the isolation of women, the gender-based division of labor, domestic violence, marital rape, lack of control over reproduction) that are central to radical feminists' understanding of "woman" as a social category or sex class do not figure in postfeminist discourse (p. 349; Stacey, 1983, pp. 568–569). Of course, statistics on wife battering, marital rape, and the research on women's "second shift" (Hochschild, 1989) at home indicate that the symptoms of these problems still exist. Some women may see such problems as the price of their freedom; 60 percent of women agreed with a *New York Times* poll statement that "most men are willing to let women get ahead but only if women still do all the housework at home" (Cowan, 1989, p. 8Y).

The retreat from analysis of the sex/gender system, when combined with an emphasis on self-reliance and the construction of "individual 'lifestyle' solutions" (Rapp, 1988, p. 26), means that the need to alter male behavior is ignored and "underlines the 'post' of 'postfeminism'" (Rosenfelt and Stacey, 1987, p. 357). This attitude is consistent with postfeminists' internalization of negative stereotypes of feminists and their assumption that feminist attitudes would worsen, rather than improve, their lives by lowering their chances for heterosexual romance and marriage (p. 348; see also Hogeland, 1994a).

The primary difference between postfeminists and antifeminist backlashers is the latter's unwillingness to allow for positive effects of women's liberation. For backlashers, women's liberation was a mistake—for women and for everyone else. Women's denial of traditional roles (i.e., fulltime motherhood and homemaking) and their increased freedom to *choose* motherhood have made them miserable and have weakened the family. The solution, for backlashers, is a return to the patriarchal family (and, not incidentally, a rollback of abortion rights [Faludi, 1991, pp. 400–421]). While postfeminists assume woman's right to work *and* to mother, one clear thrust of the backlash has been to reassert the primacy of traditional gender roles in which "woman's place is in the home" and to argue that deviation from that path leads to a variety of dire personal and social consequences, running the gamut from mental illness to the destruction of masculinity (see pp. 335–362; pp. 281–312).

The area in which postfeminism and the backlash seem to converge is in their common embrace of "difference" arguments, that is, their use of arguments supporting the notion that women and men are fundamentally different, psychologically and emotionally. For backlashers, feminism led women to deny their "true" natures and is, therefore, the cause of women's misery. Implicitly, postfeminist thought also appears to accept the inviolability of gender differences, evidenced by Friedan's espousal in *The Second Stage* of the "beta" mode, which stresses such "feminine" values as fluidity, flexibility, and interpersonal sensitivity (Stacey, 1983, p. 562) and by Hewlett's claim that motherhood is the both "the most passionate attachment" and the "deepest emotion in women's lives" (1986, p. 188).

Rosenfelt and Stacey call this a "conservative profamily vision, one that simply assumes the inevitability or superiority of heterosexual marriage and motherhood" (1987, p. 346). The central question for postfeminism, then, would be, how can women integrate the two halves of their life (and the assumed radically different values and behaviors that govern them), family and work? This question encompasses a variety of issues made central in postfeminist media coverage: toxic day-care (Faludi, 1991, p. 41–45), women's second shift (Kantrowitz, 1986, Wallis, 1989, pp. 86 and 89) the "marriage crunch" (Salholz, 1986) and the "infertility epidemic" among career women (Faludi, 1991, pp. 27–32). The dismissal of radical feminist sexual politics, and the assumption that women's entry into the labor force is the major legacy of feminism, are clear in the framing of these problems as "women's issues." The *Newsweek* cover story on work/family conflicts is entitled "A Mother's Choice" (Kantrowitz, 1986). Women's presumed overriding desire for heterosexual marriage is implied in the title of another *Newsweek* cover story on the marriage crunch, "Too Late for Prince Charming?" (Salholz, 1986).

At the very least, such rhetoric implies that despite postfeminist attitudes about the success of women's liberation, the "equality" essence of feminism has taken hold only in the public sphere (if even there) and has left traditional assumptions about responsibilities in the private sphere largely intact. Of course, to achieve equality in the private sphere would require further adjustment from men, an issue mysteriously absent in postfeminist rhetoric. However, another implication lurks in this rhetoric as well, one that is potentially more disturbing. The difference assumptions that undergird many of the arguments about women's needs for motherhood and relationships have increasingly come to be used as the basis for claims for women's superiority in a variety of arenas. As I discuss in Chapter 5, it is difficult to discuss this phenomenon solely as a result of postfeminism since such arguments formed the basis for much feminist theory in the 1980s. However, as these arguments trickled down into popular culture in various forms, they gave strength to postfeminist assumptions about essential male-female differences and responsibilities.

Ultimately, given Susan Faludi's and other feminists' (e.g., Ehrenreich, 1990a; Pollitt, 1994) able deconstruction of the faulty research and assumptions behind many of these postfeminist issues, it is difficult to tell how much of postfeminism and the backlash is "real" (i.e., reflective of the condition of women's lives or of their attitudes) and how much is media construction. For example, Press and Strathman (1993, p. 11) make a useful point about the relationships of 1970s television representations of feminism and the postfeminism that followed:

Television feminism promoted an ethic of achievement and success for women who were "making it in a man's world." It avoided the challenges of feminism to private life. . . . The "feminist" that survived was a kind of "woman in a grey flannel suit"—dressed for success but with nothing to go home to. . . . The mass media first promoted this impoverished version of feminism, then gleefully reported the discontent with that version as "postfeminism."

Press and Strathman are right in implying that postfeminist rhetoric inevitably assumes the same kind of feminist subject projected in 1970s television programming: the middle-class, heterosexual, white, career woman. Postfeminist rhetoric assumes that this kind of woman, having internalized feminist rhetoric, chose to pursue a career instead of choosing fulltime motherhood and, in the 1980s, is discontent with her life.

To me, the most meaningful aspect of this limited formulation is that it renders invisible all other kinds of women, continuing the illusion that feminism (and, hence, postfeminism) affects only a selected segment of womanhood—that segment in a position to "choose" in the first place. This is the ultimate rhetorical sleight of hand committed by postfeminist rhetoric, and it produces postfeminist thought's most powerful framing device: Patriarchy is gone and has been replaced by choice, resulting in several premises that create the postfeminist worldview. Among them: Second-wave feminists *chose* to emphasize certain issues at the expense of other issues (and media selection and interpretation of movement activity had nothing to do with this). The problems that women face today are a direct result of the *choices* that they made (and not the result of the lack of support for those choices from government, employers, partners, etc.). In a related vein, social policies that might help women combine work and family have failed because feminists *chose* not to support them (and not because of opposition from politicians, lobbyists, or business interests). Finally, the possibilities for happiness in a woman's work and personal life are a direct result of the *choices* that she makes (and not a result of the ways in which those choices are limited by her employer, the government, her economic status, her race, her sexual identity, her personal support system, etc.). In dismissing feminist ideology, postfeminism also dismisses the fundamental insight of feminist ideology: Women operate within a sex/gender system that limits acceptable choices.

As I have indicated, mediated postfeminism, like mediated feminism, is constructed in a way that limits its relevance for many women while, at the same time, declaring its relevance for every woman.[7] Rather than trying to establish that postfeminism does or does not reflect the mood of all women in the 1980s is less useful, for me, than trying to understand the implications of postfeminist rhetoric circulating in cultural products in the 1980s. The emergence of postfeminism in the news media, in popular books, and in popular movies creates an important context for understanding its emergence in popular prime-time television programming. In turn, the limits of postfeminist programming make clearer the importance of those (tele)visions of feminism that managed to survive in the 1980s.

Postfeminism in 1980s Television

The contradictory nature of postfeminism is intensified when juxtaposed with television texts and contexts in the 1980s. Television critics have argued that television participated in the postfeminist emphasis on reasserting the importance of women's familial roles (Press, 1991; Press and Strathman, 1993; Probyn, 1990). However, at the same time that television producers began to rediscover the functional nuclear family as a premise for popular programming, they also became increasingly sensitive to the need to appeal to working women as a key television audience. Television advertisers, who for years viewed the white, middle-class homemaker as their primary target, understood by the 1980s that women were in the workplace to stay. The enthusiastic pursuit of the working-women audience in 1980s television was aided by the development of a new genre of working-women's magazines, including *Working Mother, Working Woman, Savvy,* and *Self* (D'Acci, 1994).[8] The broadcast networks' loss of viewers to cable, as well as the decreasing numbers of women watching daytime television, also increased the pressure to attract an upscale female audience for prime-time fare (pp. 70–72).

One sign of this new goal was the development of prime-time genres that incorporated elements of the most popular form of daytime programming for women, the soap opera. One of these new forms was the prime-time serial, a genre that included *Dallas* (1978–91), *Knots Landing* (1979–93), *Dynasty* (1981–89), and *Falcon Crest* (1981–89) among its most successful members. For many culture watchers, these dramas, with their lavish sets, displays of wealth, and battles over power, have come to exemplify the zeitgeist of the 1980s. As Susan Douglas argues, their message stressed competitive individualism—certainly an eighties theme— and tailored it to women, who were not so subtly told that they "had to make their peace with patriarchy and learn how to fit in. They had to compete with men and with other women if they were going to fulfill their feminist aspirations" (1994, p. 238). Comparing these dramas to the media-constructed "catfight" between women over the ERA, Douglas maintains that their common function was to "put the lie to feminists' claims about sisterhood" (p. 222). Whether it was Alexis and Krystle (*Dynasty*), Abby and Laura (*Knots Landing*), or Sue Ellen and Kristin (*Dallas*), women in the prime-time soaps fought over men, money, and power with great energy.[9]

As a number of scholars have argued, these shows were contradictory and are difficult to place in terms of their meaning for women. Even though there were powerful women on these shows, that power usually came through association with a male family member and hardly challenged the power of patriarchy. As was (and is) true of traditional soap opera, prime-time soaps placed tremendous emphasis on the rituals of romance, marriage, and reproduction, making personal relationships "the core problematic of the narrative" (Ang, 1990, p. 79). Although it is possible to argue that prime-time soaps permit a subversive reading that views them as a critique of the instability of the patriarchal family, I posit that this genre comes closer than any other to representing backlash thinking. In a delightful description in *American Film*, Pat Dowell calls Alexis Carrington Colby, *Dynasty*'s resident evil matriarch, "television's nightmare of female power unleashed, a New Right vision of the liberated woman in a man's world" (1985, p. 46). Indeed, in prime-time soaps, the most successful and powerful female characters are the most evil (e.g., Angela Channing of *Falcon Crest*, Alexis Colby of *Dynasty*, Abby Ewing of *Knots Landing*), there is little sisterhood between women that is not eventually betrayed, and the happiest women (although happiness is a fleeting thing on these shows) are those who know their place and support their men (e.g., Krystle Carrington of *Dynasty*, Pam Ewing of *Dallas*, Maggie Gioberti of *Falcon Crest*).[10]

A second important programming innovation in the 1980s, and one more postfeminist in tone, was the professional serial drama, represented by programs such as *Hill Street Blues* (1981–87), *St. Elsewhere* (1982–88), and *L.A. Law* (1986–94). These dramas were generic hybrids; that is, they combined the structure of soap opera with (some of) the content of cop shows, legal shows, or medical shows. However, because the connection between characters in these shows was professional rather than personal or familial (which was always the case in prime-time soaps), the female characters faced different issues. Because of their professional settings, these dramas paid closer attention than prime-time soaps to issues of gender discrimination raised by the women's movement, and such issues often drove storylines. The influence of feminism in American culture is obvious in these shows; the female characters are competent, performing professionals who often "win" professionally, solving their cases, curing their patients, triumphing in office politics. In these ensemble dramas, female characters are far less sexualized (although they are almost always conventionally attractive and often beautiful) and far more professionally independent than the characters in the wave of 1970s female-centered professional dramas such as *Police Woman* or *Charlie's Angels* which came to be known as "jiggle" shows (D'Acci, 1994, pp. 15–16).

Yet the personal travails of professional women, specifically the personal costs and the pain of competing in a man's world, are a consistent theme.[11] Reproduction, relationship stability, and mental health are problems for successful female professionals on these shows. Joyce Davenport (*Hill Street Blues*) and Ann Kelsey (*L.A. Law*) both have fertility problems. Lawyer Abby Perkins's husband cannot deal with her success and steals their child (*L.A. Law*), and driven assistant district attorney Grace Van Owen becomes addicted to pills and has a nervous breakdown (*L.A. Law*). Sergeant Lucy Bates (*Hill Street Blues*) cannot find a decent man to date and suffers from unrequited love for her police partner. On *St. Elsewhere*, Dr. Wendy Armstrong is overcome by the pressure of her work and commits suicide.[12]

Of course, few characters on professional serial dramas (or on prime-time soaps) have consistently fulfilling personal lives; after all, the "self-replication" of serial drama "depends upon a continual disintegration of the family" (Feuer, 1986, p. 105). The women characters' problems are distinctive, however, in that they stem from an implicit (but sometimes explicitly stated) conflict between careerism and personal health and happiness, a powerful postfeminist theme.[13]

The third trend in 1980s television, a trend that traverses genres, provides an antidote to the angst of the serial dramas. I refer to this third trend as postfeminist family television, a term coined by Andrea Press (1991, p. 42), and it includes both drama (*thirtysomething* [1987–91]) and situation comedy (*The Cosby Show* [1984–92], *Family Ties* [1982–89]), *Growing Pains* [1985–92]). As is the case with episodic series that rely upon "the continual reintegration of the family" (Feuer, 1986, p. 105), these programs, which all include professional women as main characters, emphasize an idealized family life. The term "postfeminist" is fitting for these programs, argues Press, because they combine a "relatively feminist view of women in the workplace" (i.e., the women work outside the home as well as within it) with idealized versions of "the traditional nuclear family widely criticized by the feminist movement" (p. 46).

In short, postfeminist family television assumes that feminist goals have been achieved, for the most part, by women's access to the public sphere, and that "families need not change to accommodate working wives and mothers" (Press and Strathman, 1993, p. 13). This is the major difference between postfeminism in nonfictional media (and in professional serial dramas) and postfeminism in fictional family television programming, particularly sitcoms. In the former, success in the workplace has led to problems in personal life; in the latter, home life is idealized, at least for women with families.[14] Moreover, in most of these postfeminist visions, there is little bonding or support between women, implying that women's problems, and their solutions, are individual and do not require group identity.[15] Press and Strathman critique these characteristics of postfeminist family television as unrealistic, arguing that "by ignoring issues centrally important in structuring the real lives of working women, television glorifies and supports a status quo oppressive for women" (p. 14).

Analyzing postfeminism from another angle, Elspeth Probyn argues that some postfeminist television (e.g., *thirtysomething*) presents the family as the haven that protects women from the dangers and frustration of the working world (1990, p. 151). Deriving ultimate satisfaction and fulfillment from nurturing and caretaking roles is naturalized in postfeminist programming, but at the same time, such programming pays lip service to the notion of "choice" for women.[16] As Probyn puts it, "Postfeminism thus allows choiceoisie to be posed as the possibility of choosing between the home or the career, the family or the successful job" (pp. 152–153). Of course, as I discussed above, the class implications are important here. The "choice" between fulltime motherhood and combining motherhood and a career (notice the term "career" rather than "job") is not available to all women. In television entertainment, as well as in nonfictional media, postfeminist "choice" is a phenomenon discussed primarily in terms of middle-class women's lives.

Press, however, argues that *Roseanne*, a situation comedy about a working-class family, also participates in postfeminist discourse. Although "the ill-paid, dull, repetitive, demeaning aspects of working-class labor are remarkably well-presented" on *Roseanne*, Press claims that "the depiction of deep-seated conflict in the workplace . . . is balanced by a thorough idealization of working-class family life" (1991, p. 43) in which Roseanne has enormous power in the home, reinscribing visions of matriarchal power from previous representations of working-class life (e.g., *The Honeymooners, The Goldbergs*). I think this reading is too facile, as it overlooks the powerful feminist potential of *Roseanne* as a sitcom that offers a great deal of feminist commentary within the context of a nuclear family; *Roseanne* also has been praised by feminists precisely because it avoids idealizing family life (e.g., Ehrenreich, 1990b; Rapping, 1994).[17]

Although Press and Strathman make a good point about the apparent lack of realism in postfeminist representation, I am more concerned with the rhetorical functions of this programming, with the ways in which they can be "considered parables or morality plays about appropriate and inappropriate beliefs and behavior. Among other things, they teach and preach about appropriate (and ideal) social and sexual relationships and interaction" (Cantor, 1990, p. 275). Generally, I see postfeminist family television as serving two functions in its representation of feminism as "other" (Probyn, 1990): First, it diverts attention from continuing problems women face in the workplace (unequal pay, sexual harassment, discrimination), thereby "posting" feminist concerns in that arena. Second, even while trumpeting women's success at work but never showing it, it reasserts the primacy and importance of women's role in the family (Press, 1991, p. 43). This is most evident in the emphasis given to the professional concerns of wives in these shows versus their husbands. In *The Cosby Show*, for example, wife Claire Huxtable is a lawyer and husband Cliff is a physician. His office is attached to their home and figures frequently in the action, while her office is almost never seen. Likewise, in *Family Ties*, wife Elyse is an architect who is never seen doing her job, while husband Steven's job as manager of a public television station is the basis for several episodes.

One final sign of the ascendance of postfeminism in 1980s television was the decline of the primary form for representing feminism in 1970s television: the single working-woman sitcom. The longest running shows of this type in the 1980s were holdovers from the 1970s, *One Day at a Time* and *Alice*, which ended by 1985. New variations on the theme were attempted in the early 1980s (e.g., *Flo* [1980–81], *I'm a Big Girl Now* [1980–81], *Gloria* [1982–83]), but none lasted more than a couple of years (a cycle broken by the success of *Murphy Brown* in 1988). Some of the elements of single working woman sitcoms can be seen in *Who's the Boss?* (1984–92), a show about a female New York advertising executive, Angela Bower, who hires a male housekeeper, Tony Micelli, to run her Connecticut home. However, *Who's the Boss?* operates as a domestic comedy for the most part, building episodes around the antics of the "family" constituted by Angela, Angela's mother, Angela's son, Tony, and Tony's daughter.[18]

Alternatives to Postfeminist Television in the 1980s: Feminism and Female Bonding

The discussion in this chapter thus far creates the impression of virtual postfeminist hegemony in 1980s popular television. That is not entirely the case. The categories and characteristics I have discussed exclude 1980s programming such as *Cagney and Lacey* (1982–88), *Kate and Allie* (1984–89), and *Designing Women* (1986–93), all of which have been linked to feminism by the popular press and by television critics and all of which were part of television's 1980s campaign to attract a working-woman audience (see D'Acci, 1994, p. 103).[19] All three of these programs have in common an element missing from postfeminist programming: female bonding or sisterhood.[20] Each also contains some postfeminist elements. Andrea Press includes *Kate and Allie* and *Designing Women* as examples of "postfeminist 'postfamily' television." Although she notes that these sitcom "glorify female bonding and alternative family forms," she dismisses their importance by arguing that their "potentially radical perspective is undercut by their continued trivialization of the obstacles real women would face if actually attempting to achieve these goals" (1991, p. 47). Press also includes *Cagney and Lacey* as postfeminist in tone, basing this assessment largely on the argument that the gender-related issues raised in the drama "are often posed as the problems of individual women rather than of women as a collective group" (p. 40). The trouble with calling *Cagney and Lacey* postfeminist on this basis is that this characteristic is not unique to postfeminist television. Television has always individualized social problems; indeed, previous chapters have analyzed this characteristic in 1970s feminist television such as *The Mary Tyler Moore Show* and *One Day at a Time*.

Generally, I do not share Press's pessimism about all 1980s television. Although she is absolutely correct in claiming that feminism gets watered down, negotiated, and limited in many shows in the 1980s, I also believe that some programming, including the three examples named above, resists postfeminism quite vigorously in some ways. Of the three, *Kate and Allie* is easiest to categorize as postfeminist. *Kate and Allie*'s tale of two divorced mothers, friends since childhood, who share an apartment in New York City with their three (combined) children is, in many ways, another domestic comedy with a slight twist: Both parents are female. However, the two female leads slot fairly easily into the socially constructed roles of "mother" and "father." Kate is the more independent and confident of the two, and she is the breadwinner who supports the family. Allie is the traditionalist, a domestic homebody who cares for the children and the home. The contrast between the two characters' approaches to life and their negotiations of decisions and situations makes the show interesting and provides a welcome vision of sisterhood to offset the discouraging competition between women on other prime-time fare. Moreover, the sitcom's presentation of a positive alternative to the nuclear family has important feminist implications.

However, *Kate and Allie*'s uneasy balance of feminist and postfeminist ideas is illustrated by an episode in which Kate eventually decides against marrying her steady boyfriend, Ted. Initially excited by Ted's proposal, Kate balks when she realizes that Ted expects her to stay at home and bear and raise a second family for him. Kate's resistance to this idea and her belief that his expectations reflect an outmoded perspective are revealed in her comment to Allie that "he doesn't want me—he wants my mother," and her comparison of Ted's vision of marriage to *Father Knows Best*, the 1950s television icon of patriarchal family life.

The influence of feminism can easily be read into Kate's reaction, particularly in her rejection of the romantic fantasy that love can conquer all, a point she makes to both Allie and Ted. However, the dialogue from the final scene in the episode, when Kate explains her decision against marriage to Ted, reveals the slide of Kate's feminist reaction into postfeminism:

Kate: It's a beautiful dream [referring to Ted's vision of the traditional family]. . . . It's not *my* dream. I've already been through that. I loved it. But I didn't love it enough to want to do it again.
Ted: This doesn't make any sense. My mother and father met, they fell in love, they got married, they had kids. What's happening? Who changed the rules?
Kate: I don't know. A lot of people who didn't get to live out their dreams, I guess.
Ted: (Looking out the window). Well, I don't think I like what's going on out there.
Kate: Give it time. It just got started.
Ted: What am I supposed to do?
Kate: Find somebody who wants the same things you want. And you will.

Just as "the rules" Ted refers to are patriarchy, feminism is, of course, the thing that's "going on out there," the unnamed influence that has altered Kate's expectations. The most startling portion of this exchange, however, is that in answer to Ted's question about what his reaction should be, Kate does not tell him that he must change. Instead, he simply needs a different kind of woman—the kind who "chooses" the kind of life he wants. Here we have what Elspeth Probyn (1990) calls postfeminist "choiceoisie" as the alternative to feminism. This moment in *Kate and Allie* exemplifies the postfeminist retreat from sexual politics. In the postfeminist vision, men do not have to change. Ted's expectation that a woman be willing to alter her life to fulfill his desires is not about patriarchy after all; it is just about individual differences, about choice. Despite Ted's reference to changing rules, Kate never implies that Ted will have to change his expectations; he will simply have to find another woman to fulfill them. This implicit acknowledgment of feminism followed by a disavowal of its implications is the kind of negotiation at the heart of postfeminism.

In contrast, judging from the amount of attention it has received from feminist television critics, *Cagney and Lacey* would have to be judged the most explicitly feminist program in prime-time television during the 1980s.[21] Popular press coverage also made explicit connections between *Cagney and Lacey* and feminism, helped no doubt, by the fact that Gloria Steinem was an outspoken advocate of the drama (D'Acci, 1994, pp. 20– 62). *Cagney and Lacey*'s feminist aspirations did not go unquestioned, leading to the show's troubled history on prime-time and a gradual softening of its politics, a process beautifully documented and analyzed by Julie D'Acci in *Defining Women: Television and the Case of Cagney and Lacey* (1994). D'Acci partially links the program's troubles to the backlash against feminism in the 1980s. She argues that *Cagney and Lacey*'s representation of feminism "changed . . . from a criticism of institutional inequities (sexism, racism, and, to a lesser degree, classism) to an examination of women's issues (or what the industry imagined as such issues) that had the potential for dramatic intensity and exploitability" (1994, p. 155–156).

One of the points that D'Acci makes about the negotiation of feminism during this period was that the networks somehow learned their lesson from the *Cagney and Lacey* controversies and found it safer to represent feminism in sitcom, "which attracted the working women's audience with far less risk" (1994, p. 103). As I argued in Chapter 1, I too believe that comedy offers space for representing social controversy and social change that might be too threatening when encoded as realist drama. This is no doubt one of the reasons why the programming form representing feminism that has been the most long-lived on television historically has been situation comedy. D'Acci's study of *Cagney and Lacey*'s audience makes clear that many female viewers in the 1980s desired something more than the muted acknowledgment of women's progress offered in postfeminist family television. Although *Cagney and Lacey*'s sometimes explicit (for television) feminist stance had almost no peers in dramatic programming,[22] it had some company in comedy, specifically in *Designing Women.*

Cagney and Lacey and *Designing Women* have some common characteristics. Both built episodes around "women's issues." Both faced cancellation early in their runs on prime-time and were saved by viewer protest.[23] Finally, both shows emphasized female bonding, a rarity in 1980s television. Indeed, *Designing Women* and *Cagney and Lacey* were considered similar enough that, in portions of the 1986, 1987, and 1988 seasons, they were both part of the Monday evening "woman's night" counterprogramming strategy on CBS designed to provide an alternative to Monday night football.[24] Importantly, *Designing Women* was part of a lineup which contained the programming that in the network's judgment would attract the coveted working-women's audience (and it did). Moreover, this scheduling also meant that *Designing Women* was contextualized, from the beginning, by television programming that was consistently singled out by the popular press for its progressive portrayals of women's lives—*Cagney and Lacey* and *Kate and Allie.* Although *Cagney and Lacey* was canceled by the fall of 1988, *Murphy Brown* joined the CBS Monday night lineup that same season.[25]

While *Designing Women* is female centered, like its companions on "women's night," it does not have the "markers" of feminist import that characterize such programs as *Cagney and Lacey, Murphy Brown,* or even *Kate and Allie.* A sitcom focusing on the interior-design partnership of four women, *Designing Women* is not about women trying to make it in a "man's world" (e.g., law enforcement or journalism), and it does not play upon the "emerging woman" theme that characterized *One Day at a Time* and, to an extent, *Kate and Allie.*

Indeed, press reactions to *Designing Women*'s early seasons stress the sitcom's "feminine" appeal more than its feminism. Members of the press consistently note that *Designing Women* is a program created and written primarily by a woman,[26] and a common theme in press reaction to the program emphasizes its appeal for women as a show in which "women, only women, sit around and talk, only talk" (Schine, 1987, p. 144). Another writer notes that "the best episodes of *Designing Women* are primarily occasions for the five regulars to sit around getting on one another's cases and chewing the fat" (Blount, 1988, p. 29).

A female reviewer claims that *Designing Women* is part of the progress television has made in "getting the female experience right" (O'Reilly, 1989, p. 18), and there is general agreement that the appeal of the sitcom comes from the interplay of its female characters, who "talk about the things women really talk about" while "laughing, and commiserating, and teasing, and supporting one another, as women do" (Yorkshire, 1987, pp. 82, 79).

This press coverage of *Designing Women* reveals an emphasis on the *realism* of the sitcom's portrayal of adult women and their interaction. This realism, for many writers, is derived from the kinds of topics that the women discuss, such as PMS, breast size, and dating divorced men, as well as the freedom with which they discuss them. An article in *People* called *Designing Women* a "gyne-com" with "female locker room humor" (Aitken, 1986, p. 136), and one of the show's stars commented to a reporter that "I've heard women say that they love to watch the show because we talk about the things women really talk about, like men's butts" (Yorkshire, 1987, p. 82). Generally, interviews with the sitcom's stars, actresses Dixie Carter, Delta Burke, Annie Potts, and Jean Smart, continue the realism theme, consistently noting the strong friendships on the set and the supportive relationships among the co-stars.[27]

Implicit feminist elements are easily discerned from this discussion. At a basic level, *Designing Women* highlights adult female interaction, a theme that gets little attention on television. Moreover, the sitcom presents "women's talk"—frequently devalued as gossip, chatter, or bitching—as meaningful and worthwhile. Indeed, as the reviews indicate, there is little that *happens* on *Designing Women*: Most episodes are driven by conversation rather than events. That conversation, however, often turns to specific feminist issues, which are dissected and analyzed with the same vigor as the less political topics named above.[28] What emerges in many episodes is a variation on consciousness-raising, a regeneration of feminist consciousness that often vigorously resists postfeminist attitudes. *Designing Women*'s feminist discourse does not exist without contradiction. Every episode does not involve a feminist issue, and not all feminist issues are framed in the way that many feminists would like. However, as I discuss next, *Designing Women*'s rhetorical strategy of framing its feminist discourse within a conservative, even postfeminist setting, and with a collection of amusing and hardly militant characters, may increase, rather than decrease its power.[29]

The Postfeminist Workplace in *Designing Women*

The setting for *Designing Women* is Sugarbaker's, an interior design firm in Atlanta, Georgia. Officially, then, the program is set in the workplace. However, this workplace is different from most. Sugarbaker's is headquartered in the home of its senior partner, Julia Sugarbaker. The majority of the action takes place in the main room of the house, a room that closely approximates a large, comfortable, middle-class living room, dominated by a long couch with a coffee table in front of it and chairs at each end. The partners in the firm have desks in the room at which they often sit, yet they spend significant amounts of time sitting on the couch and chairs. In one corner of the room is a small bar with stools, where the characters often sit to drink coffee or eat. The room does not look like an office; the tasteful wooden desks blend with the homey decor of the room, and there are no filing cabinets or office machinery such as typewriters or computers (records, files, and design materials are kept in storerooms in the back of the house). Moreover, although the characters often discuss their work, they are seldom seen doing it. In essence, although Sugarbaker's is a business, its ambience is more like that of a home, making it an "appropriate" setting for the women's talk that drives the narrative.

The obvious tie between the five main characters is their association with the design firm, but their actual relationships are as personal as they are professional. Julia Sugarbaker, a widow in her late forties and the senior member of the firm, is intelligent, elegant, and opinionated, often displaying her indignation about some social issue. Suzanne Sugarbaker, Julia's younger sister, is a self-centered former beauty queen and "silent partner," who makes little real contribution to the firm except to serve as a foil for the other characters. Suzanne's propensity to make inappropriate racist, classist, or sexist remarks that reflect her egocentric worldview epitomizes her function as Julia's opposite.

Mary Jo Shively, a divorced mother in her thirties, is a displaced homemaker who returned to work after her divorce. Mary Jo is the "everywoman" character, attractive and bright but insecure, making her way through the travails of work and single motherhood. Charlene Frazier [Stillfield], the firm's business manager, is close to Mary Jo in age. Charlene is single for the first three seasons of the show, marries in the last episode of the third season, and has a child in the fourth season. Charlene is an attractive, friendly, and trusting person, who is naive in many ways. She is fascinated by gossip and scandal, devouring *People Magazine* and *The National Inquirer* with relish. While intellectually unsophisticated in comparison to Julia and Mary Jo, she often makes insightful comments about human nature.

The final main character in *Designing Women* is Anthony Bouvier, the firm's delivery man for the program's first four seasons. The only male, he does little to disrupt the female-centered environment. Anthony is an African-American ex-convict who is bright and often shrewd, but his generally subservient position, in terms of both social power and his job, make him no threat to the dominance of the women. In the fifth season, Anthony becomes an equal partner in the firm, but his new job equality does not affect his position within the program's interaction. Indeed, for the most part, Anthony can be characterized as a sort of eunuch within his environment—what Doty (1993, p. 58) calls a "(subtextual?) gay man." His gender is a nonissue, and as a member of another oppressed group, Anthony is well-suited to participate in the "women's talk" that takes place in Sugarbaker's. In fact, Anthony's closest relationship in the group is with Suzanne, who often uses him as a confidant. In one episode ("The Women of Atlanta"), Anthony explicitly notes that "for some reason, she [Suzanne] thinks of me as her girlfriend." The improbable relationship between Suzanne and Anthony contains no hint of sexual attraction, a situation naturalized not only by general taboos against interracial romance but by the attitudes of both characters, who would clearly consider such a suggestion absurd.

All of the characters have strong ties to one another. Although each of the women has romantic relationships with men within the course of the show and three are mothers, these relationships receive relatively little attention.[30] The communication among the women drives the narrative of the program. Their talk is the vehicle through which multiple perspectives are heard, discussed, and validated. The personalized setting of Sugarbaker's makes such talk possible.

The decidedly feminine setting of *Designing Women* also indicates accommodation to postfeminist attitudes.[31] These are not women trying to make it in a man's world; in that sense, *Designing Women* signals a retreat from the feminist challenge posed by earlier programs such as *The Mary Tyler Moore Show* or *Cagney and Lacey*. On the other hand, by sidestepping the "work versus personal life" issue, *Designing Women* also avoids depicting the misery afflicting women in 1980s professional serial dramas and the utopian visions of family life depicted in postfeminist family sitcoms. Faludi maintains that such female-centered sitcoms as *Designing Women* and *The Golden Girls* (1985–92) were the networks' safer alternative to single, working-woman shows, safer because "the heroines were confined to the home in nonthreatening roles in a strictly all-female world" (1991, p. 159).

Certainly, *Designing Women*'s premise does not confront gender politics in the same fashion as other single-woman shows. Instead, *Designing Women* essentially combines home and work through the melding of personal and professional relationships. Ethel Goodstein suggests that this characteristic is what makes *Designing Women*'s workplace a "postfeminist nirvana," in which the characters have "the best of both worlds, home and work" (1992, p. 177). The sitcom's characters are working women, but the work hardly figures in plotlines and is rarely seen. Ultimately, the work is just an excuse to get the women together and to depict their relationships. In that sense, *Designing Women* is a rare all-female version of a television staple—the workplace sitcom. After the cancellation of *Alice* in 1985, *Designing Women* was the only workplace sitcom dominated by female characters that reached the top twenty rated programs in the 1980s.[32]

With its ambiguous depiction of women in the public (but really private) sphere, *Designing Women* seemingly withdraws from the feminist battle over equality in the workplace, and some critics judge that aspect of the sitcom harshly (e.g., Goodstein, 1992, pp. 176–177).[33] However, rather than labeling *Designing Women* unquestionably postfeminist because it does not confront gender politics in the ways we have come to expect from television, I suggest in this chapter that it be examined on its own terms. Initially, rather than viewing *Designing Women*'s feminized workplace as *only* a withdrawal from issues of gender equity in the workplace, I suggest instead a focus on the subversive potential of its combination of home and work, spheres that patriarchal capitalism traditionally "insists on keeping separate, gendered, and differently valued" (Doty, 1993, p. 58). With *Designing Women*'s unique environment comes the freedom to discuss ideas and define issues solely in women's terms and based on women's experiences. This freedom is the prerequisite of consciousness raising.

"Women's Talk" and Consciousness-Raising in *Designing Women*

In Chapter 2, I explained the functions of consciousness-raising for women involved in second-wave feminism as a way of understanding the feminist resonance of *One Day at a Time*. In *One Day*, consciousness-raising was an implicit ingredient in the premise of the sitcom and in the character of Ann Romano. The heightened self-awareness of women across the country was the legacy of the consciousness-raising practiced within feminist groups and disseminated through feminist literature and women's popular culture. In the most basic sense, the function of consciousness-raising was the realization of the political status of women as an oppressed group and the ways in which sexual politics governed their lives.

In many episodes of *Designing Women*, interaction among characters parallels the essential process of consciousness-raising, disguised as "women's talk." In discussion of various "women's issues," the four women share personal experiences and perspectives, and they often reach conclusions about how those issues reflect cultural assumptions and practices that affect and shape the lives of all women (although, in many cases, "women" means white, middle-class, heterosexual women). In this sense, *Designing Women* makes the personal political in a fashion that is unusual for prime-time. The type of talk practiced by characters in *Designing Women* is likely to be familiar to many female viewers. Their interaction displays many of the characteristics that researchers have identified from their study of women's conversation in natural settings. For example, it takes place in the private sphere (or "women's space"), is based on personal experience and is highly contextualized, often uses narrative, and displays concrete rather than abstract reasoning. Some researchers have argued that the function of such talk for women is ultimately liberating because it provides them with a space, within male-dominated culture, to discuss issues of importance to them and to develop a female-centered perspective on the world that can contradict the perspective preferred by patriarchy.[34] This function of women's talk is remarkably similar to the definition of consciousness-raising offered by Jo Freeman in *The Politics of Women's Liberation* (1975, p. 118):

Women come together in small groups to share personal experiences, problems, and feelings. From this public sharing comes the realization that what was thought to be individual is in fact common; that what was thought to be a personal problem has a social cause and a political solution. . . . Women learn to see how social structures and attitudes have molded them from birth and limited their opportunities. They ascertain the extent to which women have been denigrated in this society and how they have developed prejudices against themselves and other women. They learn to develop self-esteem and to appreciate the value of group solidarity.

However, *Designing Women* is television, after all. Elements of the interaction in the sitcom do not perfectly replicate the identified characteristics of women's talk or those of the consciousness-raising groups of second-wave feminism. For example, the conversation in *Designing Women* does not always create an atmosphere of pure equality among the participants, as was the goal of leaderless consciousness-raising groups in the 1970s (Echols, 1989, pp. 88–89). Even so, what *Designing Women* accomplishes is a representation of female interaction that functions to create a woman-centered analysis of sexual politics, the ultimate goal of consciousness-raising. Emerging, as it does, from seemingly organic conversation among a group of "ordinary" women (i.e., women not clearly positioned as *feminist* representations, as opposed to, for example, *Cagney and Lacey*), this outcome is less threatening than it would be if produced in a different context. In this sense, *Designing Women* displays the rhetorical negotiation typical of television and of postfeminism. However, as I suggest later, such negotiation may be the prerequisite for the sitcom's engagement with sexual politics.

Despite the fact that it is more than ten years removed from the height of second-wave feminist activity and visibility, *Designing Women*'s featuring of feminist discourse is more explicit than that of any sitcom I have yet discussed, with the exception of *Maude*. When *Designing Women* is considered in its context, however, this difference makes sense. By 1986, the awareness of second-wave feminist issues that contextualized *One Day at a Time* had receded, not only in the culture at large but in prime-time television. In postfeminist times, "choice" had replaced sexual politics as an explanation for the problems and possibilities in women's lives. *Designing Women*'s attention to sexual politics, then, is not a sign that television became more radical in the 1980s; the opposite is more likely true. Rather, by 1986, *Designing Women* was forced to provide information and reasoning that would have been implicit for viewers ten years earlier, as it was in *One Day at a Time*.

An episode titled "Julia Drives over the First Amendment," the final episode of the 1988–89 season, exemplifies the pattern of interaction on *Designing Women*. In this episode, a newsstand down the street from Sugarbaker's has begun to display posters advertising the pornographic magazines that it sells. In conversation with Mary Jo and Suzanne one morning, Charlene expresses her discomfort at visiting the newsstand. A bit of the ensuing discussion illustrates the nature of their interaction:

Charlene: Well, you know, when they first put it [the newsstand] up last week, I thought, you know, this is great. It's gonna be so close to us and I can get all my magazines so easily—you know how I like to keep up. You know, I just have this incredible thirst for knowledge. If Madonna or Cybill Shepherd's having a fight with somebody, I'd want to know. But that newsstand just has so many dirty magazines, have you noticed? They've got a whole section.

Mary Jo: Yeah, I noticed that. I was down there yesterday getting some of their design magazines. I got a copy of *Southern Homes* and *Antiques*, and *Carpets and Drapes Monthly*, and then I saw this other copy of something that I had never seen before called *Jugs*, and I thought "Oh, how nice. A new magazine about pottery and porcelain." *Imagine* my surprise.

Charlene: Well, they've put up a great big poster now to advertise one of those magazines. A girl in black rubber underwear wearing a dog collar and chains or something. Well, frankly, I just don't want to have to look at a girl wearing black rubber underwear first thing in the morning, unless of course it *is* Madonna and there's an important news story attached.

Anthony: Oh, that's nothing, Mary Jo. There's even a magazine called *Stump* about women amputees with no clothes on.

Suzanne: Oh, great. Well, I'm telling you, we're never gonna hear the end of this one. Every time Julia enters or leaves this house, she's gonna see that picture and she's gonna be ranting and she's gonna be raving. She's gonna be carrying on like some kind of hyena, and, we're all gonna have to pretend like we care.

This snatch of conversation typifies the dynamics at Sugarbaker's. The women (and sometimes Anthony) share experiences, each of them adding details of their experience with the newsstand. These anecdotes are grounded in their personal experience and feelings about what they have seen, exemplified by Charlene's comment that she just doesn't "want to have to look at a girl wearing black rubber underwear first thing in the morning."

As was the case in feminist consciousness-raising groups, the women interact as peers, and the purpose of their interjections is not to compete or to produce a superior story, but to pool their experiences and acknowledge the contributions of the other participants. For Charlene, Mary Jo, and Suzanne, each contribution is tied to the personality of the speaker. Charlene's is tied to her affection for scandal magazines and Mary Jo's to her professional interests. Typically, Suzanne is little interested in the issue because she perceives that it does not directly affect her, except for the possibility that she will have to endure one of Julia's diatribes.

By building on one another's experience, the women validate one another's perspectives. While Charlene and Mary Jo give what might be considered irrelevant information during their brief narratives, each is able to express her personal views in her own fashion without interruption or commentary from others.[35] Indeed, Mary Jo answers even Suzanne's typically self-centered comment without censure, saying, "Well, you know, Suzanne, Julia feels very deeply about the issue of pornography and if she has a statement about something that she sees, then you can bet that it's going to be rational and intelligent."

Mary Jo's final comment foreshadows Julia's entrance into the narrative. Driving down the street, Julia sees the offensive poster and drives her car over it, causing damage to the newsstand. Discussing the incident later in Sugarbaker's, Julia adds her opinion to the dialogue on pornography:

Julia: You know what really infuriates me? That man at the newsstand kept talking about how that poster is protected by the First Amendment right of free speech. That is an argument that's wearing a little thin with me. I believe in the First Amendment as much as anybody else. But I also know that when our forefathers were fighting and dying at Valley Forge, they were not really doing it to protect a publication called *Hot Tushies.*

Charlene: You know, isn't it amazing how specific those magazines are?

I mean there is something for everybody. There's one out there that's all about feet. I mean, can you believe that? I've never seen anything like it in my life. I mean, if a person liked that they could just get a Kinney's catalogue and have a real good time. I mean, it's like "Girls Who Eat Chicken" or "Girls with Big Ones Who Think That Oswald Acted Alone."

Julia: Charlene! What I was trying to say is, that every sleazy rag in the country hides behind the First Amendment and I am sick and tired of it.

Mary Jo: Well, I hate to say this, Julia, and you know that I hate that poster just as much as you do, but what you're talking about is censorship.

Julia: Do you honestly believe that anyone has a constitutional right to show a poster of a woman being degraded, chained up with a dog collar and whipped? You couldn't show a black man being depicted that way because it would be considered incenditory [sic] speech. So why would we demand any less for women? The First Amendment was designed to protect *political speech* and everybody knows it. Now, we've already wasted enough time on this silliness and I don't want to discuss it any more.

This excerpt demonstrates the change in conversational dynamics that takes place when Julia enters the dialogue. Julia takes the issue out of the private sphere, placing it squarely within the public debate over pornography. Her references to the First Amendment and the Constitution demonstrate her greater public awareness and her view of the issue as one that extends beyond the personal experiences of the individual women. Moreover, Julia adds an element of competition to the conversation through her impassioned refutation of Mary Jo's comment about censorship. Finally, Julia assumes control of the situation with her proclamation that the conversation is over.

Julia's behavior positions her in a different role from that of the other women. On a basic level, this is understandable. Julia is older than the others, and, as the senior partner, she is technically their superior. However, her persona in conversation reflects a more complex function for her character. Julia speaks as the representative of the public sphere within the group. Julia's discourse is more impersonal, reflecting abstract rather than personal reasoning, and she acts more as a lecturer than a conversational peer. Less interested in validating the others' perspectives than airing her own point of view, Julia translates private concerns into public advocacy.

Julia's role as public advocate grows in this episode as she drives over the poster again the next day. She is subsequently imprisoned after the publisher of the magazine that owns the poster sues her for violation of civil rights. Eventually, the publisher assumes that Julia has learned her lesson and drops the charges. However, before Julia is released, the publisher, a woman, comes to the jail to meet with her. Julia takes the opportunity to debate the woman on the pornography issue, having obtained the public face-off she desires:

> This country will let the Nazis speak, and we will let the Ku Klux Klansmen speak, because as despicable as their statements are, they are speaking their mind. But when you publish your magazine, you're not speaking your mind. You'd shut that magazine down tomorrow if it wasn't turning a profit. You know it and I know it. Pornography is not free speech, it's commerce. Otherwise you couldn't zone it out of certain nice areas of the city.

As this speech illustrates, Julia perceives and talks about the issue of pornography in abstract rather than concrete terms, offering an economic analysis that goes beyond the case at hand.

In one sense, Julia's integral involvement in the plot for "Julia Drives over the First Amendment" makes it understandable that she should be the character to take a public stand. However, other episodes demonstrate that Julia plays this role even when she is less personally affected by the issue than another character, or even when the other characters have the opportunity to take a stand, yet wait for Julia to articulate it for them. An episode titled "The Women of Atlanta" illustrates the latter case.

In this episode, the designers have the opportunity to be photographed by a men's magazine (similar to *GQ* or *Esquire*) for a pictorial on "The Women of Atlanta" in which they will be depicted in their jobs as interior decorators. While Charlene and Suzanne are excited by the prospect, Mary Jo and Julia are resistant to the idea, and Mary Jo voices her reservations:

> There's some thing about it that just doesn't sound right. . . . Something about the title, you know, "The Women of Atlanta." It just sounds like. . . . Well, I mean, they usually feature women from the same geographical location, you know, and they photograph them at home or in the office, and they always have some girl named "Karin," who spells her name KAR*I*N, and they show her studying at her local junior college, and she'll have her books spread all around her, except she won't have any clothes on except knee socks and a little red tam! I mean, like that's the way I always study for my exams. Or they'll have some enterprising nymphet named "Chardonnay," who's starting up a catering business, and they'll show her slaving over a hot stove with

nothing but a silk teddy and high heels on. I mean, like doesn't everybody cook dinner that way. Or they'll have just a simple housewife named Lois, who's, you know, laying on the laundry room floor having a real good time while her clothes dry. Not only do they look stupid, but do these women really get any work done?

Mary Jo's objections are a classic example of a personal approach to the issue, an approach based in her past experiences with such pictorials, and the contrast between such public representations of women and her lived experience. Her description does not go beyond a personal objection to analyze the cultural assumptions that lead to such depictions of women. Her reaction serves as a contrast to Julia's later reaction.

When the photographer arrives the next day, Mary Jo and Julia are still uncertain about whether they will participate in the pictorial, but the male photographer flatters them so adroitly that they agree to be photographed. However, during the session, the women find that they are being manipulated. The photographer supplies seductive clothes for them to wear and poses them suggestively. Slowly, the women begin to realize that they are being exploited, expressing their concern to one another in side comments, although they do not confront the photographer directly.

Despite their doubts, Mary Jo, Charlene, and Suzanne complete their portion of the session, allowing the photographer to pose them seductively. However, when Julia's turn comes, and the photographer tells her to assume a provocative pose (he tells her to take a string of pearls between her teeth and suck them), she instantly rebels and proceeds to express the indignation that all of the women feel:

> I want you and your equipment out of here now! If you are looking for somebody to *suck pearls*, then I suggest you try finding yourself an oyster. I am not a woman who does that. As a matter of fact, I don't know any woman who does that. Because it's stupid! And it doesn't have anything more to do with decorating than having cleavage and looking sexy has to do with working in a bank. These are not pictures about the "Women of Atlanta." They're about just the same things they're always about, and it doesn't matter if the clothes are on or off, it's just the same old message. And I don't care how many pictures you've taken of movie stars. When you start snapping photos of serious, successful, businessmen like Donald Trump and Lee Iocacca in unzipped jumpsuits, with wet lips, straddling chairs, then we'll talk!

Again, it is Julia who shifts their experience to the political level. In contrast to Mary Jo's earlier personal analysis, Julia treats the issue in terms of larger cultural norms about the divergent messages surrounding men and women. As "the personal becomes political" in this episode, it follows the general pattern for consciousness-raising in women's groups. The private experiences of the women are translated into a larger realization about the sexual politics surrounding all women.

This process is also evident in "Julia Drives over the First Amendment," as Julia translates the women's discomfort with the newsstand into a statement on the politics of pornography. However, regardless of whose experience triggers discussion of an issue, it is often Julia who will translate that experience into the language of public advocacy. For example, in an episode titled "Stand and Fight," Mary Jo is mugged, triggering discussions about women's powerlessness against assault. Each of the women shares her personal feelings about the issue, but it is Julia who combines their observations to make a general statement about the issue:

That's what the rapists and muggers count on, Charlene. They count on my having too good of taste [to fight back], and your not wanting to hurt anybody, and Suzanne not wanting to roll around on the sidewalk, Mary Jo being so terrified she can't move—they count on *all* of that. It is unbelievable to me that every sixty seconds in this country a woman is sexually assaulted. . . . You know, I think women are just about ready to say "We're mad as hell and we're not going to take it anymore. If you come up to us with a gun or a knife, you'd better be prepared to use it right then and there, because we're not going anywhere with you. And we're not going to be dug up, raped and mutilated, months later on some rural road. We are going to be prepared to stand and fight! With dignity, in the parking lots and the shopping centers, and the driveways of America! But buddy, you better be prepared to do the same, because even at the very least, one of us is gonna be walking funny!"

In yet another episode, "The Candidate," all of the women are outraged by the sexist remarks made by a male candidate for Atlanta's Board of Commissioners, but it is Julia who takes a public stand by running against him.

There are different ways to interpret the function of Julia's role within the group. As the oldest, most secure, most knowledgeable, and most powerful member of the group, Julia speaks in a hierarchical fashion that sometimes resembles lecturing rather than supportive interaction. Because she speaks of issues in a more analytical, abstract fashion, Julia could be interpreted by some viewers as the most "sensible" of the women, concomitantly devaluing the more personal discourse of the others. That Julia is usually the one to make generalizations from their experiences could leave the impression that the other women are unable to make such connections themselves or that Julia's role inhibits them from doing so. Or, conversely, giving the majority of feminist resonance to Julia's character could be seen as a way of isolating her as the most "radical" of the women for those antifeminist viewers who wish to read her character against the grain. This reading would take quite a bit of work, however, given the way that the laughter and applause tracks in *Designing Women* clearly support Julia's opinions.[36]

In my reading of the sitcom, I prefer to emphasize the ways that Julia's role exemplifies the expected function of consciousness-raising. She takes the personal and makes it political, validating the feelings and experiences of the other women by placing them in a larger cultural context: in short, she takes their gender consciousness and attempts to transform it into a form of feminist consciousness. The talk of the other women creates the context for Julia's speeches; although Julia frequently takes the dominant role, the other women's experiences often provide the initiative for her monologues. In this way, they maintain a significant role in the creation of the positions that Julia proclaims.

Taken generally, the content of *Designing Women*, the issues it addresses, and the viewpoints expressed on those issues posit a reality that challenges postfeminist denial of sexual politics. Although Julia's position as the greater authority on many issues prevents true equality in the interaction (a goal of consciousness-raising groups), it is also true that the viewpoints she expresses are not those of the dominant culture. For example, Julia's resistance to First Amendment arguments against the suppression of pornography is based in a woman-centered analysis that rests on the belief that pornography's primary function is the degradation of women, a perspective advanced by radical feminists such as Andrea Dworkin and Catherine MacKinnon (see MacKinnon, 1987). Julia's definition of pornography as commerce reflects a belief that pornography is allowed to exist because of cultural assumptions about women as sexual commodities. Her objections in "The Women of Atlanta" are based in similar notions about consistently portraying women, but not men, in sexual contexts. Finally, her rejection of women's traditional submissiveness in the face of sexual assault in "Stand and Fight" is another example of resistance to patriarchal norms.

Given these realizations, it is possible to see Julia as a character that simply illustrates one possibility in the range of communicative strategies performed by women. For example, in their individual ways, the other characters also reject patriarchal definitions. Mary Jo's speech about the seductive portrayal of women in men's magazines at the beginning of

"The Women of Atlanta," although not explicitly acknowledging the cultural forces that work to make such depictions permissible, rejects the definition of women which these portrayals offer on the basis that they are simply unrealistic and ridiculous in comparison to her experience. Similarly, in "Julia Drives over the First Amendment," Charlene challenges the belief that pornography is undefinable with a typically "feminine" analysis that pits abstract concepts against personal, practical experience:

> You know, I personally can't understand one thing about all this. You know, they can't make any rules for pornography because they can't define what it is. . . . Well then, how come the guy down at the Kit'n Cat Theater knows exactly which movies to show? I mean, it's not like he gets all confused and starts showing *Ghandi*! I mean, he knows what pornography is. And the guy down at the Triple X Bookstore, he knows just what to stock. He knows what pornography is. So if there's anybody out there who can't figure it out, why don't they just talk to those two guys?

Even Suzanne, in a confrontation with the pornographic publisher in this same episode, manages to find a way to counter the publisher's arguments for the validity of her magazine:

> Well, I just think you should know that I have been backstage at the Miss America pageants, and I have seen some of the most beautiful young women in this country wearing nothing but high heels and hot rollers. So, I am not shocked by seeing someone buck naked. . . . But, I was just wondering. If you think it's so peachy keen, honey, how come we don't see you airbrushed and spreadeagled in a centerfold? Just asking.

These examples illustrate that while they couch their arguments differently from Julia's, each of the women enacts resistance to the reasoning that the dominant culture offers. The means by which they do this, through a contrast between their experience and what they are told by the dominant culture, is a testament to the uniqueness and validity of women's personal experience and perspective and mimics a consciousness-raising process. Most situation comedies, because of their unrelenting focus on the individual, rarely acknowledge the role that cultural biases play in the problems faced by their characters. *Designing Women*, in its acknowledgment of cultural responsibility for women's problems, challenges this generic characteristic.

Narrative Structure and Ideology in *Designing Women*

Two additional elements of the structure of *Designing Women* stretch generic constraints of situation comedy and, in the process, offer additional possibilities for subverting hegemonic notions of femininity and feminism. First, *Designing Women* offers multiple opportunities for character identification. While ensemble casts are not unusual for situation comedy, the ensemble cast consisting primarily of women is more distinctive.

For example, in other situation comedies perceived as "feminist," such as *The Mary Tyler Moore Show* or *Murphy Brown*, the lead characters are signaled by the titles of the programs and are positioned for primary identification within the narrative. As a result, viewers are encouraged to see Mary Richards or Murphy Brown as *the* representation of "woman" or "feminist" in these programs. The focus on a single lead character privileges a mode of character reading in which the viewpoint posited by the lead character is the most influential, offering fewer opportunities for the viewer to resist the dominant message of the program. This characteristic is another manifestation of the individualistic philosophy of situation comedy.

In contrast, *Designing Women*, by virtue of its focus on a group of women rather than a single lead character, offers a multiplicity of viewpoints. Each character is a distinct personality, and the perspective offered by each is valued within the program. Even Suzanne, whose egocentric world view is often the source of humor, is loved and supported by the other characters, and when she has problems they are taken seriously.[37] The departure from *Designing Women* in 1991 of Delta Burke, the actress playing Suzanne, was a serious blow to the appeal of the sitcom in the eyes of many fans. Suzanne was referred to by one fan as the "comedic center of the show" (Littwin, 1991, p. 7); indeed, the ironic function of Suzanne's self-centered beauty queen persona was a consistent source of humor in *Designing Women*. Suzanne not only provided comic relief during storylines treating serious issues, she also acted as a foil to facilitate the contrast between individualistic prefeminist interpretations of an issue and the feminist perspectives offered by other characters. For example, in an episode titled "Hard Hats and Lovers," the women discuss the construction workers who have been whistling and yelling at them on their way to work in the morning:

Suzanne: Julia always gets that kind of stuff. I'm telling you, it's that cocky little way she walks.

Julia: Suzanne, it has nothing to do with the way I walk. It has to do with a culture that encourages some men to embarrass women as public sexual objects with the dim hope that somehow it will allow the men in question to cling to their ill-imagined superiority.

Mary Jo: That's right. And furthermore, a woman has a right to walk down the city street any way she wants to without being sexually harassed. And I don't care if she's a nymphomaniac and naked.

Suzanne's offering of the individualistic explanation for sexual harassment (i.e., individual women are responsible because their behavior invites harassment) is the opening for Julia and Mary Jo's refutation. Julia specifically denies that her experience is individual, instead connecting it to the attitudes that are attached to all women. Mary Jo states that sexual harassment of *any* woman is wrong. As the straight woman in the ensemble, Suzanne often facilitates such feminist moments.

Although Julia is most often the character who takes the lead in interpreting the larger meaning of the women's experiences, she is not the focus of every narrative. Different episodes focus on the problems of different characters, offering opportunities for different types of identification. Each of the characters has attractive and sympathetic qualities, and the approach to the world that each represents is not consistently devalued for the benefit of others.[38] In this sense, *Designing Women* encourages rejection of monolithic definitions of femininity or feminism, allowing multiple opportunities for female identification.

A second noteworthy element of the structure of *Designing Women* is the program's frequent use of what I term *open endings*. Situation comedy narrative is traditionally oriented toward resolution and narrative closure within its half-hour format, producing an assurance that all problems have been resolved and leaving the characters and the situation intact. *Designing Women* frequently challenges this generic characteristic with the use of endings that imply that the problem has *not* been completely resolved, or that if the problem has been resolved on an individual level, it still remains on a larger level. In this way, *Designing Women* resists the simplistic views of problem-solving offered by most situation comedy, a genre that consistently implies that all problems can be resolved through individual action in a context of familial support and understanding. *Designing Women* thus offers its comedy with a serious twist that indicates awareness that women's problems are often social rather than individual.

Each of the episodes discussed at length in this chapter features an open ending. In "Julia Drives over the First Amendment," the final scene shows Mary Jo, Charlene, and Suzanne discussing Julia's release from jail as they wait for her to return home. The dropping of the charges against Julia would seem to resolve the problem of the episode. Yet, just as the other characters begin to wonder why Julia has not yet returned, the screech of brakes and the sound of an impact are heard from outside. On her way home, Julia has again run over the pornographic poster at the newsstand. At this point, the credits begin to roll. Though Julia's personal problem was seemingly resolved when the charges were dropped, she refuses to give up. While viewers do not know the effect of Julia's final act of resistance, the act itself reinforces the message that the problem that pornography represents for women remains unresolved.

The open ending in "The Women of Atlanta" takes a different form. After throwing out the photographer, Julia expresses her regret at the narrow view of women that he holds:

> You know, I've been thinking. It's too bad he's [the photographer's] not doing the *real* women of Atlanta. The *real* women of Atlanta are the blue-haired ladies who still play bridge at Merrimac's tearoom. The old bag lady named Ruby who sits out in front of the Capitol building, and Miss Millie Mae Richie who runs a plantation outside of town where her grandfather was once a slave, and the debs who come out every year in their white gowns at the Beaumont Driving Club.

As the episode ends, the scene cuts away from Sugarbaker's and the Atlanta skyline is pictured with the title "The Women of Atlanta" over it. As the song "Beautiful Girls" is heard, black and white photographs of the women whom Julia has just described are shown, each fading into the next. When the pictorial concludes, the credits begin. These photographs obviously are external to the program's narrative; there is no indication that the photographer actually took or used these photographs. However, the pictorial provides a powerful ending for the episode, reinforcing the message that women are unique and interesting in their own right and resisting the photographer's belief that all women are alike as sexual objects.

In "Stand and Fight," the problem that drives the narrative is Mary Jo's reaction to being mugged. She and the other women enroll in a self-defense class, but Mary Jo does poorly in the class and is unable to shake her feelings of fear and powerlessness. Late in the episode, however, a man comes up to Mary Jo in a parking garage. Assuming he is going to attack her, she rebuffs him fiercely, and he is frightened away. Mary Jo later tells Julia that she has overcome her fear, and the problem of the episode is seemingly resolved, at least on a personal level. However, the final scene that immediately follows reinforces the resistance that Mary Jo has just enacted. That scene shows all of the women at their self-defense class alternately yelling an aggressive "No!" at a man representing a would-be attacker. Mary Jo is last in line, and as she screams "No!" with ferocity, the other women cheer and the credits begin.

This final scene was not necessary to resolve the problem of the episode; Mary Jo and Julia's earlier discussion accomplished that. However, as in the other cases, the final scene reinforces the raised consciousness that the larger narrative enacts. The final image of the self-defense class, with its variety of women, demonstrates that the problem of women's feelings of powerlessness goes beyond one woman's experience and requires continued resistance. Moreover, the fact that it is Mary Jo that takes the public action in this episode by standing up to her would-be mugger offers some balance to Julia's consistent public role.

Although every episode of *Designing Women* does not feature an open ending, such endings occur often enough to be noticeable, particularly within episodes that focus on the problems of women in a patriarchal system. Such a strategy is consistent with the viewpoint expressed in various episodes that the problems the women face are not simply individual crises but are related to their position within the culture, a position that requires continued resistance and that cannot be ameliorated by simple narrative closure. This connection between the *personal* problems of the characters and the larger *political* culture is enactment of the consciousness-raising process.

Negotiating Feminism and Postfeminism in *Designing Women*

On a basic level, the kind of interaction between women that *Designing Women* depicts works to reduce the demarcation between the personal and public spheres because "the recognition that the personal is political rejects the disjunction of private and public discourse" (Langellier, 1989, p. 269). Obviously, to suggest that all women's talk is subversive to patriarchy is an overstatement; but such talk "becomes subversive when women begin to attach importance to it and to privilege it over their interactions with men" (Cameron, 1985, p. 157). Such privileging occurs both among the characters on *Designing Women*, who clearly place importance on their interaction, and in the program as a whole, which allows few men to disrupt its woman-centered narrative and which emphasizes women's talk within that narrative. Thus, the focus on personal interaction and women's talk in *Designing Women*, the possibility for identification with multiple characters, and the resistance encouraged by some episodes' open endings contribute to construction of feminist discourse that challenges postfeminist assumptions in popular culture and in other television programming. *Designing Women* undermines easy postfeminist conclusions about what *kind* of women are feminists, about the lack of sisterhood among women, and about the declining relevance of sexual politics.

Although I have labeled the constructions of feminism in earlier chapters as "lifestyle feminism" (*Mary Tyler Moore*), or "therapeutic feminism," (*One Day*), *Designing Women* does not lend itself as easily to a particular label. It is perhaps closest to what Julie D'Acci has called "women's issue" feminism in her study of *Cagney and Lacey*. As she describes it, women's-issue feminism "was associated with particular issues that, although they actually signalled major social problems, . . . were presented as *specific to* women rather than to society as a whole" (1994, p. 155). *Designing Women* does and does not participate in this kind of feminist discourse. The fact that so-called "women's issues" such as sexual harassment, wife abuse, or women's position as sexual objects appear as problems that crop up in an episode, are analyzed, solved on some level, and then disappear, is an indication of the women's-issue approach. This kind of "issue of the week" structure implies that such problems can be solved solely through women's action and that they are anomalies in women's otherwise "normal" lives (D'Acci, 1994, p. 160).

However, particularly when the constraints of sitcom are taken into account, *Designing Women* also goes beyond a strict women's-issue approach. As I suggest in my discussion of some of the content of the characters' interaction, as well as the series's use of open endings, the sitcom introduces ambiguity about the extent to which the problems it addresses are "female concerns" that can be "restricted to historically constructed women" (D'Acci, 1994, p. 167).

"Stand and Fight" is perhaps the most women's-issue oriented episode analyzed in this chapter. Its solution—that women learn to defend themselves against violence—leaves the problem and the solution squarely in the laps of women themselves, disregarding the larger questions of modifying men's behavior or questioning the cultural acceptance of violence against women. However, in the dialogue quoted from "Hard Hats and Lovers" above, Julia and Mary Jo reject the suggestion that women's behavior is relevant to understanding sexual harassment, which they explicitly term a cultural and not an individual problem. In different episodes and on different issues, *Designing Women* vacillates between the individualistic, self-help perspective of much liberal feminism and the identification of sexual politics derived from radical feminism. And, of course, all of the feminist discourse produced in the sitcom is framed by its collection of highly feminine characters and their decidedly feminized setting.

I have chosen, in this chapter, to stress those aspects of *Designing Women* that resist postfeminist attitudes toward women's lives. Yet the sitcom's sometimes explicitly feminist rhetoric is countered in various ways within individual episodes and across the series. For example, in those episodes in which characters express a position stressing the presence of sexual politics in women's lives, there is often a subplot that not only provides additional comedy to balance the seriousness of the political plotline (thus keeping *Designing Women* from overstepping the boundaries of sitcom), but also can be viewed as contradicting the political message offered.[39] Moreover, not all *Designing Women* episodes have plotlines that deal as explicitly with feminist issues as the ones I have analyzed here. Some episodes focus on the ridiculous situations and humorous misunderstandings that fuel most sitcom narratives. *Designing Women*, like all popular television, is contradictory, operating within a complex web of hegemonic and potentially subversive elements that create a tension between discourses of postfeminism and feminism.

At the most visible level, the potential for reification of hegemonic notions of femininity in *Designing Women* is evident in the lead characters' consistent enactment of traditional white, middle-class femininity. Andrea Press has argued that such "commercial femininity" is a hallmark of postfeminist television, in which women are given the freedom to work but not the freedom to disregard conventional standards for physical attractiveness (1991, p. 39; see also Wolf, 1992). All four characters in *Designing Women* are conventionally attractive, their appearances enhanced by cosmetics, hairstyling, and fashionable clothing, and it is clear that they are invested in their visual appeal. One small but interesting exception is the significant weight gain experienced by Suzanne Sugarbaker in the third and fourth seasons of the show. The fact that the characters, and Suzanne herself, do not alter their evaluations of Suzanne as an attractive, glamorous woman presents some resistance to the "tyranny of slenderness" (Bartky, 1990, p. 73) that is part of hegemonic notions of femininity.[40] However, by generally performing their status as objects of heterosexual appeal, the characters of *Designing Women* do little to challenge the belief that "femininity as spectacle is something in which virtually every woman is required to participate" (p. 73).[41]

The visual femininity that the characters enact is supported by the "appropriately" feminine nature of their occupation and their workplace. Interior designing, its concern with the aesthetics of private places, and its general unaffordability except by those with large incomes, as well as the "homey" nature of the Sugarbaker offices, contribute to the reification of hegemonic notions of white, middle-class womanhood that place even working women in a privatized environment. Even the title of the program, "*Designing Women*," while obviously connected to the profession of the characters, contains a double meaning with its connection to the conventional stereotype of women who have "designs" on men.[42]

Finally, although the show's narrative does not focus on this aspect of their lives very often, all of the women except for Suzanne are, or become, mothers during the series. Unlike postfeminist family television, *Designing Women* does not focus on maternal concerns very often, but the majority of its characters have fulfilled the postfeminist biological imperative. And, with rare exceptions, the sexual politics highlighted in various episodes steer clear of interrogating family politics specifically.[43]

Given these elements, it is clear that *Designing Women* challenges some postfeminist assumptions and not others. Moreover, in the last two years of *Designing Women* (1991–93), the replacement of Suzanne and Charlene by new characters altered the dynamics between the women and lessened the appeal and feminist potential of the sitcom. Although *Designing Women*'s producer, Linda Bloodworth-Thomason, claimed that the replacements, Alison Sugarbaker (Suzanne and Julia's cousin from New York) and Carlene Dobber (recently divorced sister of Charlene), were designed to fit easily into the slots vacated by Suzanne and Charlene (i.e., Alison is willful and self-centered, Carlene is naive and ingenuous), the new characters were different enough to alter the dynamics of the sitcom (Harris, 1991).

For example, Suzanne was not necessarily opposed to the feminist politics of the other characters; she simply viewed them as irrelevant to her life. Alison, in contrast, is a competitive businesswoman with a conservative ideology that is decidedly opposed to the liberal feminist politics of Julia and Mary Jo, and she serves, in most episodes, as a caricature of conservative Republican beliefs. Suzanne was egocentric and oblivious of politics, but she was not mean-spirited. The sarcasm directed at her by other characters, and her appeal for the audience, came from the humor generated by her prefeminist disdain for sexual politics and her perception that being beautiful and wealthy was all the protection a woman needed.

Alison's character is much more definitively postfeminist; she firmly believes in her own right to compete and succeed in the public sphere but does not see solidarity with other women or feminist activism as necessary factors in that success. Indeed, Alison makes repeated references to the idea that feminists whine too much, that, as she says to Julia and Mary Jo in a 1991 episode, what dissatisfied women "really need are dates," and that women just need to work harder if they wanted to succeed. Generally, Alison's character is much harsher, more judgmental, and more ideological than Suzanne's. In turn, Julia and Mary Jo's reactions to her are genuinely combative in a way they had not been with Suzanne. This dynamic is perhaps clearest in "The Strange Case of Clarence and Anita," the 1992 episode devoted to the women's reactions to the Thomas/Hill hearings on sexual harassment, in which Alison wears a t-shirt that reads "She Lied," while Mary Jo wears a t-shirt that reads "He Did It."

In the sitcom's treatment of the hearings, Alison is the mouthpiece for the perspective that Hill's charges were a feminist plot against Thomas and that sexual harassment is a feminist chimera. In a scene at the end of the episode in which Alison is being interviewed by a local television station for a story on reaction to the hearings, she says:

I think Miss Hill lied. Anyway, what if he did throw a few *bon mot* her way? I mean, I think Miss Hill herself is attractive, but the way some of these feminists look, they should be grateful for any kind of attention they get. I'm sorry, but we won! If you don't like it, you can just go and have yourselves a big old brassiere bonfire.

Mary Jo's response to this statement is to put the hearings into a context emphasizing sexual harassment's place in continuing discrimination against women:

All we want is to be treated with equality and respect. Is that asking too much? I'm sorry, I don't mean to be strident and overbearing, but, you know, nice just doesn't cut it anymore. I'm mad because we're fifty-one percent of the population and only two percent of the United States Senate. . . . I'm mad because in a Seminole, Oklahoma, police station, there's a poster of a naked woman that says "women make bad cops." I'm mad because in spite of the fact that we scrub America's floors, wash the dishes, have all the babies, and commit very little of the crime, still we only make fifty-eight cents on the dollar. I don't know about the rest of you women out there, but I don't give a damn anymore if people think that I'm a feminist or a fruitcake.

As is the case with most prime-time television, the term "feminism" is rarely heard on *Designing Women*, despite the clear sympathies of Mary Jo and Julia. This speech is noteworthy for its use of the term and for its obvious sense of frustration and refusal of a postfeminist attitude.[44]

In addition to the harsher note introduced by Alison, the new character of Carlene also altered the dynamic between the women. Although she was designed to represent the same kind of gentle innocence earlier represented by Charlene, Carlene is much more provincial than her sister; she is not very bright and seems not to have a mind of her own. Unlike Charlene, who added useful experiences and insight to the interaction at Sugarbaker's (and frequently participated in the creation of feminist perspectives), Carlene functions as a sort of pet to the other women, someone to be nurtured and guided, but she is not their peer. Indeed, the "shaping" of Carlene became a sort of contest in which Alison competed with Julia and Mary Jo. Alison, for instance, paid for Carlene to attend college, and expected allegiance in return.

Ultimately, the atmosphere at Sugarbaker's became much less supportive after the departure of Suzanne and Charlene. An element that had made the show appealing, the portrayal of very different women engaged in supportive interaction that often produced a woman-centered perspective on the world, was simply missing when the sitcom became a battle between liberal and conservative politics. Although the narrative generally supported Mary Jo and Julia's feminist positions,[45] it was less satisfying to watch because there was much less genuine affection among the four women characters than had been present in the sitcom's original incarnation. While Suzanne had provided gentle irony that offered comic relief, Alison was an almost thoroughly negative character that had little appeal. The producers tried for one last solution when they replaced Alison with another new character, B. J. Poteet, in the 1992–93 season, but the ratings were slipping steadily. The sitcom was moved from "women's night" to a much less favorable Friday evening time slot, and it was canceled in the spring of 1993.

Even in its first four seasons, when *Designing Women* arguably was at its best, it was inconsistent. Despite its explicitly verbalized feminist positions and its unusual portrait of female solidarity, the sitcom was a contradictory mixture of feminist and postfeminist elements. However, for viewers like myself, starved for programming about adult women who often discussed issues meaningful for women, *Designing Women* was enjoyable, often stimulating, and sometimes genuinely moving. In past work on *Designing Women*, I called the sitcom "empowering" for women because of its woman-centered perspective on the world that challenged dominant perspectives (Dow, 1992b). These days, I am inclined to soften that conclusion because, as I explained in the Introduction, I believe that critics too easily overlook the disjunction between politicized readings of popular discourse and the material and political realities in which we live.

Yet, despite its limitations, I believe that *Designing Women* deserves acknowledgment for the (admittedly negotiated) challenge that it posed to postfeminist assumptions. The 1980s return to "family values" in conservative rhetoric and prime-time sitcoms, and the mixed messages about women and professional success embedded in prime-time serials make recognition of the uniqueness of programming like *Designing Women* important. At the very least, *Designing Women* was a sitcom that, at times, made the term "postfeminism" appear rightly absurd. It also made the contradictions in women's lives amusing at the same time that it argued that these contradictions were genuinely painful for us. That is no small feat. I have never believed the old canard that feminists have no sense of humor; I do believe that we are rarely *represented* as having senses of humor. *Designing Women* offered representations of funny women; not just funny because they deprecated themselves or because they functioned as comic objects, but women funny on behalf of feminism.[46]

In the next chapter I discuss *Murphy Brown*, another posfeminist era sitcom, and one that seems to me to be a reversal of these positive aspects of *Designing Women*. That the two shows were broadcast on the same network on the same night of the week for a number of years is another example of television's ability to maintain a profitable tension between progress and perseveration, both within and across programming.

Notes

1. For example, a *Time* cover story in 1989 that asks the question "is there a future for feminism?" claims that women's dislike for the feminist label indicates that feminism "is a victim of its own resounding achievements. Its triumphs—in getting women into the workplace, in elevating their status in society and in shattering the 'feminine mystique' that defined female success only in terms of being a wife and a mother—have rendered it obsolete, at least in its original form and rhetoric" (Wallis, 1989, p. 82).

2. For examples of second-wave feminist arguments about these issues, see the following essays, all in *Radical Feminism* (Koedt, Levine, and Rapone, 1973): Judy Syfers, "Why I Want a Wife"; Jo Freeman, "The Building of the Gilded Cage"; Betsy Warrior, "Housework: Slavery or Labor of Love"; Sheila Cronan, "Marriage"; and WBAI Consciousness-Raising Group, "Men and Violence." Also see Pat Mainardi, "The Politics of Housework," and Beverly Jones, "The Dynamics of Marriage and Motherhood," in *Sisterhood Is Powerful: An Anthology of Writings from the Women's Liberation Movement* (Morgan, 1970).

3. Ruth Sidel's book, *On Her Own: Growing Up in the Shadow of the American Dream* (1990), based on interviews with more than 150 young women in the late 1980s, is an insightful description and analysis of postfeminist attitudes toward success, family, and feminism, and reveals themes very similar to those Bolotin describes.

4. Stacey (1983) actually terms the trend she is discussing as "the new conservative feminism" rather than "postfeminism." She wishes to distinguish writings such as Friedan's from antifeminism but feels the term postfeminism is too broad (see p. 579, fn. 3). With hindsight that Stacey did not have when she wrote in 1983, I believe that the profamily feminism she describes became a key part of postfeminism in the 1980s. Moreover, based on her later work with Deborah Rosenfelt (1987), I think she might agree.

5. Brenner's (1993) discussion of the changes in NOW is illustrative of this process. She notes that despite swells in membership during important national feminist battles (such as the ERA and the *Webster* Supreme Court decision), "NOW's activist base remains very small relative to the total membership. Members can be mobilized for single events or actions around highly visible issues, such as the massive demonstrations for abortion rights held between 1989 and 1992. Otherwise, the relationship between members and organizations is similar

to that of traditional interest groups—most members pay dues in order to be represented in Washington" (p. 122).

6. The 1989 *Time* article on postfeminism also asserts that there is a high level of support for abortion rights among young postfeminists. Indeed, the tremendous turnout for pro-choice demonstrations in the wake of the *Webster* decision supports such a claim (see Davis, 1991, pp. 465–467).

7. Many of the articles I have used in this discussion attempt to give credibility to their conclusions by citing statistics, like those indicating the small number of women who label themselves "feminist" and the large number of women who believe that balancing home and work is their biggest challenge. However, statistics have their own problems as a form of evidence. For a woman to reject the feminist label is not the same as rejecting belief in the need for equal rights and equal treatment for women. Moreover, these statistics do not indicate that women, in general, blame feminism for their problems. The meaning of statistics is always circumscribed by what questions are asked and how they are asked.

My everyday experience, with white, middle-class women in their thirties and forties who are my friends and colleagues, and with large numbers of "twentysomething" women in the classes I teach, makes claims about the pervasiveness of postfeminist attitudes, particularly those related to the romanticization of family life and the rejection of sexual politics, intuitively meaningful to me. At the same time, however, it is difficult to know how much of these women's subjectivity (and my own) is shaped by experience with media accounts of postfeminism. Moreover, because my world of everyday experience is largely white and middle class, I also know that generalizations that do not acknowledge the boundaries of race and class are dangerous. For example, in statistical surveys that account for race difference, support for feminist achievements and for the feminist label is higher among women of color than among white women (Kantrowitz, 1986, p. 51).

8. For analysis of the development of these magazines and their appropriation of some aspects of feminism, see McCracken, 1993, chapter 7.

9. For more detailed analyses of the themes and functions of prime-time soaps, including those that argue that these programs have powerful resonance for women, see Ang, 1985, 1990; Feuer, 1984; Geraghty, 1991; Joyrich, 1992.

10. As an experienced viewer of *Dynasty, Dallas*, and *Knots Landing*, I am compelled to offer a couple of qualifications to the generalizations about lack of female bonding that I make here. In comparison to other prime-time soaps, *Knots Landing* offers some consistent and quite positive depictions of the importance of female friendship, and includes female characters who, at various times, have taken strong stands on women's desire for equality and autonomy. These messages are not uncontradicted, but they are noteworthy, nonetheless.

11. This theme sometimes took the form of a storyline involving unwanted pregnancy. Feminist rhetoric about women's right to control their reproductive choices surfaced in episodes from dramas such as *Cagney and Lacey, Spenser for Hire*, and *St. Elsewhere*, but, as Celeste Condit (1990) has argued, it was "overlaid with a set of evaluations that described abortion as an action to be avoided wherever possible." Generally, abortion as portrayed in prime-time television "was a woman's choice but morally undesirable, especially as a practice for women in financially secure traditional marriages" (p. 139).

12. The women of professional serial dramas have some company in 1980s films focusing on women. A number of popular movies focused on successful

professional women with less than satisfying personal lives. In *Baby Boom* (1987), a successful New York City business woman inherits a child and is quickly convinced that she cannot have it all. She gives up the fast track to move to the country, sell gourmet baby food, and marry a vet. In *Crossing Delancey* (1988), an ambitious young woman in New York rebuffs the need for matchmaking by her Jewish grandmother but eventually falls for the traditional, stable pickle vendor her grandmother has chosen. In *Broadcast News* (1987), an ambitious, driven network news producer cannot manage a relationship, presumably because of her inability to separate from her work. While these movies certainly participate in postfeminist questioning of women's choices, they do not belong in the same "backlash" category as *Fatal Attraction* (1987). However, Faludi's discussion of the trends in 1980s filmmaking, including the increasing marginalization of female characters, is generally discouraging. For another perspective on "postfeminist" films, see Modleski, 1991.

13. To be fair, I should also note that, on *Hill Street Blues*, as on most cop shows, there is a recurring and often-voiced theme that the life of a police officer is detrimental to personal relationships, for both women *and* men.

14. Single career women do not fare as well. In *thirtysomething*, for example, the single female characters (Melissa, Ellyn, and Susannah, the latter two of whom were married by the time the drama left prime-time) were generally unsympathetically portrayed as bitchy, neurotic, and/or frustrated women who did not know what they wanted and had very difficult emotional lives. They were all, however, quite competent at their work.

15. Interestingly, Press and Strathman argue that "prefeminist" television included far more female bonding (e.g., Lucy and Ethel in *I Love Lucy*; Alice and Trixie in *The Honeymooners*) than feminist or postfeminist television does.

16. For another textually based analysis of the conservatism of *thirtysomething*'s treatment of women and the family, see Loeb, 1990. More recently, Margaret Heide (1995) has combined textual analysis and interviews with female viewers to provide a rich analysis of the problems and possibilities of *thirtysomething*'s vision of women's lives.

17. My decision not to include a case study of *Roseanne* in this book should not be read as a dismissal of the sitcom's feminist potential. As is the case with *Cagney and Lacey*, there has been good work done on *Roseanne* by feminist scholars (e.g., Lee, 1992; Rowe, 1995), and I decided, in this book, to concentrate on programming that has received less attention.

18. As a role reversal sitcom in which the home is run by a man and the woman is the breadwinner, *Who's the Boss?* obviously is influenced by feminism. The feminist politics of this sitcom are suspect, however. For example, the show's emphasis on the hypermasculinity of Tony, a muscled former baseball player, is an obvious attempt to refute implications of homosexuality. Moreover, the frequently reasserted incompetence of Angela in domestic matters also indicates stereotyping; that is, as a driven career woman, Angela has no domestic skills. Finally, the fact that Angela and Tony fall in love over the course of the series and are eventually married, thereby forming an "official" family, pushes it further toward postfeminism.

19. Popular media reaction to *Designing Women* will be discussed below. For discussion of popular media reaction to *Cagney and Lacey*'s feminist discourse, see D'Acci, 1994. *Kate and Allie* was noted for its feminist implications in *Ms.* (Horowitz, 1984) and for its realism in *Vogue* (Cantwell, 1985; Schine, 1984), and was

praised by feminists Barbara Ehrenreich and Jane O'Reilly in *TV Guide* (1984). For scholarly analyses of *Kate and Allie*'s feminist import, see Deming, 1992, and Rabinovitz, 1989.

20. Indeed, Doty (1993) includes both *Kate and Allie* and *Designing Women* as sitcoms with the potential for lesbian or queer readings. As he explains it, such shows centered on women "encourage, and in many ways position, audiences to read and enjoy queerly, whether they would call it this or not. Specifically, they are positioned to take lesbian or queer pleasures in the development of women's realtionships within situation comedy narratives" (p. 44).

21. The number of journal articles and book chapters devoted to analysis of the feminist dimensions of *Cagney and Lacey* is startling. See, for example, Alcock and Robson, 1990; Ang, 1990; Clark, 1990; D'Acci, 1987, D'Acci, 1992; Fiske, 1987b; Gamman, 1988, 1991; Mayerle, 1987 and White, 1987.

22. Other female-centered dramas of the 1980s included *Moonlighting* (1985–89), *Scarecrow and Mrs. King* (1983–87), and *Remington Steele* (1982–87), but each compromised its feminist possibilities in various ways and none was as progressive as *Cagney and Lacey*. See D'Acci's (1994, pp. 143–145) discussion of *Remington Steele*, Faludi's (1991, pp. 144, 157) discussion of *Moonlighting*, and Dowell's (1985, p. 48) discussion of *Scarecrow and Mrs. King*.

23. *Designing Women* was put on hiatus midway through its first season, and was in danger of being canceled. The outpouring of letters from viewers supporting the return of the show brought it back to prime-time. The drive to keep *Designing Women* on the air was led by Viewers for Quality Television, the same media interest group that was formed in 1984 during the successful effort to put *Cagney and Lacey* back on the air after it faced a similar situation. In fact, the response for *Designing Women* (some 50,000 letters) was substantially larger than the response for *Cagney and Lacey*. (See Bernstein, 1987, and Yorkshire, 1987.)

24. *Designing Women* did not become a permanent part of "women's night" until the end of its first season. The sitcom was scheduled on Mondays for the first two months of its run (September to November 1986) but was then moved around the schedule to various slots for the next three months until it came to rest on Monday nights in March of 1987. This haphazard scheduling no doubt contributed to the initially low ratings of the series, leading to its near cancellation midway through the first season.

Cagney and Lacey also had scheduling problems. After its comeback from cancellation in the spring of 1984, it was shown on Monday evenings until December 1987. It was then moved to another night and returned to Monday nights for only two months in 1988 before leaving prime-time in August of that year.

25. In the fall of 1990, Sharon Gless, one of the stars of *Cagney and Lacey*, returned to that show's Monday evening slot in *The Trials of Rosie O'Neill* (1990–91), a legal drama about a divorced female public defender in Los Angeles. *The Trials of Rosie O'Neill* was short-lived, but it certainly fit within the CBS Monday night tradition of progressive programming targeted at working women.

26. The creator and co-producer of *Designing Women* is Linda Bloodworth-Thomason. Her co-producer is her husband, Harry Thomason.

27. For examples of press coverage stressing the strong relationships on the set of *Designing Women*, see Aitken, 1986; Bernstein, 1987; Goodwin, 1987; Yorkshire, 1987.

28. Throughout its lifetime, *Designing Women* had a history of addressing controversial issues, particularly those that affect women, including episodes dealing with breast cancer ("Old Spouses Never Die"), AIDS ("Killing All the Right

People"), interracial relationships ("There's Some Black People Coming to Dinner"), sexism in religion ("How Great Thou Art"), women's body images ("Big Haas and Little Falsie" and "They Shoot Fat Women, Don't They?"), exploitation of women as laborers ("Curtains"), and sexual harassment of women ("Bachelor Suite").

29. For reasons that I make more explicit later in this chapter, my analysis here focuses on the first four seasons of *Designing Women*, when its feminist rhetoric was most visible. Changes in the show in later seasons, most notably the loss of two of the original characters and the addition of new ones, negatively altered the dynamics of *Designing Women*.

30. As Doty put it, "*Designing Women* has been rather offhand about introducing, and then marginalizing or eliminating, the men who date or marry its women characters," making it clear that "the narrative fact of straight romance and marriage does not necessarily heterosexualize lesbian sitcoms any more than being married makes actual lesbians straight" (1993, p. 57).

31. For a thorough analysis of the feminized setting of *Designing Women* as an ideological frame for the sitcom, see Goodstein, 1992. Goodstein's analysis is insightful, but I cannot totally agree with her conclusions about the conservatism of *Designing Women* because they almost completely ignore the narrative of the sitcom—the plots, dialogue, interaction, and so on—in favor of visual analysis of architecture and setting. Her analysis does, however, add depth to the recognition that *Designing Women* is a contradictory text, an issue I discuss at some length in the conclusion to this chapter.

32. Even in *Alice*, the waitresses worked under the watchful eye of their symbolic patriarch and the owner of the diner, Mel. The paradigmatic workplace sitcom for the 1980s was *Cheers* (1982–93), which was set in a bar and featured two female characters, both waitresses. One of these characters eventually left the show and was replaced by a woman manager, who was very ambitious but incompetent in both work and personal relations.

33. Goodstein (1992, p. 177) also asserts that *Designing Women* eschews "radically feminist discourse," a claim with which I disagree in this analysis. However, it is difficult to engage Goodstein directly because she never defines what she means by "radically feminist discourse."

34. For discussion of the characteristics of "women's talk" as well as its political function, see Hall and Langellier, 1987; Jones, 1980; Kramarae, 1981; Langellier, 1989; Presnell, 1989; Spender, 1985. The explanations of masculine and feminine discourse that these researchers offer are based largely in research on white, middle-class behavior. While some have argued that similar speech patterns can be found in the discourse of all oppressed groups, which would include racial/ethnic and class subcultures as well as white, middle-class women, others have argued that communicative strategies are far more specific (see, e.g., Cameron, 1985; Kramarae and Jenkins, 1987). Some research reveals that the general characteristics of women's talk I describe here also apply to the discourse of African-American girls and women (see Maltz and Borker, 1982; Treichler and Kramarae, 1983), but not all of the research I cite in this chapter accounts for racial differences. Although the women's talk I discuss in *Designing Women* is produced by white, middle-class women and thus is appropriate for juxtaposition with the research on women's communication that I use, application across subcultures should not be assumed.

35. This characteristic is in contrast to empirical research studies of women's talk, in which nondisruptive overlaps and interruptions are common (see Kal-

čik, 1986). The difference reveals the influence of the constraints of the television medium and makes clear *Designing Women*'s function as a *representation* of women's talk.

36. Interestingly, Dixie Carter, the actress who played Julia Sugarbaker, gave some support to interpretations of Julia as an "over the top" feminist. Carter claimed in interviews that she was not nearly as radical in her opinions as the character she played. For example, in a *Ladies Home Journal* article, Carter claims that, in opposition to Julia, she is not politically liberal and "not a feminist in the current sense of the word. There's no question in my mind that I'm different from men, and frankly, I *enjoy* feeling every bit like a female" (Rovin, 1990, p. 68).

37. This is particularly evident in an episode from the 1989–90 season, "They Shoot Fat Women, Don't They?" in which Suzanne must deal with reactions to her substantial weight gain at her high school reunion.

38. Although Suzanne would seem to be the least sympathetically portrayed character in *Designing Women*, the other women are not always dismissive of Suzanne's seemingly trivial concerns and obsession with appearances. For example, in "One Sees, the Other Doesn't," Suzanne is doubtful about the possibilities of dating a blind man whom she genuinely likes. Discussing this problem, the other women realize that Suzanne's reluctance is based not on prejudice against the fact that the man is blind, but on her own insecurity. Because Suzanne believes that her primary asset is her physical beauty, she is afraid that the man cannot care for her if he cannot see her. The other women support Suzanne and convince her that she has appeal for others that goes beyond her appearance.

39. In an analysis of "The Strange Case of Clarence and Anita," Jeremy Butler makes this argument. He notes that although Julia and Mary Jo are adamant in their belief in Hill's story, and although the episode's applause track supports their position, their feminist discourse is undermined by a subplot. In this subplot, Julia and Mary Jo are appearing in a local theater production of *Whatever Happened to Baby Jane?* In the final scenes of the episode, they are dressed to imitate Joan Crawford and Bette Davis, stars of the 1962 film. Describing a final diatribe in defense of her feminist position that Mary Jo addresses to a local news camera, Butler notes that "her eyes are bulging and the Bette Davis make-up looks hideous, undercutting any plea for equality or respect" (1994, p. 330). Butler concludes that "by implicitly criticizing Mary Jo's feminist position through her bizarre appearance and extreme performance style, . . . the episode contradicts its supposedly feminist discourse. It fissures that discourse and allows for a multiplicity of meanings, a variety of decoding positions" (1994, p. 331).

40. As I mentioned above, an episode of *Designing Women* focuses on how Suzanne deals with her significant weight gain in the context of her high school reunion. The other characters are supportive in their affirmation that physical attractiveness in women is overvalued, and the ending of the episode features a moving speech by Suzanne to her former classmates who have reacted insensitively and elected her "The Person Most Changed." Interestingly, such textual evidence within *Designing Women* indicating resistance to hegemonic notions of femininity was also supported by extratextual statements made by those involved in the program. Although questions were raised in the media, the *Designing Women* producers consistently maintained their position that the weight gain of Delta Burke (the actress portraying Suzanne) did not affect her importance to or status within the program (see, for example, "Odd Woman Out," 1991).

41. *Designing Women* addresses lesbianism in an episode in which Suzanne discovers that a friend of hers is lesbian. Suzanne, in keeping with her self-centered

character, wrongly assumes that the woman is interested sexually in her, leading to amusing situations. The episode concludes with frank discussion between the two through which Suzanne understands that her friend's sexual identity does not have to interfere with their friendship. I mention this episode here, however, because one of its most interesting aspects is that the lesbian character, a television newscaster, participates in "femininity as spectacle" as enthusiastically as Suzanne does; in fact, one of the interests over which they bond is their love for shopping and makeup.

42. Jeremy Butler addresses this in his analysis of *Designing Women*, in which he notes that the title of the sitcom carries a connotation that "a 'designing woman' is one with designs—designs that are presumably evil and presumably victimize an unsuspecting man. A designing woman is tantamount to a scheming, conniving, plotting woman" (1993, p. 17).

43. One exception is an episode titled "The Rowdy Girls," in which Charlene discovers that her cousin, Mavis, is a battered wife. This is a contradictory episode. Although Mary Jo cites the statistics on wife abuse in a manner that implies the vastness of the problem ("Something like every fifteen seconds a woman is beaten up in her own home. . . . Just since we started having this conversation . . . a dozen women have been beaten up or sexually abused by quote 'a loved one' "), Julia stands firm in her conviction that women should just leave men that beat them, regardless of their economic circumstances. However, a later speech by Mavis herself outlines some of the complexity surrounding women's economic dependence that Julia ignores:

> I'm thirty-five years old. I have a beautiful home, a successful husband, and a billfold full of credit cards, none of which have my name on them. So I give all that up, knowing that I don't even have a hundred dollars to call my own. I take myself, my two years of college, my three kids, and little Mavis the fourth here [she is pregnant], and step out into what?

The conclusion to this episode is emotionally powerful; the women give Mavis the money that enables her to leave her husband, and viewers are left believing that Mavis has solved her problem with their encouragement and support. The most positive message here is one about female solidarity; that is, even though the women cannot identify with Mavis, they support her and do not judge her. However, as an explanation of the larger sexual politics involved in domestic violence, "The Rowdy Girls" is less satisfactory. The episode focuses on Mavis's decision-making, facilitated by resources and support to which few women have access. Obviously, it can still be interpreted as empowering for women, but it is a limited and individualistic view of the problem in comparison to some other episodes of *Designing Women*.

44. Interestingly, this episode also features an open ending, in which scenes from the Thomas/Hill hearings are briefly seen behind the credits. In the first scene, Senator Arlen Specter states that "none of us wants to discourage women from coming forward with charges of sexual harassment." With seemingly deliberate irony, the scenes that follow feature a male participant in the hearings negatively characterizing Anita Hill: Arlen Specter accusing Hill of perjury, John Danforth accusing her of erotomania, and John Doggett accusing her of unrequited love. The next to the last scene features the swearing-in ceremony of Clarence Thomas and President George Bush's remark that America is founded on the idea that "all *men* are created equal" (my emphasis). The final scene is a

freeze frame of Anita Hill as she was testifying before the Judiciary Committee. It is the only shot in which there is no sound.

45. The feminist rhetoric that was featured in *Designing Women* episodes after the fall of 1991 was less likely to emerge in conversation among the four female characters than as an isolated statement by Mary Jo or Julia. For example, in a 1991 episode, "Real, Scary Men," Sugarbakers is pursuing a contract to decorate a men's lodge used by members of the "men's movement" popularized by Robert Bly. After repeatedly being treated as interlopers by the men at the lodge, and listening to the men's tales of having lost touch with their feelings, Mary Jo exclaims: "Men's liberation—what a concept. Oh, we're [men are] just so tired of making all the money and getting all the great jobs, and getting to be president. And never having to stand in line to go to the restroom. Boo, hoo." Moments later, Julia weighs in by noting that if the men "really want to feel like crying," they should pretend they are "one of those women who holds down a job, raises a family on the side, watches her legal rights erode year after year, and is still being told that women's liberation went too far. That ought to make you feel like crying." These statements are powerful refutation of postfeminist notions about the "success" of feminism, but they are isolated diatribes rather than the product of group interaction, as was usually the case in earlier episodes.

46. The label "feminine discourse," defined by critics such as Mary Ellen Brown and Jackie Byars, is a useful way to talk about the particular appeal of *Designing Women* that I am trying to describe here. Brown and Byars, in separate essays, attempt to explain television discourse that may have special resonance for female viewers, even when placed within a hegemonic framework. Such a perspective contains awareness that *all* commercial television reflects hegemonic influence, but also emphasizes the need to recognize "alternative discourses at work" (Byars, 1987, p. 296). Feminine discourse, one such alternative, is defined by Brown as

> a way of talking and acting among feminine subjects (usually women) in which they acknowledge their position of subordination within a patriarchal society. . . . Often feminine discourse . . . is parodic: that is, it makes fun of dominant practices and discursive notions. By playing in this way with the conventions of the dominant discourse, feminine discourse constitutes itself as "other" to it, and displays a potential resistance. (1990a, p. 190)

While such discourse may not appear explicitly feminist, in popular conceptions of the term, it works to question hegemony and to assert the power of women to create their own understanding of a world that is often hostile to their interests. Thus, the term "feminine discourse" can "acknowledge the way in which women sometimes use television, despite its problems for women" (Brown, 1990b, p. 205). *Designing Women*, I think, takes feminine discourse beyond what Brown envisions here; that is, it is more explicitly feminist and critical of patriarchy than what Brown describes. Indeed, I have some reluctance to believe that simply acknowledging women's subordination is tantamount to resisting it. However, the characters on *Designing Women* participate in the kind of parody that Brown describes *and go beyond it*, in many cases, in their specific verbalization or enactment of resistance to patriarchal norms.

Chapter 4
Murphy Brown:
Postfeminism Personified

For four years (1988–92), *Designing Women* shared "women's night" on CBS with *Murphy Brown*. Because I viewed them in tandem, I have often made sense of the two sitcoms in terms of their similarities and their contrasts with each other. For example, both were products of the growing minority of powerful female producer/writers in the 1980s; *Designing Women* was produced by Linda Bloodworth-Thomason and her husband, Harry Thomason. *Murphy Brown* was the product of the team of Diane English and her husband, Joel Shukovsky. The sheer novelty of the existence of female producers resulted in the lion's share of publicity being directed at the female members of these teams; moreover, because of their integral involvement with the actual writing of the shows, English and Bloodworth-Thomason always were featured as more directly involved with the creative aspects of the sitcoms. In short, *Murphy Brown* and *Designing Women* were frequently talked about as examples of programming written by women, about women, and for women.

Newsweek's 1989 cover story on the new "womanpower" in television, entitled "Networking Women," attributes the wave of new woman-centered programming to two factors: the heightened pursuit of the female audience for prime-time (in the wake of male viewers' defection to cable) and the presence of female talent behind the scenes (Waters and Huck, 1989, pp. 48–49). Relying on what Marjorie Ferguson (1990) has called the "feminist fallacy," the notion that media representations of women will improve as women rise in media industries, the article argues that the more powerful women on screen are "being cast in the formidable image of their behind-camera female creators" and that "only the sexual integration of TV's creative community could have blessed us with a 'Murphy Brown' " (Waters and Huck, 1989, pp. 49, 52).

"Networking Women" is a rather typical story in the "let's celebrate women's progress" media genre; it exaggerates the import of a few success stories, thereby implying that women's problems have all but disappeared. Its claim that female producers "in the post-Reagan, post-feminist '90s" are using their programming to tell women that "it's okay to work," "it's okay to be alone," "it's okay to mess up," and "it's okay to mouth off" is supported, primarily, by examples from *Roseanne* and *Murphy Brown*, hardly typical television women (Waters and Huck, 1989, pp. 50–51). Again, however, it is a media convention to highlight dramatic, deviant examples.

The tremendous attention paid to *Murphy Brown* upon its debut in the fall of 1988 is attributable to a number of factors. It starred a highly visible film actress, Candice Bergen, in her first foray into series television. It was a relative ratings success at a time when the pressure on new shows to prove themselves quickly was fierce. Finally, and most interesting to me, it was a reworking of a television staple associated with 1970s feminism—the single, working-woman sitcom. The numerous comparisons between *Murphy Brown* and *Mary Tyler Moore* made this point hard to miss; as Waters and Huck put it, "the critics . . . haven't lavished so much attention on an unmarried woman since Mary Richards walked into that other TV newsroom in Minneapolis" (1989, p. 49).[1] In the same article, Linda Bloodworth-Thomason also spoke of *Mary Tyler Moore* as the baseline for representations of working women: "When Mary Richards threw that hat in the air for the last time, it stayed up. The contemporary TV woman is making it on her own" (Waters and Huck, 1989, p. 50).

The similarities between Mary Richards and Murphy Brown, which both focus on a single woman who works in a television newsroom, are overpowered by the differences, as popular critics have hastened to note. While *Mary Tyler Moore* was firmly within what Norman Lear called the "emerging woman" genre, there is no doubt that Murphy Brown has made it. She is no struggling producer-cum-secretary in local news but, rather, a powerful network co-anchor of a prime-time news magazine. Murphy Brown presumably proves that "TV women have come a long, *long* way since Mrs. Cleaver whipped up her last breakfast for the Beav" (Waters and Huck, 1989, p. 48).

This point is made again and again in media treatment of *Murphy Brown*. Not only was a CBS special focusing on the twentieth anniversary of *Mary Tyler Moore* broadcast on a Monday evening (February 18, 1991) with *Murphy Brown* as its lead-in show, but the special was advertised as "An Evening with Murphy and Mary." *Primetime Live*, the ABC news magazine show, introduced a July 25, 1991, feature on *Murphy Brown* by placing the show on a continuum of "liberated woman" sitcoms that included *That Girl* and *Mary Tyler Moore*.

In virtually all comparisons between the two sitcoms the purpose is to demonstrate how far women have come since *Mary Tyler Moore*.[2] If Mary

Richards was the feminist television icon of the 1970s, then Murphy Brown is the postfeminist icon for the 1990s. The show's producers have claimed that they "intend Murphy to be for the 90's what Mary Richards was for the 70's" (Horowitz, 1989, p. 1H), and a headline in *USA Today* described the sitcom as "Mary Tyler Moore Updated for the Eighties" (quoted in Alley and Brown, 1990, p. 204). Critic Jane Feuer has perhaps put it most explicitly by claiming that *Murphy Brown* is a "program based almost entirely on intertextuality," and that "the two shows [*Mary Tyler Moore* and *Murphy Brown*] really represent a continuation of the same cultural theme—the earlier show riding the crest of the feminist movement, the later one detailing its ebb in the 'postfeminist' era" (1992, p. 156).

To return to my original comparison, unlike *Designing Women, Murphy Brown* was treated, from the outset, as a sitcom with feminist implications. While *Designing Women* was positioned in media accounts as a sitcom with a *gendered* consciousness (e.g., women talk to women about things women really talk about), *Murphy Brown* was treated as a show with a *feminist* (or, as I will argue, a *postfeminist*) consciousness. Several possible explanations for this reaction exist. One has to do with the power of television conventions. Previous television trained viewers and critics to see single, white, working-woman sitcoms as the paradigmatic form for feminist representation. *Designing Women*'s characters are white, single, working women, but the sitcom lacks other essential characteristics, such as the liberal feminist emphasis on women in a man's world (journalism is a masculine occupation, whereas interior design is feminine). Possibly, for critics, *Designing Women*'s feminism is undercut by its context, revealing the implicit sexism in media perceptions of women's progress; that is, media assume that feminism is being represented when women do what men traditionally do, making male values the standard for measuring women's advancement.

A second explanation is that *Designing Women* questions the reigning postfeminist ethos promulgated by mainstream media. *Designing Women*'s frequent reiteration of the ongoing need for feminism, as well as its consciousness-raising about that need, hardly fits a view of the world that increasingly saw changes wrought by women's liberation as part of the problem in women's lives rather than as the solution.

If *Designing Women* resists postfeminism, *Murphy Brown* exemplifies it, both in its validation of women's progress embodied in the power of the lead character and in its exploration of the costs of that progress. Although media treatment of *Murphy Brown* emphasizes the sitcom's progressive portrait of a professional woman, it also contains subtler themes about the lessons of liberation. The *Newsweek* article discussed above, for example, claims that "beneath their self-assured veneers," television's new, powerful women "carry stretch marks on their psyches. They've been roughed up by life and are coming to terms with their limits" (Waters and Huck, 1989, pp. 50–51). Candice Bergen adds to this theme in a 1989 *Playboy* interview in which she notes that "Murphy is at the top of her profession but . . . she is, in a very realistic way, paying the price for it" ("Candice Bergen," 1989, p. 62).

A *People* article calls Murphy Brown a "feminist figurehead" and a "merciless careerist" while contrasting the character's persona with the happy home life of the actor who portrays her (Jerome, 1991, pp. 162, 160). This issue of *People* features Candice Bergen on the cover, with a caption that reads: "*Murphy Brown* is a hoot, but her [Bergen's] heart's at home with Chloe, 6, and her French husband, Louis Malle, the man who saved her 'from the loneliness I was so used to living with.' " In fact, the many articles about Bergen consistently note the contrast between the star's happy, satisfied life as a wife and mother and the "desolate personal life" of Murphy Brown (Rosenblatt, 1992, p. 258). At another point in the *Playboy* interview, Bergen says "I don't know if I could have played this part if I weren't married and didn't have a child. It would have been too painful for me" ("Candice Bergen," 1989, p. 69).

Esquire magazine's annual "Women We Love" issue for 1992, which featured Bergen on the cover as their "Woman of the Year" adds further strength to this positioning of Murphy Brown as an example of postfeminist fallout: "A product of the Eighties backlash against women Having It All, Murphy embodies a belated recognition that it is not possible all-at-once to do the deal, cook the dinner, give a man good lovin', and still flounce about with a chirpy Mary Tyler Moore bob and a smile" ("Candice Bergen," 1992, p. 79).[3] Diane English, the sitcom's producer, perhaps put it most succinctly in her comment in a *New York Times Magazine* profile that *Murphy Brown* is "a sort of cautionary tale about getting what you wished for" (De Vries, 1993, p. 20).

I have reviewed popular press treatments of *Murphy Brown* at length here because they indicate the ambivalence of attitudes toward women's progress both in the sitcom and in reactions to it. Elsewhere, I have interpreted *Murphy Brown* solely as a "cautionary tale," connecting it to the backlash against women's liberation (see Dow, 1992a, 1995). Today, I am less sure of the totalizing power of that interpretation. As a viewer, I have always been reserved in my positive reaction to the sitcom because I felt that feminism had not come far enough for me to take comfort in a show that made a buffoon out of a powerful female character. However, continued watching of *Murphy Brown,* and the gathering of reactions from many self-identified feminist viewers who unabashedly enjoy it have confounded the simplicity of this view. *Murphy Brown* is tremendously sophisticated comedy, and it is perhaps the model of what critics mean when we say there is no such thing as a closed text.

That *Murphy Brown* has import for women's roles is something everyone seems to agree on, an interpretation that was strengthened by then-Vice President Dan Quayle's attack on Murphy's single motherhood. However, the substance or ideological content of that import is difficult to pin down. As the press coverage indicates, there is a doubleness to the perceived meaning of the sitcom; it is discussed, at once, as an affirmation of women's progress and as a reminder of the problems such progress has created. This is, of course, precisely the doubleness represented by postfeminist attitudes, as I discussed in Chapter 3. My reading of *Murphy Brown* in this chapter, then, is an exploration of this postfeminist ambivalence as it is constructed in the character of Murphy Brown and the narrative themes that fuel the sitcom. *Murphy Brown* illustrates particularly well, I think, the way in which popular texts gain appeal from exploiting and reworking cultural contradictions at particular historical moments.

Postfeminist Womanhood

The regulars on *Murphy Brown* consist primarily of Murphy's colleagues at "FYI," the weekly prime-time news magazine show of which she is a coanchor. The other primary anchor on "FYI" is Jim Dial, an older, experienced television newsman known for his rigid, uptight nature and his stiff, laconic style. Miles Silverberg, the executive producer of "FYI" and Murphy's boss, is less experienced and younger than Murphy, a situation that Murphy finds consistently irritating in early seasons of the sitcom. Two other regulars are Frank Fontana and Corky Sherwood, reporters for the program. Frank is an experienced investigative reporter and Murphy's closest friend in the group.

In contrast, Corky has little journalistic experience. She is an ex-Miss America who was hired at "FYI" for her beauty queen status. Corky is young, pretty, and perky, a softer character than Murphy, and she provides a traditionally feminine foil for Murphy's feminist character. Murphy's relation to Corky is competitive rather than cooperative. Corky's role on "FYI" is to produce "soft" news features (e.g., "Twelve Angry Women in Hairdresser Horror Stories," "Dinner with the Van Patten Family") that appeal to female viewers. Although the two women become friends over time, Murphy does not see Corky as her professional equal, and a strong theme in their relationship is Murphy's disdain for Corky's journalistic ability. Two other regulars on *Murphy Brown* are not connected to "FYI." They are Murphy's ever-present housepainter, Eldin

Bernecky, who appears in most of the scenes set in Murphy's home,[4] and Phil, the owner of a bar frequented by the "FYI" staff.

This review of characters shows kinship between *Murphy Brown* and *Mary Tyler Moore*. Like Mary Richards, Murphy is "a woman in a man's world." However, unlike Mary Richards, Murphy does not achieve success by playing a domestic role in the workplace; rather, she has adapted successfully to the masculine culture of television journalism and made her way to the top of her profession through rugged individualism. The fact that Murphy's professional competence is never an issue on *Murphy Brown* shows progress since *Mary Tyler Moore*. Murphy is a media "star," a knowledgeable, driven, investigative reporter who has won numerous awards. Unlike *Mary Tyler Moore*, in which the narrative problematic was "can she make it on her own?" *Murphy Brown* has moved beyond such a question. She has indeed made it on her own, becoming in the process what Phyllis Japp calls "a male persona in a female body" (1991, p. 71). Indeed, Murphy could be considered the fictional embodiment of the liberal feminist hegemony Hewlett and Friedan assumed when they argued that women's liberation required that women "clone the male competitive model" (Hewlett, 1986, p. 186).

Murphy Brown signifies Murphy's masculinized persona in numerous ways. Her name is not traditionally feminine; generally, "Murphy" would be more likely to refer to a man than a woman. Moreover, although Candice Bergen is a strikingly beautiful woman, her style, as Murphy Brown, is not traditionally feminine. Indeed, much of the humor that arises from Murphy's character is connected to the incongruity of Bergen's glamorous and patrician persona in combination with the deemphasized femininity, abrasive personality, and physical aggressiveness of Murphy Brown.

Murphy's clothing is severely tailored, and she tends to wear high collars and boxy suits with straight lines. Even her less formal clothes have a masculine aura; when Murphy is relaxed, she often wears a baseball cap, tennis shoes, and baggy, man-tailored slacks. The contrast of Murphy's look and manner with that of the ultrafeminine Corky give Murphy's "difference" additional weight. Reinforcing the idea that she and Corky are two extremes on a spectrum, Murphy's tendency toward black, brown, and strong colors are a clear contrast to Corky's frequent pastels, soft scarves, and bows. While Murphy often wears flats, Corky always wears high heels. Murphy's subdued makeup and hair also are striking in comparison to Corky's teased, bleached hair and bright lips. Corky's appearance is part of her general performance of femininity, while Murphy's style reflects the goal of gaining credibility in a male world.

Murphy's physical presence also is noteworthy in defining her character. Her stride is aggressive, her gestures are strong, her manner of speaking is forceful, and she commands primary attention in any scene in which she is involved. Murphy's physical and facial expressions are excessive; she often does double-takes, and her expressions of distaste, amazement, or triumph are exaggerated. She is the primary focus in most camera shots in which she is involved, and her strength and autonomy are underscored by the way in which camera angles often show her physically isolated from other characters in a scene.

Murphy's physical aura is reinforced by her aggressive communication style. She is supremely confident about her own opinions, and she expresses them easily, often with little regard for others' feelings. For example, in "The Strike"[5] (1989), Murphy is disgusted by the way the men around her are handling a management-union dispute. She accuses them of being blinded by male pride, and comments, "just pull down your pants, I'll get a ruler, and we'll settle this once and for all." This line, in fact, illustrates the double edge to Murphy's character. It can be taken, simultaneously, as a salient feminist comment on a masculine obsession with power at the expense of reasonable problem-solving *and* as further evidence of Murphy's insensitivity and her taste for harsh sarcasm.

The latter interpretation is bolstered by Murphy's habit of playing hostile practical jokes, another typically male-associated trait that defines her character. When angry at her producer, for example, she has pizzas delivered to him every half-hour all night long, later hiring a polka band to play outside his window. Upset with Corky, she sends religious missionaries to Corky's house. Even Murphy's closest friend, Frank, does not escape. When Frank finally wins a prestigious journalism award that he has coveted for years, the victory goes to his head and he becomes obsessed with his own importance. To deflate Frank's ego, Murphy hires actors to tell him that the award has been rescinded because it was based on a mathematical error.

A clear message of *Murphy Brown* is that the personality traits alluded to above, such as aggression, competitiveness, and lack of interpersonal sensitivity, are key to Murphy's professional success in a patriarchal world. For example, in "The Unshrinkable Murphy Brown" (1989) Murphy is so relentless while interviewing a subject that he has a heart attack and dies on the air. Guilt-stricken, Murphy vows to be a nicer person, and in subsequent scenes she is uncharacteristically polite and considerate to her colleagues. They are shocked and dismayed at the change in her behavior, concerned that it is affecting the quality of her work.

This episode is instructive, because it implies that Murphy's display of traditionally "nice," feminine qualities is not only shocking, but incompatible with her success as a journalist. In order to be successful she must be tough and competitive, and must reject behaviors that contradict such a persona. While other reporters on "FYI" are also capable and successful, notably Jim Dial and Frank Fontana, they do not behave as ruthlessly as Murphy. To compete in a male culture, Murphy becomes an extreme version of it, a caricature of the consequences of liberal feminism. Alison Jaggar notes that a typical liberal feminist argument is that "women are capable of participating in male culture and of living up to male values" (1983, p. 250). In *Murphy Brown*, consistent with postfeminism, this success has its costs. A theme in early seasons is Murphy's recovery from alcoholism, a disease that she attributes to her driven lifestyle. She has little success with romantic relationships and does not bond easily with other women.

All of these factors are, of course, fodder for comedy, contributing to the intriguing ambivalence of the sitcom's message. At the same time that Murphy is a "new" (read: liberated, autonomous, and powerful) woman on television, much of the humor attached to her character is derived from the incongruity of these characteristics in a woman. The prevailing tone in *Murphy Brown* is irony: Murphy is funny because she consistently acts as we do not expect a woman to act. Rather than rejecting naturalized prefeminist conceptions of "good womanhood," the sitcom depends upon them to make sense. The troubling aspect of this dynamic is that laughter is linked most often to the absurdity of Murphy rather than to the absurdity of conventional expectations for womanhood, indicating that the postfeminist presumption of women's equality is premature. As Andrea Press notes in her brief discussion of *Murphy Brown*, given that Murphy's "harsh personality becomes the focus of so much of the show's humor, . . . were a man in her role, one suspects that the humor would have to be focused entirely differently" (1991, p. 41).

The earlier seasons of *Murphy Brown* are the most direct about exploiting aspects of Murphy's stereotypical liberal feminist character. A recurring theme, for example, is that Murphy's competitiveness and ambition are excessive. In "Devil with the Blue Dress" (1988), Miles assigns Corky to assist Murphy on a difficult story, claiming that Corky needs "seasoning as a reporter." After expressing her displeasure to Miles in competitive terms ("I won't work with her on my story. I was an only child—I never learned to share"), Murphy finally agrees. Hoping to discourage Corky, Murphy sends her on various humiliating wild-goose chases (such as searching through a suspect's garbage cans), but Corky eventually discovers a piece of information that proves to be the key to the story.

Murphy dismisses the value of the information in front of Corky so that she can pursue the angle herself. Corky later discovers this maneuver but responds graciously, saying, "When I realized what you'd done with that crucial piece of information I gave you . . . there it was, the perfect example of what makes you the best. . . . I have learned so much from you and I respect you so much. Thank you for allowing me to work by your side." Murphy assuages the guilt engendered by this reaction by telling Corky that she may introduce the story during the FYI broadcast before turning it over to Murphy.

However, Corky reads the entire story and takes full credit for it. After the show, Murphy is furious, but she must admit respect for Corky, saying, "You saw your brass ring and you went for it. It took a lot of chutzpa. I have to respect a person for that." This episode illustrates a pattern in *Murphy Brown* in which Murphy's aggressive, competitive personality creates a problem that leads to her humorous comeuppance. In this episode, Murphy rejected cooperation and nurturing (qualities of traditional femininity) in favor of competition and ruthlessness (qualities of the patriarchal public sphere). While the latter qualities presumably have led to Murphy's past success, she is reproved for them in this situation, creating a classic double-bind for her. Through plotlines such as this, *Murphy Brown* exploits the perceived conflict between femininity and professional success.

That the competition is between two women is additionally interesting in this case. Murphy consistently compares herself to other newswomen, but not other newsmen, in a fiercely competitive way. In various episodes, she measures her success against that of Lesley Stahl, Connie Chung, and Linda Ellerbee, exemplifying the sitcom's reliance on humor generated by intertextual references and reinforcing the idea that there are limited spaces for women at the top. To help Corky to join such a club threatens Murphy's status rather than presents her with an opportunity for female solidarity. *Murphy Brown*'s almost total lack of realistic female community sets it apart from other examples of "postfeminist postfamily" television such as *Kate and Allie, The Golden Girls,* or *Designing Women.* These shows, to varying degrees, contain the message that female friendship and support are important and valuable to women; that message is arguably a primary reason for their popularity with women audiences and offers some resistance to postfeminism's rugged individualism. Murphy Brown, on the other hand, embraces individualism so thoroughly that she is seemingly incapable of deep emotional ties.

Murphy has none of the nurturing qualities so common in television's female characters. She is rarely physically affectionate, usually stiffening when others are demonstrative toward her. When Jim Dial comes to her for advice on a personal problem, her first response is, "Don't you have a family priest or someone?" In a later season, when Corky is married and is considering an affair, she asks Murphy for advice and receives essentially the same response: "I don't know, Corky. I'm not good at this stuff. Isn't there some all night radio station you can call?"

Murphy's interpersonal difficulties extend into her private life, where she enacts the stereotype of a driven career woman with no time or talent for relationships. Outside of the newsroom, her closest relationship is with Eldin, her housepainter. When she is not invited to the inaugural ball, she ends up spending the evening with Eldin. When she is suspended from work, it appears that Eldin is the only person to keep her company. There is no real or implied romantic connection with Eldin, but Murphy seems to have no other friends outside her job. In a 1988 episode, Murphy first thinks of becoming a single mother. However, it proves difficult to find someone to father her child. Forty years old, Murphy fears her time for motherhood is running out, and she bemoans the fact that her "most enduring relationship is with the skycap at Dulles airport."

Unmarried, childless, and without a satisfying romantic relationship, Murphy's character embodies what media constructions of postfeminism posit as the negative consequences of female independence. For example, *Time*'s 1989 cover story asking "Is there a future for feminism?" maintains that many career women resent feminists for not foreseeing the sacrifices women would have to make, noting that "the bitterest complaints come from the growing ranks of women who have reached 40 and find themselves childless, having put their careers first" (Wallis, 1989, p. 82). *Murphy Brown*'s emphasis on Murphy's barren personal life enacts this postfeminist scenario. Although Jim Dial, who is closest to being Murphy's peer, has a successful marriage (and a wife who is a fulltime homemaker), such a choice is precluded for Murphy.

Several episodes of *Murphy Brown* comment on the effect of Murphy's life choices on her personal relations, offering the message that her professional ambition precludes lasting personal relationships. For example, in a 1988 episode, Murphy's ex-husband, a political activist to whom she was married for five days twenty years earlier, appears on "FYI." They reignite their attraction and decide to marry again. However, Murphy cannot find time for a wedding and they give up on the idea. Her excuses range from "I gotta fly to Moscow to interview Gorbachev" to "I can't plan that far in advance—I've got to be ready to hop a plane at a moment's notice." Murphy's devotion to her work seems extreme in this circumstance, with the result that she sacrifices her own personal happiness.

In the 1990–91 season, Murphy began a relationship with Jerry Gold, an abrasive talk show host. In their first try at a relationship, Murphy eventually called it off, saying, "I'm good at a lot of things, but this isn't one of them. I start saying things I don't normally say, I start doing things I don't normally do. . . . Oh, God, I'm wearing an apron. See what I mean?" This remark comes after a failed dinner party that Murphy concocted to introduce Jerry to her colleagues. It is telling that Murphy equates her failure at the relationship with her unsuitability for a domestic role, reinforcing the dichotomy between the private and public spheres.

In the next season, Murphy and Jerry try again to be a couple, but it ends when Jerry takes a job in California and Murphy is too busy to pursue a long-distance romance. Again, however, this episode creates an inverse relationship between Murphy's personal happiness and her professional success. Murphy and Jerry are brought together when a new "FYI" segment requires that they debate political issues each week. Their sharply contrasting political views make this a lively and popular segment. However, after they rekindle their romance, Murphy is no longer aggressive and sharp-witted in the debate segment; instead, she exhibits traditionally feminine qualities. She is supportive, polite, and willing to compromise with Jerry's extremist views. Her colleagues are horrified, concluding that her romance with Jerry has affected her professional performance.

This episode reiterates that personal happiness and professional success are incompatible for Murphy, implicitly arguing that, for women, the qualities the public world requires are radically different from those necessary for success in the private world of relationships. Murphy simply cannot win. *Murphy Brown* implies that she must act one way to be professionally successful and another to be personally fulfilled. For many female viewers, Murphy's difficulties could strike a responsive chord. However, the episodes of *Murphy Brown* that deal with this issue present these conflicts as the result of Murphy's *choices* rather than as a result of contradictory cultural expectations. The ultimate rugged individualist, Murphy is no one's victim. Rather, she sabotages herself. This dynamic is what makes *Murphy Brown* so vividly postfeminist. Unlike *Designing Women*, *Murphy Brown* gives no "presence" to patriarchy. Instead, women's problems (or Murphy's problems) flow from their own choices.

A final, classic example of *Murphy Brown*'s depiction of Murphy's self-sabotage again highlights the personal/professional dichotomy that defines her character. In "The Morning Show" (1989), the major plotline concerns Murphy's week-long stint as the substitute co-anchor of "Today America," a program much like "Good Morning America." Murphy ridicules the "soft news" orientation of the program, and she is unhappy to discover that Corky is to be her co-host. Corky is excited by the assignment and spends significant time preparing. Murphy, in contrast, does not see the job as challenging and does no preparation.

The contrasts between Murphy and Corky as co-anchors are the context within which Corky's traditional femininity is validated, while Murphy's aggressive competitiveness only creates difficulties. In the first morning show, they interview the male author of a popular children's book. While Corky praises the inventiveness and popularity of the book, Murphy asserts that the setting of the book, "the Land of the Woogies," emulates a male-dominated society, and that the story represents the larger culture's "struggle for sexual equality in the workplace." The author protests that his characters are not gendered, but Murphy is relentless, claiming that the "Fifis," another group in the book, are female and represent "an oppressed minority of sorts." At this point, Corky steps in, soothes the author and ends the interview.

The contrast between Murphy's feminism and Corky's femininity are clear in this scene. Murphy personifies the intensity and humorlessness of the stereotypical feminist ideologue, refusing to enact the supportive, gracious role required in such a situation. While her argument that the children's book is sexist indeed may be correct (and some viewers may see it as a salient point to make), within the context of the episode, the laugh track encourages the audience to view her claim as absurd and her behavior as inappropriate for the situation. Corky, in contrast, is at home in the "soft news" format which reflects traditionally female interests.

While Corky is praised for her performance, Murphy is described by colleagues as "acerbic, humorless, inflexible, and unprepared." The next day, Murphy panics when she hears that she must participate in a segment with a bake-off champion, and she moans, "The last time I tried to bake brownies, I had to call in an industrial cleaning service." During the segment, Corky startles Murphy by separating an egg with one hand. Corky's baking expertise is manifest, and Murphy is challenged. She becomes obsessed with learning to separate eggs and annoys the bake-off champion. Murphy ruins the segment as she and the bake-off champion do verbal (and nearly physical) battle and have to be pried apart by Corky. Murphy's dearth of culinary skills, and her inability to acquiesce graciously to Corky's superiority in this arena further demonstrate her lack of stereotypical feminine qualities.

By the end of this episode, Murphy is humbled, and she must admit that Corky did the better job. Murphy is humiliated because she is not traditionally feminine enough, in terms of social facilitation or cooking skills, to fulfill the assigned role. Despite the fact that her particular traits have led to success in "hard news," when she fails at "soft news," she is punished. Again, Murphy is the victim of conflicting expectations. Corky, whose more traditionally female skills are appropriate for the situation, shines on the morning show, although she has failed in the past at "hard news" assignments.

This episode adds strength to a theme that dominates early seasons of *Murphy Brown*: a woman cannot both be professionally successful and retain traditional qualities of femininity. Murphy is rich and famous but not a "real" woman in personality or personal relationships. Corky, in contrast, is more traditionally feminine in appearance and behavior but is professionally competent only in the feminine province of lower-status "soft" news situations. In *Murphy Brown*, neither major female character can be totally complete, and the "weaknesses" of each are highlighted through contrast with the other. The sitcom allows only polar conceptions of womanhood, refusing to permit integration of traditionally bifurcated masculine and feminine qualities attached to the public and private spheres.

The sharp contrast between Murphy and Corky that feeds the dichotomy in *Murphy Brown* between professional and personal competence lessens in later seasons of the sitcom, largely as a result of the development of Corky's character through her marriage, divorce, and increasing professional ambition. Corky's ultimately unsuccessful marriage to a man from her hometown in Louisiana (resulting in the comical married name of "Corky Sherwood-Forrest") extends *Murphy Brown*'s message about the incompatibility of personal and professional success to encompass Corky's life as well. The disintegration of Corky and Will Forrest's marriage, although it receives little attention in the sitcom's narrative, is linked to the pressures of their dual careers and the fact that they rarely see each other.

Although Corky still handles only soft news features, she becomes more competent, successful, and ambitious in later seasons of *Murphy Brown*. Interestingly, one of the hallmarks of Corky's development as a journalist is her adaptation of Murphy's style of "going the distance" to get what she wants, even if it involves manipulation and/or misrepresentation. However, despite Corky's development, the disturbing element of competition that fuels Murphy and Corky's relationship is never lost. Corky frequently uses her new skills at Murphy's expense, which feeds the competition between them *and* functions to discipline Murphy for her excesses. A 1991 episode, in which Corky is given a network special of her own, is illustrative.

Corky decides to frame the special as a tea-party, in which she will interview people such as Mrs. Fields (of Mrs. Fields' cookies fame) and Mary Ann Mobley and Gary Collins (best known as hosts of the Miss America pageant). Corky also wishes for Murphy to be a guest, a request Murphy disdains ("What self-respecting journalist would let himself[6] be interviewed at a tea-party?"), until Miles manages to talk her into it by appealing to her ego. On the day the special is to be broadcast live, a newspaper columnist ridicules the special so thoroughly that Corky is completely demoralized, convinced that she can never be as good as the other members of "FYI," that she will never be able to "ask the tough questions." Uncharacteristically, Murphy offers Corky encouragement and convinces her to go ahead with the special. Corky promises that she will "try to live up to your [Murphy's] standards."

During the special, instead of asking Murphy questions about her professional experiences, Corky turns the conversation to Murphy's troubled personal life with questions such as "Earlier in your career, you were, in your own words, a 'major booze hound.' I was just wondering, could America trust your accuracy and judgment in reporting information?" Corky's relentless probing eventually leads to various highly personal revelations from Murphy, such as "Maybe I deliberately sabotage my personal relationships because I fear losing some professional edge." After the special, Murphy is completely humiliated, convinced that her reputation has been destroyed. When she confronts Corky, threatening to "kill" her, Corky's reply is that she was modeling herself after Murphy: "I did what I thought you would have done in the same situation. . . . I'm right, aren't I, Murphy?"

Murphy is hoisted on her own petard in this episode. She has disdained Corky's abilities for years while asserting her own superiority as a journalist, only to be the unwitting victim when Corky finally is able "to ask the tough questions" (it is doubly interesting, of course, that Murphy's dysfunctional personal life is the focus). Murphy suffers this kind of deflation regularly in *Murphy Brown*, frequently at Corky's hands. In true sitcom style, Murphy never really learns her lesson (to do so would eliminate the "sit"), and she keeps returning for yet more comeuppances.

I find it particularly meaningful that Corky is so often the catalyst for Murphy's symbolic punishments, feeding the postfeminist media theme of divisions among women and the implicit message that the possibility of female solidarity was a feminist fantasy. In much postfeminist pop culture, women have replaced patriarchy as women's worst enemy. Journalists lavish attention on the conflicts between mothers who work outside the home and those who do not, between women of different races, and between feminists and nonfeminists—conflicts that are strengthened by their vivid representation in television programs like *thirtysomething*; films such as *Fatal Attraction* (1987), *Jungle Fever* (1991), *The Hand That Rocks the Cradle* (1992), and *Disclosure* (1994); and public controversies like the Thomas/Hill hearings, in which much was made of Clarence Thomas's preference for women with light complexions and of the divergence in white and black women's responses to Hill's charges.[7]

Generally, the episodes I have discussed thus far illustrate what I believe to be a powerful rhetorical strategy in *Murphy Brown*: Murphy's function as a comic scapegoat representing postfeminist ills. By sacrificing Murphy through humiliation, embarrassment, or ridicule, *Murphy Brown* turns the tables on the basic project of liberal feminism, which is to critique how the public sphere excludes women. Instead, Murphy is a vision of liberal feminist success, and the scapegoating of her character is a recurring reminder of the problems that success creates. Murphy is too abrasive, confident, outspoken, and powerful (for a woman) to be left unchecked. In *Murphy Brown*'s postfeminist vision, patriarchy is no longer the problem; feminism (and the problems it creates for women) is.

Kenneth Burke argues that the general attitude of classical comedy is "charitable," designed to promote cooperation and resolution of differences (1959, p. 166). This is also the basic philosophy of television situation comedy narrative, which centers on problem-solving. The way in which problems are resolved says much about the values promoted by a series. For example, the controlling value of patriarchal authority is evident in 1950s sitcoms like *Leave It to Beaver* or *Father Knows Best*, in which the correct resolution of a problem inevitably follows the wisdom of the father (Leibman, 1995).

In *Murphy Brown*, Murphy's extreme personality and behavior most often create (or significantly contribute to) the problem that must be solved, and the solution involves some kind of symbolic discipline for Murphy as the comic scapegoat. The comic scapegoating in *Murphy Brown* is simply another example of a classic comedic strategy, in which a character serves as a representation for ideology or behavior that is ridiculed or debunked in the process of disciplining the character.[8] The treatment of Archie Bunker in *All in the Family* is the paradigmatic example of this strategy in television situation comedy. Archie was the repository for the conservative bigotry that Norman Lear wished to attack. Poking fun at Archie was a way to debunk the ideology he represented. However, audience interpretation of this strategy is unpredictable. Although critics might assume that audiences were always complicitous with Lear's intention to ridicule Archie, research shows that many viewers loved Archie *because of* his contentious conservatism (Adler, 1979).

Reaction to Murphy is similarly ambivalent, I think. Although *Murphy Brown* troubles me because of Murphy's consistent function as a sort of feminist buffoon whose ritual humiliation functions to contain the threat that a powerful woman poses, I can see why she is so appealing for many viewers with feminist sympathies. Television programming offers so few representations of powerful, funny, smart, belligerent women (the massive amounts of attention that *Murphy Brown* and *Roseanne* receive often blinds us to how unusual and outnumbered they are) that we take what pleasure we can get from the ones we have.

Patricia Mellencamp (1986) has made a similar argument about the appeal of *I Love Lucy*'s (1951–61) portrayal of Lucy Ricardo's desperate, and always futile, attempts to escape domesticity for show business. That is, although Lucy is always chastened by episode's end and returned to her traditional role, for many women this outcome does not wholly diminish the appeal of Lucy's struggle. Just so with Murphy Brown. Although my position is that the series does not encourage a view of Murphy as a victim of conflicting expectations that continue to be enforced by a patriarchal culture, it is quite possible that feminist viewers construct that interpretation for themselves, filling in a context that the sitcom's narrative does not provide. Such an interpretation would make Murphy a sympathetic character rather than a comic scapegoat. As is always the case, the possibility of such a reading of *Murphy Brown* depends upon the experiences a viewer brings to a text as well as on the work s/he is willing to do in decoding it.

The Politics of Single Motherhood

Major shifts in narrative premise often spell disaster for situation comedies. A large part of the appeal of sitcom is its regularity, circularity, and predictability in terms of character function and plotline. Major shifts in characters or in situation can diminish that appeal. Some very popular and long-running sitcoms successfully manage shifts in character (witness, for instance, the many changes in *M*A*S*H*, and to a lesser extent, in *Cheers*), but major shifts in situation are harder to manage. For example, as I discussed in Chapter 2, the appeal of Rhoda Morgenstern in *Mary Tyler Moore* was largely linked to her situation as an underdog single woman. In *Rhoda*, when she became a satisfied wife, the situational dynamics changed so much that her previous appeal for the audience was lost.

At the conclusion of the 1991 season, *Murphy Brown*'s producers presented the possibility of a drastic alteration in the narrative premise of the sitcom when Murphy discovered that she was pregnant. As I will discuss in a moment, Murphy's decision to become a single mother ultimately had little effect on the dynamics of the sitcom. However, the series of events surrounding Murphy's pregnancy and birth, both inside and outside the text of *Murphy Brown*, deserves discussion for its illustration of the intersections of postfeminism, politics, and media intertextuality.

Press reaction to Murphy's pregnancy was mixed. Rather than viewing it as shocking, some writers (e.g., Charen, 1991; James, 1991) interpreted it as part of a trend on series television, which was experiencing a spate of baby-related storylines in shows such as *Designing Women* (in which Mary Jo considered having another child through artificial insemination) and *Cheers* (Sam Malone desired a child and enlisted the aid of his platonic friend Rebecca). The stigma of unwed motherhood as a plot device presumably had been diminished by successful storylines in recent years on *Moonlighting* (1985–89) (although the pregnant character rushed into a short-lived marriage and eventually miscarried) and *The Days and Nights of Molly Dodd* (1987–91) (in which the pregnancy led to the mother and father becoming engaged, until the father unexpectedly died).

Murphy's pregnancy did spark some moral outrage, from editorial columnists who accused television producers of irresponsibly weakening "the rule against illegitimacy [that] helps to prevent women and children from being abandoned by men" (Charen, 1991, p. 15A), to viewers who protested that the show was sending the wrong message about the joys of single motherhood ("Murphy Is Not Reality," 1992, p. 10A; "Mixed Messages," 1992, p. 10A). Even Candice Bergen herself, in *TV Guide*, made a point of asserting that "I myself, as a parent, believe that the ideal is that you have a two-parent family. I'm the last person to think fathers are obsolete" (Rhodes, 1992, p. 8).

However, given the possibilities, the handling of Murphy's pregnancy within the narrative of the sitcom was remarkably conservative. In the concluding episode to the 1990–91 season of *Murphy Brown*, both of Murphy's former loves reenter her life at the same time. Jerry Gold returns from California to resume a relationship with Murphy at the same time that Murphy's ex-husband, Jake Lowenstein, reappears. Murphy juggles the two men briefly, unable to decide between them. In the episode's final scene, Murphy is shocked by the result of a home pregnancy test, creating the cliffhanger question: Who is the father?

Murphy Brown takes care, in later episodes, to downplay implications of sexual irresponsibility. When Frank chastises Murphy for having unprotected sex with two men, Murphy reminds him that it was a fluke, that she has sex about as often as Democrats are in the White House. Moreover, the father turns out to be Jake, who makes the choice not to be involved in the pregnancy or the child's life, citing his commitment to political activism around the world. Finally, although Murphy considers abortion, she ultimately rejects it. By this point, it has been established the Murphy is not promiscuous, that the child has an aura of legitimacy derived from the fact that Murphy was once married to the father, that the father is deserting her through his own choice,[9] and that Murphy will not abort the pregnancy simply to avoid the inconvenience of single motherhood. Beyond the fact that Murphy engaged in unprotected extramarital sex in the first place, the portrayal of her journey to single motherhood is relatively timid.

Indeed, Murphy's surrender to women's supposed biological imperative, is, in my view, the ultimate postfeminist moment in *Murphy Brown*, giving credence to the claims about biological clocks, about the emptiness of childless career women, and women's "natural" destiny to mother. Various characters in *Murphy Brown*, including Murphy herself, reiterate that Murphy is unsuited for motherhood. After she has decided to keep the baby, Phil comments that her decision was "pretty gutsy for a woman with no maternal instinct whatsoever," to which Murphy replies, "Not everyone is born with maternal instincts, Phil. I can get some. I'm sure there's a class." At another point, Corky comments that she is sure Murphy will "make a wonderful mother. Once she gets a little practice and maybe some estrogen supplements."

Given her personality and lifestyle, Murphy's decision to bear the child hardly seems rational. It makes sense only as a reflection of the sexist adage that all women have a deep and irrepressible desire (duty?) to reproduce that is merely waiting to be triggered. Indeed, this essentialist interpretation of Murphy's motivation is given support in the "birth" episode from the end of the 1992 season—an episode viewed by some 38 million people. In the final scene, Murphy cradles her new infant in her arms, singing to him words from one of her favorite songs, "Natural Woman," by Aretha Franklin. The lines that Murphy sings, including "I didn't know what was wrong with me, 'til you helped me name it," and "You make me feel like a natural woman," take on a powerful meaning in this context. Having given birth, Murphy is miraculously transformed, albeit briefly, from an "unnatural" (professional) to a "natural" (maternal) woman.[10]

Apparently, then-Vice-President Dan Quayle did not view this episode before making his remarks about the poverty of family values represented by *Murphy Brown*. If he had, he might have noticed how closely it dovetailed with his wife's (and presumably his own) view, expressed at the Republican National Convention a few months later, that, contrary to feminist claims, "women do not wish to be liberated from their essential natures."

Given my position that *Murphy Brown*'s treatment of Murphy's pregnancy and birth is hardly radical, the most interesting aspects of the Quayle / *Murphy Brown* media phenomenon to me is the way in which a popular sitcom, and the underlying values of the entertainment industry, became the dominant focus in reaction to a speech that was predominantly an attack on poor women. Focusing on the theme of family values, as though its implications were gender, race, and class neutral, both mainstream media and the text of *Murphy Brown* itself (through its intertextual appropriation and interpretation of Quayle's statement) created a debate that left untouched what bell hooks (1994) usefully calls "white supremacist capitalist patriarchy."

Quayle's famous comment about *Murphy Brown* occurred in a May 19,

1992, speech to the Commonwealth Club of California, an elite political group dominated by white men.[11] Attempting to make sense of the recent Los Angeles riots, Quayle argued that "the lawless social anarchy which we saw is directly related to the breakdown of family structure, personal responsibility, and social order in too many areas of our society." He went on to note that, while baby boomers such as himself participated in the "war against traditional values" waged in the 1960s and 1970s, now that the boomers are "middle-aged and middle-class . . . the responsibility of having families has helped many recover traditional values."

Quayle maintains that the poor, unfortunately, have never managed to regain those traditional values. The result is that "the intergenerational poverty that troubles us so much today is predominantly a poverty of values. . . . The anarchy and lack of structure in our inner cities are testament to how quickly civilization falls apart when the family foundation cracks." The Vice-President then asserts the necessity of male role models for inner-city children, touts marriage as "the best antipoverty program of all," and calls for a return to the moral stigmatization of illegitimacy.

At this point he mentions *Murphy Brown*, claiming that "it doesn't help matters when prime-time TV has Murphy Brown—a character who supposedly epitomizes today's intelligent, highly paid, professional woman—mocking the importance of fathers by bearing a child alone and calling it just another 'lifestyle choice.' " Moments later, Quayle extends his censure to the "cultural leaders in Hollywood, network TV, the national newspapers" who "routinely jeer" at moral values.

Quayle's remarks made the front pages of national newspapers—notably the *New York Times* and *USA Today*—and became the lead story on ABC's *World News Tonight*, the most popular national television newscast in America. In its May 20 edition, *USA Today* ran a photograph of Murphy Brown holding her baby next to the headline: "Quayle: Murphy No Role Model." The following day, the *New York Times* ran the same photograph of Murphy Brown on its front page, juxtaposed with photos of Quayle and White House spokesperson Marlin Fitzwater and the headline "Appeal of 'Murphy Brown' Now Clear at White House." The *New York Times* article made clear the extent to which Quayle's brief comment about Murphy Brown was influencing reaction to his speech, noting that in his tour of Los Angeles, "Mr. Quayle was greeted at every stop and in six local television interviews with questions about the 'Murphy Brown' program" (Wines, 1992, p. A12). Press coverage of President Bush's trade talks with Canadian Prime Minister Brian Mulroney also was dominated by questions about the *Murphy Brown* issue (pp. A1, A12).

Generally, reports on Quayle's remarks were dominated by analysis of the White House campaign strategy to emphasize family values, by the comical contradictions in Quayle's and Fitzwater's follow-up remarks, and by reactions from *Murphy Brown* producers. Fitzwater, for instance, noted that Murphy's decision to bear the child " '[exhibits] pro-life values which we think are good' " (Wines, 1992, p. A1), an opinion that Quayle later countered, claiming that *Murphy Brown* " 'does not represent pro-life policies' " ("Quayle vs. Brown," 1992, p. A1). Quayle's disagreement with Fitzwater was no doubt prompted by the widely reported response of Diane English to the Vice-President's attack: " 'If the Vice-President thinks it's disgraceful for an unmarried woman to bear a child, and if he believes that a woman cannot adequately raise a child without a father, then he'd better make sure abortion remains safe and legal' " (Rosenthal, 1992, p. A11).

English's comment was one of the few that made it into coverage of the incident that indicated even a slight sense of the substance and the politics of Quayle's speech. However, even English overlooked Quayle's classism. Quayle did not suggest that *women in general* could not raise children adequately without fathers; rather, he suggested that *poor women*, in particular, were "bearing babies irresponsibly." Murphy Brown's contribution to the crisis was that she was failing to provide a worthy role model for poor women, apparently a key issue in the "trickle-down theory of values" which holds that prime-time television is a major influence on inner-city mothers (Pollitt, 1994, p. 32). A point that was never raised in the debate over Hollywood's poverty of values was that, in fact, the overwhelming majority of families on television have always been headed by two parents, a factor that has apparently made little difference in checking the "anarchy and lack of structure in our inner cities."

Quayle's claims in his speech that poverty is traceable to a lack of moral fiber, that single, poor women are inadequate mothers, that poor mothering is responsible for inner-city problems, and that marriage will save the inner city from decline are the most interesting and disturbing claims in his speech to the Commonwealth Club. That these claims were largely overlooked is fairly easy to explain. First, the mass media loves to inflate its own importance and found it far more interesting to highlight its own minor role in Quayle's speech than to examine the implications of the Vice-President's remarks for welfare and urban policy. Second, it is a media convention to focus on an individual—even a fictional one— rather than to grapple with the structural problems (e.g., lack of economic opportunity, racism, sexism) that contribute to inner-city poverty.

Media emphasis on the "Murphy Brown angle" transformed a vicious attack on poor, presumably black (given the emphasis on the inner cities and the L.A. riots) women into a debate about Hollywood liberalism, middle-class morality, and the constitution of the nuclear family.[12] *Mur-*

phy Brown itself, in its famous and much hyped response to Quayle in the premiere episode of the 1992 fall season, frames the debate in this fashion. Continuing the series tradition of intertextual references (which had been seen most recently in a baby shower for Murphy attended by Katie Couric, Joan Lunden, and other real-life newswomen), this episode's pivotal moment is a scene in which Murphy and Frank see Quayle's remarks on the evening news. Murphy, who has been struggling to learn to care for her new infant, is frustrated, exhausted, and unkempt in her pajamas, having recently moaned that "this mother stuff is the hardest thing I've ever done. And I'm one of the fortunate ones. I have a secure job, a fairly stable life, I'm educated—last night I bit the head off a stuffed bunny." [13]

Indeed, this episode establishes that almost everyone around Murphy (all men, interestingly enough) is better at motherhood than she is. Murphy is incompetent at interviewing nannies in the beginning of this episode, and Eldin eventually takes over that task. When Murphy shows up at the office, it is Miles who tells her that she is not ready to come back. Later, Frank must show her how to hold her baby so that he will stop crying, prompting the following exchange:

> *Murphy*: Oh, great, Frank, you've got better maternal instincts than I do.
> *Frank*: Murphy, would you stop writing this stuff down? You can't go at it like a reporter. You've gotta just feel your way through it.

This episode is the first indication that motherhood will not alter Murphy's personality and that postbaby episodes will retain the earlier comedic dynamic of deriving humor from Murphy's lack of feminine qualities and of placing her in situations where her failure is humorous.

After hearing Quayle's brief remarks about her "lifestyle choice," Murphy explodes:

> Glamorize single motherhood? What planet is he on? Look at me, Frank, am I glamorous? . . . And what was that crack about just another lifestyle choice? I agonized over that decision. I didn't know if I could raise a kid myself. I worried about what it would do to him, I worried about what it would do to me. I didn't just wake up one morning and say "Oh, gee, I can't get in for a facial, I might as well have a baby!"

Murphy's debunking of Quayle's characterization of her motives is humorous, but it takes Quayle's comments largely at face value and ignores their context, as did media accounts. As the controversy escalates (in additional intertextual moves, *Murphy Brown* visually features several of the actual headlines following Quayle's remarks), Murphy decides that she must make a response to the Vice-President on "FYI." Although media accounts positioned this episode as an oppositional response to the Vice-President, the substance of Murphy's argument on "FYI" is consistent with the framing of the debate as a referendum on the proper definition of a family:

> These are difficult times for our country, and in searching for the causes of our social ills, we could choose to blame the media, or the Congress, or an administration that's been in power for twelve years, or we could blame it on me. . . . I doubt that my status as a single mother has contributed all that much to the breakdown of Western civilization. . . . The Vice-President says he felt it was important to open a dialogue about family values, and on that point we agree. Unfortunately, it seems that for him, the only acceptable definition of family is a mother, a father, and children, and in a country where millions of children grow up in non-traditional families, that definition seems painfully unfair. Perhaps it's time for the Vice-President to expand his definition and recognize that, whether by choice or circumstance, families come in all shapes and sizes, and ultimately what really defines a family is commitment, caring, and love.

Following this speech, Murphy proceeds to introduce a group of adults and children (from various racial backgrounds, but predominantly white) representing a variety of definitions of family.

By the time that this episode aired in September of 1992, both the White House and the producers of *Murphy Brown* were enjoying the fruits of the publicity the incident had created. Candice Bergen, only partly tongue-in-cheek, thanked Quayle in her acceptance speech after she won the Emmy for best actress in a comedy series. Quayle obtained yet more attention when he arranged to watch the episode with a group of single mothers. The producers of *Murphy Brown* benefited from the ratings boost and the rise in advertising prices that the incident gave the sitcom (Elliott, 1992; "Murphy to Dan: Read My Ratings" 1992), and the Bush administration gained publicity for its "family values" campaign agenda. The only losers were the poor women of the inner cities, who became invisible in a debate that began with an assertion of their moral failings.[14]

Despite *Murphy Brown*'s relentless topicality and media characterization of it as a forum for liberal values (Zoglin, 1992), the sitcom is actually much less likely than *Designing Women* to engage with feminist politics, particularly when they are complicated by race. Like *Designing Women, Murphy Brown* built an episode around the Thomas/Hill hearings. In this episode, Murphy is called before the Senate Ethics Committee to testify about how she obtained a leaked Senate report that she used in a story. The episode takes a number of shots at the senators who question Murphy (who are thinly veiled caricatures of the members of the Senate Judiciary Committee that grilled Anita Hill), and Murphy delivers an entertaining diatribe denouncing them for their "grandstanding and shameless self-promotion." For all this, however, the issues of gender, race, and sexual harassment that were central to the Thomas/Hill hearings (and that figured in the *Designing Women* episode) are completely ignored. Similarly, a 1994 *Murphy Brown* episode, modeled on O. J. Simpson's then alleged murder of his wife and his flight down an L.A. freeway, is recast as a plotline about "FYI"'s difficulties covering a story about a famous white astronaut who has allegedly murdered his brother. Again, race and sex, central to the O. J. case, were eliminated from the narrative.

Postfeminist Politics in *Murphy Brown*

Despite all of the controversy, Murphy's child, Avery, makes little difference in the patterns of Murphy's character or in the narrative of *Murphy Brown*. Avery is not featured in every episode, and Murphy's personality remains largely unchanged. Generally, the child functions as a comic device to provide plotlines for Murphy's antics. Various episodes center on child-derived plotlines, such as Murphy's attempt to create a perfect, traditional Christmas for Avery (which turns into an exploration of her dysfunctional extended family), the problems that result when Murphy takes Avery to the White House Easter egg hunt, or the difficulties she creates when she attempts to join a mothers' play group.

In fact, at least one article, originally published in the *Los Angeles Times*, featured complaints from a number of women and child-care experts (including baby guru T. Berry Brazelton) that Murphy was unrealistically well-adjusted to working motherhood and that she was not "guilty, anguished, or exhausted" enough. The consensus among those interviewed in this article was that *Murphy Brown*, having defended Murphy's right to be a single mother, has "failed to prove Dan Quayle wrong" by neglecting to portray Murphy as a classically "good" mother and refusing to focus on "what [her] child's life was like" (Smith, 1993, p. E6). Harry Stein, critic for *TV Guide*, made a similar argument in an article in which he claimed that *Murphy Brown* featured "parenthood as designed by people with zero love for children. . . . Say what you will about the much-mocked Ozzie and Harriet, in their world the kids came first. In Murphy's, as in ours, they far too often come last." Indeed, Stein comments in this same column that he had looked forward to the possibility that Murphy, whom he views as overly self-involved, would change:

"Would she—like most real moms, working and otherwise—have a visceral understanding of the depth of her child's needs, and, in meeting them, take on a new depth of her own?" (Stein, 1992, p. 31).

Putting aside the obvious arguments that could be made about the possibilities for realism in television, I find a number of fascinating postfeminist contradictions at work in critiques of Murphy's motherhood. The postfeminist working mothers who dominated television in the 1980s never inspired such a reaction, even though they were hardly realistic in that their highly paid professional jobs never seemed to interfere with their constant availability for family matters. However, these women were characters in sitcoms about *family*, not work. *Murphy Brown*, in turn, has always been a sitcom about *work*, not family.

However, the possibility that, after initial adjustment, Murphy's professional life might continue largely unaffected by her maternity is interpreted by critics of *Murphy Brown* as irresponsibility on the part of the show's producers (as if Dan Quayle was really concerned about the maternal fitness of white, wealthy, career women in the first place). For some reason, Murphy's motherhood should dominate her life. Such a move would have brought *Murphy Brown* even closer to the "unstated but ever-present normative implication of postfeminist television . . . that women should combine work with family, and that normal women prioritize the latter" (Press, 1991, p. 146).

To its credit, in one of its rare refusals of postfeminist ideology, *Murphy Brown* refuses to provide this satisfaction. After a brief flirtation with essentialist womanhood in the "natural woman" scene, the sitcom seems to take the position that Murphy's dedication to her job, and her personality as a strong-willed, belligerent woman, will not be drastically altered by motherhood. In a sense, *Murphy Brown* is simply being consistent with its original premise—that Murphy approaches life much like a man would. Her brand of parenting is more stereotypically masculine than feminine in that her life as a professional and her life as a mother seem rather compartmentalized (the masculine model) rather than overlapping (the feminine model). However, her ability to do this is as much a product of class (i.e., her ability to afford a fulltime mothering substitute) as a product of personality. Like postfeminist family television, *Murphy Brown* generally avoids dealing with integration of an employed woman's personal and professional lives. In family-based sitcoms, such as *The Cosby Show*, viewers see only the mother's home life. *Murphy Brown*, in contrast, focuses on the mother's work life. There is little attention, in either case, to the difficulties of juggling the two spheres and their different demands.[15]

In the 1994–95 season, *Murphy Brown* toyed with the idea of Murphy marrying an "FYI" correspondent, Peter Hunt, who became a recurring character in the 1993–94 season and with whom she had been having an on and off romance. Their relationship was a focus in only a few episodes, as Peter was often out of town on assignment. However, in a spring 1995 episode when the two are caught in a hurricane, Peter asks Murphy to marry him and she accepts. In the final episode of the 1995 season, however, with the wedding only days away, both have doubts. They finally conclude that they are too impulsive and that neither really wants marriage. This is a rather unsatisfying episode; the romance was never well developed and there is little investment in its outcome. Certainly, Murphy's marriage would have complicated the show's narrative going into its eighth season.

The most interesting aspect of this episode is its last scene. After Peter and Murphy agree marriage would be a mistake and Peter leaves Murphy's home, Avery comes downstairs, complaining that he cannot sleep. Murphy picks him up and dances around the room with him to a song for which the refrain is "You're all I need to get by." The clear message here is that Murphy has all the family that she needs, and that her son, rather than marriage, will supply her emotional satisfaction. As it did in the birth episode, *Murphy Brown* descends here into a profound romanticization of motherhood, and one that rings rather false, given Avery's near invisibility in the series narrative. The ending claim of this episode, that Murphy can reject marriage and find fulfillment in motherhood instead, does little but reinforce the general message of the series that a successful career cannot be the basis for a satisfying life for a woman.

This interpretation of Murphy's motherhood has a number of ideological edges, as does Murphy's character generally. *Murphy Brown* gives in to the postfeminist notion that a woman's life is incomplete without reproduction, but does not, in turn, use Murphy's motherhood to further essentialist ideas about the effect of maternity on women's thinking and/or behavior. Nor does it argue that careerism and motherhood are incompatible (for those of us who would have preferred that Murphy remain child-free, this is meaningful and keeps us watching). Likewise, Murphy's difficulties with the tasks of motherhood and her lack of "maternal instincts" can be interpreted as subtle debunking of essentialized constructions of motherhood *or* as further demonstration of how Murphy's stereotypical feminist lifestyle has "defeminized" her and made her (humorously) unsuitable to be a mother—furthering her general function as a comic scapegoat.

More than any other popular television show, *Murphy Brown* represents and comments on various strands of postfeminist thought in the late 1980s and early 1990s: the personal costs of professional success, the conflicts between work and motherhood, and the emphasis on the "choices" women make. Despite the clear coding of its main character as a liberal feminist success story—prompting even Katha Pollitt to call it "the most feminist sitcom in TV history" (1994, p. 32)—*Murphy Brown* still leaves room for ambivalence.[16]

For profeminist viewers, Murphy is a rare and satisfying portrait of a powerful woman. From this perspective, even Murphy's frequent come-uppances, from which she always bounces back to endure yet more of them, can be viewed as evidence of the continuing discomfort of Americans with powerful women and of the need for continued feminist struggle (certainly, media obsession with Hillary Clinton's persona provides intertextual support for this idea). However, for an audience uncomfortable with the confrontation that feminism presents for many cherished assumptions, Murphy's function as a comedic character, whose extreme personality traits are often the source of humor, provides the relief necessary to keep her character appealing. The fact that Murphy "suffers" for her success makes it easier to accept her rejection of traditional womanhood. Ultimately, *Murphy Brown*'s potential to satisfy viewers from both camps (if only partially) tells us something about why it is so popular.

However, a sitcom's potential to enable diverse evaluations by viewers does not necessarily mean that any of those evaluations are powerfully oppositional; it is possible that "popular texts offer viewers a multiplicitous but *structured* meaning system in which instances of multivocality are complementary parts of the system's overall hegemonic design" (Cloud, 1992, p. 313). Even with its potential doubleness, *Murphy Brown* stops far short of offering any substantive challenge to postfeminism in the same way that *Designing Women* does. For example, *Murphy Brown* reiterates the profoundly disturbing silences of mass-mediated postfeminist discourse on issues such as male responsibility, female solidarity, sexual politics, *and* the significant differences in women's experiences and problems created by race, class, and sexual identity. *Designing Women*, in contrast, gave some attention to all of these factors, though in differing degrees.

This emphasis on individualistic solutions and women's "choices" is classic postfeminism, and it is sustained in the text of *Murphy Brown* and in reactions to it. *Murphy Brown* appears to eschew any acknowledgment of women's collective problems or of the need for collective action to solve them.[17] To me, the fact that so much of the humor generated by Murphy's character derives from her failure to meet conventional expectations for womanhood indicates that we are far from living in post-patriarchy. However, as *Murphy Brown* tells it, Murphy sabotages herself and pays the price for it. Even those critics of *Murphy Brown* who claim that Murphy integrates motherhood and work too easily are not motivated by a desire to dramatize the need for structural change to benefit working mothers. Rather, they are concerned that Murphy is failing to fulfill adequately her responsibility as a postfeminist role model. The onus is not on a workplace, or government, or cultural mindset that has failed to adapt to the realities of women's lives; it is on the woman, the character (or those who write her).

Indeed, it is difficult to view someone as privileged and powerful as Murphy as a victim because she is the kind of woman who has benefited the most from the liberal feminist advances of the past two decades: she is white, wealthy, and well educated. For me, this is the ultimate problem of uncritically accepting Murphy Brown as a representation of what feminism hath wrought: In doing so, all we are gaining is the possibility for a kind of rugged individualism on the part of exceptional women whose lives are cushioned by privileges of education, race, and class. In doing so, we are encouraged to overlook the profound inequalities that burden women who are *not* like Murphy Brown (a category that, in fact, includes most women). The Quayle/*Murphy Brown* incident reveals, at once, just how easily Murphy Brown has been accorded status as the icon of liberated womanhood *and* how different her circumstances are from the poor, black women who have benefited little from liberal feminism and who were Quayle's primary target.

Murphy Brown is a popular sitcom because it taps into the postfeminist anxieties of both those who think feminism went too far and those who think it did not go far enough. In the end, however, I view *Murphy Brown* as a sitcom which, beyond the "lifestyle feminism" popularized more than twenty years ago by *Mary Tyler Moore*, has no genuine feminist politics of its own, no sense that women's problems can be understood "not as symptoms of individual failure but as symptoms of oppression by a system of male dominance" (Jaggar, 1983, pp. 85–86). That *Murphy Brown* can be so widely interpreted as a vision of feminist success is a testament to how firmly postfeminist attitudes and expectations have taken hold of popular consciousness.

Notes

1. Although many articles on *Murphy Brown* stressed the comparison with *Mary Tyler Moore*, particularly noteworthy is a review of *Murphy Brown* in *The Christian Century* which builds its entire analysis of the sitcom around the comparison, concluding that Murphy is a substantial improvement over Mary (Rebeck, 1989).

2. For other examples of press coverage that make this claim, see Alley and Brown, 1990; Elm, 1989; Horowitz, 1989; O'Connor, 1989; O'Reilly, 1989; Wisehart, 1989.

3. *Esquire*'s connection of *Murphy Brown* with the backlash mentality is interesting—and ambiguous. That is, while the comment seems to cast the backlash as unfair, it also seems to agree with the substantive claim of the backlash—that women simply cannot have it all. Moreover, like backlashers, *Esquire* does not

explore how the continuance of patriarchy limits women's capacity to "have it all." Equally interesting is the fact that in *Backlash, Murphy Brown* is one of the few television programs that Susan Faludi does not critique as antifeminist (1991, p. 158).

4. In the 1994–95 season, Eldin left *Murphy Brown* (the actor that played him, Robert Pastorelli, began his own sitcom). By this point, Eldin's primary purpose was serving as the nanny for Avery, Murphy's child, and he was replaced in this position by his mother.

5. The names that identify episodes used in this analysis are from Alley and Brown, 1990.

6. Remarkably, Murphy does indeed refer to herself with a masculine pronoun in this comment.

7. For excellent discussion of these issues in relation to the Thomas/Hill hearings, see Crenshaw, 1992; Lubiano, 1992; Painter, 1992.

8. Hugh Duncan, drawing on Burke, explains the function of a comic scapegoat as a representation of values that pose a threat to the dominant social order (1962, p. 395). Functioning as a caricature of the values in contention, the scapegoat is comically sacrificed, through ridicule, embarrassment, or humiliation, and the social order is protected from the threat it represents (Duncan, 1962, pp. 401, 378).

Such a comic strategy ultimately is aimed at acceptance of the scapegoated character; however, that acceptance must come on the terms set by the dominant cultural group. As Duncan notes: "There is hostility in our laughter, but it is not the hostility of derisive laughter which ends in alienation and hate. . . . Such joking is really a form of instruction, a kind of social control, directed at those we intend to accept once they learn to behave properly" (1962, p. 389). As Duncan explains it, this is the conservative function of comedy; it requires sacrifice of the scapegoat so that authority can be maintained (1962, p. 380).

9. After Jake leaves, Murphy and Jerry Gold make a brief attempt to live together, but they cannot get along. Murphy decides that their relationship makes her feel too dependent and "needy." Murphy's most consistent companion throughout her pregnancy is Eldin, her housepainter, who is motivated, he claims, by the realization that whereas Murphy would be a rotten mother, he would be an excellent one. Indeed, Murphy eventually hires Eldin to be the child's nanny. While Eldin's skill at child-rearing could be viewed as a feminist statement (i.e., men can be caretakers as well as women), it can also be viewed as underscoring Murphy's maternal incompetence (i.e., an itinerant housepainter can be as good a mother as she can).

10. The troubling implication of this scene was not lost on some viewers. In response to a *USA Today* editorial about *Murphy Brown*'s glorification of single motherhood, at least two viewers wrote letters expressing their dissatisfaction with the sitcom's message. One wrote, "Television writers, take a hint: Not every woman has to be fulfilled through the joys of motherhood" ("Aghast at Writers," 1992, p. A10), while another had a more expansive analysis:

Why can't she "feel like a natural woman" without a child? Why does the entertainment industry insist on showing childless women as less than whole? . . . Is having a child supposed to "tame" Murphy and make her softer and more feminine? The entertainment industry's message seems to be that liberation has made women unhappy and unfulfilled. What's wrong with exalting an intelligent female character who is happy with her life and her choices?" ("A 'Natural Woman'?" 1992, p. A10)

11. All quotations from the Quayle speech that I use here are from "Excerpts from the Vice-President's Speech on Cities and Poverty," the *New York Times*, May 20, 1992, p. A11.

12. For example, the *Chicago Tribune*, alongside an analysis of the response to the *Murphy Brown* flap from politicians and members of the television community, ran a story entitled "Single Mom: Quayle Stance Is Ludicrous," which featured a single, white, female business executive describing the joys of single motherhood. The woman concludes that "she knows 'other single women who have children and who are strong and financially able—and they deserve to have a child if they want to' " (Kleiman, 1992, p. 1:2). By featuring a white, economically privileged woman, even this seemingly oppositional story fails to challenge the politics of race and class raised in Quayle's speech and, in fact, implicitly participates in the distinction between deserving and undeserving mothers that Quayle creates.

13. This remark, in which Murphy refers to herself as "fortunate," is the closest this episode comes to acknowledging the differences between Murphy and the women Quayle was attacking.

14. Katha Pollitt, one of the few journalists to point out the race, class, and gender politics that infused Quayle's speech, offered an incisive analysis of the Quayle / *Murphy Brown* incident that has greatly influenced my thinking about the issues involved. See Pollitt, 1994, pp. 31–41.

15. A few episodes following the birth did pay some attention to the difficulties created by a new baby. In the 1992 season premiere, a running joke concerns Murphy's inability to find time to take a shower. In another episode, the opening sequence of shots shows Murphy being forced to change her shirt three times because the baby keeps spitting up on it. Another plotline is driven by the problems caused when Murphy brings the baby to the office. After the 1992–93 season these issues largely go away, and there are many episodes when the baby is never seen or mentioned.

16. I use the term "ambivalence" for two reasons. First, I do not see much potential for denotative flux in *Murphy Brown*; hence my avoidance of the term "polysemous." The issue, for me, is not whether viewers are encouraged to see Murphy as carrying meaning about the progress of American women (I think it is clear that they are) but, rather, how they might *evaluate* Murphy's representation of that progress. Second, following Dana Cloud's (1992, p. 314) arguments about depiction of racial difference in *Spenser: For Hire*, I see potential evaluations of *Murphy Brown* "as contained within a *binary* meaning system"; hence the term "ambivalence" rather than "polyvalence."

17. It's useful to note here that Robert S. Alley and Irby B. Brown, in their book-length study of the making of *Murphy Brown*, claim that "the fictional characters on *Murphy Brown* relate to one another as if feminism had succeeded. . . . In the world of *FYI* . . . Murphy and her colleagues have transcended sexism. They probably do reside in a postfeminist world, a world we would argue rests firmly on the causes championed by the feminist movement" (1990, p. 100).

Chapter 5
The Other Side of Postfeminism: Maternal Feminism in *Dr. Quinn, Medicine Woman*

Dr. Quinn, Medicine Woman, an hour-long drama centering on the life of a woman doctor in the frontier town of Colorado Springs in the late 1860s, debuted as a midseason replacement on CBS in January of 1993. It was an immediate success, boasting the highest "TVQ" rating of any television program in recent history.[1] The success of *Dr. Quinn* took industry pundits by surprise; they had predicted that it was doomed to fail. It was a so-called "soft" drama geared to family viewing, it was a period piece set in the old West, and, perhaps most damaging, it depended upon a female lead (Carter, 1993; Kilday, 1993). These characteristics are, for example, exactly opposite those of *NYPD Blue,* the other big success story of 1993. Even worse, CBS scheduled the drama on Saturday, a graveyard slot for prime-time network television because programmers and advertisers are convinced the audience defects to cable.

Dr. Quinn's surprising success, and its ability to attract precisely the kind of audiences that advertisers on network television yearn for— women between eighteen and forty-nine—has attracted relatively little attention from the popular press. Critics do not see the drama as particularly complex or interesting, and most have dismissed it. They have called it historically inaccurate and melodramatic (Stein, 1993), attacked it for its "political correctness" and "anachronistic moralizing" (Kilday, 1993, p. 108; see also Kaufman, 1993), and one critic has labeled it "frontier hooey" (quoted in Schindehette, 1993, p. 74). Reviewers seem to agree that the program is neither "true to the form [of the western] nor true to the time [it depicts]" (quoted in Kilday, 1993, p. 108).

Such complaints take notice of a number of unusual elements for a historical western: black and Native American primary characters, and a female lead character, the central authority figure. The latter factor is given the most attention in the publicity surrounding *Dr. Quinn*'s star, Jane Seymour. The consensus is that a major draw for the show (which has a large number of adolescent girls in its audience) is the female role model provided by Dr. Michaela Quinn. Dr. Quinn is a thirty-five-year-old virgin (until her marriage in the 1995 season), a characteristic apparently so remarkable it was mentioned in *Newsweek* (Hamilton, 1994, p. 44), and in most profiles of Jane Seymour, the actress who plays Dr. Quinn (e.g., McLellan, 1994; Schindehette, 1993; Schwarzbaum, 1994). Jane Seymour herself stresses other positive aspects of the lead character in interviews: She has claimed that *Dr. Quinn* shows that "women can be productive without being victims or sex objects" (Schindehette, 1993, p. 74) and that "it lets little girls aspire to being more than just mothers [or] being married" (Liebman, 1994, p. 28). An *Entertainment Weekly* story on Seymour and *Dr. Quinn* called the drama a "feminist western" that "brought a feminist agenda to the classic Hollywood interplay between cowboys and Indians" (Schwarzbaum, 1994, p. 28).

The feminist dimensions of *Dr. Quinn* seem readily apparent. The title character is a white, thirty-five-year-old, unmarried woman in an unconventional profession for her gender, particularly for the time period (indeed, the recognition that she inhabits a conventionally masculine role is signaled by the fact that her nickname, which is used by all characters, including two of her children, is "Dr. Mike").[2] These characteristics are quite common for female characters representing feminism on prime-time dramatic television: recall the plethora of female lawyers, doctors, and police officers in contemporary dramas like *Hill Street Blues, L.A. Law, Cagney and Lacey, Hunter,* or *St. Elsewhere* who fit these general characteristics. *Dr. Quinn* seems to fit easily into the liberal feminist tradition of television in which women's progress is showcased by allowing them to occupy traditionally masculine professional roles—what Julie D'Acci (1992, p. 174) calls the "role reversal" strategy.

Yet there are also key differences that separate *Dr. Quinn* from television's feminist tradition and from the other programs discussed in this book. First, *Dr. Quinn* is a western, a genre that brings with it, as I discuss later in this chapter, a distinct *ethos*. Second, this drama melds the spheres of home and work in ways that are unusual in female-centered postfeminist television. Finally, *Dr. Quinn* adapts and illustrates some key themes in recent postfeminist and feminist thought that radiate from the concept of woman's "difference"; that is, the idea that inherent qualities of womanhood (often linked to motherhood) should be valued for their positive application in the public sphere.

Feminism, Postfeminism, and Woman's "Difference"

As early as 1983, Hester Eisenstein critiqued the influence of work by cultural feminists such as Mary Daly (1978) and Susan Griffin (1978), work that made claims for woman's superiority based on, in Eisenstein's view, a suspicious biologism, a false universalization of women's experience, and "a retreat from the fundamentally liberating concept of woman as agent, actor, and subject" (1983, p. 135). As Alice Echols argues in her history of radical feminism, cultural feminism that stressed woman's superiority and the creation of a separate woman's culture was evolving by the late 1970s out of some branches of radical feminism (1989, pp. 243–265). The process by which difference arguments became part of popular consciousness in the 1980s and 1990s, however, is most evident in the intersections between postfeminist idealization of family life and the dissemination of the work of feminist scholars like Carol Gilligan and Sara Ruddick, who stressed, respectively, women's "different voice" and their capacity for "maternal thinking."

As I discussed in Chapter 3, a primary issue in media constructions of postfeminism has been the difficulty of reconciling women's expanded roles in the public sphere with their traditional responsibilities in the private sphere. Key postfeminist texts, such as Friedan's *The Second Stage* (1981) and Hewlett's *A Lesser Life* (1986) gained notoriety for their common accusation that the emphasis of second-wave feminism on workplace equality failed to account for women's supposedly innate desire to bear and raise children. Friedan and Hewlett claim that feminism's demonization of motherhood led to the neglect of family issues in the feminist agenda. As I have argued, this interpretation of feminism's relationship to family issues is rather incomplete in that it dismisses the relevance of the questions that radical feminists raised about the sexual politics of the traditional family, and it also adopts a perspective on feminism drawn from mass media accounts rather than from actual movement efforts.[3] Regardless of their accuracy in describing feminist ideology, however, Friedan and Hewlett made significant contributions to the romanticization of motherhood that became a postfeminist trend.

Although the rise of the New Right and conservative control of the White House were major factors in the renewed emphasis on family values in the 1980s, feminist thinkers also played a role in the resurgence of attention to women's "natural" maternal qualities and their implications (Faludi, 1991, pp. 325–332). Ann Snitow (1992) has constructed a rough timeline delineating phases in feminism's relationship to motherhood since 1970.[4] In the first phase, between 1963 (the year the *Feminine Mystique* was published) and 1975, she argues that feminists attempted to denaturalize motherhood from a given for every woman to a choice;

however, she also notes that relatively little attention was paid to mothering during this period because most movement activists and writers were young and were not yet mothers (pp. 36–37). By the second phase, 1976–79, "the feminist work of exploring mothering took off, and books central to feminist thinking in this wave were written, both about the daily experience of being a mother and about motherhood's most far-reaching implications" (1992, p. 38). The most influential of these books, such as Adrienne Rich's *Of Woman Born* (1976) and Nancy Chodorow's *The Reproduction of Mothering* (1978) deconstruct motherhood and mothering as patriarchal *institutions*, attempting to separate them from mothering as a *practice* and an *experience* for women.

The third and final phase, and the one of interest to me in this chapter, began in 1980 with the publication of Sara Ruddick's influential article "Maternal Thinking" (1980) which became part of a book by the same title in 1989. Although, as Snitow (1992, p. 40) points out, "it was not part of Ruddick's intention to publish her work in the same year Reagan was elected," Ruddick's claims for mothers' special capacities for nurturance, sensitivity, and connection with others can be used to reinforce the regressive roles for women preferred by the New Right.

"Maternal Thinking" was followed in 1982 by Carol Gilligan's *In a Different Voice*, which argued that women's moral reasoning differs from men's and is more likely to be guided by "a standard of relationship, an ethic of nurturance, responsibility, and care" (p. 159). Although Gilligan does not stress motherhood as a factor, her conclusions echo Ruddick's in significant ways. Both Ruddick and Gilligan argued for the feminist implications of their work; for example, Ruddick argued that "mothers who acquire a feminist consciousness and engage in feminist politics are likely to become more effectively nonviolent and antimilitarist. By increasing mothers' power to know, care, and act, feminism actualizes the peacefulness latent in maternal practice" (Ruddick, 1989, p. 242). Gilligan claimed that recognition of the variation in moral reasoning demonstrated by her work would refute a belief in psychological theory that women, because they appear to reject abstract modes of reasoning, are morally underdeveloped. Such thinking, she argued, results from the sexist "assumption that there is a single mode of social experience and interpretation" that is based on the behavior of men. By arguing for the importance of the "different voice" of women, Gilligan maintained that women's experiences should not be subordinated to men's (1982a, pp. 173–174).

The works of Ruddick and Gilligan dovetail in their emphasis on the "differences" that women embody in psychological, relational, and perhaps political terms. Although written with feminist goals in mind, their conclusions were ripe to be appropriated for antifeminist goals, particularly during the aggressively pronatal 1980s. Indeed, Snitow argues, even feminist abortion politics were colored by the romance of motherhood:

On the political front it's been some time since feminists demanding abortion have put front and center the idea that one good use to which one might put this right is to choose not to have kids *at all*. Chastised in the Reagan years, pro-choice strategists—understandably—have emphasized the right to wait, the right to space one's children, the right to have each child wanted. They feared invoking any image that could be read as a female withdrawal from the role of nurturer. (1992, p. 41)

Moreover, in a bid to adapt to the political climate and gain wider support, many feminists recast their demands for women in the 1980s as "family issues," a label with a double edge. On the one hand, it removes the taint of special interest politics attached to "women's issues."[5] On the other hand, "the danger in focusing on the family was the lack of discussion of power within families, or the obscuring of women's oppression within these social arrangements" (Stearney, 1994, p. 150).

The pronatalism of the 1980s prompted analyses of the resurgence of maternal yearning in mainstream women's magazines such as *Mademoiselle* and *Glamour* (see, e.g., Angier, 1989; Lague, 1990) as well as in *Ms.*, which presented contrasting views in a 1988 issue. The two articles were entitled, interestingly enough, "Womb Worship" (Weideger, 1988), and "Mother's Choice" (Quindlen, 1988).[6] A number of popular movies also dramatized the appeal of nurturing, for both women (*Baby Boom* [1987], *She's Having a Baby* [1988], *For Keeps* [1988]) and men (*Author! Author!* [1982], *Three Men and a Baby* [1987]).[7]

Clearly, the valorization of motherhood and woman's difference that grew from work by feminist academics did not stay in the academy.[8] Attention to "woman's difference" became a hot topic in mainstream media in the 1980s and into the 1990s, as books and articles appeared in a variety of arenas arguing for recognition of women's special qualities. Bestselling self-help books like Deborah Tannen's *You Just Don't Understand: Men and Women in Conversation* (1991b) and John Gray's *Men Are from Mars, Women Are from Venus* (1992) echoed Gilligan by arguing that the communication problems between men and women evolve from their differing value structures and ways of seeing the world and relationships. Tannen became a frequent guest on talk shows targeted at women and in women's magazines (e.g., Tannen, 1991a). Gilligan became a star in both feminist and mainstream media: she published a summary of the conclusions of *In a Different Voice* in *Psychology Today* (Gilligan, 1982b), she became *Ms.* magazine's "Woman of the Year" in 1984, and she was the subject of a 1990 cover story in the *New York Times Magazine* (Faludi, 1991, p. 327). *Time*'s 1990 special issue, "Women: The Road Ahead" included a story on Gilligan's conclusions entitled "Coming from a Different Place" (Toufexis, 1990).

In business, books like *The Female Advantage: Women's Ways of Leadership* (Helgesen, 1990) used Gilligan to argue that women have a different leadership style; they are "intuitive, anti-hierarchical, process oriented, tolerant of ambiguity, and not invested in power" (Noble, 1993, p. 3:6). Helgesen's work also was the subject of an article in *Time*'s special issue (Rudolph, 1990) and was debated in magazines like *Fortune* (Fierman, 1990) and in the *New York Times* (Noble, 1993).[9] Theories of women's greater comfort with cooperation rather than competition have influenced educational theory as well. The arguments of *Women's Ways of Knowing* (Belenky et al., 1986), which theorizes that women are "connected" knowers rather than competitive "separate" knowers (the masculine model), have been influential in calls for development of cooperative, experiential, group learning rather than traditional hierarchical methods.

Although some used Gilligan's work "to bolster arguments that independence was an unnatural and unhealthy state for women" (Faludi, 1991, p. 331), Gilligan's and Ruddick's conclusions have generally resulted in claims for valuing women's special capacities in private *and* public arenas. This is not a new feminist strategy. In the late nineteenth century, a number of feminist reformers rooted their claims for increased rights for women in difference arguments. Social feminists such as Frances Willard, president of the Woman's Christian Temperance Union, argued that women's special capacities for caring and moral guidance uniquely equipped them to contribute to "public housekeeping" (Bordin, 1986; Dow, 1991).[10]

These historical resonances lead me to the implication of postfeminist thought that I wish to emphasize in this chapter: its nostalgia. Just as scholars have argued that much of the power of the Reagan presidency derived from Reagan's evocation of a mythic past (Lewis, 1987; Wills, 1987), the postfeminist ethos that arose in tandem with Reagan's America also drew on nostalgia. Difference feminism, wittingly or not, contributed to that effect. A consistent theme in popular media's exploration of postfeminist anxiety is the contrast with a simpler past, when women's responsibilities were contained within the home. Their choices were fewer, but their lives were easier.[11] Such a claim is, in fact, true only for a segment of America women—married, middle-class, predominantly white mothers who did not work outside the home. Less privileged women have always combined paid work with motherhood, but, consistent with postfeminism's elision of class differences, their history is generally ignored. Moreover, although many have argued that economic pressures, as much as feminism, led to the increase in the number of women combining work outside the home with motherhood (Ehren-reich, 1990a, pp. 196–207; Phillips, 1990), the postfeminist mantra of "choice" usually elides this distinction as well.

Postfeminism's idealization of motherhood and its refusal of sexual politics means that postfeminist questioning of women's "choices" usually emphasizes women's anxieties about the impact of work on motherhood, that is, the ways in which postfeminist women may be failing their families because of their pursuit of fulfillment in the public sphere. Even as media treatment of these themes pays lip service to women's desire or need to work, it also reifies traditional notions that their most important work is at home. With that in mind, the intersections of postfeminism and difference feminism become important. Although difference feminism may advocate the extension of women's qualities from the private sphere to the public sphere, it further naturalizes women's responsibilities in the private sphere. Even if the difference feminist utopia is eventually achieved and traditionally female qualities are valued in public life, it is not clear whether that shift will entail necessary material changes such as federally subsidized day-care or pay equity.

Westerns, Nostalgia, and *Dr. Quinn*

These tensions, between public and private spheres, between nostalgia and contemporary angst, and between utopian feminist visions and women's material realities, make *Dr. Quinn, Medicine Woman* a compelling (tele)vision of feminism. As I said at the beginning of this chapter, popular critics have accused the drama of transporting contemporary social issues backward in time. The most obvious and useful response to that objection is that there is no such thing as a historically accurate western. All westerns—on film *and* television—are *fantasies* about the frontier, guided in no small part by the needs of the culture that produces them (see Brauer, 1975; Cawelti, 1971; Tompkins, 1989). Indeed, it is this realization that highlights the unique quality of westerns—their placement in a mythic past. Although there are strong differences between westerns in different media—novels, films, and television series—they are all fundamentally nostalgic, and this characteristic allows them to perform specific ideological functions which, at different times in American history, have been very powerful for their audiences.

My contention in this chapter is that *Dr. Quinn*'s use of nostalgia strategically frames the drama's reworking of contemporary feminist and postfeminist themes. The retreat into nostalgia as a strategy for addressing contemporary cultural anxieties has become increasingly evident on television in recent years in such dramatic series as *Homefront* (1991–92), *I'll Fly Away* (1991–92), and *The Young Riders* (1989–93), but *Dr. Quinn* has been the most successful of these efforts. Common sense tells us that nostalgia is especially appealing in troubling or confusing times. A number of theorists of postmodern culture have discussed the emergence of nostalgia as a cultural strategy, arguing that, in many cases, the use of nostalgia is an antidote to the perceived instability and incoherence of postmodernism. In this case, postmodernism is a label used to refer to the instability of contemporary times, in which the viability of "real" stable meanings is called into question, all judgments are relativized, and notions of transcendent truth are dismissed. Instead, we are awash in images, representations without referents, and an ever expanding field of "culture" in which commodification rules (see Baudrillard, 1992; Connor, 1989, pp. 50–62; Jameson, 1991). In the words of philosopher Jean-François Lyotard, "the Enlightenment narrative, in which the hero of knowledge works toward a good ethico-political end," is obsolete, which means that the search for overarching consensus about truth, morality, and "the good" is pointless (1984, pp. xxiii–xxiv).

The implications of pronouncements about the "postmodern condition" continue to be debated, and I do not wish to enter that debate here. However, even without an awareness or acceptance of a postmodern condition, it is no stretch to acknowledge that symptoms of cultural instability surround us. The rising tide of violence, the proliferation of challenges to white male ethnocentric hegemony enacted by feminism and multiculturalism, the waning belief in the promise of democracy and the American Dream, and, last but not least, the pervasive decentering effects of globalized media, are hard to ignore. The point of this admittedly reductionist summary is to provide the context in which Jameson and others produce their arguments about the uses of nostalgia. Through nostalgic cultural products, we search for a "reassuring anchor" through representations of an earlier, simpler time (Joyrich, 1992, p. 238) and find an "authentic way of confronting our own current political dilemmas in the present" (Jameson, 1991, p. 25). From this perspective, nostalgic cultural forms go beyond simple sentimentality; they are reactions to and symptoms of postmodernity that are both opposed to and inflected by the times in which they are produced. This perspective provides a useful way of understanding the revival of westerns generally, and the appeal of *Dr. Quinn*, specifically.

In the late 1970s and early 1980s, it became a truism in the film and television industries that the traditional western was a dormant genre. Various explanations were offered for the decline of the TV western, and a common refrain was that the genre was too simplistic and limited by its historical setting. Hence, it could not compete against the rise of sophisticated and topical serial melodramas such as *Hill Street Blues, St. Elsewhere*, or *L.A. Law*. Consistent with this train of thought, Michael Barson

(1985, p. 68) has argued that the television western's demise derives from the fact that it "does not and did not offer anything truly different on a dramatic level than several other television genres did," and, by the late 1970s, viewers preferred their drama to have a contemporary setting. According to Barson, cop shows, private detective shows, and other dramas that reworked the themes of justice, morality, and communal behavior replaced westerns in the hearts of television viewers.

However, now that we are experiencing a seemingly lasting revival of the western, in both film and television, this conclusion appears dubious. Despite the fact that prime-time television still has several powerful contemporary dramas holding their own (e.g., *NYPD Blue* [1993–present], *Law and Order* [1990–present], *E.R.* [1994–present]), the enormous success of the *Lonesome Dove* (1989) miniseries and the *Gambler* made-for-TV movies (1980, 1983, 1987, 1993), coupled with the respectable performance of the *Young Riders* drama series (which is now syndicated on the Family Channel) and the continuing production of western TV movies by cable and broadcast networks, indicates that the western has staged a comeback. Moreover, the success of recent western feature films such as *Silverado* (1985), *Young Guns* [I and II] (1988), *Posse* (1993), and, most notably, *Dances with Wolves* (1991), *Unforgiven* (1992), and *Tombstone* (1993) (not to mention a small trend of female-centered westerns such as *Bad Girls* [1994] and *The Quick and the Dead* [1995]) lends considerable strength to the idea that the western genre has reasserted its appeal.

I offer this list of western pop culture trivia because I believe Barson misapprehends the appeal of westerns. The western is a distinctive form of drama, and certain of its generic characteristics allow a kind of storytelling that contemporary, primarily urban, dramas cannot achieve. From this perspective, westerns declined because audiences began to want something different that the western did not provide, and, along the same lines, westerns are reviving because they fill needs that other forms of drama cannot.

The appeal of westerns in the late 1980s and early 1990s can be explained, then, as a method of compensating for the instability of contemporary lived reality. The moral polarization, unfettered individualism, and frontier simplicity depicted by the western not only are comforting in a basic sense; they also offer the western relatively uncluttered ground upon which to represent contemporary conflicts. Like *Dr. Quinn*, other members of the recent wave of westerns (e.g., *Silverado, Dances with Wolves, Young Riders, Posse*) have explored contemporary issues such as racism (against blacks and Native Americans), sexism, and environmental issues. Moreover, following a line of thinking begun by Fredric Jameson which holds that our nostalgia for a better past translates into appropriation of the cultural forms or aesthetic styles of that past (Connor 1989, p. 177), it is interesting that the original heyday of the film and television western was the 1950s, a period of time in America history mythologized for its placidity, safety, conformity, and optimism.

Westerns, I suggest, perform two somewhat contradictory functions: First, they allow us to escape the complexity of contemporary life by returning us to a simpler time. Second, they reconstruct contemporary conflicts in a historical context, a strategy that can have a powerful effect on perceptions of these conflicts. Both functions will be central to my reading of *Dr. Quinn* because they provide the foundation for the drama's legitimation of a maternal feminism that draws on contemporary reassertion of notions of woman's difference.

Historicizing Feminism in *Dr. Quinn*

The most obvious historicizing device in *Dr. Quinn* is its use of the trappings of the television western. I use the word "trappings" purposely, for, beyond setting, *Dr. Quinn* has little resemblance to such popular television westerns as *Gunsmoke* (1955–75) or *Bonanza* (1959–73), although it has been compared to *Little House on the Prairie* (1974–83) (see Schindehette, 1993). *Dr. Quinn* has little or none of the violence, gunplay, and territorial disputes that characterized past westerns. What it does display, however, is the vital ingredient of the western *ethos*: setting, both geographic (the rural frontier) and temporal (late nineteenth century). In westerns, the frontier performs a leveling function; it strips life to its essence in a context that has few institutional pressures. There are only localized codes of justice, education is rudimentary, and most work is entrepreneurial. The West is a world in which every person, supposedly, is measured and valued by what s/he does and what s/he can contribute. As Kitses notes, "What gives [the western] a particular thrust and centrality is its historical setting; its being placed at exactly that moment when options are still open, the dream of primitivistic individualism . . . still tenable" (1969, quoted in Brauer, 1975, p. 14).

Westerns, then, offer the ultimate context for discovering the authentic self, and it is no coincidence that all westerns take, as some part of their theme, the testing or definition of manhood (Tompkins, 1989). This central quest, adapted for womanhood, is the western's principal legacy to *Dr. Quinn*. With this loose foothold in a nostalgic genre, *Dr. Quinn* interweaves feminist and postfeminist discourses drawn from various cultural sources, not the least of which is television itself. As I noted above, *Dr. Quinn* makes use of televisual conventions of liberal feminism in its focus on a woman in a traditionally masculine occupation. Moreover, the title character's rejection of a conventional life for a woman of her period is signaled by the premise of the drama. Dr. Michaela Quinn travels west from Boston in 1867 after the deaths of her father and her fiancé, the only two people who supported her quest to practice medicine. She graduated from a female medical college in Philadelphia and received substantial training from her father, a famous surgeon. Her credentials, in short, are good, and the first episode makes clear that she leaves Boston, her family, and the only life she has ever known, so that she can practice medicine in an area that will value her as a doctor rather than as a woman.

While such a "journey tale" is compatible with the traditional western, it is equally recognizable as the symbol for a woman's emancipation in past television discourse about feminism. In *The Mary Tyler Moore Show* (1970), for instance, Mary Richards left home for a new life in Minneapolis as a working woman after breaking up with her fiancé; in *One Day at a Time* (1975), Anne Romano moves from the suburbs to the city of Indianapolis after her divorce; in *Alice* (1976), the title character moves to Phoenix to start a new life after the death of her husband. In each case, the journey to a new place symbolizes the liberation of the character, and it is replayed in the opening credits of these programs for at least their first season, just as in *Dr. Quinn*. Indeed, my decision to include *Dr. Quinn* in a book focused almost exclusively on situation comedy was influenced by the fact that the drama draws so clearly on the conventions of representing feminism that originated in sitcom.

In the first season of *Dr. Quinn*, the opening credits that depict Dr. Mike on her journey west included narration that said: "I was told a woman doctor couldn't survive alone on the frontier. But I won't give up—and I'm not alone anymore. I've inherited a family, and that may be the biggest challenge of all." The first episode promptly sublimates the individualistic premise of the drama. Dr. Mike's only friend in her new town dies, leaving the care of her three children to the doctor, and Dr. Mike is immediately, literally, domesticated. This turn of events—and its reiteration in the opening narrative as perhaps her "biggest challenge"—is key to *Dr. Quinn*'s incorporation of postfeminist discourse. The placement of the heroine's professional struggles within a family context provides the opportunity to engage with a central issue in postfeminist gender anxiety: can women do it all? Moreover, the central place of these children—Matthew, Colleen, and Brian—in various "life lesson" subplots, clearly figures in *Dr. Quinn*'s attraction of a family audience and in its popularity with adolescent girls.

At the same time that *Dr. Quinn* firmly situates its lead character in the middle of contemporary feminist debates (at least as television defines them), its careful inclusion of easily decodable discourses of femininity works to exempt her from certain stereotypes that have afflicted other television characters representing feminism (see D'Acci, 1992). Dr. Mike is not antifamily values or antimotherhood. Other discourses of conventional femininity are even clearer. Jane Seymour brings enough heterosexual glamour to the role, through her own striking beauty and the intertextual associations with her persona as the highly sexualized "Queen of Television Miniseries," to compensate for Dr. Mike's rather plain, functional wardrobe and deemphasized sexuality.[12]

Dr. Mike also has a steady, heterosexual love interest with whom her relationship is emotionally, although not physically, intense. He is, in fact, quite a feminized character in many ways, making him a suitable partner for an idealized representative of contemporary feminism. Sully, a mountain man and sometime Indian agent, is sensitive, caring, and supportive of Dr. Mike; most importantly, her higher status in the community does not threaten him. More than any other character, Sully supports Dr. Mike's moral vision for the community. However, these feminized aspects of his character are compensated for by his other, hypermasculine traits, illustrating what Lynne Joyrich has called "an excess of 'maleness' that acts as a shield" against the implications of feminization (1990, p. 165). He is handsome and muscled, and dresses in rough furs and leather. He is also a quintessential outdoorsman who lives in the wild, speaks only when he has something important to say, and feels most comfortable in his group of all-male Cheyenne companions. Many of the townspeople view him as something of a savage, and only Dr. Mike and her children truly understand him.

Following Dr. Mike and her family (including Sully), the other characters in *Dr. Quinn* exist in a kind of hierarchy, descending from the white townspeople, to the black townspeople, to the Indians and the immigrants. Their likelihood of appearing in any given episode is signaled by their place in the hierarchy. The townspeople include the white town merchant, Loren Bray, whose bigotry against the Indians, the immigrants, and the blacks who populate the town is manifest. In the first season, Loren's sister, Olive, a generally positive character, runs the store with him and runs a ranch as well (although viewers never see her doing so). In *Dr. Quinn*'s second season, the character of Olive leaves the program and is replaced by another woman, Dorothy, who also runs the store with Loren. However, instead of running a ranch she edits the town paper.

Loren's bigotry is shared by the other white businessmen in town: Hank, the saloon and brothel owner who often terrorizes the prostitutes who work for him, and Jake, the alcoholic and illiterate barber (who is eventually elected mayor). The town's minister, Reverend Johnson, also participates in the bigotry. He is a minor character, and his weakness characterizes him. Horace, the town's postmaster and telegraph operator, is a likable and compassionate person. His love for Myra, one of the town prostitutes with a proverbial heart of gold, is an ongoing subplot that culminates in their marriage in the 1994 season. However, the townspeople treat Horace as a lovable milquetoast unworthy of much respect.

The town's recurring black community includes Robert E., a blacksmith, livery owner, and former slave. The only black woman character, who becomes Robert E.'s wife, is Grace, who operates her own cafe. Both are thoroughly positive characters.[13] Members of the Cheyenne tribe that live on a reservation outside the town appear regularly, although only one, Cloud Dancing, has a consistent speaking role. In stark contrast to earlier TV westerns, the depiction of the Cheyenne as proud, intelligent, and peaceful discredits the bigotry toward them by many of the townspeople.[14] Finally, an immigrant community lives in a tent city on the outskirts of town. Some of the immigrants work in the nearby silver mines, but their existence is precarious. The immigrants are also the target of prejudice by the townspeople, a prejudice largely based on their poverty and supposed stupidity because of their poor English. The narrative of *Dr. Quinn* depicts the immigrants as good people caught in difficult circumstances. One of them, a young Swedish woman, is Dr. Mike's eldest son's fiancé.

This diverse roster of characters is a unique element in *Dr. Quinn*'s adaptation of the western, and represents another facet of the drama's incorporation of contemporary themes. While past TV westerns often used such characters as the external "problem" to be resolved in a given episode, they did not have the status of continuing characters. In *Dr. Quinn*, such characters not only serve as a nod to multiculturalism but also serve a vital function in the construction of Dr. Mike's character by providing her with a ready-made constituency to champion. Indeed, the emphasis on antiracism in *Dr. Quinn* can be taken as an indication of the linkage of antiracism and feminism in the 1980s and 1990s that has resulted from the influential work of feminists of color (e.g., Collins, 1990; hooks, 1989; Lorde, 1984). Dr. Mike is always at the center of disputes that concern the oppressed groups in her town, implicating their fate in the gender politics that define her function in the narrative. For example, plotlines have centered around Dr. Mike's support for striking local miners (most of whom are immigrants), her attempts to prevent the lynching of an immigrant for suspected cattle rustling, her battle to save the Cheyenne tribe from a typhus epidemic purposely visited upon them by the U.S. cavalry, and her effort, against serious opposition, to make sure that a celebratory town photograph encompasses all of the town's inhabitants, including Indians, immigrants, and blacks.

At this point, it makes sense to return to the implications of *Dr. Quinn*'s historicization of discourses of feminism and multiculturalism. The consistent, and, according to critics, often heavyhanded critiques of sexism, racism, and xenophobia in *Dr. Quinn* indicate its utopian potential. As Jameson argues, mass culture texts can incorporate "our deepest fantasies about the nature of social life, both as we live it now, and as we feel in our bones it ought rather to be lived" (1979, p. 147). *Dr. Quinn* offers the television version of the argument from history as a legitimation device (see Cox, 1990; Lipsitz, 1990). The drama offers alternative history that destabilizes assumptions about a mythical, harmonious past when consensus ruled. If struggles against racism, sexism, and classism have always existed, our struggles with these issues in the present become part of a historical trajectory; rather than a symptom of cultural fragmentation, they become a sign of cultural evolution. Anxieties about cultural instability are reframed and normalized through their presence in a fictional past.

However, the placement of these issues within the parameters of the television western reveals the second function of historicization in *Dr. Quinn*—as nostalgia appeal. In Jameson's terms, this function is more ideological than utopian. Nostalgia can function as a kind of collective wish-fulfillment fantasy, satisfying an "unconscious yearning for a simpler and more human social system" (Jameson, 1991, p. 283). At this point, the ideological functions of the western become relevant. Jameson describes genre as "essentially a socio-symbolic message," or "immanently and intrinsically an ideology in its own right. When such forms are reappropriated and refashioned in quite different social and cultural contexts, this message persists and must be functionally reckoned into the new form" (1981, p. 141). Indeed, *Dr. Quinn* synthesizes convention and invention within the limits of the western.

Westerns return us to a simpler locale, where the stakes are clear and the autonomy of the self is a given. Dr. Mike's journey from Boston to Colorado draws upon this appeal. What she becomes in the West will answer the question that plagues us in the present: "What is woman?" Because of the context in which it is enacted, the answer provided takes on a powerful ring of truth that characterizes nostalgia appeals. This function, which I will return to later, is strengthened in *Dr. Quinn* by the show's reliance on the conventions of melodrama. Melodrama is also a fundamentally nostalgic mode, as Lynne Joyrich explains:

As the political, social and aesthetic representations of modern society lose their legitimacy, we are forced again to find new stakes of meaning, and melodrama is the form to which we turn. In a simulated society which typically stages reality in order to "prove" its existence, melodrama offers a way to assert the "actual" drama of life. . . . Melodrama helps us place ourselves in a confusing world—its insistence on the validity of moral or experiential truths and its faith in the reality of the stakes creates a space from which to act. (1992, pp. 236, 245)

Melodrama excels at transporting social and political conflicts into the realm of the personal, where they can be managed through emotional connection and personal sentiment. Dr. Mike's decision to go west, as an escape from the stultifying sexism of civilized Boston, is a feminist revision of the western myth in which a man's ability to survive on the frontier is the ultimate test of his mettle. However, this individualistic premise borrowed from the western is domesticated by its translation into melodrama, a form that seeks affiliation and moral order (Deming, 1990, pp. 54–55). The great "challenges" for the heroine are not physical hardship, renegades, or gunfights; they are, instead, self-doubt, moral choices, and, most importantly, motherhood.

Domestication of the Western and Maternal Feminism

To the postfeminist question, What is woman?, *Dr. Quinn* offers the ultimate transhistorical answer: a woman is a mother. Not an unusual answer for prime-time television, obviously. What makes *Dr. Quinn* unique, however, is its integration of liberal feminist assumptions with a sentimentalized affirmation of motherhood (and the attendant virtues of empathy, caring, and emotional fulfillment) within a familial context. In this case, however, the family is the entire town, and maternal virtues, in the person of Dr. Mike, inform every aspect of community life.

In *Dr. Quinn*, in typical melodramatic fashion, most problems arise within, or ultimately slide into, the family; they are rarely raised by outsiders. The crises that Dr. Mike faces are internal challenges to either her own family or the family that the small town represents. This is why it is key that the disenfranchised characters in *Dr. Quinn*, the blacks, immigrants, and Indians, are regular characters, not episodic problems. As members of the community, they cannot be transformed into the "other" as easily as they were in past westerns (or as easily as they are in contemporary American life). Dr. Mike's literal and figurative maternal functions often facilitate the "continual re-integration of the family" typical of episodic series (Feuer, 1986, p. 105). This characteristic of the drama illustrates particularly well the domestication of the traditional western narrative. In past westerns, the challenges to law and order in towns such as Dodge City were embodied by outsiders, and the often violent expulsion of those outsiders resolved the crisis and restored the integrity of the town (see Brauer, 1975). In *Dr. Quinn*, the most serious threats to the town are internal, and they are transformed, by Dr. Mike's maternal logic, from abstract issues of justice into specific problems of empathy and understanding.[15] Dr. Mike's moral authority is bolstered by the absence of a sheriff, marshal, or judge. In fact, the resolution of an episode in which the townspeople finally decide to hire a sheriff demonstrates the superiority of maternal insight over law and order.

In this first season episode, one of the immigrants, the brother of Dr. Mike's son's fiancée, has been accused of stealing and butchering a cow from Olive's ranch. Moreover, unbeknownst to the town, Dr. Mike's son Matthew aided in the theft, which brings the problem literally within her family. The townspeople are determined to lynch the immigrant, but Dr. Mike convinces them to hire a sheriff and send for a judge so that the young man can be properly tried for his crime. The judge cancels, and the sheriff, an aging gunslinger played by Johnny Cash, has a difficult time restraining the lynching party. After Matthew admits his part in the crime, Dr. Mike takes the floor:

He [Matthew] and John stole a cow. They know what they did was wrong, but they did it because someone they both cared for was starving. I don't know what it's like to be hungry—so hungry I'd steal. I hope I never know. If that day came, I'd hope that my friends and family would see me in need and help me. I've come to love this town and the people in it. I want it to be a good safe place for my children. And what we're deciding today is what kind of a place this town will be. A place where we all look out for ourselves or a place where we look out for one another. And that means all of us, whether we've been here for ten years, one year, or one month. Whether we're from Ireland, Sweden, or Boston.[16]

After this speech, Olive drops the cattle-rustling charge, instead allowing the boys to pay off the price of the cow by working at her ranch. The sheriff, clearly recognizing Dr. Mike's moral authority, decides to move on. Significantly, he turns in his badge to her, leaving the fate of the town in her hands.

The extension of maternal reasoning from the private into the public realm often is key to Dr. Mike's battles to improve and to preserve the town, and it is a central element in her function as a moral authority. For example, in "The Train," a 1994 episode in which Colorado Springs campaigns to be chosen as a site for the extension of the railroad, Dr. Mike refuses to participate in the other townspeople's misrepresentation of the charms of the town (e.g., they claim that they have an opera house, a library, and a bank that do not exist). Accused by Jake of betraying the town to uphold her "high and mighty ideals," Dr. Mike disagrees, explaining that her reasoning is pragmatic, and that it would be counter-productive to destroy the trust of potential visitors to the town:

> What if people came here under false pretenses? Believing that we have a bank and a library, an opera house and miracle cures? Well, they'd find out soon enough that it wasn't true and they'd be terribly disappointed. The word would spread that our town was a fraud, and no one would ever want to come here again.

As Dr. Mike expresses it, the problem with lying is its effect on potential relationships. The "ethic of care" evident in this statement is also key to the resolution of the narrative enigma: will the town get the railroad? The railroad official, having seen through the townspeople's inflated claims, has left town, and it looks as though Colorado Springs will not get the railroad. However, he returns because his Chinese companion is ill and the doctor in the next town "doesn't treat Chinamen." Dr. Mike, of course, treats the man and saves his life. Impressed by her compassion, the official asks Dr. Mike if *she* thinks Colorado Springs should get the railroad. She says that she does, and the official persuades the company to change its mind. In the last scene of this episode, Dr. Mike is asked to drive the silver spike at a ceremony celebrating the new railroad. Her moral superiority has benefited the town yet again.[17]

In many cases, however, the legitimacy of Dr. Mike's moral leadership results from absence as much as presence. Unlike other town-based westerns, such as *Gunsmoke, Bonanza,* or *The Big Valley, Dr. Quinn* has no recurring representative of law and order—no sheriff, no marshal, no judge. There is not even a representative of centralized economic power, such as a banker. The closest substitute would be Jake Slicker, the mayor, but his position is featured only on ceremonial occasions, such as running town meetings. *Dr. Quinn* thus manages to avoid pitting Dr. Mike's authority directly against institutionalized patriarchy; she triumphs by default. This realization also is useful for understanding Dr. Mike's position as the town's only doctor. Although Dr. Mike often interprets the townspeople's trust in her as evidence that sexism can be overcome, her claim is true on only one level. Her proven abilities have overcome their reluctance to trust a woman doctor, but the townspeople also had no real alternative. She has never had to compete with a male doctor (although she faced some competition early in the series from Jake the barber, who served as the town's resident medical expert before she arrived). Her victory, again, is partially a product of the fact that she is the only game in town.

However, it is always the case that Dr. Mike's expertise as a doctor is enhanced by her sensitivity and relationship skills as a woman and, in particular, as a mother.[18] As she describes it, medicine is about treating "the whole person." Indeed, in her position as a frontier doctor, there is no distinction between the scientific authority and status of a doctor and the traditional caring role of a nurse; she is both. Moreover, because her patients are the townspeople, a tightly knit group, her relationship to them is always simultaneously professional and familial.

An early episode exemplifies this integration of professional and familial roles. Dr. Mike's mother, Elizabeth Quinn, comes from Boston for a visit and criticizes the nontraditional life her daughter has created, creating a narrative problematic about Dr. Mike's struggle for independence and respect. Mrs. Quinn's clear position as the matriarch of the Quinn family is helped intertextually by the fact that she is played by Jane Wyman, who represented the 1980s most powerful matriarch on the prime-time soap opera *Falcon Crest.*

Mrs. Quinn arrives in the episode's first scene, and the viewer quickly becomes aware of the animosity between mother and daughter resulting from Mrs. Quinn's disapproval of her daughter's choice of career and frontier lifestyle, including the fact that Dr. Mike has acquired three children. For example, she tells the children to call her "Mrs. Quinn" rather than "Grandma." The threat to Dr. Mike's independence that her mother represents is clear when Loren Bray, the town merchant, asks Mrs. Quinn if she has come "to take that headstrong daughter of yours back to Boston so's she can find a husband and do what a woman should?"

Of course, a number of subplots complicate the central storyline. In the first of these, a banker from Denver forecloses on the building that Dr. Mike uses as a clinic (the owner of the building was the mother of Dr. Mike's children), and he refuses to grant her a mortgage so that she might buy it. This subplot provides a concrete manifestation of the threat to her independence that her mother represents, particularly when the banker tells her that he will not grant her a mortgage because "folks don't have much confidence in a woman doctor." The banker concludes that Dr. Mike should marry so that her husband can acquire a mortgage for her.

In the second subplot, the town's African-American blacksmith, Robert E., is badly burned in an explosion. Because Dr. Mike's clinic has been closed by the bank, she asks Jake, the town barber, if she can treat Robert E. in his shop. Jake refuses because Robert E. is black and will offend his customers. Dr. Mike explicitly attacks Jake's racism ("Are you saying that Robert E. is good enough to shoe your horse but not good enough to be in your shop?") but when this does no good, she is forced to take the patient to her home. Finally, this episode also involves a third storyline about Dr. Mike's thirteen-year-old daughter, Colleen, who is experiencing the onset of menstruation, an event that Dr. Mike has not prepared her for and fails to notice.

The episode entails a full range of melodramatic potential: obstacles to be overcome, moral statements to be made, and relationships to be explored and repaired. However, the central issue here is Dr. Mike's identity as an independent woman, and it is explored through negotiation of her relationship with her mother. All of the central issues of the episode are hashed through in three important confrontations with her mother. These scenes position Mrs. Quinn as the ultimate judge of Dr. Mike's fitness as an independent woman, a narrative move that makes sense, given the drama's actual audience and the presumed feminine spectator for melodrama (Joyrich, 1992). Framing the negotiation of Dr. Mike's identity as an issue between two women is compatible with postfeminist discourse, in which the problems of women are no longer located in the external battle against patriarchy but in women's internal struggle to define themselves.

The lack of common ground between Dr. Mike and her mother is set up in an early scene in which Mrs. Quinn questions Dr. Mike's decision to keep the children. Explaining her attachment to the children's mother, Dr. Mike replies, "There are some women you meet and it's as though you've known them forever." Looking meaningfully at her mother, she continues, "Other women you can know for a lifetime and it's as though you're complete strangers." Their later confrontations range across the spectrum of postfeminist angst. In the first, Mrs. Quinn accuses Dr. Mike of failing as a mother because she did not notice or attend to Colleen's confusion about menstruation ("Like father, like daughter. He never noticed anything that went on in his home—he was so preoccupied with his *profession*."). Dr. Mike's distress over her failure as a mother is visible in the close-up of her face that ends this scene.

The second confrontation deals with Dr. Mike's credibility as a professional. Mrs. Quinn reacts to the arrival of a patient by saying "At least your father didn't bring his patients into the parlor," which leads to the following exchange:

Dr. Mike: Do you think I like working under these conditions? I tried buying a boarding house for a clinic but they wouldn't give me a mortgage.
Mrs. Quinn: I could have told you it was a waste of time even to discuss it.
Dr. Mike: Just like you told me they wouldn't accept me in medical school?
Mrs. Quinn: Well, they didn't, did they? You went to a "ladies" medical college.

Dr. Mike: They taught me medicine!

Mrs. Quinn: But they didn't teach the people how to accept a woman doctor.

Dr. Mike: The people of Colorado Springs accept me.

Mrs. Quinn: A few desperate souls. What you should be doing is dancing in Boston and meeting young, eligible men.

Dr. Mike: . . . . I've made a new life for myself out here.

Mrs. Quinn: Ha, and what a life.

Dr. Mike: Why can't you accept me for what I am?

Mrs. Quinn: And what are you? You're an unmarried woman raising three children, in a shack, in the middle of nowhere, offering your medical services to a bunch of backwoodsmen who pay you in potatoes and in chickens!

Mrs. Quinn's evaluation emerges in the dialogue; Dr. Mike's life lacks an acceptable purpose. Dr. Mike is, in Mrs. Quinn's estimation, neither a good mother nor a successful doctor, and the combination of these roles, as Mrs. Quinn expresses it, is absurd. In the final confrontation, Mrs. Quinn explicitly resorts to the grounds of maternal judgment and authority when Dr. Mike asks her for the money to buy the clinic. Mrs. Quinn replies that "I would be failing you if I encouraged you in this ridiculous scheme." Their differences become evident in the following exchange:

Dr. Mike: I never wanted a life of convention.

Mrs. Quinn: You mean a life like mine?

Dr. Mike: That's right. I never did and I never will.

Dr. Mike begs her mother for the money, promising to pay it back. Mrs. Quinn's reply is that the money is irrelevant; she will not help Dr. Mike ruin her life. This scene ends on an emotional note as Dr. Mike exclaims, "Sometimes I think you must really hate me, Mother," and storms away.

This scene resonates in a number of ways. It is the first time that Dr. Mike verbalizes disdain for her mother's choice of a conventional life—a loaded moment, I think, given that postfeminist discourse often emphasizes values conflicts between employed mothers and mothers who do not work for wages (see Rosenfelt and Stacey, 1987; see also Faludi, 1991). The second theme in this scene is Mrs. Quinn's treatment of her thirty-five-year-old daughter as a misguided child. She seems unable to acknowledge that her daughter has an independent identity of any kind. This scene reveals the themes of a classic mother/daughter separation story. Mrs. Quinn's inability to allow her daughter adult status results from her daughter's seeming refusal to validate her mother's life by reproducing it.

The confrontation that I have just described takes place before the episode's final commercial break, and, in the pattern of episodic melodrama, it reveals the core of the problem to be solved in the program's final segment. In this segment, Mrs. Quinn, through a series of experiences, comes to accept what the viewer already knows—that Dr. Mike has not repudiated her mother's life but enacts it in a different context. Dr. Mike's seemingly purposeless life (in her mother's eyes) gains coherence and meaning from the discourse of motherhood that flows through each part of it. Dr. Mike's literal maternal function for her children and her figurative maternal function for her patients are juxtaposed in two key scenes involving her mother.

In the first of these scenes, Robert E., the burn victim, takes a turn for the worse. He assumes the status of a fourth child in the family because of his presence in the home and the constant care he requires. Dr. Mike, who refuses to leave his side, falls asleep in a chair at his bedside late at night. Mrs. Quinn enters the room, feels touched by Dr. Mike's exhausted vigil, and relieves her. At this point, Brian, Dr. Mike's six-year-old son, enters and climbs up on Mrs. Quinn's lap, asking to hear a story. Mrs. Quinn begins a story about a daughter who leaves her mother to go to a dangerous place, when Brian interrupts her and finishes the story, saying, "And her name was Dr. Mike. She came to Colorado. . . . After my real ma went to heaven, Dr. Mike got to be my ma here on earth. And she loves me just the same. She told me so." Mrs. Quinn visibly reacts to this conclusion to the story.

In this scene, Mrs. Quinn finally empathizes with Dr. Mike's maternal devotion to her patients. Moreover, she also understands the real devotion of Dr. Mike to her children and vice versa. Significantly, in the story that Mrs. Quinn and Brian tell, Dr. Mike is a daughter in the beginning and a mother in the conclusion, representing the path that Dr. Mike travels, in her mother's eyes, over the course of the episode. The themes of professional and personal motherhood are also concurrent in the episode's final scene in which Mrs. Quinn is preparing to leave on the stagecoach.

In a revision of a similar scene early in the episode, Loren Bray asks Mrs. Quinn if she is taking Dr. Mike home with her. She replies that she is not, adding, "She's too independent and stubborn. She takes after me in that respect." At this point, Mrs. Quinn has realized the similarities between herself and her daughter.[19] Her overt gesture of reconciliation occurs when she leans out of the stagecoach and hands Dr. Mike the money to purchase the clinic. A moment later, the basis for Mrs. Quinn's new appreciation of her daughter is revealed by the last bit of dialogue in the episode. As the stagecoach pulls away, Brian calls out, "Bye, Mrs. Quinn." Mrs. Quinn quickly corrects him, saying, "You can call me 'Grandma,'" demonstrating her acceptance of the family that Dr. Mike has created. The episode closes with a long shot of Dr. Mike surrounded by her children in the middle of the town's main street. The camera then zooms in to focus on a close-up of Dr. Mike's radiant face.

In the context of the struggle with her mother, the importance of Dr. Mike's maternal persona is most clear. She ceases to be a daughter controlled by her mother's authority at the point that she becomes a mother herself. By moving into an adult female relational role, she ceases to be a child and is worthy of her own life. As her mother realizes, what Dr. Mike left Boston to escape, she has found in the West in modified form. As a doctor, she saves lives in virtually every episode, but her medical skills take a back seat to her relational skills and her ability to maintain understanding, health, and harmony within her "family." [20]

This ultimate message is apparent in the 1993 Christmas episode, in which Dr. Mike suffers an identity crisis over conflict between her work and her family, a plotline laden with contemporary overtones of postfeminist working mother's guilt. When Dr. Mike finds herself spending Christmas Eve with an expectant mother rather than with her family, she begins to consider if she has made a mistake by becoming a doctor because it takes her away from her family. The ghost of her children's biological mother visits her during this period of self-doubt and takes her on a tour of Christmases past, present and future, so that Dr. Mike can decide if she would like to change her life. This is, yet again, a television retelling of *A Christmas Carol.*

What makes it particularly interesting, however, is that the rightness of Dr. Mike's choice to be a doctor, which is in question here, is not demonstrated by the lives she has saved or improved as a professional. Rather, the vignettes she sees from her life impress upon her the importance of her familial functions. She comes to realize that if she had not become a doctor she would not have come to Colorado and would not be a mother. When she is reunited with her family at the end of the episode, after the baby has been born, her children lament her imperfect Christmas Eve. In reply, she obviously speaks to larger issues as she says, "I wouldn't have it turn out any other way. You see I'm so glad you're all here. What more could I want? I have your love. You were and will continue to be the best Christmas present I ever received."

By the third season of *Dr. Quinn,* more and more episodes revolve around preservation of the family that Dr. Mike has created. A major theme in 1994 episodes is the romance of Dr. Mike and Sully. At the end of the spring 1994 season, they decide to marry, and in a 1995 episode they attempt to adopt Dr. Mike's three children legally. These issues are magnified in importance because each is the subject of separate two-hour episodes promoted by CBS as "Special Presentations." They are also filled with melodramatic complications, liberal feminist overtones, and paeans to motherhood.

In "Return Engagement," shortly after Dr. Mike and Sully decide to marry, an obstacle appears. Dr. Mike's fiancé, David, presumed killed in the Civil War, reappears in Colorado Springs, having assumed the identity of another man. However, Dr. Mike eventually recognizes him and realizes that she still has an attraction for him. At this point, the narrative enigma of the episode becomes clear: Which man will she choose (and on what basis)? The case for David rests on their shared history (in Boston, his family and hers are old friends), intellectual companionship (they are both doctors), and passion for social justice (they worked for abolition together in the past, and both want to protect the environment in Colorado). As Dr. Mike puts it to her friend Dorothy, "We come from the same world. When I'm with him my mind works more quickly. There are thing we can talk about—things I could never share with Sully. And yet Sully knows me in a way that David never has. Sully stirs something inside me, something I can hardly put into words. . . . What am I to do?"

The viewer, of course, knows that she will choose Sully eventually; the interesting issue is how she will arrive at that conclusion. Fairly quickly, it becomes evident that Dr. Mike will not choose between two men as much as she will choose between a man and a family. During the period of her decision-making, Sully appears only in the context of the family: at Dr. Mike's home, at the children's school program, teaching Dr. Mike's youngest son how to ride a bicycle. The moment that ultimately leads Dr. Mike to choose Sully, however, occurs when it becomes clear that he will *not* use his influence with the children to pressure her. When Dr. Mike tries to explain her quandary to her children, they interrupt her, and explain that Sully has counseled them about the situation:

> *Colleen:* Sully told us to be fair—to try to get along with him [David].
> *Matthew:* Yeah, he told us you've got to think about your whole life, not just the next few years.
> *Colleen:* He said we're going to grow up and move away so you better do what's best for you.

There are contradictory discourses at work here. On the one hand, the verbal message is that marriage is a decision Dr. Mike should make based on her own needs, not the desires of her children (who clearly prefer Sully). On the other hand, she is clearly impressed by Sully's sensitivity and fairness in dealing with her children ("Sully said that?"). The next day, as she and David discuss marriage again, he suggests that they "can simply carry on where we left off." Dr. Mike responds with "I was younger then, without attachments. I have children now and responsibilities." Dr. Mike then goes to find Sully and asks *him* to marry *her.*

This episode illustrates a recurring pattern in *Dr. Quinn, Medicine Woman*; the drama mixes liberal feminist rhetoric with implicit and sometimes explicit maternalist reasoning, affirming the principles of equality at the same time it displays the significance of difference. That is, the dialogue in this episode affirms Dr. Mike's right to choose a husband based on her own needs, and then shows her taking the lead in her choice by proposing to Sully (a reversal of the process from the first time they became engaged). This is certainly a progressive message about women's ability to take charge of their fates. Yet the subtler message, shown visually in this episode as well as in previous ones, is that she and Sully and the children are already a *de facto* family; to reject him would be to reject that family. Even though she appears to make a choice, there is, in reality, no choice: family comes first.

The importance of the family that she has created becomes clear in the 1995 episode "Cooper vs. Quinn," in which she battles for custody of the children from their biological father, Ethan Cooper. Years ago, Cooper deserted his first wife, the children's mother, and was revealed as a thief and a general scoundrel in a brief visit in an earlier episode. Dr. Mike and Sully have decided to adopt the children legally, but when Cooper learns of this intention, he returns with his new wife. He initially agrees to the plan, having played no role in the children's lives for years. However, when Dr. Mike diagnoses his wife's infertility, Cooper decides he wants the children back. His wife is heartbroken that she cannot bear children; moreover, Cooper needs children in order to inherit money from his wife's wealthy father.

Cooper and Dr. Mike act as their own attorneys in the custody trial before a district judge. Cooper attacks Dr. Mike's maternal fitness as a working mother and compares her to his wife, who is willing "to devote herself to looking after them full-time." Dr. Mike attacks Cooper for his absence, reminding the court that Charlotte Cooper gave the children to her because the father had deserted them, and giving an impassioned speech about parenthood consisting of practice rather than biology:

What makes a family is not merely blood—it's the days, the hours, the weeks we spent together, through thick and thin. Before I had these children, I thought that being a doctor was the most important thing. They've shown me that there is one thing more important than all else—that's your family. When Charlotte Cooper was dying . . . she asked me to take care of them, and I'm asking you to honor her wishes.

The judge rules for Cooper, reasoning that Cooper's biological parenthood gives him the right to the children regardless of his poor character. Dr. Mike and Sully are denied an appeal, and Cooper prepares to take the children to San Francisco. As they ride out of town after tearful farewells, Cooper's wife stops the carriage, saying, "we can't do this," and returns the children to Dr. Mike. The law may not be on Dr. Mike's side (an accurate depiction of custody rulings in the 1860s, when fathers had presumption), but the wisdom of another woman saves her.

This episode has obvious contemporary themes, including the contrast between fulltime and employed mothers, the issue of biological versus emotional parenthood, and the problem of "deadbeat dads." *Dr. Quinn* obviously comes down on the side of maternal practice superseding biology, a position consistent with the themes of the series as a whole. In this episode, given Ethan Cooper's unsavory character, the conclusion is uncomplicated and emotionally satisfying. In similar real-life situations in recent years, these issues have been much more complicated, particularly for feminists, in, for example, the Baby M case, the Baby Jessica case, or the case of Jennifer Ireland, a young Michigan mother who lost custody of her child to its father (to whom Ireland had never been married and had never lived with) because she put the child in day-care while she attended college. In the Ireland case, the judge ruled for the father in the custody dispute because the child's paternal grandmother was willing to care for the child fulltime, a situation preferable, in the judge's eyes, to the "part-time" motherhood of Ireland ("Day Careless?" 1994). Interestingly, in both the Ireland case and *Dr. Quinn*, a conflict that is framed as one between mother's rights and father's rights is, in actuality, a conflict between mothering alternatives. Ethan Cooper has a wife who will do the fulltime mothering. Likewise, in the Ireland case, the father's custody was not premised on his own ability to be a fulltime parent but on his ability to come up with a mothering surrogate in the person of the child's grandmother.

The resting of ultimate accountability for children's welfare in the hands of women has been replayed in the other high-profile custody cases of recent years—the battles over Baby M and Baby Jessica. In each of these cases, the father made the strongest legal claim, but the discourse of mothering framed the debate. For example, Bill Stern was the biological father of Baby M, who was conceived through artificial insemination with Stern's sperm in the body of Mary Elizabeth Whitehead, the so-called "surrogate" mother. Both the custody battle between Stern and Whitehead and Whitehead's book about it devoted significant attention to the mothering qualifications of Whitehead versus those of Elizabeth Stern, Bill Stern's wife (Kaminer, 1990, pp. 157–161; Pollitt, 1994, pp. 63–80).[21] To a large extent, the same situation prevailed in the Baby

Jessica case which began in 1991, in which the biological parents of a child fought for custody from the couple who had hoped to adopt her.[22]

Despite claims by observers that interest in such high-profile custody cases reflects "the general state of instability in American families" (Collins, 1993, p. 25), treatment of these cases by the media communicates one quite stable assumption: Motherhood is the central role in women's lives, and they will go to great lengths to preserve it. A 1993 *TV Guide* article pointed out that there was a veritable rash of television movies about "the baby wars" that year (Collins, 1993, p. 24), most of them centered on true stories of women's battles to retain custody of children under difficult circumstances. The article quotes a network executive as saying that the trend in television movies has shifted from an emphasis on "women in jeopardy" to " 'stories that hit at the emotions, stories about families in conflict' " (Collins, 1993, p. 24). However, given that the majority of these movies concern *women's* battles to retain their identities as mothers, it is an oversimplification to say that they are not about "women in jeopardy." Moreover, because the presumed and actual audience for most television movies is female (Rapping, 1992), it is likely the case that the appeal of these movies is as much linked to their romanticization of motherhood as it is linked to increasing angst about the welfare of children.

Dr. Quinn exists among, and I suggest should be read within, these discourses about noble motherhood, a discourse that is embraced by many feminists. As I will discuss in the conclusion, I find this kind of discourse highly problematical, especially as a platform for feminist politics. However, I do not dismiss the key role that motherhood plays in women's lives; to do that, as Ann Snitow has said, "would be to trivialize the complexity of wishes, to call mothering a sort of false consciousness—a belittling suggestion" (1992, p. 42). Yet, like Snitow, I question the woman = mother equation and the implications of the naturalization of that move in popular culture. My concern, then, is with a powerful tendency that I see in popular culture and in feminist work of recent years to use motherhood as the lens through which women's lives are viewed and to posit threats to identity as a mother as the most salient ones a woman faces in the postfeminist 1990s. This hegemonic emphasis crowds out of popular debate those issues that affect women's lives regardless of their relational roles—for example, economic discrimination, harassment, violence, and sexual identity. Moreover, as I discussed earlier, this tendency normalizes women's central caretaking roles and makes more difficult and less likely needed critiques of the constraints of those roles. An additional effect is the continuing lack of attention to men's capacity for and responsibility for change.

Television has long glorified motherhood, to be sure. Yet the function of discourses of motherhood has taken on a new dimension in postfeminist popular culture, a dimension very much linked, I think, to the postfeminist glorification of "choice" and to the embrace of "maternal thinking" by some feminists. *Dr. Quinn* illustrates this new dimension, and its troubling implications, particularly well.

Utopian Fantasies and Social Realities

Although I have stressed the intersections between *Dr. Quinn* and contemporary issues, I think it equally important to emphasize the drama's function as *fantasy*. I came to study *Dr. Quinn* because of conversations with committed viewers, mostly adolescent girls and older women. The young girls discuss their admiration for Dr. Mike's combination of desirable qualities: she is beautiful, smart, a good mother, and has a handsome, sensitive, and supportive partner in Sully. Older women, perhaps aware of how difficult that combination of qualities is to achieve, tend to talk about the appeal of Dr. Mike's role in her community, particularly her triumphs over small-mindedness and bigotry, and the validation that Dr. Mike's success provides for women's moral leadership.

Indeed, there is much for feminists to admire about *Dr. Quinn*. Easily decodable markers of feminist import run throughout the drama. Its premise is that of a journey toward liberation, and, as in the episode where she is refused a mortgage because she is female, storylines frequently emphasize the problems of sexism. A recurring theme in the second season, for example, is Colleen's training as her mother's medical assistant. While Matthew, the eldest son, rejects Dr. Mike's wish for him to attend college, deciding instead to become a farmer, Colleen dreams of college and medical school (dreams that, in Dr. Mike's vision of Christmas future, she achieves). *Dr. Quinn*'s purpose as positive socialization for young girls is evident in speeches such as the following, in which Dr. Mike responds to Colleen's statement that she wishes to do more with her life than "get married and have babies": "There are no rules, Colleen. Look at me. Never hide behind the fact that you're a girl—a woman. And don't give up on your dreams just because you're afraid you won't achieve them in a man's world. You just have to fight even harder to make them come true."

At such moments, *Dr. Quinn* is, as Jameson writes, "critical of the social order from which . . . it springs" (1979, p. 144), and its placement of contemporary liberal feminist ideology in the past lends historical weight to feminist goals. The same is true for *Dr. Quinn*'s featuring of multiculturalism and its commitment to an inclusive vision of community. These elements are part of the drama's utopian dimension, its fantasy about the possibilities of social life (Jameson, 1979, p. 147), and they are facilitated by *Dr. Quinn*'s placement in a mythic past. The success of the drama's maternal feminist vision and the function of Dr. Mike as a feminist role model are dependent upon its frontier setting.

Dr. Quinn's maternal feminist vision relies on "seeing relations formed in the private, domestic, and particular realm as reasonable models for, or the first steps toward, some forms of public spirit" (Mansbridge, 1990, p. 133), the basis for the political prospects of maternal thinking. However, all of the obstacles and pitfalls accompanying such a vision are absent in *Dr. Quinn*'s frontier setting. Patriarchy gains power through institutionalization, which the frontier lacks. Opposition to Dr. Mike's vision for the town is expressed as character flaws of particular people rather than as a self-interested, organized politics. Moreover, in a small frontier town, where the inhabitants live in such interdependency that they become family, a philosophy of public decision-making based in the value of nurturance, or "making the other's good your own" (Mansbridge, 1990, p. 132), makes sense. In a less cohesive setting, its possibilities are unclear.[23] Finally, Dr. Mike's role as an authority figure is a product not simply of her maternal insight but of her status as a professional woman whose services are important to the town's well-being: she is the town's only doctor. In this way, *Dr. Quinn* continues television's typical focus on white, privileged women as feminist figureheads, obscuring the realization that such women are unusual in the number of choices they have and in their capacity to exercise them.

Dr. Mike's integration of her personal and professional lives is facilitated by similarly utopian elements. She is a single mother, but one with a community-wide support system and a flexible schedule. Her children are known by everyone in town, and the townspeople care for them at various times, offering advice and guidance. Her children are welcome in her workplace, and one of them, Colleen, becomes her assistant in the medical practice.

Perhaps the most interesting utopian moves come in Dr. Mike's central romantic relationship with Sully. Their relationship appears to be a model of egalitarianism: Sully respects her opinion and supports her in her work and in her public moral stands. They have differences of opinion and manage to compromise without sacrificing the other's autonomy. Sully shares in domestic duties, including child-care. Yet, it can be argued that the possibility of this arrangement comes from *Dr. Quinn*'s reversal of traditional familial politics. In their relationship, Dr. Mike is the one with social power and a steady income. Sully's role is much more like that of a traditional wife; he does not bring in money so much as provide services that keep the family operating smoothly: chopping wood, hunting for meat, watching the children, repairing Dr. Mike's home.[24]

Sully is, in many ways, precisely the kind of man that Betty Friedan envisioned in *The Second Stage*: the kind of man who is willing to give up economic dominance in order to spend time with his family and who is willing to share in domestic labor (the kind of man that Arlie Hochschild argued is mostly fantasy in *The Second Shift*). Of course, the key difference between Sully and a traditional wife is that he is not economically dependent. On the frontier, he provides for himself through hunting, trapping, etc., and he has no economic stake in his relationship with Dr. Mike, a situation that is rarely the case for women in traditional marriages.

The wedding of Sully and Dr. Mike in a special two-hour episode at the end of the 1994–95 season combined several of *Dr. Quinn*'s previous themes. For example, in this episode, the conflicts between Dr. Mike and her mother and their differing views of a proper life for a woman surface again as they plan the wedding. Mrs. Quinn, who has brought supplies from Boston, wants a highly formal wedding, in which all the traditional etiquette is observed. Dr. Mike wants her wedding to include the friends and the life she has created in Colorado. As she has in previous episodes, she is battling for her independence and the right to her own choices.

This episode has some nice liberal feminist touches: Dr. Mike wants Sully to wear a wedding ring (a radical idea for the time period), she does not wish to change her name, and she wishes for her mother to give her away. In the end, these various conflicts are handled through understanding and compromise, facilitated by Dr. Mike. She and Sully create a trade-off: he will not wear a ring, and she will not change her name (of course, this is not exactly an even trade, since Dr. Mike will still wear a ring and there is never any question that Sully might change *his* name). With the help of her sisters, Dr. Mike creates a new dress that is a combination of the one her mother brought her and the one her friends in Colorado have made. After an earlier refusal on the grounds of impropriety, Mrs. Quinn appears to escort her daughter up the aisle at the last minute. Of course, these are symbolic issues that have little relation to a serious feminist critique of marriage (which was legally quite an oppressive arrangement for women in the nineteenth century), yet they give a feminist veneer to the narrative, offering some balance to the episode's profound romanticization of heterosexual romance and marriage.

In the end, Dr. Mike's wedding could satisfy any young girl's dreams. She is a vision in white attended by several bridesmaids, she is marrying a handsome man surrounded by friends and family in a lovely outdoor setting, and she dances the day away as the most beautiful woman in the room. These fantasy elements reach their zenith in the final, steamy scene in which Dr. Mike and Sully begin to make love on the train that is taking them to their honeymoon (their train car has been outfitted as a bedroom). It is clear that, now properly married, Dr. Mike will lose her virginity at last.

In this episode, Dr. Mike has no doubts about her decision to get married, and she has complete faith in Sully. Her mother, and, to some degree, her sisters are the ones who threaten her independence and her happiness. At various points they attempt to undermine her trust in Sully and to dismiss the importance of the life and the choices she has made. Sully, who is off on a mission to save the life of his friend Cloud Dancing, is absent for most of these machinations. The wedding and its problems are primarily Dr. Mike's concern, just as its eventual success is her triumph. On the journey toward this happy ending, *Dr. Quinn* reiterates several postfeminist themes that have fueled the drama since it began, including the notion that conflicts between women have replaced patriarchy, that individual choice has supplanted analysis of sexual politics, and that choosing the right man can solve most of women's problems. For viewers invested in the culmination of Dr. Mike's and Sully's long-running romance (and interest in the nuptials was great enough for *TV Guide* to do a cover story on them [Hall, 1995]), this episode was doubtless quite satisfying.

My deconstruction of the unique circumstances that underlie *Dr. Quinn*'s utopian vision are meant not only to point out its lack of resemblance to contemporary reality. As I have said, all westerns have utopian elements. My larger intention here is to highlight the *strategic* nature of *Dr. Quinn*'s nostalgic frame—that is, the ways in which its maternal feminist politics depend upon its frontier setting. However, it is possible that to compare *Dr. Quinn*'s fantasy to lived reality is to miss the appeal of the drama. Ien Ang (1990) has argued that it may be a mistake to view the possibility of realistic identification as the attraction of melodrama. Instead, she has claimed that melodrama can be enjoyed as fantasy, and that "the pleasure of fantasy lies in its offering the subject an opportunity to take up positions which she could not do in real life: through fantasy she can move beyond the structural constraints of everyday life and explore other situations, other identities, other lives. It is totally unimportant here whether these are realistic or not" (1990, pp. 83–84). From this perspective, the lack of reality in *Dr. Quinn* may be precisely what attracts its predominantly female audience.

I support Ang's conclusions about the appeal of fantasy; however, I am less sanguine about the total divorce of such fantasies from viewers' experiences of and attitudes toward lived reality. In order for a viewer to enjoy and to participate in a televisual fantasy, that fantasy must live out premises that are somehow meaningful to the viewer. In short, fantasies, and their appeal, are not random; they respond to felt needs and desires. As Probyn argues, "The prime-time discourses of the family or the home or of women are affective precisely because they lodge in the real; they are attached to other ideological frameworks" (1990, p. 158). *Dr. Quinn* is powerful for female viewers because it addresses and resolves questions that are circulating constantly in other cultural discourse. Thus, even if we disregard all of the utopian elements of *Dr. Quinn*'s vision of female power and community, we can still examine the fundamental premises of its fantasy, premises that I think are very much salient to women's lived realities and to attitudes toward feminism in postfeminist times.

One such fundamental premise is that of heroic individualism, a theme consonant with both liberal feminism and postfeminism (as well as with the *ethos* of the western). Dr. Mike *chooses* to go west to practice medicine, she *chooses* to mother (quite literally, since she does not bear the children herself), and she *chooses* the right man with whom to share her life. It is clear that many who praise the drama for its positive female role model do so on this basis: that Dr. Mike is a woman who takes charge of her own life. At face value, this is an important message for young girls. At the same time, however, this message contains the seeds of what is most problematic about postfeminism: the belief that women's choices are free from constraints and that they have the same freedom to make choices as men do.

Until significant structural changes are made in American society, the notion of postfeminist choice is, at base, a rhetorical fiction that generally denies the continued need for feminism and specifically denies the need to challenge the idealization of the traditional family. As Mary Frances Berry has succinctly said, "This ideal legitimates gender relations that continue to restrict women's economic opportunities, reproductive choice, sexual freedom, and sense of independent identity" (1993, p. 27). Although *Dr. Quinn* depicts the integration of a woman's personal and professional life in a manner that is unusual for television (which usually prefers to show one side or the other, but not both), it avoids dealing with the politics of the traditional family ideal by reversing them in Dr. Mike's favor. Yet hers is an individualistic solution based on an unusual relationship with a unique man; to say that women's problems in handling postfeminist conflicts will be solved by choosing the right man is a satisfying fantasy for many young women (see Sidel, 1990), but it is only a stop-gap solution.

Even in *Dr. Quinn*, Sully is quite obviously unusual; he is practically a token positive white male character, and his whiteness is camouflaged by his strong ties to the Native American community (many viewers I have spoken with think he is actually Native American). The other white male characters in *Dr. Quinn* are flawed through bigotry (Loren, Jake, Hank) or weakness (Horace, Reverend Johnson). In fact, only the black and Native American male characters (Robert E., Cloud Dancing) are as positively portrayed as Sully; of course, they are also the least visible. It surprises me that I have not read popular criticism of *Dr. Quinn* that lambasts the drama's shabby treatment of white male characters, who approach caricature at times in their exaggerated bravado, machismo, prejudice, and disdain for femininity. These kinds of characterizations have a lot of resonance for me, and even I have found it excessive.

Of course, the shortcomings of these men allows Dr. Mike's moral leadership to triumph, which is a symptom of a larger problem linked to the second troubling premise behind *Dr. Quinn*'s fantasy: its reification of motherhood as the central element in women's identity and power both within the family *and* within the community. At the same time that *Dr. Quinn* offers utopian moments legitimating women's struggle to define themselves through their own choices, it locates Dr. Mike's victory in that struggle in her embrace of the ultimate patriarchal role for women—the idealized mother. In various storylines, the drama emphasizes maternal reasoning and its benefits for conflict resolution, environmental protection, and empathy for the oppressed. The appeal of nostalgia is critical here. The western is an aesthetic form that conjures up a mythical past in which contemporary conflicts can be played out in satisfying ways. The ideological stability offered by the western, rather than by any sense of 1860s Colorado as a specific historical referent, is what gives power to *Dr. Quinn*'s resolution of the crisis in woman's identity that postfeminism attempts to articulate. In this context, Dr. Mike's enactment of literal and figurative motherhood becomes timeless, transhistorical, and thoroughly naturalized. Given the option of self-definition in a setting where anything is possible, women will choose to mother.

Rather than taking the patriarchal path of compelling women to play the role of mother, postfeminist discourse presents that role as the "natural" choice, a kind of framing which implies, as Elspeth Probyn (1990) notes, "Why or how would anyone even consider anything else?" (p. 152). For instance, in Chapter 1, I argued that Mary Richards often acted as a mother toward other characters, and I concluded that that implicit role contradicted the sitcom's liberationist premise. However, the difference between *Mary Tyler Moore* and *Dr. Quinn* is that for Mary Richards, maternal functions represented submission; for Dr. Mike they represent power and authority. In many ways, Mary Richards is *made* to mother by the demands of others; Dr. Mike apparently *chooses* motherhood as a vocation.

Moreover, Dr. Mike's embrace of motherhood gives her credibility in myriad areas. It provides a connection with her mother, it gives meaning to her life during an identity crisis, and it becomes so powerful that it outweighs Ethan Cooper's wife's own desire for children, compelling her to return the children to Dr. Mike. Again, at face value, the message that motherhood is an important role is hardly upsetting. Feminists have argued for years that mothering is undervalued, socially and economically. However, the romanticization of mothering also serves a profoundly patriarchal purpose: It encourages women to become so invested in mothering that they fail to question the oppressive social and economic arrangements that traditional ideals of mothering uphold.[25] It obfuscates the fact that "imposing child care responsibilities principally on one parent rather than both is a deprivation of rights. The issue of child-care is really an issue of power, resources, and control among adults; it is not a battle over who is more suited for care" (Berry, 1993, p. 41). Postfeminist rhetoric—inside and outside of television—never really questions the idea that women are more suited for caring for children, and that this arrangement is most fulfilling for children *and* for mothers. Given these parameters, the absence from the discussion of men's roles in child care seems only natural. *Dr. Quinn* is more progressive than most television in its depiction of shared child care; however, its ultimate and repetitive message is not that Sully finds meaning for his life in his family role; it is that Dr. Mike does.

Yet, in *Dr. Quinn* the insights gained from maternal thinking are demonstrably effective in solving problems not only in the family but in the community as well. If we *value* the work and the ethics of mothering, claim some feminist theorists, then we can redeem its oppressive aspects.[26] This is the third and final premise of *Dr. Quinn*'s fantasy that I find troubling. I have no objection to "maternal" values per se; as Patricia Boling (1991) has noted, "the notion of a public life committed to 'maternal' values such as peace, preserving the world, living in harmony with nature, and nurturing healthy and well-educated children is surely an appealing one" (p. 608).[27] What I find disturbing, in difference feminist theory and in *Dr. Quinn*, is the idea that women are uniquely suited for implementing such a vision. *Dr. Quinn* takes this position fairly consistently. Dr. Mike is somehow always the one to see the greater good for the whole town, while her neighbors are caught up in bigotry and self-interest. If she has support for her position, it comes from other women and sometimes from members of other oppressed groups: the blacks and/or the Native Americans.

Although such a construction may positively imply that "women's world is full of superior virtues and values, to be credited and learned from rather than despised" (Alcoff, 1988, p. 414), it can be counterproductive in its implication that such virtues can be exercised only by women. Indeed, while postfeminism seems to stress the constant adjustment and adaptation of women to an ever-changing world, men's position remains curiously static, as if they cannot change (which would seem to admit the permanence of patriarchy) or there is no need to demand that they do so (which is patently unfair).

A belief in women's innate special difference has a variety of negative consequences. The first is that we veer dangerously close to making women the primary hope for salvation in a brutal postmodern world. At the point that feminists support a vision of womanhood that claims superior morality (a mistake that woman suffragists made a century ago),[28] we absolve men of responsibility for changing their ways. There is nothing wrong with women creating a vision of a more humane world, but it seems to make more sense to enlist everyone in such a cause rather than to claim that only women (or mothers) can achieve it. Such a move discourages potential allies and denies that "the capacity to love, to cherish, to nurture and to empathize belongs equally to the domain of men and women, and is, in part, what makes us human" (Stearney, 1994, p. 157).[29] Promoting women's entry into the public sphere on the assumption that they will improve it because of their moral superiority undermines the principle that they deserve such access regardless of their motives: "No one asks that other oppressed groups win their freedom by promising to be extra-good" (Pollitt, 1994, p. 61).

Moreover, celebration of maternal thinking often occludes the recognition that women's "special" capacities were developed in the context of oppressive social practices, and to argue for the value of those special capacities motivates adherence to that oppression (Boling, 1991, p. 609). There is a troublesome connection between valuing the strengths and attributes developed in oppressive circumstances and continuing to promote "the restrictive circumstances that gave rise to those attributes: forced parenting, lack of physical autonomy, dependency on survival for mediation skills, for instance" (Alcoff, 1988, p. 414). For women to develop maternal thinking, or the qualities of "difference," do they not have to continue to be socialized as other-centered, and to function as primary caretakers? How liberating is such a vision?

This vision also neglects the realization that women's responsibility for caretaking kept them out of the public sphere in the first place. Revaluing women's work without making the concrete structural changes to free them from its constraints is unlikely to change that situation. As Boling (1991) points out,

under present social conditions, the paths to public power rarely include primary parenting. Changing the world so that men are commonly responsible for raising children and women are commonly responsible for public decision making is the only way in which we are likely to introduce values of care, relationship, and world preservation into political life. (p. 610; see also Berry, 1993)

Dr. Quinn illustrates particularly well Wendy Kaminer's observation that "we've managed to enter a postfeminist world without ever knowing a feminist one" (1990, p. 1). *Dr. Quinn*'s rhetorical strategies, particularly its use of a nostalgic setting, allows it to persuasively reiterate all of the problematic assumptions of postfeminism: that patriarchy is over, that liberal feminist individualism can solve women's problems, and that our "choices" are what really determine our fates. These assumptions presuppose the notion that second-wave feminism "worked," that it leveled the playing field so that what some contemporary feminists (like me) see as evidence of continuing oppression (such as excessive pronatalism and the romanticization of motherhood) is really an expression of what women want rather than an expression of the continuing constraints on women's options and identities. Difference feminism feeds this perception, making it even more difficult to insist on the essential humanity of women, a goal first- and second-wave feminism have shared and that, despite postfeminist claims, we are still working to achieve.

Notes

1. A "TVQ" rating is a measure of popularity derived by dividing the percentage of people who like a show by the percentage of people who are familiar with it. The rating for *Dr. Quinn* is significant because, although the show is quite young, it has strong appeal among those who watch it. Advertisers are attracted to programming with a high "TVQ" rating because they believe that viewers watch more of the shows that they like, including the commercials. In addition, *Dr. Quinn* scores highest among the most coveted audience in television, women age eighteen to forty-nine (Mandese, 1993).

2. In the rest of this chapter, I will also refer to this character as "Dr. Mike," primarily so that the reader can easily differentiate mentions of the character from mentions of the program title.

3. For a discussion of second-wave feminism's efforts on behalf of family policy designed to make it easier for women both to mother and to work outside the home, see Davis, 1991, chapter 14. Importantly, Davis notes that feminists did not abandon the family as Friedan and Hewlett charged, but that, beginning in the early 1970s, "feminists did what seemed doable. Their demands for child care and family leave met enormous resistance from conservatives, and they made little progress on those issues" (1991, p. 279).

4. Although quotations from Snitow that I use in this chapter are from the version of her essay published in *Feminist Review*, a substantially similar version was published a year earlier in *Ms.* (see Snitow, 1991).

5. An example of such a move during the 1980s was U.S. Representative Patricia Schroeder's "Great American Family Tour" in January and February of 1988. Schroeder, a self-proclaimed feminist and long-time advocate for women, used this speaking tour to publicize the need for government support for child care, medical leave, flextime, and pay equity. All of these issues have been traditionally perceived as "women's issues" which would primarily benefit women, but, in her

rhetoric on the tour, Schroeder made a point of redefining them as "family issues" (see Szpiech, 1991).

6. For a useful and thorough look at discourses of motherhood in the popular press from 1970 to 1990, see Kaplan, 1992, chapter 9.

7. For an analysis of these and other "pro-motherhood" movies, see Haskell, 1988. For an analysis of 1990s films that continue to romanticize motherhood as the central role for women, see Rapping, 1995.

8. For example, "woman's difference" found its way into feminist activism outside the academy, particularly ecofeminism. In 1993, *Ms.* published an essay by ecofeminist Ynestra King, entitled "Where Nature Meets Nurture: Reflections on Ecofeminist Motherhood." Moreover, as Lynn Stearney has argued, "One of the central metaphors of the ecofeminist movement is the use of motherhood to characterize women's unique capacity to care for and nurture the earth," bringing with it the danger of returning women "to a primary identification as mothers and reinforc[ing] the notion of women's roles and natures as inextricably connected to their reproductive capacity" (1994, pp. 145, 146).

9. The dissemination of difference feminism was aided by the news media's renewed emphasis on scientific investigation of sex differences, resulting in, for example, cover stories in *Time* and *U.S. News*, entitled, respectively, "Sizing Up the Sexes" (Gorman, 1992), and "Men vs. Women: The New Debate over Sex Differences" (McLoughlin, 1988). In February of 1995, ABC News broadcast a special entitled "Boys and Girls Are Different," which also made the case for biological differences between the sexes. This special, interestingly, positioned its conclusions as refuting the conventional wisdom of feminism. Its representatives of feminist thinking were Gloria Steinem, Gloria Allred, and Bella Abzug.

10. Willard was also active in the social purity movement, designed to provide sexual protection for women, providing an interesting link to another arena in the 1980s and 1990s in which woman's difference has figured: the debate over pornography. The arguments of antipornography activists such as Catherine MacKinnon and Andrea Dworkin have caused dissension in feminist ranks because they are interpreted as favoring censorship and of promoting "the most regressive protectionist stereotypes of male and female sexuality that egalitarianism challenged—images of feminine docility, purity, and submission and male aggression" (Kaminer, 1990, p. 183).

11. Wendy Kaminer (1990) has persuasively argued that woman's difference has functioned as a convenient way of explaining women's lack of progress in the workplace and the concomitant romanticization of motherhood and domesticity. As she explains it, the postfeminist conflict between home and work is not an indication that feminism was wrong about women's capacity/desire for rewarding work but, rather, is a reflection of continuing sexism and discrimination.

12. Much of Dr. Mike's sexual appeal is linked to her luxurious, waist-length brown hair, which, in contradiction to nineteenth-century norms for women, is often worn flowing down her back rather than pinned up.

13. Both of these characters are portrayed as intelligent, productive, and talented entrepreneurs who recognize and often actively resist the racism that surrounds them. In one episode, Robert E., the blacksmith, is excluded from the design process for a new schoolhouse, although he is generally acknowledged as the most skilled artisan in town. He recognizes the racism but also notes that he is not particularly eager to design a schoolhouse that would not welcome black children. However, the white businessmen who are given the project are exposed

as either illiterate or incompetent, and the project stalls. In the end, of course, Robert E. saves the day, and the schoolhouse is completed.

14. Positive aspects of Native American culture are consistently highlighted in *Dr. Quinn*—including, for example, native medicines, agricultural abilities, and spirituality. In various episodes the Indians' natural fever tea helps save victims of typhus, their understanding of water-bearing plants helps the town deal with drought, and Dr. Mike's son matures through the experience of a Cheyenne vision quest.

15. As I have said, in comparison to past westerns, *Dr. Quinn* has few problems generated by "evil outsiders." In those cases where a visitor to the town does cause a problem, however, he or she is most likely to be rehabilitated by Dr. Mike rather than expelled. For example, in a 1993 episode, a traveling medicine show comes to Colorado Springs. Dr. Mike discovers that the alcoholic doctor who runs the show is in fact a well-known former surgeon who has given up practicing medicine because of the horror of his experiences in the Civil War. While he challenges her medical authority by claiming that his patent medicine can solve all medical problems, she does not take it upon herself to expose him. Rather, she rehabilitates him by asking him to advise her on a difficult piece of surgery she must do. The operation is a success, and the two doctors part as friends.

16. When I presented an early version of this chapter to a women's studies group at my university, an audience member pointed out that this speech of Dr. Mike's neatly transforms the issue along lines that fit Carol Gilligan's claims about woman's different voice. An issue of justice (how should the rustlers be punished?) is transformed into one of care, in which the central issue is the relationships between the townspeople and the immigrants. My thanks to Sarah Jacobson.

17. Dr. Mike's superior moral vision in comparison to the rest of the town is illustrated by an early scene in this episode in which Hank refuses to serve the Chinese man in his saloon. His racial prejudice is not challenged by the other men in the saloon.

18. This reading is illustrated by a 1994 episode, "Ladies Night," in which Dr. Mike's friend, Dorothy, has a lump in her breast. She resists Dr. Mike's medical diagnosis of cancer and her recommendation of a mastectomy, and disregards Dr. Mike's advice that the medical odds are that she will die without the surgery. However, at the point that Dr. Mike tells Dorothy that she loves her and wants her to have the operation so that she will not lose a friend, Dorothy agrees.

19. Significantly, in a conversation with Loren earlier in the episode, Mrs. Quinn claimed that Dr. Mike took after her father.

20. In fact, this analysis has not even exhausted the examples of her maternal function from this one episode. For example, like a good mother, Dr. Mike upbraids Jake the barber for his self-centered response to Robert E.'s injury. You will recall that he refused to let Dr. Mike treat Robert E. in his shop for fear of offending his customers. When he later asks about Robert E.'s condition, Dr. Mike scolds him with a sarcastic reply ("A private expression of concern is appreciated, Mr. Slicker. A public stand would have done him more good"), and he is shown looking appropriately chastened.

21. After bearing the child, for which she was paid by the Sterns, Whitehead refused to give her up. Officially, then, the dispute was between Bill Stern and Mary Elizabeth Whitehead, the two people with biological claim to the baby. However, the standard contrast drawn in media coverage was between Elizabeth Stern, the white, middle-class career woman who did not want to undergo preg-

nancy herself for health reasons, and Whitehead, the fulltime mother of two children and wife of a truck driver. Feminists have astutely analyzed the class issues that permeated the debate over Baby M (see, e.g., Pollitt, 1994, pp. 63–80); I am more interested in the reification of gendered parenting assumptions in the debate. In contrast to the interrogation of both Whitehead's and Elizabeth Stern's maternal fitness, speculations about Bill Stern's emotional health, obsession with his career, or self-centered motives for fatherhood, were largely absent.

22. Cara Clausen, Jessica's biological mother, signed away her rights to the child soon after birth, as did the man Clausen claimed was the father, and Roberta and Jan DeBoer took the baby home, preparing to adopt her. However, Clausen quickly had a change of heart, and she revealed that the true father of Jessica was Dan Schmidt, a former boyfriend. Because Schmidt had not signed away his parental rights, he sued for custody of Jessica from the DeBoers.

In 1993, after a two-year battle, the DeBoers lost custody of Jessica and she was returned to her biological parents, who had since married. Public sympathy, according to polling, was very much with the DeBoers (Cowley, 1993, p. 54), a situation perhaps traceable to the fact that much of the discourse about the case in the media was filtered through the perspective of Roberta DeBoer's narrative about mothering Jessica. Roberta DeBoer's anguish over losing Jessica was retold in stories in *People* (Hewitt, 1993) and *Newsweek* (Cowley, 1993), in an ABC television movie (*Whose Child Is This?: The War for Baby Jessica*, 1993), and in her book about the case, *Losing Jessica*, which was excerpted in *Redbook* (DeBoer, 1994). In these narratives, DeBoer cast the battle over Jessica largely as a dispute between herself and Cara Schmidt, despite Dan Schmidt's central legal role (see, e.g., DeBoer, 1994). In a similar fashion, in the 1994 follow-up stories about Jessica's progress after being returned to her biological parents, Cara Schmidt, rather than her husband, assumed the central speaking role (see, e.g., Ingrassia and Springen, 1994; "She's Anna Now, 1994).

Interestingly, in "Cooper vs. Quinn," although Sully and Dr. Mike are requesting to adopt the children *as a couple* and Sully's parenting role is referred to in the court case, Sully never speaks to the court; that role is reserved for Dr. Mike.

23. For a useful critique of "the democratic potential of mothering," see Boling, 1991.

24. In fact, in "Money Trouble," Sully and Dr. Mike are in conflict about the money needed to finish building their new home in which they plan to live after marriage. Sully cannot afford to buy needed supplies, and Dr. Mike volunteers the money. Sully is too proud to take it, so Dr. Mike makes a list of all of the daily labor that he does for her and her family, claiming that the money she gives him will be compensation for his work on their behalf.

Dr. Mike's position about the conflict is that "if you measure everything in money, it becomes crazy. How much is a hug worth? A kind word at the end of a troubling day? How much is it worth to know that you believe in me?" Interestingly, what she does here is make the argument that is often made by couples in traditional marriages: that the wife's (Sully's) most valuable role is to provide emotional support for the husband and breadwinner (Dr. Mike).

25. Ann Snitow (1992) offers an insightful analysis of why women cling to the mothering prerogative, including the "psychological power mothers have," and the feeling that "we give up something, a special privilege wound up in the culture laden word 'mother' which we will not instantly regain in the form of freedom and power. . . . Giving up the exclusivity of motherhood is bound to feel to many like loss" (pp. 42, 43).

26. Of course, what "value" means is also difficult to define. If we "value" mothering, shouldn't one of our goals be to increase the notoriously low pay of day-care providers? Does "valuing" the ethic of care mean that we will work to upgrade the status of the myriad lowly paid "helping" professions that women dominate? The contradictions that arise when one considers this issue are, for instance, illustrated well by the conservative positions on welfare reform. At the same time that conservatives advocate "family values," meaning that white, middle-class women should stay home with their children, they also characterize poor, black women who do so as lazy, shiftless welfare mothers (see Pollitt, 1994, pp. 31–41).

27. In fact, Mari Tonn and I have argued elsewhere that in some situations, the use of such values in public discourse can be quite powerful and can contribute to what we call a "feminine" rhetorical style. However, the label "feminine" is a pragmatic one for us, and does not reflect our belief that these values are inherent in or restricted to women (see Dow and Tonn, 1993).

28. Those familiar with feminist history are aware of the political costs of grounding female power in beliefs about the special nature of woman. If women's exercise of public power is legitimated by their likelihood to do good works, they are still less powerful than those people, specifically men, who have public power as a birthright. This is the hard lesson learned by nineteenth- and early twentieth-century woman suffragists who saw their political capital dissipate when female voters failed to deliver the promised social transformation linked to their supposed greater virtues (see Dow, 1991).

29. Subscribing to a maternal feminist vision also causes problems for alliances *within* feminism. An emphasis on woman's difference potentially alienates feminists who are not or do not plan to be mothers as well as feminists who simply do not see the ascribed characteristics of "difference" as descriptive of themselves (Pollitt, 1994, pp. 42–43). Moreover, some analysts have pointed out that maternal thinking may not resonate with the experiences of mothers who are not white and middle class. Alison Bailey (1994), for example, has compared Ruddick's "white, Anglo-American, middle-class" vision of mothering with Patricia Hill Collin's description of black mothering (p. 192). Bailey observes major differences, primary among them that whereas Ruddick "describes maternal practice as defined by preservative love, nurturing, and social training," Collins "describes racial-ethnic motherwork as defined by survivial, identity, and empowerment" (1994, p. 194).

Afterword: Feminist Images, Feminist Politics

In the public discourse of the 1990s, feminism appears to be entering yet another period of reckoning, one similar to the emergence of post-feminism in the 1980s. Books such as Naomi Wolf's *Fire with Fire: The New Female Power and How It Will Change the 21st Century* (1993), Katie Roiphe's *The Morning After: Sex, Fear, and Feminism on Campus* (1993), and Christina Hoff Sommers's *Who Stole Feminism?: How Women Have Betrayed Women* (1994) have not only sold respectable numbers of copies for their main-stream trade publishers, but their authors also have received significant media attention for their supposed bravery, as self-proclaimed feminists, in laying bare the faults of feminist orthodoxy. The attacks on feminism embedded in Camille Paglia's *Sex, Art, and American Culture* (1992) and the tidal wave of publicity that Paglia's flamboyance has attracted (leading to, for instance, a profile in *Vanity Fair* entitled "Paglia's Power Trip" [Wolcott, 1992]), also have contributed to the perception that the back-lash against feminism in the 1990s is coming from within its own ranks.

Although these books differ in their emphases and in the proclaimed motivations of their authors (this is particularly true for Naomi Wolf, as I discuss in a moment), they share some striking similarities. All see femi-nism strangling in the grip of an ideology that claims all women are pas-sive victims of sexual violence, economic exploitation, beauty images, or sexual harassment (in particular, they share a profound distaste for antipornography feminists such as Catharine MacKinnon and Andrea Dworkin, to whom they attribute hegemonic power over feminist ide-ology). All reject difference feminism and claim for women the right to be as sexually aggressive and power seeking as men are presumed to be, and all have a tendency to cite the discourse of academic feminists as evidence of the feminist "party line" they are critiquing.[1] Finally, all of these authors are privileged, well-educated, white women, and they clearly presume their target audience to be much like themselves.

Media affection for "trend" stories has resulted in the lumping together of these books in various cover stories purporting to examine the
state of feminism in the 1990s. Publications as diverse as *Esquire, Cosmopolitan, The Atlantic,* and *Newsweek* have hyped the issue on their covers.
These magazines offer stories with titles like "The Rise of 'Do Me' Feminism" (Friend, 1994); "Can You Be a Feminist and Love Men, Too?"
(Wolf, 1994); "Feminism's Identity Crisis" (Kaminer, 1993); and "Sexual
Correctness: Has It Gone Too Far?" (subtitled "Will the new rules of
feminist politics set women free—or set them back?" [Crichton, 1993]).

Feminism, for good or ill, appears to have become a hot commodity
once again, leading to speculation about whether or not we are entering
a "Third Wave" and, if so, what it means (Kaminer, 1995). I am not sure
it is possible to make that judgment (and even if it is, I do not want to
make it here), but it is possible to speculate about the peculiarly visible
intersections of feminism, television, and media culture in the 1990s,
how they compare to what has gone before, and what they mean for our
understanding of what feminism is all about. To call feminism a "hot
commodity" is a deliberate and literal choice for me. Today, just as in
1970, mass-mediated feminism is as much about marketability as ideology. Susan Faludi's *Backlash* appeared in the fall of 1991, fortuitously
coinciding with the Thomas/Hill hearings and reestablishing the commercial viability of books about, or informed by, feminism. Ironically,
Faludi, whose book offers a depressing litany of feminism's losses in the
1980s, is often a target of those authors who are now benefiting from the
market that *Backlash* revived.[2]

As I have maintained throughout this book, the various media feed off
one another. The debates over feminism are given renewed relevance by
the rash of events (and resulting rash of media coverage) in the 1990s
that have spotlighted gender politics. From the Thomas/Hill hearings
to the Tailhook scandal, from the murders of abortion doctors and clinic
staff to the controversy over *Thelma and Louise,* from the emergence of
Hillary Clinton in the 1992 presidential campaign (and the much hyped
"Year of the Woman" in politics) to the trial of O. J. Simpson on the
charge of murdering his ex-wife, Nicole Brown Simpson, the last five
years have offered myriad opportunities for pundits to speak to and for
media to comment on what feminism does or should mean. Importantly,
however, the debate most often revolves around feminist *representation*
rather than feminist politics or feminist activity, thus focusing on questions such as "Does the violent feminism of *Thelma and Louise* go too
far?" or "Do Hillary Clinton's opinions (as reported in the press) alienate stay at home mothers?"

This emphasis on a feminism that does or does not "sell well" is at the heart of the current popular debate. Wolf, Paglia, Sommers, and Roiphe, for example, all hold in common a belief that the emphasis on victimization that they claim has overtaken feminism is driving away the movement's potential constituency: for example, women will refuse to "buy" a feminism that makes them look helpless (this is, for instance, why Wolf calls her proposal "power feminism"). If feminism does not shape up, these critics claim, it will continue to alienate heterosexual women, women who like sex, women who don't hate men, or women who don't believe in what Sommers calls the "backlash myth" (1994, p. 227).[3]

These books are the antidote to the depressing evidence of women's continued victimization that, long known by feminists, has become impossible for media to ignore as they go about reporting on Anita Hill's accusation of sexual harassment, Paula Coughlin's charges against the military's routine acceptance of sexual assault on women officers, Senator Bob Packwood's repeated harassment of female staff, or O. J. Simpson's battering of his ex-wife. Media, willingly or not, have contributed to a kind of literacy about women's victimization, a widespread awareness that women face distinct dangers in the nuclear family and in the workplace (Dow and Hogeland, 1995). However, in a nation dedicated to family values and the presumption of equal opportunity (indeed, opportunities are so equal now that we are told affirmative action is unnecessary), the motivation to deny or explain away that victimization is quite strong. This is the need that Paglia, Sommers, and Roiphe fill, enacting a scenario remarkably similar to the postfeminist recantations of the 1980s. As white, middle-class women confronted the difficulties of combining family responsibilites and paid work (difficulties less privileged women have always faced), Betty Friedan and Sylvia Hewlett emerged to blame these troubles on women's liberation rather than on a workplace or governement that refused to adjust to the needs of women.

Similarly, Sommers, Roiphe, and Paglia have emerged with the comforting message that patriarchy is over and women have achieved equality, that the victimization of women is exaggerated and/or all in feminists' minds, and that feminist orthodoxy is disempowering women by encouraging them to see themselves as victims (Wolf shares only the last of these beliefs). There are some holes in this position. For instance, Catharine MacKinnon, the antipornography activist and sexual harassment expert that all of these authors love to demonize, was ABC News's resident expert during the Thomas/Hill hearings. MacKinnon spread her doctrine of "victimology" during her segments, emphasizing the breadth of sexual harassment, the ways in which it reflected the institutionalized power differences between men and women (read: patriarchy) and damaged women's careers. Yet as Katha Pollitt noted in a review of Roiphe's book, "if focusing on 'victimhood' reduces women to passivity . . . the experience of Anita Hill would have sent feminists off weeping, en masse, to a separatist commune. Instead it sparked a wave of activism that revitalized street-level feminism and swept unprecedented numbers of women into Congress" (1994, p. 167). In the two months following the Thomas/Hill hearings, thirteen thousand women joined the National Organization for Women (WAC Stats, 1993, p. 23). They must have been watching CNN.

There are many levels on which the visions presented by these feminist dissenters could be critiqued. Their motivations, the accuracy of their research, the veracity of their claims about feminist hegemony, and the implicit heterosexism, classism, and racism of their perspectives have been dissected in various forums.[4] As a feminist, I disagree quite strongly with many of the claims that they make; however, as a media critic I am intrigued by the ways in which the arguments they offer make use of and reproduce media logic.

As I have said, I am convinced that for many readers, these works provide a welcome alternative to confronting the powerful and unsettling evidence of women's continued victimization. However, the wide circulation of the ideas of these authors through popular media has a great deal to do with their media friendliness (Faludi, 1995). First, all of these authors, while claiming to be feminists, are critiquing aspects of the movement harshly. That move alone establishes their deviance and makes them newsworthy at a basic level. Even more interesting, however, is the use of media logic in the dramatic narrative they construct. Sommers, and Roiphe, in particular, support their case for feminist hegemony with examples of feminist behaviors or discourses that are considered extremist or controversial even within the movement.[5] They charge feminism with intolerance, conspiracy, and other offenses to American values, while claiming for themselves the high ground of objectivity that they charge other feminists with abandoning. Their examples of feminists' abuse of the truth, of common sense, and of the university curriculum are vivid and full of drama, as when, for instance, Christina Hoff Sommers argues that the "gender-feminized" colleges and universities should print a warning to parents in their bulletins that says, in part:

We will help your daughter discover the extent to which she has been in complicity with the patriarchy. . . . She will very likely reject the religious and moral codes you raised her with. . . . She may change her appearance and even her sexual orientation. She may end up hating you (her father) and pitying you (her mother). After she has completed her reeducation with us, you will certainly be out tens of thousands of dollars and very possibly be out one daughter as well. (1994, p. 91)

With such moves, Sommers, Roiphe, and Paglia attribute enormous power to their enemies and make their struggle even more heroic. The symbolic battle they construct provides good copy; even more important, their solution is for feminists to abandon the structural analysis of patriarchal power, to embrace individualism, and to reach out to the millions of women (all feminists in their hearts, they imply) who have been turned off or disempowered by the emphasis on victimage. In this analysis, "exaggerated feminist propaganda, not material inequity, is responsible for the oppression of women in contemporary society" (McDermott, 1995, p. 671). The media, which greatly prefers a dualistic worldview and has always had a hard time understanding the complexity of feminist ideology (Rhode, 1995), has found this story an easy one to write, casting it as a battle between the rigid, irrational ideologues of victim feminism (Sommers calls it "gender feminism") and the rational, commonsensical approach of their detractors.[6]

The media-friendly feminism of these books shares some of the same shortcomings as prime-time feminism: a white, middle-class, heterosexual bias, an assumption that a "seize the power" mindset and more vigorous individualism will solve all women's problems, and a conflation of feminist *identity* with feminist *politics*. As I have argued throughout this book, television entertainment has hedged its bets by representing feminism through the lives of white, middle-class, heterosexual women: the women who have benefited the most from the movement's gains and who are in the best position to practice individualist feminism. This allows the medium to substitute lifestyle questions for political ones and drives its central, implicit, question: What kind of woman is a feminist and what "choices" does she make? Inevitably, those choices are about lifestyle questions, not political ones. Yet, to give television some credit, these lifestyle questions demonstrate some progress over time, due to television's thirst for the "new," shifts in social attitudes, and changes in popular awareness of feminism.

In sitcom, for instance, the single, working woman of *Mary Tyler Moore* gives way to the divorced working mother of *One Day at a Time*. Likewise, *Designing Women*'s woman-centered work community and *Murphy Brown*'s mature, powerful, belligerent professional at the top of her field present alternatives to the office wife/mother/daughter of *Mary Tyler Moore*. In a woman-centered drama (unusual in itself for prime-time), *Dr. Quinn*'s focus on the thorough integration of a working mother's professional and personal life is unusual. Moreover, there is evidence that progress is continuing. As I write this, there are three new woman-centered sitcoms in prime-time on two of the "big three" networks (ABC, CBS, NBC) doing quite well. *Cybill* (1994–present), which debuted in a spot following *Murphy Brown* on CBS's "woman's night" on Monday, focuses on a forty-something, working actress in Los Angeles with two daughters and two ex-husbands, one of whom is unemployed and lives over her garage. Like Murphy Brown, Cybill Sheridan is beautiful, committed to her career, strong-willed, and has a sharp tongue. However, she is a much more round character than Murphy, and the sitcom's narrative gives far more attention to her relationship with her best friend, a wealthy divorcée, than it does to either her romantic life or her life as a mother. Moreover, *Cybill* gains some additional feminist resonance because of the outspoken feminist politics of its star, Cybill Shepherd.

In 1994, ABC created its own "women's night" by pairing *Roseanne* with two other sitcoms about women. The first, about a working class woman, is *Grace Under Fire* (1993–present). Its main character, Grace Kelly (the irony is a nice touch), is an attractive, divorced mother of three in her thirties who works in an oil refinery. She is also a recovering alcoholic and has been a battered wife, issues that get responsible attention in the show's narrative. Grace is witty, often cynical, and fiercely intelligent; her commentary on relations between the genders is sharp with a strong feminist flavor. *Grace Under Fire* is frequently compared to *Roseanne*, primarily because of its working-class focus, its strong female lead, and the similarities between the stars of the two sitcoms, both of who are former stand-up comics with troubled pasts (Brooke, 1994; Salzberg, 1995; Seibel, 1993). Certainly, there is room on television for two blue-collar heroines, especially given that they are still far outnumbered by privileged feminist figureheads.

The other sitcom making up ABC's "women's night" line-up, *Ellen* (1994–present),[7] is also built around a former stand-up comic, Ellen DeGeneres, called Ellen Morgan in the series. Ellen Morgan runs a bookstore in Los Angeles, and the sitcom centers on her life in the store and with her two close friends, a man and a woman. Ellen is in her thirties and her parents pressure her heavily toward marriage, but her romantic life is, to say the least, comically unsuccessful. The sitcom has a great deal of physical comedy and sight gags; as one reviewer has said, Ellen is a combination of Lucy Ricardo and Mary Richards (Jacobs, 1995). Ellen is not particularly assertive or opinionated; she is a sort of bumbling, post-feminist heroine. *Ellen* has almost no feminist edge, although it fits the basic conventions of "single woman on her own" shows. Its claim to progressivism is based almost entirely on its lesbian following, which can be linked to Ellen's androgynous style, to the refusal of DeGeneres to answer questions about her romantic preferences (Jacobs, 1995), and to the speculation that Ellen's romantic relationships with men lack chemistry because she is a closet lesbian (Millman, 1995).[8]

Television has come a long way from *Father Knows Best*. The medium's focus on women's lifestyle permutations has enhanced awareness and acceptance of the range of choices women can make about how to lead their lives. However, lifestyle politics go only so far, and progress in representing lifestyle choices is not the same as progress in representing feminist politics. There are, of course, political implications to lifestyle choices: the emphasis on women's economic independence derived from television's focus on working women is an example, as is the valorization of supportive, noncompetitive female relationships (particularly evident in *Mary Tyler Moore* and *Designing Women*), as is Ann Romano's rejection of the politics of traditional marriage in *One Day*. As feminists have claimed for a quarter century now, the personal is political. However, this adage was meant to describe *patriarchy*, not *feminism*. That is, it encapsulated the idea that what women viewed as personal, individual problems could be traced to the political status of women living in a male-dominated and male-defined society. Television entertainment, for the most part, has taken this idea in precisely the opposite direction in representing feminism: The political is personal, it tells us, as a set of political ideas and practices is transformed into a set of attitudes and personal lifestyle choices. Feminist politics become feminist identity. Feminist identity, in turn, is defined by appearance, by job, by marital status and by personality, not by political belief or political practice.

This obsession with feminist identity is what links media coverage of feminism, prime-time feminism, and the current wave of books examining the state of feminism in the 1990s. Since the beginning of the second wave, media have struggled to find ways to embody feminism in particular women and their lifestyles or attitudes. This desire is evident in titles of early articles on feminism such as "The Women of the Revolution, 1969" (featuring a profile of feminist Robin Morgan) and in the proliferation of press profiles, in the 1970s, of feminists such as Kate Millett, Betty Friedan, and, of course, Gloria Steinem. In the 1980s, media descriptions of postfeminism inevitably turned to descriptions of what feminists were supposedly like (rather than what feminism, as a politics, stood for) to make the case for women's disenchantment with the movement. Feminists were bitter and unhappy, journalists quoted young women as saying, arguing that "hairy legs haunt the feminist movement, as do images of being strident and lesbian" (Wallis, 1989, p. 81). Betty Friedan and Sylvia Hewlett claimed that feminism had been taken over by women who wanted fast-track careers and eschewed motherhood. Even *Ms.*, before its 1990 advertising-free reincarnation, went through a phase of attempting to sell feminism through personality appeal, putting women such as Cher, Glenn Close, and Cyndi Lauper on its cover, attempting to transfer their popularity to the movement.

Prime-time feminism has drawn from and capitalized on this general tendency to turn feminist politics into feminist identity. This basic hegemonic strategy is evident in each of the series I have discussed in this book, beginning with the conventions of the liberated-woman lifestyle established by *Mary Tyler Moore*. Mary Richards had brief moments of indignation about sexism, but her resonance as a "new woman" came from the fact that she lived alone, had a career, and had premarital sex. Ann Romano's awareness of patriarchy (in its figurative *and* literal sense, given that she rejected her marriage) went much further. Yet her nascent feminism was always eventually translated into psychological, not material, terms. *Designing Women* went further than any other sitcom, I contend, in offering feminist rhetoric that carried some expression of women's collective oppression and of the material forces that perpetuated it. Even so, *Designing Women*'s intensified femininity (in both setting and character), its heterosexuality, and its often absurd subplots worked to contradict and cushion its often radical (for television) feminist polemic.

The popularity of *Murphy Brown* as a symbol of feminist success is perhaps the ultimate bit of evidence that the distinction between feminist politics and feminist identity is in danger of completely disappearing. *Murphy Brown* functions as a parody of feminism as easily as it functions as an affirmation of feminism. Yet I cannot take the sanguine position of those cultural critics who see the possibility for such divergent readings as inherently progressive. Even if we assume that millions of people are "reading" Murphy Brown as a thoroughly positive feminist character, all that means is that feminism, for these readers, is a combination of power dressing, economic success, belligerence, self-confidence, and female chromosomes. In short, it is a lifestyle, an attitude, an identity. Indeed, *Murphy Brown*, for all its topicality and allusions to current events, assiduously avoids reference to feminist politics. In addition to its whitewashed treatment of the Quayle incident, the sitcom has modeled plotlines on the Thomas/Hill hearings and the O. J. Simpson case without ever mentioning the gender politics (or, for that matter, the racial politics) involved in these events. *Dr. Quinn*, which often offers more explicit, verbalized liberal feminist rhetoric than *Murphy Brown*, combines that rhetoric with a thorough romanticization of motherhood and heterosexuality and a quite utopian vision of the ease with which institutionalized patriarchy can be subverted (particularly if one lives on the frontier).

I suspect that Sommers, Roiphe, and Paglia would see these visions of white, middle- and upper-class, heterosexual heroines who are adept at finding personal solutions to the problems they face as ideal role models for feminism in the 1990s. As these critics describe it, feminism is being undermined by an emphasis on collective victimization, and the individualism that has always ruled television's representations is precisely what they claim the movement needs. As Susan Faludi put it, "By posing for the TV cameras with their 'postideological' message that women have 'made it' and can relax, they have become the nineties real-life equivalents of the blissed-out fashion models adorning the old Virginia Slims ads" (1995, p. 39). Even Naomi Wolf, whom Faludi does not include as a "faux feminist" and whose work has been taken much more seriously within the movement, is quite explicit about how media logic and a more commodified approach would benefit feminism. Wolf's book, *Fire with Fire*, in fact illustrates the precise dangers of conflating media's commodified, popularized feminism with the complex political analysis that fuels feminist movements.

Wolf's specific guidelines to fix the problems of feminism are perhaps why her book has been the most warmly received, particularly by feminists themselves. In *Fire with Fire*, Wolf does not completely share the broadly negative view of feminism put forth by Sommers, Paglia, or Roiphe; indeed, she critiques Paglia and Roiphe's dismissal of feminist perspectives on rape. Wolf does believe that patriarchy exists, and she is much more sympathetic and accurate about what feminism has tried to do; hers is the only one of these books with a positive blurb by Gloria Steinem on its cover. However, like the other authors, she is particularly concerned with feminism's emphasis on victimization, and she sees women's internalization of an identity as victims as the primary obstacle to be overcome. Wolf's endorsement by mainstream feminist leaders like Steinem and the editors of *Ms.* (she was featured on the cover of the magazine's September/October 1993 issue in a bit of prepublicity for the publication of *Fire with Fire*) and the positive review of her book in *The Women's Review of Books* (Hazleton, 1994), a widely circulated feminist journal, have given her the inside track to become a feminist leader for the "third wave."

What the movement needs, claims Wolf, is a feminism that "fit[s] every woman, and every man who cares about women, comfortably" (1993, p. 132). The clothing metaphor here reveals Wolf's desire to package feminism as a "theory of self-worth" rather than as a political practice (p. 139).[9] While equally concerned as Roiphe or Paglia with making feminism safe for vigorous heterosexuality, she claims that the real danger is not (totally) in feminist antisex propaganda but in women's psychology, specifically their fear of power.

According to Wolf, the danger women face is succumbing to "victim feminism," which "charges women to identify with powerlessness," "is sexually judgmental, even anti-sexual," "sees money as contaminating," and "believes sensuality cannot coincide with seriousness; fears that to have too much fun poses a threat to the revolution." What these women need to do is to embrace "power feminism," which "knows that a woman's choices affect many people around her and can change the world," "encourages a woman to claim her individual voice rather than merging her voice in a collective identity," "knows that poverty is not glamorous," "is unapologetically sexual," and "knows that making social change does not contradict the principle that girls just want to have fun" (1993, pp. 136–138). This is the feminism of enlightened self-interest, and Murphy Brown is its ideal representation. Without irony, Wolf describes how women have told her that "a version of feminism that could capture their aspirations" is best expressed through an advertising slogan—the Nike "Just Do It" campaign, which according to Wolf, "present[s] images of competition, even victory, and a motto of basic self-reliance" (p. 44). Advertising's goal of selling lifestyles, attitudes, and identities to women has much in common with Wolf's program for feminist renewal as well as with the prime-time feminist visions of the last quarter century.

Wolf's power feminism is an amalgam of the visions presented by *One Day*'s therapeutic feminism and *Murphy Brown*'s rugged individualism (with a dash of *Dr. Quinn*'s pioneer, "can do" spirit thrown in). Like the television networks, Wolf has discovered that the quickest way to make feminism attractive enough to be easily sold is to package it as a depoliticized attitude. The result, as bell hooks notes, is that "this movement can embrace everyone, since it has no overt political tenets. This 'feminism' turns the movement away from politics back to a version of individual self-help" (1994, p. 98). To add luster to the package, its spokesperson is a woman who possesses the same attributes that made Gloria Steinem a media favorite in the early 1970s; Wolf is young, pretty, heterosexual, and hip.

Just as advertisers and television producers have struggled for feminist representations that could attract the consumers they desired and to whom they wished to sell products, Wolf advocates a feminist representation that will help sell the movement. Despite the subtitle of her book, *The New Female Power and How It Will Change the 21st Century*, Wolf's project is hardly original. Her message—that feminism is safe for women who love men and sex, for women who want economic success, for women who wear makeup and buy clothes, and for women who want to use their resources to better their lives—has been generally available in popular culture, and specifically available in the programs discussed in this book, for many years. That brand of feminism has always sold well—particularly in the pages of *Cosmo*. It is rather telling that at least two reviewers of *Fire with Fire* have commented that its tone is "shockingly similar to women's magazine advice" (Chesler, 1994, p. 56; see also Schwarzbaum, 1993). For the paperback edition released in 1994, the subtitle of

Fire with Fire became *The New Female Power and How to Use It,* a change that gave additional emphasis to the book's self-help and therapeutic dimensions.

A feminism driven by representational concerns and commodity logic, and that is willing to sacrifice specific political objectives in the quest for a more attractive image, is a feminism with little hope of making a material difference in the lives of all women. It would be nice if the majority of women in this country felt comfortable saying, "Yes, I am a feminist"; but if the way to make that happen is to empty the term of all political implications so that all it really means is "I like myself," then feminism has not gained much.[10] There is no guarantee that revamping feminism's image (and the lifestyles, attitudes, and identities attached to it) is going to protect women from patriarchy. For example, making feminism safe for heterosexual women will not help lesbians who lose custody of their children for practicing their sexuality. Freeing women to claim their heterosexual desire—what Wolf calls "radical heterosexuality"—will hardly protect them from rape (Chesler, 1994, p. 58). Further, it may be freeing for Wolf's white, middle-class compatriots to embrace their economic clout, but it is hardly a comfort to the women on welfare who *know* poverty is not glamorous (hooks, 1994) and who are punished economically for practicing heterosexuality by living with a man.

Celebrating individual choice and achievement is satisfying and necessary: it shows what is possible for some women and what feminism wants to make available to all women. There is little evidence that feminists (or women at large) eschew individualism in their daily lives. However, women have the resources to practice individualism to different degrees, and an "every woman for herself" philosophy denies feminism's core as a collective social movement created to ameliorate the collective wrongs that afflict women. Television gives us only glimpses of this aspect of feminism, and the medium's rare images of female solidarity, while important, are rarely politicized. Yet those moments when women realize that their political interests are collective are the moments when meaningful activism occurs, such as the pro-choice marches after the *Webster* decision or the collective cry of protest after the Thomas/Hill hearings that sent money into feminist coffers and helped elect women to Congress and the Senate in record numbers (of course, the Republican "revolution" of the 1994 midterm elections indicates how fragile such gains can be). It is the *collective* feminist work—in feminist advocacy groups such as Fund for the Feminist Majority or NARAL, in feminist direct action groups such as WAC (Women's Action Coalition) or Lesbian Avengers, in women's studies programs and feminist bookstores, in rape crisis centers and battered women's shelters, in feminist publishing houses and feminist media—that keeps the movement going through those periods when media declares its demise (Dow and Hogeland, 1995).

The great weakness that Wolf's vision shares with prime-time feminism is the danger of confusing lifestyle, attitudinal feminism with the hard political and intellectual work that feminists have done and continue to do. Only because there is a feminism behind the image and outside media has popular culture been able to appropriate and commodify it in the first place (Dow and Hogeland, 1995). Yet pop culture feminism is not always and inevitably antifeminist, as some critics might charge. Rather, it is simply very limited. There is powerful feminist resonance in the programming analyzed in this book. These series, particularly *Designing Women*, have often made a good case, within their limitations, for why feminism is necessary. To use the term "feminist" to describe them is not a mistake: within the limits of commercial television, they offer a version of feminist ideology. However, that ideology is one suited to television's needs, not to the needs of a feminist politics committed to the future of all women regardless of race, class, sexuality, or life situation.

No feminist viewer should attempt to deny her pleasure in these prime-time feminist visions: they offer sophisticated, entertaining, often quite satisfying images of the personal struggles and triumphs of women. The danger is not in enjoying them but in mistaking them for something more than the selective, partial images that they are. Likewise, it is no sin for writers such as Wolf to worry about feminism's image;[11] the danger is in believing that image is equal to politics and material change. Wolf wants us to learn from media and pop culture, and she takes positive lessons from sources as varied as *Fried Green Tomatoes*, the novels of Jackie Collins, and the post-Donald media image of Ivana Trump (1993, pp. 41–44). I also think it is vital that feminism learn from pop culture; my goal, however, is a bit different. Like Wolf, I think we need to appreciate media for what it can do in giving us images of strong women; yet, at the same time, we need to maintain a very keen sense of the limitations of media logic.

This book has tried to explain why some television programming is hailed as feminist, what feminism means in that context, and how it interacts with the meanings of feminism offered by the larger media culture. What this book reveals, I think, is that media has been quite sophisticated in its adaptations of feminism for its own purposes. This is why feminist analysis must be equally as sophisticated in understanding the strategies that create mediated visions of feminism and in reminding ourselves and our students of the reflection, selection, and deflection of reality (Burke, 1968) on which these visions rely. Particularly for media critics, there is a strong temptation to succumb to the postmodernist adage that "image is everything," and to celebrate media discourse as always potentially resistant, empowering, and politically meaningful. As the analysis in this book illustrates, television can, at different times and to different degrees, be all of these things. For feminist critics, however, embracing this perspective too strongly can blind us to the fact that feminism is a politics with material consequences that entails hard choices, hard work, and a commitment to collective action. Images can and have contributed to that struggle, but they cannot substitute for it.

Notes

1. Difference feminism has, in fact, been the subject of much debate among feminists in the academy, and much of the feminist theory I cite in Chapter 5 is part of this debate (e.g., Alcoff, 1988; Boling, 1991). Contrary to the claims of these authors, difference feminism is by no means hegemonic in the academy, and it has lost much of its popularity with academic feminists. The prominence of difference feminist assumptions in *Dr. Quinn* is an indication of how popular culture lags behind academic trends.

2. Indeed, Faludi has become the central defender of feminism in these debates. She refuted Roiphe's claims about "date rape hype" in an article in *Newsweek* (Faludi, 1993a); she replied to Karen Lehrman's (1993) attacks on women's studies in a subsequent issue of *Mother Jones* (Faludi, 1993b); and she published an essay in *Ms.*, titled "Faux Feminists," about the spate of "what's wrong with feminism" books, including those by Roiphe, Paglia, and Sommers (Faludi, 1995).

3. A telling clue that the concern here is with representation rather than politics is that none of these critics have solid credentials in terms of feminist politics or movement activity. None have led feminist organizations or worked in feminist institutions, with the exception of Wolf, who has worked in a rape crisis center. Paglia and Sommers are academics and Roiphe (who is in her late twenties) and Wolf (who is in her early thirties) base many of their conclusions on their experiences as undergraduates or graduate students at elite universities. All of these writers are, largely, media creations: their common qualification to speak for feminism is that their ideas are marketable at this particular historical moment (Faludi, 1995).

However, Sommers has since parlayed her book into an organizational identity. Following publication of *Who Stole Feminism?*, she helped to found and became a board member of the "Women's Freedom Network," which described its first national conference in October of 1994 as committed to two conclusions: "that [1] intelligent life cannot continue under the presumption that all men are beasts and all women helpless victims and [2] journalists seeking commentary on feminist issues require a third alternative to the radical PC feminist left and the far-out Phyllis Schlafly Right." According to the WFN newsletter, the conference was attended by "more than 100 people" (Starr, 1994. p. 1).

4. See, for example, Susan Faludi's (1995) essay mentioned above, bell hooks's excellent essays on Paglia's, Roiphe's, and Wolf's work in her *Outlaw Culture* (1994), as well as Katha Pollitt's essay on Roiphe's work in *Reasonable Creatures* (1994), Phyllis Chesler's (1994) essay on Wolf in *Patriarchy: Notes of an Expert Witness*, the essay on Sommers and Roiphe in the forum on "Feminism and the Me-

dia" in *Signs* (McDermott, 1995), and the special issue of *Democratic Culture* on Sommers's book (Wilson, 1994).

5. As McDermott (1995) points out, these writers conveniently elide the vigorous debate *within* feminism over issues such as "the limits of female agency in oppressive contexts, the dangers of 'victim ideology,' and the inherent problems embedded in feminist constructions of female sexuality" (p. 670).

6. McDermott (1995) discusses in more detail the ways in which these attacks on feminism share the "positivist assumptions" preferred by media, which she contrasts to the "perspectival" approach, "always situated in the material world and involved in distributions of power," that feminist scholars work from. She argues that it is this "epistemological disjuncture that makes it easy for popular press representations to 'mark' feminist scholarship as a suspect entity whose content and intentions are distorted by its politics" (p. 673).

7. The sitcom was originally conceived as an ensemble show and was called *These Friends of Mine* when it premiered in March of 1994. At the beginning of the fall 1994 season, it was renamed *Ellen* because it had steadily become more focused on its star, Ellen DeGeneres (Jacobs, 1995).

8. On prime-time television, explicit (rather than "subtextual") representations of lesbians are increasing slowly, although they are still still outnumbered by representations of gay men. In recent years *L.A. Law, Roseanne, Northern Exposure,* and *HeartBeat* have created storylines about lesbians or bisexual women. Currently, there is a recurring lesbian couple on the popular ABC sitcom *Friends* (1994–present). There are limits to the progress this represents, however, given that the primary function of the lesbian characters is to serve as fodder for a main character's angst about his masculinity (he used to be married to one of them and fathered the child they are raising). This approach is illustrative of a general media strategy of portraying lesbians and gays in ways that highlight the impact of their "deviance" on heterosexuals (Gross, 1991). Interestingly, in an *Entertainment Tonight* feature that I viewed about the actor who portrays one of the lesbians on *Friends,* the actor's happy, heterosexual homelife was a major focus, and one of the questions she was asked was how her husband felt about her job playing a lesbian.

As has long been the case, the "big three" networks devote little attention to the lives of African American women. In an article that also discusses *Cybill, Grace Under Fire,* and *Ellen,* Susan Douglas discusses the status of African American women on network television. She points out that the only comedy centered on the lives of African American women, *Living Single,* is broadcast on the Fox network, which has "targeted African American women as a critical market" (Douglas, 1995b, p. 76).

9. Wolf also says that feminism may be understood as a "broad movement for social justice" (1993, p. 139). However, she eschews political "litmus tests" or any sort of specific feminist political platform (p. 126), with the result that feminism means that every woman should practice feminism as she sees it. The only "first principle" that Wolf offers is that "a woman is entitled to define herself, express her beliefs, and make her own life" (p. 127), a definition that fits Phyllis Schlafly as comfortably as it fits Gloria Steinem. As I discuss below, it is easy to see why Wolf is fond of advertising slogans.

10. Assuming that every woman who respects herself is a feminist also overlooks the extent to which women, particularly the white, middle-class women who are clearly Wolf's target, can have a stake in systems of domination. Some aspects of feminist ideology—antiracism, antihomophobia, commitment to economic

justice for women of *all* classes—are perceived by many women as against their interests. Such women may be very committed to improving *their own* lives, but that does not make them feminists (Dow and Hogeland, 1995).

11. In fact, some of Wolf's (1993) analysis is quite useful. Her discussion of how feminism and women's issues are excluded from mainstream news media and her analysis of the constraints on women's media and women journalists is insightful (see her chapter 7, pp. 76–93).

References

Adler, Richard. 1979. *All in the Family: A Critical Appraisal*. New York: Praeger.

———, ed. 1981. *Understanding Television: Essays on Television as a Social and Cultural Force*. New York: Praeger.

"Aghast at Writers." 1992. *USA Today*, May 20, p. 10A.

Aitken, Lee. 1986. "Delta Burke Hits on a Winning Pattern in TV's *Designing Women*." *People*, November 3, pp. 135–138.

Alcock, Beverley, and Jocelyn Robson. 1990. "*Cagney and Lacey* Revisited." *Feminist Review*, 35: 42–53.

Alcoff, Linda. 1988. "Cultural Feminism versus Post-Structuralism: The Identity Crisis in Feminist Theory." *Signs: Journal of Women in Culture and Society*, 13: 405–436.

Allen, Robert. 1992. "Audience-Oriented Criticism and Television." In R. Allen, ed., *Channels of Discourse, Reassembled: Television and Contemporary Criticism*, 2nd ed., pp. 101–137. Chapel Hill: University of North Carolina Press.

Alley, Robert S., and Irby B. Brown. 1989. *Love Is All Around: The Making of The Mary Tyler Moore Show*. New York: Delta.

———. 1990. *Murphy Brown: Anatomy of a Sitcom*. New York: Delta.

Althusser, Louis. 1971. *Lenin and Philosophy and Other Essays*. London: New Left Books.

Amory, Cleveland. 1976. "Review of *One Day at a Time*." *TV Guide*, February 21, p. 27.

Ang, Ien. 1985. *Watching "Dallas": Soap Opera and the Melodramatic Imagination*. London: Methuen.

———. 1990. "Melodramatic Identifications: Television Fiction and Women's Fantasy." In M. E. Brown, ed., *Television and Women's Culture: The Politics of the Popular*, pp. 75–88. Newbury Park, CA: Sage.

Angier, Natalie. 1989. "Baby Chic: What's Behind the New Diaper Rush?" *Mademoiselle*, June, pp. 194, 220, 222.

"Are Women's Minds or Lives Really Changing?" 1972. *Mademoiselle*, May, pp. 124–125, 178–181, 183.

Aristotle. 1954. *Rhetoric*. Trans. W. R. Roberts. New York: Modern Library.

Arlen, Michael J. 1975. "The Media Dramas of Norman Lear." *The New Yorker*, March 10, pp. 89–94.

Attallah, Paul. 1984. "The Unworthy Discourse: Situation Comedy in Television." In W. D. Rowland, Jr. and B. Watkins, eds., *Interpreting Television: Current Research Perspectives*, pp. 222–249. Beverly Hills, CA: Sage.

Babcox, Peter. 1969. "Meet the Women of the Revolution, 1969." *New York Times Magazine*, February 9, pp. 34–35+.

Bailey, Alison. 1994. "Mothering, Diversity, and Peace Politics." *Hypatia*, 9: 188–198.

Barkin, Steve M., and Michael Gurevitch. 1987. "Out of Work and on the Air: Television News of Unemployment." *Critical Studies in Mass Communication*, 4: 1–20.

Barson, Michael. 1985. "The TV Western." In B. G. Rose, ed., *TV Genres: A Handbook and Reference Guide*, pp. 57–72. Westport, CT: Greenwood.

Bartky, Sandra L. 1990. *Femininity and Domination: Studies in the Phenomenology of Oppression*. New York: Routledge.

Bathrick, Serafina. 1984. "*The Mary Tyler Moore Show*: Women at Home and at Work." In J. Feuer, P. Kerr, and T. Vahimagi, eds., *MTM: "Quality Television,"* pp. 99–131. London: British Film Institute.

Baudrillard, Jean. 1992. "From *Simulations*." In P. Waugh, ed., *Postmodernism: A Reader*, pp. 186–188. London: Edward Arnold.

Beale, Lewis. 1992. "Maude Was a Pioneer: Decision on Abortion was Watershed in TV History." *Star Tribune* (Minneapolis), November 21, p. 1E.

Becker, Samuel. 1984. "Marxist Approaches to Media Studies: The British Experience." *Critical Studies in Mass Communication*, 1:66–80.

Belenky, Mary F., Blythe M. Clinchy, Nancy R. Goldberger, and Jill M. Tarule, eds. 1986. *Women's Ways of Knowing: The Development of Self, Voice, and Mind.* New York: Basic Books.

Berman, Susan K. 1975. "Primetime Almost Comes of Age with 'Phyllis' and 'Fay.'" *Ms.*, November, pp. 61–62.

Bernays, Anne. 1970. "What Are You Supposed to Do If You Like Children?" *Atlantic Monthly*, March 3, pp. 107–109.

Bernstein, Fred. 1987. "Pulling Itself Out of the Ratings Heap, *Designing Women* Becomes TV's Trashy New Smash." *People*, April 20, pp. 63–66.

Berry, Mary Frances. 1993. *The Politics of Parenthood: Child Care, Women's Rights, and the Myth of the Good Mother.* New York: Viking.

"The Best Comic Actress." 1993. *TV Guide*, April 7, p. 22.

Bianculli, David. 1992. *Teleliteracy: Taking Television Seriously.* New York: Touchstone.

Bird, Caroline. 1971. "Myths that Keep Women Down." *Ladies Home Journal*, November, pp. 68–70.

Blount, Roy. 1988. "My, How They Kiss and Talk." *TV Guide*, July 2, pp. 26–29.

Bodroghkozy, Aniko, 1992. "'Is This What You Mean by Color TV?': Race, Gender, and Contested Meanings in NBC's *Julia*." In L. Spigel and D. Mann, eds., *Private Screenings: Television and the Female Consumer*, pp. 143–167. Minneapolis: University of Minnesota.

Boeth, Richard. 1971. "Gloria Steinem: The New Woman." *Newsweek*, August 16, pp. 51–55.

Boling, Patricia. 1991. "The Democratic Potential of Mothering." *Political Theory*, 19: 606–625.

Bolotin, Susan. 1982. "Voices from the Postfeminist Generation." *New York Times Magazine*, October 17, pp. 29–31+.

Bordin, Ruth. 1986. *Frances Willard: A Biography.* Chapel Hill: University of North Carolina Press.

Bosworth, Patricia. 1986. "ABC Special on Women's Lives." *Working Woman*, August, p. 110.

Brauer, Ralph. 1975. *The Horse, the Gun and the Piece of Property: Changing Images of the TV Western.* Bowling Green: Popular Press.

Brenner, Johanna. 1993. "The Best of Times, the Worst of Times: U.S. Feminism Today." *New Left Review,* July/August, pp. 101–159.

Brooke, Jill. 1994. "Brett Butler: True Grit." *Ladies Home Journal,* April, pp. 150+.

Brooks, Tim, and Earl Marsh. 1985. *The Complete Directory to Prime Time Network TV Shows, 1946–Present,* 3rd ed. New York: Ballantine.

———. (1992). *The Complete Directory to Prime Time Network TV Shows, 1946–Present,* 5th ed. New York: Ballantine.

Brown, Helen Gurley. 1962. *Sex and the Single Girl.* New York: Bernard Geis.

Brown, Mary Ellen. 1990a. "Motley Moments: Soap Opera, Carnival, Gossip, and the Power of the Utterance." In M. E. Brown, ed., *Television and Women's Culture: The Politics of the Popular,* pp. 183–200. Newbury Park, CA: Sage.

———. 1990b. "Consumption and Resistance—The Problem of Pleasure." In M. E. Brown, ed., *Television and Women's Culture: The Politics of the Popular,* pp. 201–210. Newbury Park, CA: Sage.

Brownmiller, Susan. 1970a. " 'Sisterhood Is Powerful': A Member of the Women's Liberation Movement Explains What It's All About." *New York Times Magazine,* March 15, pp. 26+.

———. 1970b. " . . . Woman Is Often Her Own Worst Enemy—the Enemy Within." *Mademoiselle,* February, pp. 184, 267–268.

Brunsdon, Charlotte. 1983. "*Crossroads*: Notes on Soap Opera." In E. A. Kaplan, ed., *Regarding Television—Critical Approaches: An Anthology,* pp. 76–83. Frederick, MD: University Publications of America.

———. 1990. "Television: Aesthetics and Audiences." In P. Mellencamp, ed., *Logics of Television: Essays in Cultural Criticism,* pp. 59–72. Bloomington: Indiana University Press.

Bryant, Donald. 1953. "Rhetoric: Its Functions and Its Scope." *Quarterly Journal of Speech,* 39: 401–424.

Budd, Mike, Robert M. Entman, and Clay Steinman. 1990. "The Affirmative Character of U.S. Cultural Studies." *Critical Studies in Mass Communication,* 7: 169–184.

Burke, Kenneth. 1953. *Counter-Statement,* 2nd ed. Los Altos, CA: Hermes.

———. 1959. *Attitudes Toward History.* Boston: Beacon Press.

———. 1968. *Language as Symbolic Action: Essays on Life, Literature, and Method,* 2nd ed. Los Angeles: University of California Press.

———. 1973. *The Philosophy of Literary Form,* 3rd ed. Berkeley: University of California Press.

Butler, Jeremy. 1993. "Redesigning Discourse: Feminism, the Sitcom, and *Designing Women.*" *Journal of Film and Video,* 45: 13–26.

———. 1994. *Television: Critical Methods and Applications.* Belmont, CA: Wadsworth.

Byars, Jackie. 1987. "Reading Feminine Discourse: Prime-Time Television in the U.S." *Communication,* 9: 289–303.

Cameron, Deborah. 1985. *Feminism and Linguistic Theory.* New York: St. Martin's Press.

Campbell, Karlyn Kohrs. 1973. "The Rhetoric of Women's Liberation: An Oxymoron." *Quarterly Journal of Speech,* 59: 74–86.

———. 1980. "Stanton's 'The Solitude of Self': A Humanistic Rationale for Feminism." *Quarterly Journal of Speech,* 66: 304–312.

"Candice Bergen." 1989. *Playboy,* December, pp. 61–81.

"Candice Bergen." 1992. *Esquire*, August, p. 79.

Cantor, Muriel G. 1990. "Prime-Time Fathers: A Study in Continuity and Change." *Critical Studies in Mass Communication*, 7: 275–285.

Cantwell, Mary. 1985. "Kate & Allie & Cagney & Lacey & Krystle & Alexis & Me." *Vogue*, February, p. 334.

Carragee, Kevin M. 1990. "Interpretive Media Study and Interpretive Social Science." *Critical Studies in Mass Communication*, 7: 81–96.

Carter, Bill. 1993. " 'Dr. Quinn, Medicine Woman' Cures CBS' Case of the Saturday Night Programming Blues." *New York Times*, January 25, p. D8.

Cawelti, John. 1971. *The Six-Gun Mystique*. Bowling Green, OH: Popular Press.

Charen, Mona. 1991. "Sitcoms Treat Unwed Motherhood as Laughing Matter." *The Cincinnati Post*, October 3, p. 15A.

Charlton, Linda. 1970. "Women Seeking Equality March on 5th Avenue Today." *New York Times*, August 26, p. 44.

Chesler, Phyllis. 1994. *Patriarchy: Notes of an Expert Witness*. Monroe, ME: Common Courage Press.

Chodorow, Nancy. 1978. *The Reproduction of Mothering: Psychoanalysis and the Sociology of Gender*. Berkeley: University of California Press.

Clark, Danae. 1990. "*Cagney and Lacey*: Feminist Strategies of Detection." In M. E. Brown, ed., *Television and Women's Culture: The Politics of the Popular*, pp. 117–133. Newbury Park, CA: Sage.

Cloud, Dana. 1992. "The Limits of Interpretation: Ambivalence and the Stereotype in *Spenser: For Hire*." *Critical Studies in Mass Communication*, 9: 311–324.

Cohen, Marcia. 1988. *The Sisterhood: The True Story of the Women Who Changed the World*. New York: Simon and Schuster.

Collins, Monica. 1993. "The Baby Wars." *TV Guide*, September 25, pp. 24–26.

Collins, Patricia Hill. 1990. *Black Feminist Thought*. New York: Routledge.

Comer, Nancy A. 1972. "Women! The Next Thing You Know They'll Be Running for Office." *Mademoiselle*, May, pp. 188–189, 246–247.

Condit, Celeste. 1989. "The Rhetorical Limits of Polysemy." *Critical Studies in Mass Communication*, 6: 103–122.

———. 1990. *Decoding Abortion Rhetoric: Communicating Social Change*. Urbana: University of Illinois.

Connor, Steven. 1989. *Postmodernist Culture: An Introduction to Theories of the Contemporary*. Oxford: Basil Blackwell.

Cowan, Alison L. 1989. "Poll Finds Women's Gains Have Taken Personal Toll." *New York Times*, August 21, pp. 1, 8.

Cowley, Geoffrey. 1993. "Who's Looking After the Interests of Children?" *Newsweek*, August 16, pp. 54–55.

Cox, Robert. 1990. "Memory, Critical Theory, and the Argument from History." *Argumentation and Advocacy* 27: 1–13.

Crenshaw, Kimberle. 1992. "Whose Story Is It Anyway? Feminist and Antiracist Appropriations of Anita Hill." In T. Morrison, ed., *Race-ing Justice, En-gendering Power: Essays on Anita Hill, Clarence Thomas, and the Construction of Social Reality*, pp. 402–440. New York: Pantheon.

Crichton, Sarah. 1993. "Sexual Correctness: Has It Gone Too Far?" *Newsweek*, October 25, pp. 51–56.

D'Acci, Julie. 1987. "The Case of *Cagney and Lacey*." In H. Baehr and G. Dyer, eds. *Boxed In: Women and Television*, pp. 203–226. London: Routledge and Kegan Paul.

———. 1992. "Defining Women: The Case of *Cagney and Lacey*." In L. Spigel and

D. Mann, eds. *Private Screenings: Television and the Female Consumer*, pp. 169–202. Minneapolis: University of Minnesota.

———. 1994. *Defining Women: Television and the Case of Cagney and Lacey*. Chapel Hill: University of North Carolina.

Daly, Mary. 1978. *Gyn/ecology: The Metaethics of Radical Feminism*. Boston: Beacon.

Davidson, Bill. 1976. "It *Wasn't* So Nice to Have a Man Around the House." *TV Guide*, December 11, pp. 24–27.

———. 1981. "Careful Now, Don't Slip Off the Pedestal." *TV Guide*, October 3, pp. 28+.

Davidson, Sara. 1969. "An 'Oppressed Majority' Demands Its Rights." *Life*, December 12, pp. 66–78.

Davis, Flora. 1991. *Moving the Mountain: The Women's Movement in America Since 1960*. New York: Touchstone.

"Day Careless?" 1994. *Time*, August 8, p. 28.

DeBoer, Roberta. 1994. "Losing Jessica." *Redbook*, August, pp. 97–99+.

Deming, Caren. 1990. "For Television-Centred Television Criticism: Lessons from Feminism." In M. E. Brown, ed., *Television and Women's Culture: The Politics of the Popular*, pp. 37–60. Newbury Park, CA: Sage.

Deming, Robert. 1992. "*Kate and Allie*: 'New Women' and the Audience's Television Archive." In L. Spigel and D. Mann, eds., *Private Screenings: Television and the Female Consumer*, pp. 203–214. Minneapolis: University of Minnesota Press.

De Vries, Hilary. 1993. "Laughing Off the Recession All the Way to the Bank." *New York Times Magazine*, January 3, pp. 19–21, 24, 26.

Donovan, Josephine. 1993. *Feminist Theory: The Intellectual Traditions of American Feminism*, 2nd ed. New York: Continuum.

Doty, Alexander. 1993. *Making Things Perfectly Queer: Interpreting Mass Culture*. Minneapolis: University of Minnesota.

Douglas, Susan J. 1994. *Where the Girls Are: Growing Up Female with the Mass Media*. New York: Random House.

———. 1995a. "Signs of Intelligent Life on TV." *Ms.*, May/June, pp. 78–81.

———. 1995b. "Sitcom Women: We've Come a Long Way, Maybe." *Ms.*, November/December, pp. 76–80.

Dow, Bonnie J. 1990. "Hegemony, Feminist Criticism, and *The Mary Tyler Moore Show*." *Critical Studies in Mass Communication*, 7: 261–274.

———. 1991. "The 'Womanhood Rationale' in the Woman Suffrage Rhetoric of Frances. E. Willard." *Southern Communication Journal*, 56: 298–307.

———. 1992a. "Femininity and Feminism in *Murphy Brown*." *Southern Communication Journal*, 57: 143–155.

———. 1992b. "Performance of Feminine Discourse in *Designing Women*." *Text and Performance Quarterly*, 12: 125–145.

———. 1995. "Prime-time Feminism: Entertainment Television and Women's Progress." In C. Lont, ed., *Women and Media: Content, Careers, Criticism*, pp. 199–216. Belmont, CA: Wadsworth.

Dow, Bonnie J., and Lisa Maria Hogeland. 1995. "Feminist Literacy." Unpublished manuscript.

Dow, Bonnie J., and Mari Boor Tonn. 1993. " 'Feminine Style' and Political Judgement in the Rhetoric of Ann Richards." *Quarterly Journal of Speech*, 79: 286–302.

Dowell, Pat. 1985. "Ladies Night." *American Film*, January/February, pp. 44–49.

Dudar, Helen. 1970. "Women's Lib: The War on 'Sexism.' " *Newsweek*, March 23, pp. 71–74, 78.

Duncan, Hugh D. 1962. *Communication and Social Order*. New York: Oxford University Press.

Durbin, Karen. 1972. "The Sexual Confusion." *Mademoiselle*, July, pp. 90–91, 162.

Echols, Alice. 1989. *Daring to Be Bad: Radical Feminism in America, 1967–75*. Minneapolis: University of Minnesota Press.

Ehrenreich, Barbara. 1983. *The Hearts of Men: American Dreams and the Flight from Commitment*. New York: Doubleday.

———. 1990a. *The Worst Years of Our Lives: Irreverent Notes from a Decade of Greed*. New York: Pantheon.

———. 1990b. "The Wretched of the Hearth." *The New Republic*, April 2, pp. 28–31.

Ehrenreich, Barbara, and Deirdre English, eds. 1978, rpt. 1989. *For Her Own Good: 150 Years of the Experts' Advice to Women*. New York: Anchor.

Ehrenreich, Barbara, and Jane O'Reilly. 1984. "No Jiggles, No Scheming. Just Real Women as Friends." *TV Guide*, November 24, pp. 6–10.

Eisenstein, Hester. 1983. *Contemporary Feminist Thought*. Boston: G.K. Hall.

Elliott, Stuart. 1992. "Contretemps Lifts Ad Rate for 'Murphy.'" *New York Times*, September 17, p. C8.

Elm, Joanna. 1989. "What TV's Real Newswomen Think of Murphy Brown." *TV Guide*, December 23, pp. 4–7.

Epstein, Barbara. 1981. *The Politics of Domesticity: Women, Evangelism, and Temperance in Nineteenth Century America*. Middletown, CT: Wesleyan University Press.

Evans, William A. 1990. "The Interpretive Turn in Media Research: Innovation, Iteration, or Illusion?" *Critical Studies in Mass Communication*, 7: 147–168.

"Excerpts from the Vice-President's Speech on Cities and Poverty." 1992. *New York Times*, May 20, p. A11.

Faludi, Susan. 1991. *Backlash: The Undeclared War Against American Women*. New York: Crown.

———. 1993a. "Whose Hype?" *Newsweek*, October 25, p. 61.

———. 1993b. "Faludi Lashes Back." *Mother Jones*, November/December, p. 4.

———. 1995. "I'm Not a Feminist but I Play One on TV." *Ms.*, March/April, pp. 30–39.

Femia, Joseph V. 1981. *Gramsci's Political Thought: Hegemony, Consciousness, and the Revolutionary Process*. Oxford: Clarendon Press.

Ferguson, Marjorie. 1983. *Forever Feminine: Women's Magazines and the Cult of Femininity*. London: Heinemann.

———. 1990. "Images of Power and the Feminist Fallacy." *Critical Studies in Mass communication*, 7: 215–230.

Feuer, Jane. 1984. "Melodrama, Serial form, and Television Today." *Screen*, 25: 4–16.

———. 1986. "Narrative Form in American Network Television." In C. McCabe, ed., *High Theory/Low Culture: Analysing Popular Television and Film*, pp. 101–114. New York: St. Martin's Press.

———. 1992. "Genre Study and Television." In R. Allen, ed., *Channels of Discourse, Reassembled: Television and Contemporary Criticism*, 2nd ed., pp. 138–160. Chapel Hill: University of North Carolina Press.

Feuer, Jane, Paul Kerr, and Tise Vahimagi, eds. 1984. *MTM: "Quality" Television*. British Film Institute.

Fierman, Jaclyn. 1990. "Do Women Manage Differently?" *Fortune*, December 17, pp. 115–118.

Firestone, Shulamith. 1970, rpt. 1971. *The Dialectic of Sex: The Case for Feminist Revolution.* New York: Bantam.

Firestone, Shulamith, and Anne Koedt, eds. 1970. *Notes from the Second Year: Radical Feminism.* New York: New York Radical Women.

Fiske, John. 1986. "Television: Polysemy and Popularity." *Critical Studies in Mass Communication*, 3: 391–408.

———. 1987a. *Television Culture.* London: Methuen.

———. 1987b. "*Cagney and Lacey*: Reading Character Structurally and Politically." *Communication*, 9: 399–426.

———. 1992. "British Cultural Studies and Television." In R. Allen, ed., *Channels of Discourse, Reassembled: Television and Contemporary Criticism*, 2nd ed., pp. 284–326. Chapel Hill: University of North Carolina.

Fiske, John, and John Hartley. 1987. "Bardic Television." In H. Newcomb, ed., *Television: The Critical View*, 4th ed., pp. 600–612. New York: Oxford.

Fosburgh, Lacey. 1970. "Traditional Groups Prefer to Ignore Women's Lib." *New York Times*, August 26, p. 44.

Freeman, Jo. 1975. *The Politics of Women's Liberation.* New York: Longman.

French, Marilyn. 1977. *The Women's Room.* New York: Summit.

Friedan, Betty. 1963. *The Feminine Mystique.* New York: Norton.

———. 1973. "Up from the Kitchen Floor." *New York Times Magazine*, March 4, pp. 8–9, 28–37.

———. 1981. *The Second Stage.* New York: Summit.

Friend, Tad. 1994. "The Rise of 'Do Me' Feminism." *Esquire*, February, pp. 48–56.

Frye, Northrop. 1957. *Anatomy of Criticism: Four Essays.* Princeton, NJ: Princeton University Press.

Gamman, Lorraine. 1988. "Watching the Detectives: The Enigma of the Female Gaze." In L. Gamman and M. Marshment, eds., *The Female Gaze: Women as Viewers of Popular Culture*, pp. 16–18. London: Women's Press.

———. 1991. "Response: More *Cagney and Lacey*." *Feminist Review*, 37: 117–121.

Geraghty, Christine. 1991. *Women and Soap Opera: A Study of Prime-Time Soaps.* Cambridge, UK: Polity Press.

Gilligan, Carol. 1982a. *In a Different Voice: Psychological Theory and Women's Development.* Cambridge, MA: Harvard University Press.

———. 1982b. "Why Should a Woman Be More Like a Man?" *Psychology Today*, June, pp. 68–77.

Gitlin, Todd. 1980. *The Whole World Is Watching: Mass Media in the Making and Unmaking of the New Left.* Berkeley: University of California Press.

———. 1982. "Prime-Time Ideology: The Hegemonic Process in Television Entertainment." In H. Newcomb, ed., *Television: The Critical View*, 3rd ed., pp. 426–454. New York: Oxford University Press.

———. 1983. *Inside Prime-Time.* New York: Pantheon.

———. 1990. "Who Communicates What to Whom, in What Voice and Why, about the Study of Mass Communication?" *Critical Studies in Mass Communication*, 7: 185–196.

Goldman, Robert, Deborah Heath, and Sharon Smith. 1991. "Commodity Feminism." *Critical Studies in Mass Communication*, 8: 333–351.

Goodstein, Ethel. 1992. "Southern Belles and Southern Buildings: The Built Environment as Text and Context in *Designing Women*." *Critical Studies in Mass Communication*, 9: 170–185.

Goodwin, Betty. 1987. "Annie Potts: Let Her Tell You About the Time She Had Dinner with Dan Rather." *TV Guide*, April 25, pp. 16–18.

Gorman, Christine. 1992. "Sizing Up the Sexes." *Time*, January 20, pp. 42+.

Gray, Herman. 1994. "Television, Black Americans, and the American Dream." In H. Newcomb, ed., *Television: The Critical View*, 5th ed., pp. 176–187. New York: Oxford University Press

Gray, John. 1992. *Men Are from Mars, Women Are from Venus: A Practical Guide to Improving Communication and Getting What You Want in Your Relationships*. New York: Harper Collins.

Greer, Germaine. 1971. *The Female Eunuch*. New York: McGraw Hill.

Griffin, Susan. 1978. *Woman and Nature: The Roaring Inside Her*. New York: Harper.

Gross, Amy. 1970. "Women's Lib Loves You." *Mademoiselle*, February, pp. 232–233, 282–288.

Gross, Larry. 1991. "Out of the Mainstream: Sexual Minorities and the Mass Media." *Journal of Homosexuality*, 21: 19–47.

Hall, Carla. 1995. "We've Got the Wedding Bell News." *TV Guide*, May 6, pp. 11–18.

Hall, Deanna, and Kristin Langellier. 1987. "Storytelling Strategies in Mother-Daughter Communication." In B. Bate and A. Taylor, eds., *Women Communicating: Studies of Women's Talk*, pp. 107–126. Norwood, NJ: Ablex.

Hall, Stuart. 1982. "The Rediscovery of 'Ideology': Return of the Repressed in Media Studies." In M. Gurevitch, T. Bennett, J. Curran, and J. Woollacott, eds., *Culture, Society, and the Media*, pp. 56–90. London: Methuen.

Hamamoto, Darrell. 1989. *Nervous Laughter: Television Situation Comedy and Liberal Democratic Ideology*. New York: Praeger.

Hamilton, Kendall. 1994. "A Year as Pure as the Driven Snow." *Newsweek*, January 10, p. 41.

Haralovich, Mary Beth. 1992. "Sit-coms and Suburbs: Postitioning the 1950s Homemaker." In D. Mann and L. Spigel, eds., *Private Screenings: Television and the Female Consumer*, pp. 111–142. Minneapolis: University of Minnesota Press.

Harris, Mark. 1991. "*Designing Women*." *Entertainment Weekly*, October 4, pp. 22–29.

Hartmann, Heidi. 1979. "Capitalism, Patriarchy, and Job Segregation by Sex." In Zillah R. Eisenstein, ed., *Capitalist Patriarchy and the Case for Socialist Feminism*, pp. 206–247. New York: Monthly Review Press.

Haskell, Molly. 1988. "Hollywood Madonnas." *Ms.*, May, pp. 84–87.

Hazleton, Leslie. 1994. "Power Politics." *Women's Review of Books*, February, pp. 1, 3, 4.

Heide, Margaret. 1995. *Television Culture and Women's Lives: thirtysomething and the Contradictions of Gender*. Philadelphia: University of Pennsylvania Press.

Helgesen, Sally. 1990. *The Female Advantage: Women's Ways of Leadership*. New York: Doubleday.

Hewitt, Bill. 1993. "The Battle for Baby Jessica." *People*, May 31, pp. 32+.

Hewlett, Sylvia Ann. 1986. *A Lesser Life: The Myth of Women's Liberation in America*. New York: Warner.

Hochschild, Arlie. 1989. *The Second Shift*. New York: Avon.

Hogeland, Lisa Maria. 1994a. "Fear of Feminism." *Ms.*, November/December, pp. 18–21.

———. 1994b. "'Men Can't Be That Bad': Realism and Feminist Fiction in the 1970s." *American Literary History*, 6: 287–305.

———. 1995. "Sexuality in the Consciousness-Raising Novel of the 1970s." *Journal of the History of Sexuality*, 5: 601–632.

hooks, bell. 1989. *Talking Back: Thinking Feminist, Thinking Black*. Boston: South End Press.

———. 1994. *Outlaw Culture: Resisting Representations*. Routledge, 1994.

Horowitz, Joy. 1989. "On TV, Ms. Macho and Mr. Wimp." *New York Times*, April 19, pp. 1H, 36H.

Horowitz, Susan. 1984. "Life with 'Kate and Allie'—The Not So Odd Couple on TV." *Ms.*, September, pp. 32–33.

———. 1987. "Sitcom Domesticus: A Species Endangered by Social Change." In H. Newcomb, ed., *Television: The Critical View*, 4th ed., pp. 106–111. New York: Oxford.

Ingrassia, Michele, and Karen Springen. 1994. "She's Not Baby Jessica Anymore." *Newsweek*, March 21, pp. 60–66.

Jacobs, A. J. 1995. "Will the Real Ellen Please Stand Up?" *Entertainment Weekly*, March 24, pp. 18+.

Jaggar, Alison M. 1983. *Feminist Politics and Human Nature*. Totowa, NJ: Rowman and Allanheld.

James, Caryn. 1991. "A Baby Boom on TV as Biological Clock Ticks Cruelly Away." *New York Times*, October 16, pp. B1, B7.

Jameson, Fredric. 1979. "Reification and Utopia in Mass Culture." *New Left Review*, 1: 130–148.

———. 1981. *The Political Unconscious*. Ithaca, NY: Cornell University Press.

———. 1991. *Postmodernism, or the Cultural Logic of Late Capitalism*. Durham, NC: Duke University Press.

Jamieson, Kathleen H., and Karlyn K. Campbell. 1988. *The Interplay of Influence: Mass Media and Their Publics in News, Advertising and Politics*, 2nd ed. Belmont, CA: Wadsworth.

Janeway, Elizabeth. 1970. "Happiness and the Right to Choose." *Atlantic Monthly*, March 3, pp. 118–126.

Japp, Phyllis. 1991. "Gender and Work in the 1980s: Television's Working Women as Displaced Persons." *Women's Studies in Communication*, 14: 49–74.

Jerome, Jim. 1991. "Murphy's Laws." *People*, December 2, pp. 157-166.

Jones, Deborah. 1980. "Gossip: Notes on Women's Oral Culture." In C. Kramarae, ed., *The Voices and Words of Women and Men*, pp. 193–198. New York: Pergamon Press.

Jones, Gerard. 1992. *Honey, I'm Home!: Sitcoms, Selling the American Dream*. New York: Grove Weidenfeld.

Joyrich, Lynne. 1990. "Critical and Textual Hypermasculinity." In P. Mellencamp, ed., *Logics of Television: Essays in Cultural Criticism*, pp. 156–172. Bloomington: Indiana University Press.

———. 1992. "All That Television Allows: TV Melodrama, Postmodernism, and Consumer Culture." In L. Spigel and D. Mann, eds., *Private Screenings: Television and the Female Consumer*, pp. 227–252. Minneapolis: University of Minnesota.

Kalčik, Susan. 1986. "' . . . like Ann's Gynecologist or the Time I Was Almost Raped': Personal Narratives in Women's Rap Groups." In Claire M. Farrer, ed., *Women and Folklore: Images and Genres*, pp. 3–11. Prospect Heights, IL: Waveland.

Kaminer, Wendy. 1990. *A Fearful Freedom: Women's Flight from Equality*. Reading, MA: Addison-Wesley.

————. 1993. "Feminism's Identity Crisis." *The Atlantic*, October, pp. 51–68.

————. 1995. "Feminism's Third Wave: What Do Young Women Want?" *New York Times Book Review*, June 4, p. 3.

Kanter, Rosabeth Moss. 1977. *Men and Women of the Corporation.* New York: Basic Books.

Kantrowitz, Barbara. 1986. "A Mother's Choice." *Newsweek*, March 31, pp. 46–51.

Kaplan, E. Ann. 1987. "Feminist Criticism and Television." In R. Allen, ed., *Channels of Discourse*, pp. 211–253. Chapel Hill: University of North Carolina Press.

————. 1992. *Motherhood and Representation: The Mother in Popular Culture and Melodrama.* New York: Routledge.

Kaufman, Joanne. 1993. "The Woman Who Saved Saturday Night." *Ladies Home Journal*, June, pp. 140–141, 192–194.

Kilday, Greg. 1993. "Lady Jane." *Lears*, October, pp. 78–80, 108.

"King Lear." 1976. *Time*, April 5, pp. 74–75.

King, Ynestra. 1993. "Where Nature Meets Nurture: Reflections on Ecofeminist Motherhood." *Ms.*, July/August, pp. 41–43.

Kitses, J. 1969. *Horizons West.* Bloomington: University of Indiana Press.

Kleiman, Carol. 1992. "Single Mom: Quayle Stance Is 'Ludicrous.' " *Chicago Tribune*, May 21, p. 2.

Klemesrud, Judy. 1970a. "A Herstory-Making Event." *New York Times Magazine*, August 23, pp. 6+.

————. 1970b. "The Lesbian Issue and Women's Lib." *New York Times*, December 18, p. 47.

Koedt, Anne, Ellen Levine, and Anita Rapone, eds. 1973. *Radical Feminism.* New York: Quadrangle.

Kolodny, Annette. 1985. "Dancing Through the Minefield: Some Observations on the Theory, Practice, and Politics of a Feminist Literary Criticism." In E. Showalter, ed., *The New Feminist Criticism*, pp. 144–167. New York: Pantheon.

Komisar, Lucy. 1970. "The New Feminism." *Saturday Review*, February 21, pp. 27–30, 55.

Kraditor, Aileen. 1981. *The Ideas of the Woman Suffrage Movement, 1890–1920.* New York: W.W. Norton.

Kramarae, Cheris. ed. 1980. *The Voices and Words of Women and Men.* New York: Pergamon.

————. 1981. *Women and Men Speaking: Frameworks for Analysis.* Rowley, MA: Newbury House.

Kramarae, Cheris, and Mercilee M. Jenkins. 1987. "Women Take Back the Talk." In J. Penfield, ed., *Women and Language in Transition*, pp. 137–156. Albany: State University of New York Press.

Lague, Louise. 1990. "10 Things Motherhood Has Taught Me." *Glamour*, May, pp. 122–131.

Langellier, Kristin. 1989. "Personal Narratives: Perspectives on Theory and Research." *Text and Performance Quarterly*, 9: 243–276.

Lear, Martha W. 1968. "The Second Feminist Wave." *New York Times Magazine*, March 10, pp. 24+.

Lee, Janet. 1992. "Subversive Sitcoms: *Roseanne* as Inspiration for Feminist Resistance." *Women's Studies*, 21: 87–101.

Lehrman, Karen. 1993. "Off Course." *Mother Jones*, September/October, pp. 45–51, 64–68.

Leibman, Nina. 1995. *Living Room Lectures: The Fifties Family in Film and Television.* Austin: University of Texas Press.

Leo, John. 1986. "Motherhood vs. Sisterhood: A New Book Challenges Feminist Attitudes Toward the Family." *Time*, March 31, pp. 61–63.

Leonard, John. 1970. "The Subversive Mary Tyler Moore." *Life*, December 18, p. 8.

Levine, Richard M. 1975. "As the TV World Turns." *New York Times Magazine*, December 14, pp. 6:20+.

Levitt, Leonard. 1971. "She: The Awesome Power of Gloria Steinem." *Esquire*, October, pp. 88–90+.

Lewis, William F. 1987. "Telling America's Story: Narrative Form and the Reagan Presidency." *Quarterly Journal of Speech*, 73: 280–302.

Lichtenstein, Grace. 1970. "For Most Women, Strike Day Was Just a Topic of Conversation." *New York Times*, August 27, p. 30.

Liebman, Lisa. 1994. "The Savior of Saturday Night." *New Woman*, February, p. 28.

Lipsitz, George. 1990. *Time Passages: Collective Memory and American Popular Culture*. Minneapolis: University of Minnesota Press.

Littwin, Susan. 1991. "The Delta Factor." *TV Guide*, October 26, p. 7.

Loeb, Jane. 1990. "Rhetorical and Ideological Conservatism in *thirtysomething*." *Critical Studies in Mass Communication*, 7: 249–260.

Lorde, Audre. 1984. *Sister Outsider*. Trumansberg, NY: The Crossing Press.

Lubiano, Wahneema. 1992. "Black Ladies, Welfare Queens, and State Minstrels: Ideological War by Narrative Means." In T. Morrison, ed., *Race-ing Justice, Engendering Power: Essays on Anita Hill, Clarence Thomas, and the Construction of Social Reality*, pp. 323–363. New York: Pantheon.

Lyotard, Jean François. 1979, rpt., 1984. *The Postmodern Condition: A Report on Knowledge*. Minneapolis: University of Minnesota.

MacKinnon, Catharine. 1987. *Feminism Unmodified: Discourses on Life and Law*. Cambridge, MA: Harvard University Press.

Mainardi, Pat. 1970. "The Politics of Housework." In A. Koedt and S. Firestone, eds., *Notes from the Second Year*, pp. 28–31. New York: New York Radical Women.

Maltz, Daniel N., and Ruth A. Borker. 1982. "A Cultural Approach to Male-Female Miscommunication." In J. J. Gumperz, ed., *Language and Social Identity*, pp. 196–216. Cambridge: Cambridge University Press.

Mandese, Joe. 1993. "'Dr. Quinn' Could Cure CBS' Blues on Saturday." *Advertising Age*, February 15, pp. 3, 61.

Mansbridge, Jane J. 1986. *Why We Lost the ERA*. Chicago: University of Chicago Press.

———. 1990. "Feminism and Democracy." *The American Prospect*, 1: 126–139.

Marc, David. 1984. *Demographic Vistas: Television in American Culture*. Philadelphia: University of Pennsylvania Press.

———. 1989. *Comic Visions: Television Comedy and American Culture*. Boston: Unwin Hyman.

"Mary Tyler Moore." 1989. *People*, Summer [extra], p. 35.

Mayerle, Judine. 1987. "Character Shaping Genre in *Cagney and Lacey*." *Journal of Broadcasting and Electronic Media*, 31: 133–151.

McCracken, Ellen. 1993. *Decoding Women's Magazines: From Mademoiselle to Ms*. New York: St. Martin's Press.

McDermott, Patrice. 1995. "On Cultural Authority: Women's Studies, Feminist Politics, and the Popular Press." *Signs: Journal of Women in Culture and Society*, 20: 668–684.

McLellan, Diane. 1994. "Lady Jane." *Ladies Home Journal*, May, pp. 162–163+.

McLoughlin, Merrill. 1988. "Men vs. Women." *U.S. News & World Report*, August 8, pp. 50–56.

McRobbie, Angela. 1991. *Feminism and Youth Culture: From "Jackie" to "Just Seventeen."* Boston: Unwin Hyman.

Medhurst, Martin, and Thomas Benson. 1984. "Rhetorical Studies in a Media Age." In M. Medhurst and T. Benson, eds., *Rhetorical Dimensions in Media: A Critical Casebook*, pp. ix-xxiii. Dubuque: Kendall/Hunt.

Meehan, Diana. 1983. *Ladies of the Evening: Women Characters of Prime-Time Television.* Metuchen, NJ: Scarecrow.

Meehan, Eileen. 1986. "Conceptualizing Culture as Commodity: The Problem of Television." *Critical Studies in Mass Communication*, 3: 448–457.

Mellencamp, Patricia. 1986. "Situation Comedy, Feminism and Freud: Discourses of Gracie and Lucy." In T. Modleski, ed., *Studies in Entertainment: Critical Approaches to Mass Culture*, pp. 80–95. Bloomington: Indiana University Press.

Mercer, Marilyn. 1972. "Gloria: The Unhidden Persuader." *McCall's*, January, pp. 68–69+.

Meyerowitz, Joanna, ed., 1994. *Not June Cleaver: Women and Gender in Postwar America, 1945–1960.* Philadelphia: Temple University Press.

Miller, Carolyn. 1984. "Genre as Social Action." *Quarterly Journal of Speech*, 70: 151–167.

Millett, Kate. 1970, rpt. 1971. *Sexual Politics.* New York: Avon Books.

Millman, Joyce. 1995. "Ellen Comes Subtly Out of the Closet in 'Friends of Mine.'" *Fargo Forum*, March 23, p. A13.

Mintz, Lawrence. 1985. "Situation Comedy." In B. G. Rose, ed., *TV Genres: A Handbook and Reference Guide*, pp. 107–129. Westport, CT: Greenwood Press.

Mitz, Rick. 1980. *The Great TV Sitcom Book.* New York: R. Marek.

"Mixed Messages." 1992. *USA Today*, May 20, p. 10A.

Modleski, Tania. 1991. *Feminism Without Women: Culture and Criticism in a "Postfeminist" Age.* New York: Routledge.

Morgan, Robin, ed. 1970. *Sisterhood Is Powerful: An Anthology of Writings from the Women's Liberation Movement.* New York: Vintage.

"Murphy Is Not Reality." 1992. *USA Today*, May 20, p. 10A.

"Murphy to Dan: Read My Ratings." 1992. *Time*, October 5, p. 25.

"A 'Natural Woman'?" 1992. *USA Today*, May 20, p. 10A.

Newcomb, Horace. 1974. *TV: The Most Popular Art.* New York: Anchor.

Newcomb, Horace, and Paul Hirsch. 1987. "Television as Cultural Forum." In H. Newcomb, ed., *Television: The Critical View*, 4th ed., pp. 455–470. New York: Oxford University Press.

"The New Feminism." 1970. *Ladies Home Journal*, August, pp. 63–71.

Nightingale, Virginia. 1990. "Women as Audiences." In M. E. Brown, ed., *Television and Women's Culture: The Politics of the Popular*, pp. 25–36. Newbury Park, CA: Sage.

Noble, Barbara P. 1993. "The Debate Over *la différence*." *New York Times*, August 15, p. 3:6.

North, Sandie. 1970. "Reporting the Movement." *Atlantic Monthly*, March 3, pp. 105–106.

Nothstine, William L., Carole Blair, and Gary A. Copeland. 1994. "Invention in Media and Rhetorical Criticism: A General Orientation." In W. L. Nothstine, C. Blair, and G. A. Copeland, eds., *Critical Questions: Invention, Creativity, and the Criticism of Discourse and Media*, pp. 3–14. New York: St. Martin's Press.

O'Connor, John J. 1975. "One Day at a Time." *New York Times*, December 16, p. 79.

———. 1989. "An Updated Mary Richards in 'Murphy Brown.' " *New York Times*, November 27, p. 17Y.

"Odd Woman Out." 1991. *People*, July 29, pp. 46–50.

O'Reilly, Jane. 1989. "At Last! Women Worth Watching." *TV Guide*, May 27, pp. 18–21.

Paglia, Camille. 1992. *Sex, Art, and American Culture*. New York: Vintage.

Painter, Nell Irvin. 1992. "Hill, Thomas, and the Use of Racial Stereotype." In T. Morrison, ed., *Race-ing Justice, En-Gendering Power: Essays on Anita Hill, Clarence Thomas, and the Construction of Social Reality*, pp. 200–214. New York: Pantheon.

Phillips, Kevin. 1990. *The Politics of Rich and Poor: Wealth and the American Electorate in the Reagan Aftermath*. New York: Random House.

Pogrebin, Letty Cottin. 1972. "The Working Woman." *Ladies Home Journal*, May, pp. 32–34.

Pollitt, Katha. 1994. *Reasonable Creatures: Essays on Women and Feminism*. New York: Knopf.

Powell, Lee. 1986. "Feminist Sylvia Hewlett Argues That the Women's Movement Forgot Someone Special: Mother." *People*, October 20, pp. 101–103.

Presnell, Michael. 1989. "Narrative Gender Differences: Orality and Literacy." In K. Carter and C. Spitzack, eds., *Doing Research on Women's Communication: Perspectives on Theory and Method*, pp. 118–136. Norwood, NJ: Ablex.

Press, Andrea. 1991. *Women Watching Television: Class, Gender, and Generation in the American Television Experience*. Philadelphia: University of Pennsylvania Press.

Press, Andrea, and Terry Strathman. 1993. "Work, Family, and Social Class in TV Images of Women: Prime-Time Television and the Construction of Postfeminism." *Women and Language*, 16: 7–15.

Prial, Frank J. 1970. "Feminist Philosopher Katharine Murray Millett." *New York Times*, August 27, p. 30.

Probyn, Elspeth. 1990. "New Traditionalism and Post-Feminism: TV Does the Home." *Screen*, 31: 147–159.

"Quayle vs. Brown." 1992. *The Cincinnati Post*, May 21, pp. 1A, 8A.

Quindlen, Anna. 1988. "Mother's Choice." *Ms.*, February, pp. 55-57.

Rabinovitz, Lauren. 1989. "Sitcoms and Single Moms: Representations of Feminism on American TV." *Cinema Journal*, 29: 3–19.

Radway, Janice. 1984. *Reading the Romance: Women, Patriarchy and Popular Literature*. Chapel Hill: University of North Carolina Press.

Rapp, Rayna. 1988. "Is the Legacy of Second Wave Feminism Postfeminism?" *Socialist Review*, 18: 31–37.

Rapping, Elayne. 1992. *The Movie of the Week: Private Stories, Public Events*. Minneapolis: University of Minnesota.

———. 1994. "In Praise of Roseanne." *The Progressive*, July, pp. 36–38.

———. 1995. "Movies and Motherhood." *The Progressive*, July, pp. 36–37.

Rebeck, Victoria A. 1989. "From Murphy to Mary: Codependent No More." *Christian Century*, October 25, pp. 948, 950.

Reed, J. D. 1983. "Postfeminism: Playing for Keeps." *Time*, January 10, pp. 60–61.

"A Report on a Consciousness-Raising Group." 1970. *Mademoiselle*, February, pp. 80+.

"Rhoda and Mary—Love and Laughs." 1974. *Time*, October 28, pp. 58–68.

Rhode, Deborah L. 1995. "Media Images, Feminist Issues." *Signs: Journal of Women in Culture and Society*, 20: 685–710.

Rhodes, Joe. 1992. "When Baby Makes Two." *TV Guide*, September 19, pp. 6–10.

Rich, Adrienne. 1976. *Of Woman Born: Motherhood as Experience and Institution.* New York: W.W. Norton.

———. 1979. *On Lies, Secrets, and Silence: Selected Prose, 1966–1978.* New York: W.W. Norton.

———. 1986. *Blood, Bread, and Poetry: Selected Prose, 1979–1985.* New York: W.W. Norton.

Roiphe, Katie. 1993. *The Morning After: Sex, Fear, and Feminism on Campus.* New York: Little, Brown.

Rosen, Diane. 1971. "TV and the Single Girl." *TV Guide*, November 6, pp. 12–16.

Rosenblatt, Roger. 1992. "Candy Can." *Vanity Fair*, December, pp. 223–227+.

Rosenfelt, Deborah, and Judith Stacey. 1987. "Second Thoughts on the Second Wave." *Feminist Studies* 13: 341–361.

Rosenthal, Andrew. 1992. "Quayle Says Riots Arose from Burst of Social Anarchy." *New York Times*, May 20, pp. A1, A11.

Rossi, Alice. 1970. "Job Discrimination and What Women Can Do About It." *Atlantic Monthly*, March 3, pp. 99–102.

Roush, Matt. 1994. " 'Roseanne' Boldly Refusing to Kiss Up." *USA Today*, March 1, p. 3D.

Rovin, Jeff. 1990. "Dishing with the *Designing Women*." *Ladies Home Journal*, October, pp. 60, 67–71.

Rowe, Kathleen. 1995. *The Unruly Woman: Gender and the Genres of Laughter.* Austin: University of Texas.

Ruddick, Sara. 1980. "Maternal Thinking." *Feminist Studies*, 6: 342–367.

———. 1989. *Maternal Thinking: Toward a Politics of Peace.* New York: Ballantine.

Rudolph, Barbara. 1990). "Why Can't a Woman Manage More like . . . a Woman?" *Time*, Fall [special issue], p. 53.

Ryan, Barbara. 1992. *Feminism and the Women's Movement: Dynamics of Change in Social Movement Ideology and Activism.* New York: Routledge.

Said, Edward W. 1983. "Opponents, Audiences, Constituencies and Communities." In H. Foster, ed., *The Anti-Aesthetic: Essays on Postmodern Culture*, pp. 135–159. Port Townsend, WA: Bay Press.

Salholz, Eloise. 1986. "Too Late for Prince Charming?" *Newsweek*, June 2, pp. 54–61.

Salzberg, Charles. 1995. "Brett Butler Mouths Off." *Redbook*, January, pp. 57+.

Schatz, Thomas. 1981. *Hollywood Genres: Formulas, Filmmaking, and the Studio System.* Philadelphia: Temple University Press.

Schindehette, Susan. 1993. "What's Up, Doc?" *People*, February 25, pp. 74–80.

Schine, Cathleen. 1984. "Real Women." *Vogue*, August, pp. 75–76.

———. 1987. "Don't Weep for Me, CBS." *Vogue*, March, p. 144.

Schwarzbaum, Lisa. 1993. "She Wolf." *Entertainment Weekly*, December 17, p. 62.

———. 1994. "Love, Medicine and Miracles." *Entertainment Weekly*, April 8, pp. 28–30.

Seibel, Deborah S. 1993. "Will Brett Butler Be the New Roseanne?" *TV Guide*, October 2, pp. 16–23.

"She's Anna Now." 1994. *Redbook*, August, p. 121.

Shilts, Randy. 1987. *And the Band Played On: Politics, People, and the AIDS Epidemic.* New York: St. Martin's Press.

Shreve, Anita. 1989. *Women Together, Women Alone: The Legacy of the Consciousness-Raising Movement.* New York: Viking.

Shulman, Alix Kates. 1978. *Burning Questions*. New York.

Sidel, Ruth. 1987. *Women and Children Last: The Plight of Poor Women in Affluent America*. New York: Penguin.

———. 1990. *On Her Own: Growing Up in the Shadow of the American Dream*. New York: Penguin.

Smith, Lynn. 1993. "Critics Say Selfish 'Murphy Brown' Is Failing as a Career Mother Who Wants It All." *Saint Paul Pioneer Press*, January 24, p. 6E.

Snitow, Ann. 1991. "Motherhood—Reclaiming the Demon Texts." *Ms.*, May/June, pp. 34–37.

———. 1992. "Feminism and Motherhood: An American Reading." *Feminist Review*, 40: 32–51.

Solomon, Martha. 1979. "The 'Positive Woman's' Journey: A Mythic Analysis of the Rhetoric of Stop ERA." *Quarterly Journal of Speech*, 65: 262–274.

Sommers, Christina Hoff. 1994. *Who Stole Feminism? How Women Have Betrayed Women*. New York: Simon and Schuster.

Spender, Dale. 1985. *Man Made Language*, 2nd ed. London: Routledge & Kegan Paul.

Spigel, Lynn. 1992. *Make Room for TV: Television and the Family Ideal in Postwar America*. Chicago: University of Chicago Press.

Spigel, Lynn, and Denise Mann. 1992. "Introduction." In L. Spigel and D. Mann, eds., *Private Screenings: Television and the Female Consumer*, pp. vii–xiii. Minneapolis: University of Minnesota Press.

Stacey, Judith. 1983. "The New Conservative Feminism." *Feminist Studies*, 9: 559–584.

———. 1987. "Sexism by a Subtler Name? Postindustrial Conditions and Postfeminist Consciousness in the Silicon Valley." *Socialist Review*, 17: 7–28.

Starr, Tama. 1994. "WFN's First Conference: Liberation From Stereotypes." *The Women's Freedom Network Newsletter*, Fall, pp. 1–2.

Stearney, Lynn. 1994. "Feminism, Ecofeminism, and the Maternal Archetype: Motherhood as a Feminine Universal." *Communication Quarterly*, 42: 145–159.

Stein, Harry. 1992. "Our Times." *TV Guide*, November 14, p. 31.

———. 1993. "*Dr. Quinn* Should Shrink from New Age Nonsense." *TV Guide*, March 6, p. 43.

Steinem, Gloria. 1969. "After Black Power, Women's Liberation." *New York*, April 7, pp. 8–10.

———. 1970. "What It Would Be like If Women Win." *Time*, August 31, pp. 22–23.

———. 1990. "Sex, Lies, and Advertising." *Ms.*, July/August, pp. 18–28.

Streeter, Thomas. 1989. "Polysemy, Plurality, and Media Studies." *Journal of Communication Inquiry*, 13: 1–33.

Szpiech, Kimberly M. 1991. "A Critical Analysis of Representative Patricia Schroeder's Rhetoric on the 'Great American Family.'" Unpublished M.A. thesis. University of Cincinnati.

Tannen, Deborah. 1991a. "How to Close the Communication Gap Between Men and Women." *McCall's*, May, pp. 99–102, 140.

———. 1991b. *You Just Don't Understand: Men and Women in Conversation*. New York: Ballantine.

Taylor, Ella. 1989. *Prime-Time Families: Television Culture in Postwar America*. Berkeley: University of California Press.

Theroux, Phyllis. 1987. "TV Women Have Come a Long Way, Baby—Sort Of." *New York Times*, May 17, p. H35.

Thorne, Barrie, Cheris Kramarae, and Nancy Henley, eds. 1983. *Language, Gender and Society.* Rowley, MA: Newbury House.

Tichi, Cecilia. 1991. *Electronic Hearth: Creating an American Television Culture.* New York: Oxford University Press.

Tompkins, Jane. 1989. "West of Everything." In D. Longhurst, ed., *Gender, Genre and Narrative Pleasure,* pp. 10–30. London: Unwin Hyman.

Toufexis, Anastasia. 1990. "Coming from a Different Place." *Time,* Fall [special issue], pp. 64–66.

Treichler, Paula A., and Cheris Kramarae. 1983. "Women's Talk in the Ivory Tower." *Communication Quarterly,* 31: 118–132.

WAC Stats: The Facts about Women. 1993. New York: The New Press.

Wallis, Claudia. 1989. "Onward, Women!" *Time,* December 4, pp. 80–89.

Walters, Suzanna Danuta. 1992. *Lives Together/Worlds Apart: Mothers and Daughter in Popular Culture.* Berkeley: University of California Press.

Waters, Harry F., and Janet Huck. 1989. "Networking Women." *Newsweek,* March 13, pp. 48–55.

Weideger, Paula. 1988. "Womb Worship." *Ms.,* February, pp. 54–57.

Weller, Sheila. 1978. "Will 'One Day at a Time' Convert Bonnie Franklin?" *Ms.,* November, pp. 45+.

Westover, Ted. 1980. "One Fray at a Time." *TV Guide,* March 17, pp. 26+.

White, Mimi. 1987. "Ideological Analysis and Television." In R. Allen, ed., *Channels of Discourse,* pp. 134–171. Chapel Hill: University of North Carolina Press.

Whitney, Dwight. 1970. "You've Come a Long Way, Baby." *TV Guide,* September 19, pp. 34–38.

"Who's Come a Long Way, Baby?" 1970. *Time,* August 31, pp. 16–21.

Wilkes, Paul. 1970. "Mother Superior to Women's Lib." *New York Times Magazine,* November 29, pp. 27–29, 140–150, 157.

Willis, Ellen. 1984. "Radical Feminism and Feminist Radicalism." In S. Sayres, A. Stephanson, S. Aronowitz, and F. Jameson, eds., *The 60s Without Apology,* pp. 91–118. Minneapolis: University of Minnesota.

Wills, Garry. 1987. *Reagan's America: Innocents at Home.* Garden City, NY: Doubleday.

Wilson, John K., ed. 1994. "Special Issue: A Symposium on *Who Stole Feminism?*" *Democratic Culture,* 3, no. 2.

Wines, Michael. 1992. "Appeal of 'Murphy Brown' Now Clear at White House." *New York Times,* May 21, pp. A1, A12.

Wisehart, Bill. 1989. "Murphy and Mary: Similar But So Unalike." *Star Tribune* (Minneapolis), December 24, p. 39.

Wolcott, James. 1992. "Paglia's Power Trip." *Vanity Fair,* September, pp. 238–241, 300–303.

Wolf, Naomi. 1992. *The Beauty Myth.* New York: Anchor.

———. 1993. *Fire with Fire: The New Female Power and How It Will Change the 21st Century.* New York: Random House.

———. 1994. "Can You Be a Feminist and Love Men, Too?" *Cosmopolitan,* May, pp. 202–204.

"Woman of the Year." 1972. *McCall's,* January, p. 67.

"Woman's Place." 1970. *Atlantic Monthly,* March 3, pp. 81–126.

"Women's Lib: A Second Look." 1970. *Time,* December 14, p. 50.

Yorkshire, Heidi. 1987. "Those Remarkable *Designing Women.*" *McCall's,* November, pp. 79–87.

Zoglin, Richard. 1992. "Sitcom Politics." *Time,* September 21, pp. 44–47.

Index